THE
BIBLIOGRAPHIC
RECORD
AND INFORMATION
TECHNOLOGY

THE BIBLIOGRAPHIC RECORD AND INFORMATION TECHNOLOGY

Ronald Hagler
Peter Simmons
School of Librarianship
The University of British Columbia

AMERICAN LIBRARY ASSOCIATION

Chicago 1982

Designed by Vladimir Reichl

Composed by Automated Office Systems, Inc.
  in Times Roman on a Text Ed/VIP
  phototypesetting system

Printed on 50-pound Warren's 1854,
  a pH-neutral stock, and bound
  in B-grade Holliston linen cloth
  by Braun-Brumfield, Inc.

Library of Congress Cataloguing in Publication Data

Hagler, Ronald.
  The bibliographic record and information technology.

  Includes bibliographical references and index.
  1. Machine-readable bibliographic data.
  2. Library materials—Bibliography—Theory, methods, etc.
  3. Information storage and retrieval systems.
  I. Simmons, Peter Alan, 1936–   . II. Title.
  Z699.H264 1982   025.3′028′54   82-14706
  ISBN 0-8389-0370-3

To the Teachers' Teachers:

> *the students of the School of Librarianship*
> *The University of British Columbia*
> *over the years,*
> *the instigators of this book.*

CONTENTS

APPENDICES

LIST OF CHAPTER
HEADINGS

PREFACE

For many years a goal of library administration has been the development of integrated systems for technical services to permit the completely automated handling of bibliographic data from selection through ordering, receiving, cataloguing, processing, and circulation. Though this goal has rarely been achieved during the past twenty years, a number of individual libraries, as well as the centralized processing facilities and some commercial companies, are well on their way to developing such systems. The basis of any such system, and its major component, is the bibliographic record: the identification of each individual item in the library's collection. The tool is, of course, the computer, now a familiar "member" of any library's staff whether it is housed within the library, in a municipal hall or campus administration building, in the offices of a commercial jobbing or processing agency, or at the headquarters of a consortium half a continent away.

This book grew out of the authors' experiences in teaching a core-curriculum course at the School of Librarianship, The University of British Columbia, on basic bibliographic information and its automated handling. They sought, but could not find, a timely text or texts to introduce novices to computer functions in the context of bibliography, to deal with manual and automated bibliographic databases of all kinds as part of a single coordinated system of bibliographic control, and to analyze the technical, administrative, and economic aspects of a rapid transition from older rules, practices, and techniques to present-day ones. Most of all, they wanted material addressed more directly to the increasing numbers of professionals who *use* existing bibliographic data than to the diminishing numbers of professionals who *create* bibliographic records.

These and related concepts were developed over a period of years into a text/workbook produced and used in-house. But a workbook written for a particular course in a particular school is not transferable directly to any other academic programme. When invited by the American Library Association to attempt a revision for publication, the authors accepted the charge of expanding their core-curriculum text into a treatment of all aspects of the creation, storing, assembling, and dissemination of bibliographic data in the context of both manual and computer-based techniques.

The focus of this book has not strayed far from that of the course which gave it birth, namely the bibliographic record in all its manifestations. But here the attempt is to touch on all its ramifications as they concern every professional librarian. If the result forms an acceptable text in support of part of the content of one or more graduate library school courses, the authors will be well rewarded for their efforts. Their greater hope, however, is that this integrated approach may further the destruction of the barriers between public, technical, and administrative services personnel in libraries by emphasizing their common reliance on sound bibliographic practices.

It is the authors' intention neither to linger over clerical routine nor to solve the specialist's bibliographic problems. Whether one works in a large or a small library, in an academic, special, school, or public library, in an archive, for an indexing company, or as a free-lance information specialist, there is an area of professional decision-making in the use of bibliographic data which all exercise in common. That is this book's area of concern.

Although this is not a book on how to catalogue, how to plan for the production of bibliographic tools, or how to develop a computer-assisted reference service, it is an introduction to the bibliographic and technological concepts needed before embarking on such tasks. Today, every librarian must be familiar with a variety of obsolescent, current, and future-oriented bibliographic practices in both a manual and a computer-based context. It is even more important to understand the *reasons* for the older and for the newer practices and technologies. Only in the context of such understanding is it possible to justify the specific methods and techniques prescribed by any one cataloguing rule, any one computer-based method of input/output, or any one institution's policies.

Objectives

On completing this book, the reader may be expected to be conversant with

1) the purposes of bibliographic identification as one of the many component parts of library service
2) the organization of typical catalogues, bibliographies, indices, and automated databases
3) the use of computer hardware, both in general and for specific library

applications, and the nature and application of computer software (or programs) as they are needed for the management of bibliographic data

4) the nature of a format for the identification and manipulation of elements of bibliographic data; and the uses of formats in both manual and computer systems

5) the use of manual and computer-based systems, and of pre- and post-coordinate techniques, for searching and browsing bibliographic lists and databases of all kinds

6) the purposes and the general effects, though not the detailed practical application, of a number of standards widely used in bibliographic control in English-speaking areas, namely:

   a) style manuals intended for the preparation of footnotes and citations in research papers, abstracting journals, etc.

   b) the International Standard Bibliographic Description

   c) the MARC format for the communication of bibliographic data in machine-readable form

   d) the *Anglo-American Cataloguing Rules* and their immediate predecessor rules, as they have been implemented in national bibliographic services over the past half century

   e) the *Library of Congress Subject Headings, Sears List of Subject Headings,* the PRECIS system, and the concept of the thesaurus, as examples of verbal subject analysis

   f) the *Dewey Decimal Classification* and the *Library of Congress Classification* as examples of classification principles

   g) common present and past principles of alphanumeric arrangement as incorporated into filing rules

7) enough of the history of bibliographic practices to understand earlier purposes and methods and the reasons for changes from them to present-day ones

8) some of the administrative and economic consequences of continuing developments in the areas of

   a) bibliographic technology

   b) interlibrary and international cooperation

   c) the identification of bibliographic needs at the local, regional, and national levels.

The concepts introduced in this book all have immediate practical application, but this is not a how-to book. The student, particularly one who has not previously worked in a library or other bibliographic situation, must gain confidence in putting these concepts to work by means of practical exercises. Many texts on how to catalogue offer such exercises, but practice in locating and analyzing bibliographic records in actual manual and automated sources is the authors' recommended method for reinforcing the ideas developed herein.

Readings

This is not a work which analyzes only one type of bibliographic practice, for example library cataloguing imitating that of the Library of Congress. Rather, it attempts to provide the context for understanding the many practices, standards, and rules now being applied where bibliographic information on current publications is created and disseminated—principally libraries, national bibliographic agencies, and the abstracting and indexing services. Bibliographic entries in a variety of styles, old and new, have been deliberately chosen as illustrations.

This book also is being published at a time when major upheavals in techniques and rules have forced bibliographic control into a new context. An annotated reading list of the extensive literature describing the status ante quo, the upheavals themselves, and their results would occupy a book not much shorter than this one. To be useful to the novice such a reading list would have to document, and identify as such, the uninformed or misleading commentary, the speculation on possible future activities which never came about, the descriptions of dead-end experiments, and the information which, though once valid, is now obsolete. Much material of this kind now exists in the literature alongside the writings describing the mainstream of events as they actually took place and/or interpreting these events from one or another informed and legitimate point of view. The authors and publisher have agreed that to compile such a reading list must remain a task for a later effort, not for incorporation into this broad introductory survey.

A large proportion of the published literature relevant to the concerns of this book has been cited systematically in (1) the annual "Year's Work" articles in *Library Resources & Technical Services* since 1958, particularly the surveys of "Serials" and of "Cataloging and Classification" (now separately "Descriptive Cataloging" and "Subject Analysis"), and (2) the literature surveys which comprise most of the articles in the *Annual Review of Information Science and Technology* since its inception in 1966.

The authors' sources of the present work can be documented in general terms. They are (1) first-hand knowledge derived from involvement in some of the activities whose results are described herein, (2) many valued personal contacts, gratefully acknowleged but too numerous to specify here, and (3) a scanning of journal material in their specialties over the whole of their professional careers. In the following pages, citation of specific sources has been limited to (1) instances where a specific quotation or fact had to be documented, (2) a few surveys of broad scope useful as background, and most importantly (3) the primary sources of bibliographic control, the rules and standards which form the basis of the practices described in the accompanying text.

Vancouver, British Columbia
April 1982

I The Purposes and Methods of Bibliography

1

BIBLIOGRAPHIC CONTROL

Identifying and locating items of recorded communication, whether for information, for cultural enhancement, or for recreation, is the common purpose of bibliographic control. This is the core function of large numbers of people. Their job titles are varied: Librarian, Information Scientist, Director of Learning Resources, Media Specialist, to name a few. Their formal training may have been taken at a graduate library school, a faculty of education, a commercial computer facility, a business college, or by apprenticeship in a working situation. Many have no specific formal training for information work, but were self-educated through experience.

Abstractors, indexers, cataloguers, and bibliographers establish bibliographic control over the world's store of documentary information. Reference librarians, readers' advisers, and information searchers interpret the methods of this control to the ultimate users of documents. The institutional library (public, special, academic, etc.) is a major focus of these activities, but far from the only one. Individual freelance efforts and commercial enterprises have always played an important role in the creation and dissemination of bibliographic information. Thus there is no common designation applied to the occupations described above because bibliographic control is only a part of each, and because each is concerned with it in a different context.

Bibliographic control in its broadest sense may be described as (1) recording the existence and identity of all types of documents, printed and other, as they are produced, (2) systematically acquiring these materials in libraries, archives, and other depositories, (3) providing name and subject access to them, and (4) locating copies of the documents through catalogues which show the holdings of various libraries and other collections. Critical *selection,* whether for any ad hoc use of an item or for its inclusion in a collection, is *not* a function of

3

bibliographic control. Selection is based on value judgements and other subjective criteria. To bring the item and its user together may be the raison d'être of an information specialist, but this can only be accomplished once the existence of relevant items has been objectively defined.

Bibliographic control is an unending task. The information explosion adds to the number of extant documents at an alarming pace, and what has been accomplished at any given time is under constant threat of obsolescence because it is never sufficiently complete, detailed, and error-free. The obsolescence of many existing methods of bibliographic control is particularly evident today because of the application over the past two decades of a new and radically different technology to solve the age-old problems.

There are two tangible results of bibliographic control: (1) actual collections of items made available for use, and (2) lists describing items, wherever those items may be. The remainder of this book deals not with the collections, but with the identification of documents in all kinds of bibliographic lists. Its focus is the technical, economic, and administrative concerns underlying the listing of a document in a bibliography or catalogue.

The Study of Bibliographic Control

An identification of a document is commonly called a citation or an entry. A bibliographic citation is at once a very simple and a very complex thing. When stripped to its essentials (title, author, and imprint of a printed monograph), it is readily understood by almost anyone and composed daily by students of all ages who have had little specific training for the task. The conscious study of bibliographic data and their organization is already pursued in the elementary grades, where recognition of simple information on a catalogue card is taught. Surprisingly few user instructions are required in the prefatory pages of a bibliography or at a library card catalogue, considering the complexity of those tools. It is a measure of the success of the art of bibliography over the ages that both a bibliographic citation and the means of locating it in a group of them are essentially self-explanatory.

By high school the student is formulating footnotes and citations of consulted sources. Here difficulties multiply rapidly for two reasons: (1) the need to create or apply some standard of consistency in the selection and arrangement of data, and (2) the seemingly infinite variety of ways in which the desired data are displayed (or concealed) by the item to be cited. In college, consultation of bibliographic data is an almost daily requirement, the need to make one's own citations is almost as frequent, and specified rules must be consulted and adhered to more rigidly. At the same time, concerns such as judging the merits of an edition, disputing an attributed authorship, or evaluating a rare book's historical significance as a physical item blur the line between purely bibliographic issues and the neighbouring studies of critical evaluation.

In graduate library education the ramifications of the bibliographic citation become a frightening ogre occupying a strikingly large part of a two-year academic programme in one guise or another. They occupy part or all of courses variously entitled "Organization of Materials," "Cataloguing and Classification," "Administration of the Technical Services," "Library Automation," etc. In most schools, all students are required to take some courses dealing with bibliographic data in general. Elective courses proliferate in ever-increasing detail: "The Cataloguing of Audiovisual Materials," "Special Problems in Technical Services Automation," etc. Finally, a detailed study of the format of bibliographic records is an increasingly important part of courses devoted to automated reference work, such as "Introduction to Online Searching." The growing complexity of the presentation and use of bibliographic data in libraries encourages fragmentation of its study, but in any programme of professional librarianship, information science, or archives management, the nature of bibliographic control must be presented in its most abstract and general principles.

A library technology programme can concentrate on the clerical detail: recognition of the data in existing lists, application of specific rules, neat and accurate input/output of the data (whether on a typewriter or a computer terminal), and file maintenance (filing, correcting, revising, etc.) The clerk or paraprofessional is only expected to recognize the particular situation predicted when the job was described. The professional is expected to be able to abstract from past practice to desirable future policy, particularly at times of rapid change such as the present. Therefore, studies at the graduate level, although they incorporate familiarization with the clerical functions of bibliographic work, quickly proceed to the more generalized objectives outlined for this book in the Preface.

The Computer in the Context of Bibliography

Technology has always influenced, and often dictated, practical applications. Electronic technology has had such impact on bibliography for the past twenty years that modern librarians' dependence on computers removes them from the category of casual computer users. They have already passed through the period of applying computer-based techniques developed for other purposes to the automation of their existing practices. Librarians are now well into the stage of analyzing the future of bibliographic service and developing a computer-based methodology to support innovative services. The various automated techniques described throughout this book have been initiated by, or developed with the help of, librarians since the mid-1960s. Some of them are automated copies of manual routines; others anticipate a future which is as yet but dimly seen.

It is not important that most computer users even attempt to understand what is going on within the equipment to which a terminal provides a window. For them, the computer is a "black box," a term suggesting that the machine is a sealed unit which one may use without needing to see or understand it. The request is put in; the response emerges. The student of librarianship may wonder whether it is necessary to study the working of electronic computers at the level of detail introduced in Chapter 2, or machine-readable data formats at the level of detail in Chapter 5 or Appendix I. Many librarians are not even remotely aware of how computers came to exist, and it is common for librarians, especially those without experience in the management of automated systems, to believe that details of internal computer operation and data formatting will be looked after satisfactorily by others such as the systems analysts and computer programmers.

Yet systems analysts and programmers very rarely approach librarianship with any knowledge of the nature of bibliographic data, and all too few have any experience of the technical and administrative range of problems presented by bibliographic records. Only misinterpretation and decision-making based on incomplete evidence can result when a librarian who knows too little of machine operation designs any part of an automated system in consort with a computer expert unfamiliar with the purposes and problems of bibliographic control. Perhaps worse, when the computer expert is left largely alone to design the system or part, the librarian is in danger of losing control of a system for whose effective operation he or she is responsible. For those who would participate in the design and effective use of automated systems, a black box is unsatisfactory. It is incumbent upon every information professional to be able to analyze in detail the contexts, computer-based as well as manual, in which bibliographic records are created, stored, manipulated, and retrieved. What might at first seem simple may in fact not be, and what seems impossible today may be commonplace tomorrow.

Models and Standards

In the past, certain individual institutions have seemed (although rarely to their own staffs) to come so close to acquiring, housing, and listing *all* the significant materials within a broadly defined area that their practices have served as models for others to imitate. The Bodleian Library, the Library of Congress, the British Museum Department of Printed Books, and others have all determined in their day what constitutes good bibliographic control and have transmitted their rules and detailed practices to others for imitation. Some of these single-institution practices have, over the years, taken on the guise of basic principles, even when they were never intended as such.

Today, it is easier to see that no one institution can accomplish the complex task of bibliographic control in isolation, or even hope to be pre-eminent in any absolute terms. In many countries there is now more than one "national" library, each serving a separate subject area or function. Commercial and nonprofit firms known as *abstracting and indexing services* (a & i services) share in the task of assembling bibliographic data on the book, conference, research report, and journal literature of various fields of interest. Institutions have ways undreamed of a generation ago for cooperating with one another, both within a country and internationally.

At a more personal level, it is increasingly true that all workers in information agencies, not only those involved in acquisitions, cataloguing, and interlibrary loan, have a strong interest in improved bibliographic control. It is no longer largely the role of the cataloguer to dictate how a library's bibliographic function should operate. If that was ever the case, it was by default. It is the reference librarian, reader's adviser, or information researcher who is directly affected by the consequences of good (or poor) bibliographic control. The debates of the mid-1950s, and again of the late 1970s, over the introduction of new cataloguing codes in the English-speaking world testify to the fact that administrators, too, are faced with serious and costly decisions concomitant on any change in the rules or methods of bibliographic control.

Thus all now share in establishing the standards and the models for bibliographic control, as well as in formulating the entries themselves. The library world has had a very difficult period of adjustment to this fact over the past fifteen years. North American librarianship in particular was, for all practical purposes and through most of the twentieth century, tied to policies set by the Library of Congress for its own internal purposes. The result was what has to be honestly described as a love-hate relationship with those policies and with that library. The supremacy of the Library of Congress has been seriously and suddenly challenged since 1970. Librarians are now groping toward decentralization of applications, while at the same time reinforcing their adherence to ever more general standards. The implications of this trend are analyzed in Chapter 9.

International expression of the need for a decentralized model of bibliographic control has taken the form of two major programmes: (1) UNISIST, sponsored by Unesco and the International Council of Scientific Unions, and (2) the programme of Universal Bibliographic Control (UBC) of the International Federation of Library Associations and Institutions (IFLA). Neither is a new concept, but both have been given institutional shape during the 1970s and have resulted in major developments in standards for bibliographic control.[1]

---

1. On UNISIST, see the special issue, v. 2, no. 2 (1977) of *International Forum on Information and Documentation*. UNISIST's principal contributions to bibliographic control to date are the International Serials Data System (ISDS) and the *Reference Manual for Machine-Readable Bibliographic Descriptions* (see page 63 for the former, pages 147–148 for the latter). On UBC, see Dorothy Anderson, *Universal Bibliographic Control,* 2nd ed., Occasional Papers, no. 10 (London: IFLA International Office for UBC, 1982). Its principal contribution is the International Standard Bibliographic Description (ISBD), for which see pages 113–121.

Conservatism versus Change

Bibliography is an extremely conservative art. It is true that a subject bibliography or a set of footnotes may be a one-time effort, and that internal consistency is all that is required. At the other extreme, however, are library catalogues, typically created over a period of decades (if not centuries) by a large number of individuals. The interchange of information on their catalogue entries among different libraries is a specific purpose of interlibrary cooperation; hence standardization is of some consequence. Between the single bibliography and the library catalogue there are dozens of serially issued bibliographies in which a change of the terms or rules of compilation from volume to volume would be quite jarring. An inherent resistance to significant change is therefore reasonable and even desirable.

Change may, however, be forced for a number of reasons. These have been operating with particular vigour during the past generation, following a lengthy previous period of relative stability. Changes in the physical means of storing and communicating bibliographic data are called for by the new technology described in Chapter 2. Changes in economic circumstances dictate elaboration, or retrenchment, of bibliographic services. Changes in the relationship between public-sector institutions and commercial agencies have altered the balance of services provided by each, as described in part in Chapter 9.

Changes to rules governing the content of the bibliographic record are always more controversial, since they are presumably within the control of those applying the rules; but the situations to which the rules must be applied are themselves changing rapidly today, and are part of the focus of Chapters 5, 7, and 8. In 1950, serial publications were fewer and bibliographically simpler. Conference proceedings, except for those of regularly held society meetings, were virtually unknown. Corporate names followed patterns quite unlike today's. New forms of nonprint materials incorporate means of self-identification unknown to rule-makers then. The rules of 1950 are simply inadequate today, no matter what the technology involved in their application. Even the rules of 1967 have not survived the transition to computer technology unscathed. Library users have learned from commercial sources the new methods of access to indexed materials described in Chapter 6. Since these are much more sophisticated than those accepted a generation ago, the users are now making greater and different demands on bibliographic services.

When changes to bibliographic standards, procedures, and products are suggested by such external circumstances, a period of uncertainty and of policy conflict among institutions is inevitable. The present is such a period. When a more stable and ''conservative'' period will again return is another uncertainty, but its return is certain because of the very nature of the art.

Comprehensiveness, Fragmentation, Integration

Unrealizable dreams, such as a single universal bibliography or a union catalogue of the holdings of all significant collections, have tantalized bibliographers through the ages. From the uncompleted *Registrum Librorum Angliae* of the thirteenth century through Gesner's one-volume *Bibliotheca Universalis* of the sixteenth century to the serial *National Union Catalog* of the twentieth century, there have been serious attempts at comprehensiveness.[2] When the potential universe is sufficiently circumscribed, as in an author, country, or subject bibliography, comprehensiveness may be realistically attempted. However, even national bibliographies with the avowed aim of listing all documents originating within a jurisdiction are frequently limited in scope: technical documents, house organs, items of fewer than a given number of pages, ephemeral materials (variously defined), even research reports and categories of government publications are excluded from one or another supposedly comprehensive national bibliography. Any bibliographic list must in practice be supplemented by other lists, sometimes clearly complementary but often inefficiently overlapping in coverage.

The pity is that as the lists have become more numerous and more specialized, conventions governing their compilation and production have often diverged one from another. That the modern world of business has found some aspects of bibliography to be profitable only increases the strain on standardization. Despite the commendable attention of most of the commercial firms to recognized standards, and even more, their willingness to subsidize and to participate in the establishment of those standards, the appeal of the nonstandard unique feature with which to beat the competition has at times been too strong to resist.

The potential for elements of incompatibility has suddenly been greatly increased by the introduction of computer hardware and computer software into the creation, production, and consultation of bibliographic lists. The ension between the centrifugal force of standardization and the opposing force of individualism in bibliographic control is never quite in balance. At present there appears to be a unifying tendency.

It is easy for a library user to be beguiled into thinking that a catalogue, a subject bibliography, a periodical index, and a computer-based search of a bibliographic database are essentially different tools for research. In reality they are parts of a single tool which happens (for purely economic, historic, and technological reasons) to be fragmented into many physical parts requiring a

2. The *Registrum* is also called "the first co-operative catalogue" in Dorothy May Norris, *A History of Cataloguing and Cataloguing Methods 1100–1850, with an Introductory Survey of Ancient Times* (London: Grafton, 1939), p. 30. She notes that "Gesner also marks another step in the history of co-operative cataloguing, since he suggested that his work . . . should be used by librarians instead of compiling author catalogues themselves." (Ibid., p. 132).

variety of access techniques. Even librarians still sometimes distinguish functionally three kinds of bibliographic lists: (1) the in-house catalogue(s), (2) published enumerative bibliographies of all types purchased for the collection, and (3) machine-readable databases accessible by telephone and computer terminal. The first category is the responsibility of the cataloguers; the second, that of the general reference librarians; and the third, perhaps that of the new breed of systems personnel. Fortunately, such artificial distinctions are increasingly rare among professionals.

Terminology

The terminology of any field is a living thing, subject to change. This has been particularly true in recent years of the traditional vocabulary heard around library circulation counters, bibliographic centres, information desks, and cataloguing departments. Words and terms which describe the manual processes of searching for bibliographic information have a technical and slightly antique air about them ("check the card catalogue," "a list of citations"). Terms relating to automated routines may have a futuristic ring and probably sound even more technical ("do a COM look-up," "a bibliographic databank"). People of average education use both the older and, increasingly, the newer terminology as parts of their normal vocabulary. However, they usually use such technical terms, either old or new, with a minimum of precision. When pushed to define such a term exactly, they suddenly lose the focus of its meaning.

Part of the problem of discussing bibliographic practices technically is that the same words must often be used at several different levels of meaning. In addition to its rather vaguely defined meaning for the average person, "edition" means one specific thing to a publisher, possibly another to a cataloguer, and very likely something else again to a rare book librarian. "Index" is understood by everyone, but in a specialized context a librarian would likely have to qualify it as, for example, a name index, a concept index, an index to periodical articles, or a keyword index, since in many respects these are all very different from one another.

Today's growing variety of methods of information transfer has added considerably to the vocabulary of bibliography. Conversely, many terms widely used only a decade ago have become obsolescent or are now dangerously misleading because of changed contexts. The gradual imposition of automated techniques on manual routines has merged two vocabulary streams with consequent changes to both. Older bibliographic terminology, like the word "bibliography" itself, is etymologically related to the book, particularly the printed book. Deliberate attempts to find terms free of this connotation for nonbook or nonprint materials (themselves very book-oriented terms), or for a combination of print and other media, have produced inelegant replacements, new definitions, and much frustration. Earlier works dealing with the topics of this one have been able to speak of "the title of the book," but in the following pages the reader will more frequently find "the title of the item," "the document's publisher," etc.

This book is about bibliographic data and their uses in general; yet there does not exist in English a set of generic terms widely understood as embracing the common functions of catalogues, bibliographies, and computer-held databases. Hence somewhat pedantic terms such as "bibliographic record," "access point," and "bibliographic list" are often used to reinforce the authors' premise that bibliographic data per se share common internal characteristics, common processing techniques, and common retrieval patterns no matter what kind of item they describe or what medium conveys the data to the user.

Finally, the compromises involved in increasing internationalization (both in traditional bibliography and in automation) have had a marked effect on vocabulary. The old terms "entry" and "heading," for example, have divided British and American cataloguers for generations without most cataloguers on either side of the Atlantic consciously realizing it.

Terms have been chosen for use in this book based on Anglo-American usage at the time of writing; where a widely used term lacks specificity or sharp focus in the context, or could be ambiguous, a term capable of greater precision has been defined and substituted, even if it does not seem the most natural one. A term used technically is italicized on its first appearance in the text of this book unless it has already occurred as a section heading. The usage in this book conforms to meanings found in the technical glossaries in the current standards, for example the second edition of the *Anglo-American Cataloguing Rules,* the nineteenth edition of the *Dewey Decimal Classification,* and the various manual and machine-readable bibliographic formats described and cited in Chapter 5; as well as more general glossaries such as Harrod's.[3]

One caution about terminology is worth emphasizing at this early stage, namely that some technical terms in bibliography are simply not objectively definable, even though conflicting practical results may follow from two differing subjective interpretations of a definition. Good examples of the problem may be found in the use of "title," "work," "edition," and "serial." Anyone can give a working definition of one of these words, or claim to recognize a given title, work, etc., as such. But when distinctions are needed to resolve conflict, the term suddenly becomes subjective, or determinable only in a

3. *Anglo-American Cataloguing Rules,* 2nd ed. (Chicago: American Library Association; Ottawa: Canadian Library Association; London: Library Association, 1978), pp. 563–572; Melvil Dewey, *Dewey Decimal Classification and Relative Index,* 19th ed., 3 vols. (Albany, N.Y.: Forest Press, 1979), 1:lxxvii–lxxxii; *A Glossary for Library Networking,* prepared by Dataflow Systems Inc. for the Network Development Office, Network Planning Paper, no. 2 (Washington: Library of Congress, 1978); Leonard Montague Harrod, *The Librarians' Glossary of Terms Used in Librarianship, Documentation, and the Book Crafts, and Reference Book,* 4th rev. ed. (London: Deutsch, 1977).

specified context. For example, "serial" almost invariably means something slightly different within the same library to reference librarians looking for a serial, to persons in the serials check-in unit, to those in serials cataloguing, to those who select serials, to those who budget for expenditures on serials, and to those in the library's bindery. No common definition is functionally useful within the organization as a whole. As another example, the difficulty of defining a title is illustrated in Figure 11 on page 57. The keys to interpreting the meaning and most appropriate application of bibliographic terms are experience and context.

The Bibliographic Temperament

The use and making of bibliographic lists, and even more the planning and implementation of computer-based applications, require constant concentration on noticing facts and interpreting their relationships, no matter how inconsequential they may appear at first glance. To be effective in bibliographic control, one must develop the detective instinct of a Sherlock Holmes. People are not born with this instinct. It comes more easily to some than to others, but anyone who consciously rejects this type of mental discipline will find neither self-fulfillment nor much success in the information-handling professions.

Nevertheless, no single detail of the information in this book is of consequence in itself. Its *context* is what makes it significant. Therefore, the reader should consciously attempt to relate what is presented here to (1) its application to past personal experiences in looking up information in bibliographic tools of all kinds, (2) practices observed in all types of libraries and archives, (3) the practical application of the concepts presented here through specific rules, institutional policies, network operations, etc., and (4) information gained in studying about all other aspects of librarianship. The study of bibliographic control is laden with detail, which generally seems confusing and irrelevant until one acquires through careful observation and experience the context in which to judge which details are significant for a particular purpose.

It bothers many students beginning a graduate library school programme that there is so little in the study of bibliographic theory or practice which is absolute or tangible: everything is presented as being relative. This is particularly disturbing to those who had been led to believe that bibliographic citation and library cataloguing consist of the application of concrete and tangible rules to situations which exactly fit those rules. As teachers, the authors have always found the student question "But what is the *right* way?" to be the most frequently asked (in one guise or another) and the most difficult to answer. The only professionally honest answer is almost always, "It depends on. . . ." One of the things "it depends on," for better or for worse, is so often someone's personal assessment of the issues involved and of the priorities to be applied. Any opinion is the "right" one if its premises are conceded.

Today in bibliographic work there are fewer premises conceded than ever before. The recent changes most difficult to deal with were caused neither by new cataloguing codes nor by the computer, but by the fact that today a library rarely acts alone in the purchase or creation of bibliographic services. The politics of compromise and consensus-seeking among cooperating libraries, the politics of lobbying with government for the support of expensive large-scale ventures, and the politics of arriving at commercial decisions in an environment of competitive and sometimes profit-motivated enterprises have become integral parts of the provision of bibliographic data in libraries.

This book cannot usurp the prerogative of others in determining what is "right" in any given situation. What it can do is show what reasoning in what circumstances has led to what practical applications. The authors are more concerned to analyze what *has* been done and what *can* be done than to presume to describe what *should* be done. Early in this century, Charles Ammi Cutter feared that the influence of the Library of Congress for standardization might mark the close of "the golden age of cataloguing." But despite that influence, and despite the more recent application of modern electronic technology to bibliographic control, Cutter's view of cataloguing (and by implication all of bibliography) as "an art, not a science" is as valid as ever.[4] This view has one overriding implication for the reader and student: one does not learn to deal with bibliographic information by studying it, but by experiencing it.

4. Charles A. Cutter, *Rules for a Dictionary Catalog,* 4th ed., rewritten, U.S. Bureau of Education, Special Report on Public Libraries, Part II (Washington: Government Printing Office, 1904), p. 6. (This exists in a reprint edition published in London by the Library Association.)

2

THE TECHNOLOGY
OF BIBLIOGRAPHY

The intelligent assemblage of bibliographic data into files from which selected data can be retrieved on demand requires many professional and judgemental operations, such as establishing formats, analyzing the subject(s) of a document for various potential uses, determining policies regarding what should be listed and in what detail, etc. Some of these are unique to bibliographic work, some are not. Such matters occupy most of the following chapters of this book, where they are treated only in the context of bibliographic work. Other procedures are required which must be described as clerical, though in the best sense of that word: producing information in some visible form, maintaining and housing files, arranging data alphanumerically or in some other predetermined sequence, locating specified data in a prearranged file, transferring data from one place or medium of communication to another, etc. None of these functions is unique to bibliography, although their operation in the bibliographic context may require slight modifications of standard business practice.

These clerical functions, the "technology of bibliography," have an effect on the judgemental, or professional, functions—perhaps a greater effect than most librarians thought about until very recently. Why do some libraries opt to keep a catalogue of serial publications physically separate from that of monographic publications? Why is it likely that the *National Union Catalog* will eventually change from a basically single-entry listing (see page 159–160) of unit records to a register format (see page 170)? Why do so few libraries now produce their own catalogue cards locally? These and scores of other questions may reflect professional and administrative decisions; but the basis for the decisions, and the reason the questions arise at all, are rooted more in the technology and economics of bibliography than in its theory.

The Manual Technology

From the production of the earliest bibliographies or catalogues until the mid-twentieth century, there was no physical means of keeping track of thousands of documents other than to keep written, typed, or printed records of them. In order to ensure *multiple access* to these records, that is, access by various names, titles, subjects, dates, or any other point of interest, it was necessary manually and separately to incorporate the desired names, etc., as filing elements in the list itself or in an appended index or indices to the list.[1]

Lists in Book Form

A finite catalogue or bibliography can be printed and distributed in multiple copies and consulted in many places, but it can only be brought up to date by a re-edited revision or by cumulating or noncumulating supplements. How frequently supplements or a new edition can be produced is determined by economic factors, including the foreseen sales potential if the bibliography or catalogue is commercially produced. These production and updating methods are still used for many published bibliographies, notably the printed versions of periodical indices and abstracting tools emanating from the abstracting and indexing services (for example the H.W. Wilson Company indices).

For the first thousand years of the existence of organized libraries in Europe, the most common library catalogue format was also such a *book catalogue*. Things were less hurried, library collections grew more slowly, and users did not object to searching a catalogue in several parts or to checking marginal annotations to determine whether an item was listed. It was considered acceptable to have a single new complete catalogue only every few years. Major libraries such as that of the British Museum retained such updating practices well into the twentieth century.

Lists in Card Form

By contrast, a file in which each bibliographic record occupies a separate card can be continually and instantly updated, but at the cost of considerable disadvantages. A card catalogue is relatively costly in materials to produce, and particularly costly to file and house on a continuing basis. Thus, although individual cards can be easily and cheaply reproduced, it is normally impracticable to reproduce and maintain a whole card file, especially a large one, for consultation in different places. The file exists as many physically separate pieces and, in the case of a library's card catalogue, normally in only one copy;

1. An analysis of manual and machine-based technologies for indexing, or accessing, the entries in a bibliographic file begins in Chapter 6. Only the physical characteristics of the whole file as they affect production are at issue in this chapter.

there is little security against vandalism, fire, etc. The likelihood of misfiled, and hence lost, entries is great compared to any other form of bibliographic file. A filing error of one percent in a card file is considered extremely low; but this means a thousand misplaced entries in a tiny file of a hundred thousand! A large card file is of inconvenient size to users who are deterred merely by the prospect of walking from A to Z. It hinders their comprehension of its arrangement and structure by presenting to their scrutiny only one entry at a time, rather than a page of related entries for browsing and comparison. This makes a misfiled entry an even more serious problem, since the searcher is effectively distracted from the established searching pattern.

From the late nineteenth century, however, the demand for immediate updating in rapidly growing library catalogues, particularly in North America, made it likely that the one great advantage of the card form would override all its disadvantages in the minds of library administrators. Then the production and low-priced sale of bibliographic records by the Library of Congress on 7.5 × 12.5 cm. card stock beginning in 1901 settled any last doubt: the card form of catalogue became supreme in North American libraries and many others for most of the twentieth century.

Bancroft, Hubert Howe. 1832—.
    Chronicles of the builders of the common-
    wealth. With index. San Francisco, 1891–92.
    8 v. 8°.   4596

→ —— History of the Pacific states of North
    America. San Francisco, 1882–90. 34 v. 8°.
                                               3502

Contents.

Alaska, 1730–1885, v. 28.	Nevada, 1540–1888, v. 20.
Arizona, 1530–1888, v. 12.	New Mexico, 1530–1888, v. 12.
British Columbia, 1792–1887, v. 27.	North Mexican States and Texas, 1531–1889, v. 10.
California, 1542–1890, v. 13–19.	Northwest coast, 1543–1846, v. 22, 23.
Central America, 1501–1887, v. 1–3.	Oregon, 1834–88, v. 24, 25.
Colorado, 1540–1888, v. 20.	Texas, 1801–89, v. 11.
Idaho, 1845–89, v. 26.	Utah, 1540–1886, v. 21.
Mexico, 1516–1887, v. 49.	Washington, 1845–89, v. 26.
Montana, 1845–89, v. 26.	Wyoming, 1540–1888, v. 20.

Pacific states of North America, History of
        the. 34 v. Bancroft, H. H.   3502

British Columbia.
    Bancroft, H. H. British Columbia, 1792–
    1887. 1887. (*In his* Hist. of the Pacific states,
    v. 27.   3501

FIG. 1. Entries for the same item under different access points in the *Second Catalogue of the Library of the Peabody Institute of the City of Baltimore* (1896-1905). The most complete entry is filed under the author's name; briefer entries, differently formatted, appear under other access points. One of these is an analytic entry for a single part of the complete item (see pages 102–104).

The Unit Entry

When more than one entry for the same item was desired for filing in a multiple-access list, it originally appeared logical to reformat the elements of the entry, whether fully or more briefly, as shown in Figure 1. In the case of a list in "book" form, economy of space was often an object in this reformatting; in the case of the card catalogue, however, almost every entry occupies the same amount of physical space (one card) though there may be few or many lines of data on the card. Since individual cards can easily be reproduced by stencil, photographic, or print methods, the *unit entry system* quickly became the favoured practice in card catalogues.

This means that identical copies of a single bibliographic record are made for a multiple-access list as shown in Figure 2. One of them is filed under whatever

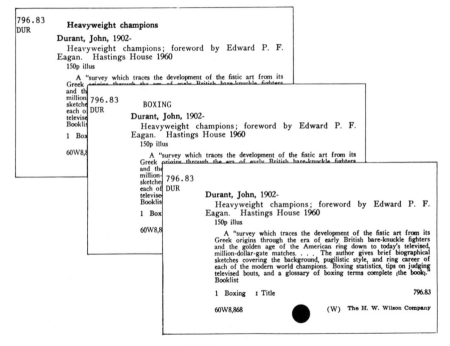

FIG. 2. Unit entries as produced on card stock by the H.W. Wilson Co. from 1938 to 1975. They have been prepared for filing in a card catalogue by the overprinting or typing of secondary access points above the main entry heading, and by the addition of a call number at the upper left corner. The secondary access points are indicated by "tracings" (1.Boxing. I.Title) at the bottom of the unit entry. Similar unit entries prepared by the Library of Congress still predominate in North American library catalogues, and are illustrated in many later figures.

appears on its own top line. This is called the *main entry heading* and is usually an author's name (see pages 217–220). It is still common practice to type or print at the top of each additional copy of the unit entry the required *added entry heading* or *subject heading* under which it is to be filed, as shown in the figure. As labour costs increased, however, libraries began to indicate some or all such additional filing elements on unit cards in a less time-consuming way, such as by marking titles, subject headings, etc., for the filer with a highlight pen.

Purpose and Cost

The manual technologies briefly described above were suited to the materials and methods for presenting bibliographic data available in their time. However, they had to be effected within the frame of reference of priorities and budgets, just as is true today. The size and expense of maintaining card catalogues, and the expense of revising and/or cumulating printed bibliographies, made it necessary to control the scope and depth of the service which could be offered. For example, there has always existed some administrative predisposition against giving contents notes if they would extend the entry beyond a single card, and against using as many cross-references and subject entries as might be desirable because of their almost uncontrollable numbers. Many of these supposed limitations which have come to be taken for granted are based solely on the physical and economic aspects of the manual technologies.

The physical/economic problem of the large size of a card catalogue could be overcome by miniaturizing it onto microform, but only with the sacrifice of its greatest advantage: the ability to interfile new entries into it. A microform catalogue is, in effect, a miniaturized book catalogue, even if it consists of photographed cards. At first, therefore, filmed catalogues were only made to take advantage of other purposes, such as to provide a back-up security copy or for transport to another location. Microform catalogues only became a viable alternative for regular public use when it became possible to produce them with computers, as discussed later in this chapter.

Both the manual technologies, and more importantly the psychology of their use, have been well entrenched: card catalogues held sway for a century, book-form catalogues and bibliographies have been used for over a millennium. It is no surprise that their features were initially simply transferred to the machine mode of handling bibliographic data. It will take more than a decade or two to demonstrate which are the beneficial features of the old technologies to be preserved and developed in the new, and which are the enforced features to be rejected as soon as possible.

The Climate for Change

Soon after World War II, a quiet revolution began, at first almost unnoticed. The King County (Washington) Library began producing catalogue entries from punched cards.[2] Information keypunched only once was interpreted by the electromechanical accounting machinery of the day and reformatted over and over again to produce lists arranged under different elements: once author(s), then title(s), then subject(s), without further individual effort by human workers dealing with single cards. Unit entry output with headings was possible, but so was reformatted output. However, the Hollerith-card technology only made it feasible to manipulate very brief bibliographic records in this way.

Around the same time, C. Dake Gull, Calvin Mooers, Ralph Shaw, and others were experimenting with machine-based searching techniques which would replace human scanning and comparison of entries in subject files. At the time, these were expensive and uncertain experiments, but the increasing cost of all human activity has long since surpassed the rapidly declining cost of equivalent machine (now computer) operations. Libraries, conservative though they may be in these matters, have been forced to the same conclusion as banks, utilities, and stores: it is no longer economically feasible to use people to perform the repetitive tasks involved in storing, sorting, comparing, copying, and otherwise manipulating the data pertaining to a large number of things or transactions. These are the clerical operations which bulk so large in bibliographic control, and which have long been distinguished by librarians from the professional work of creating and formatting bibliographic data.

Computer technology in general will already be quite familiar to many readers. They should merely scan or even bypass the rest of this chapter. For readers to whom the computer is still something of a mystery, the remainder of this chapter introduces those computer basics needed as a background to the study of its application to bibliographic control.

The Beginnings of Electronic Technology

Despite numerous attempts in the eighteenth and nineteenth centuries to devise manual or steam-powered machines to solve mathematical problems, it was the military needs of the 1940s that created the impetus for developing today's electronic devices. To produce large accurate weapons required sophisticated high-speed calculators. By 1949 an electronic (having no moving parts), digital (number-handling), programmable (able to act sequentially on prior instructions) computer was in use in the United States. It occupied fifteen hundred square feet, weighed more than thirty tons, and contained miles of

2. The earliest circulation system using punched cards was actually tested in the 1930s at the University of Texas, but the technology of the day was not adequate to forward the idea.

wire transmitting great amounts of electricity to power almost two thousand vacuum tubes used as switches.

Immense vacuum tube computers were soon manufactured in limited numbers, and by the early 1950s somewhat smaller ones were being made for business use. Although these commercial machines still consumed many kilowatts of electricity, they were an improvement on the earliest machines in one major respect: they stored programs within the machine, and programs could be run sequentially without the assistance of a skilled engineer.

Computers of that period accepted data and instructions in the form of punched cards. A rectangular card which conveys information by means of spaces punched out of the card is in fact an old technology for the storing of coded data. Punched cards were used to instruct machine-driven weaving looms in 1801, and to input data into Charles Babbage's unsuccessful steam-powered calculators and computers in the middle of the nineteenth century. By 1890 a company had been set up to sell punched card machines as mechanical calculators, and by the 1920s that company had taken the name International Business Machines Corporation.

Even IBM's marketing skills could hardly have promoted vacuum tube machines beyond extremely limited use. The vacuum tube's replacement, the transistor, was invented in 1948. Like the tube, it is an electronic switch; they both perform exactly the same function. But there the similarity ends. The tube is large, unreliable, and expensive; the transistor is small, simple, and cheap. It is virtually unbreakable, uses little electricity, and emits no heat during operation. This last fact is one of its most important attributes. The lack of heat emission coupled with its small size allows large numbers of transistors to be packed into a small area, with the result that electronic signals follow much shorter paths in transistor machines than in tube machines.

Thus an important practical result of miniaturization is faster operation. An early transistorized computer occupied about one one-hundredth of the space of its vacuum tube ancestor, and operated at speeds one thousand times greater. The vacuum tube computer could carry out a single instruction in a few milliseconds (thousandths of a second); its transistor replacement operated in microseconds (millionths of a second).

Later improvements in computer components resulted in large numbers of transistors being fabricated on a single *chip* of silicon, technically called an *integrated circuit*, which measures a small fraction of an inch on each side. The number of transistors incorporated on a single chip has increased from a dozen or so in the early 1960s to several thousand in the early 1970s, and has now reached several hundred thousand. This development of the technology continues to have a truly significant impact on the size, and therefore the speed and cost, of computers. The size of circuits, and therefore their production costs and power requirements, have been reduced to the point where high-density microcircuits form the basis of radios, calculators, wristwatches, and control units within other machines. An integrated circuit the size of an aspirin tablet operates in nanoseconds (billionths of a second), and faster devices are already in the design stages.

What Is a Computer?

Before discussing computers and their component parts, it is important to draw some distinctions between general-purpose computers and other electronic machines which, strictly speaking, may be computers, but which cannot be programmed to perform a number of different tasks. Some of these may be of value in library operations, but they serve no useful purpose in bibliographic control per se. They include calculators, television games, language translators, and a host of special-purpose devices containing microprocessors. The microprocessor is a miniature electronic circuit which manipulates data according to the instructions it receives; some instructions will have been built into the chip by its manufacturer, while others may be changed according to the use that is made of it.

The processor is only part of the computer. To be of any use in bibliographic control, a computer must also be able to receive, store, and output data. Therefore at least one input device, some capability for data storage, and an output device must be associated with the processor. Together, these physical components are called the computer *hardware*. Any or all of the other devices may be of one physical piece with the processor, or any or all of them may be physically separate *peripheral devices*. The one requirement is that all must be able to communicate with each other.

Communicating with the Computer

In order to get information into a computer it must be input, either by means of a keyboard-operated device or by transfer from another computer. The transfer of data from one computer to another is discussed on pages 39–42 under Inter-Computer Communication, but the data had to be entered into a computer at some point for the first time, and that requires a keyboard.

Input Devices

In the earliest days of computers, input was accomplished by electrically linking a typewriter keyboard directly to the computer and using it to key in commands and data. Only a single user had access to the machine at a time, and inputting large amounts of information tied up the computer for hours or even days. The solution to this input bottleneck was to interpose a temporary data storage medium, usually punched cards or paper tape. A mechanical reader then transmitted information in "batches" from the storage medium to the computer thousands of times more quickly than a single individual could key it in using a single keyboard. Batch input could also be scheduled for times when the computer was not busy with other activities. These paper media have now faded from popularity, because of rising paper prices and the inflexibility inherent in their use. Keyboard operators are attracted to modern alternatives that permit the correction of a mistake with greater ease than by sticking a paper label over a very small hole.

Some of the more sophisticated input devices still make use of an intermediate storage medium. *Optical character recognition* (OCR) is a system in which information is typed onto plain sheets of paper or cards, usually with a special type font, although new readers can interpret virtually any typeface. Data on the sheets are transmitted to the computer by a page reader which identifies each character optically by its shape. OCR is a convenient method of input for text that has been printed or typewritten clearly and consistently.

Another kind of keyboard device often used is a form of magnetic recording which may be thought of as a combination of typewriter and tape recorder. The typewriter unit has a standard keyboard and produces paper copy; in addition the signals from the keystrokes are recorded on magnetic cards, reels of tapes, tape cassettes, or disks. Unlike punched cards, paper tape, or even OCR images, these magnetic media are easy to erase and re-record. The magnetic cards, tape, or disks are then carried to a computer-controlled electromechanical reader which inputs the data to the computer.

Numeric data are now frequently input using *bar coding*. Labels containing codes very similar to those now seen on grocery items and magazines can be purchased in pre-numbered rolls as unique identifiers of library books for circulation systems. Bar codes have several advantages. They are relatively foolproof: it is possible to make one unreadable, but it is very difficult to change the code. They are read into the computer by very simple equipment: either a stationary sensor past which the label is moved or a small hand-held *light pen* moved across the stationary label. In either case, a number is transmitted to the computer where it is later matched up to the person, item, or activity represented by the code. A severe limitation is that it is not feasible to store any significant amount of alphanumeric data on a bar code. Figure 3 illustrates the common nonmagnetic physical media described above for storing coded information for batch input into a computer.

OCR and bar coding have significant uses in library operations, but the online terminal is now the most common means of computer input today for bibliographic records. It is the original idea of a keyboard attached directly to the computer, but modern computers are no longer restricted to receiving signals from a single source at any one time. As a result, the direct keyboarding of information no longer requires exclusive use of the computer as it once did. An online terminal inputs information to only part of the machine's internal storage, thus other parts are available for other purposes, including accepting input

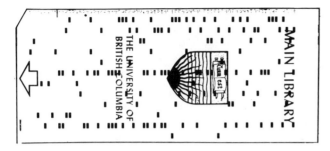

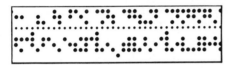

```
ΔSETΔ(¶ARKIV Fⱴ11ⱴOR MATEMATIK,⊦BD. 7, NR. 15)⅀
ΔPRIΔ4.00⅀
ΔNBNΔ¶S68-11⅀
ΔNOBΔ¶BIBLIOGRAPHYⱴ7Aⱴ P. 209.⅀
ΔSUTΔ¶BANACH SPACES.⅀
ΔSUT/2Δ¶TOPOLOGY.⅀
ΔDDCΔ517/.5⅀⅀
ΔCRDΔ72-350760⅀
ΔLANΔENG⅀
ΔFFDΔ1.1 5.X 20.S 21.1968 23.ENK⅀
ΔCALΔ¶J¶N234⊦1968.¶█G7⅀
ΔMEPΔ¶GRIMOND, ¶JOSEPH.⅀
ΔTILⱠCΔ¶THE NATURE OF POLITICS⊦BY ¶JO ¶GRIMOND.⅀
ΔIMPΔ¶LONDON,⊦¶FRIENDS OF THE ¶HEBREW ¶UNIVERSITY OFⱤ█████Ⱡ█Ɽ██
¶JERUSALEM⊦ⱴ3Eⱴ1968ⱴ3Fⱴ⅀
ΔCOLⱠCΔⱴ3█Eⱴ1ⱴ3Fⱴ, 10 P.⊦22 CM.⅀
ΔSETΔ(¶HERBERT ¶SAMUEL LECTURES,⊦1967)⅀
ΔPRIΔUNPRICED⅀
ΔNBNΔ¶B68-06155⅀
ΔSUGⱠXYΔ¶GT. ¶BRIT--¶POLITICS AND GOVERNMENT█--1945-⅀
ΔDDCΔ3██20/.0942⅀⅀
ΔCRDΔ76-350796⅀
ΔLANΔENG⅀
ΔFFDΔ1.1 5.X 2█0.S 21.1968 23.ENK 26.B⅀
ΔCALΔ¶H¶C2█58.¶H34⊦¶Y67⅀
ΔMECNΔ¶YORKSHIRE AND ¶HUMBERSIDE ¶ECONOMIC ¶PLANNING ¶COUNCIL.¶
```

FIG. 3. Some nonmagnetic storage media: a punched eighty-column ''Hollerith'' card, two types of bar code, some punched paper tape, and some bibliographic data reproduced in typical OCR characters.

from other terminals. A terminal may be equipped with a display screen, in which case it is referred to as a *CRT* (cathode ray tube), a *VDT* (video display terminal), or some similar acronym. It may be equipped with or accompanied by a printer, in which case it is simply called a *print terminal* or a typewriter terminal.

A method of input very useful for question-and-answer dialogues between an individual and a computer is the touch-sensitive screen, or *touch terminal*. The computer is programmed to display a number of choices, called a *menu,* to the user on a display screen, in a manner described on page 176. The user responds by touching that part of the screen where the desired answer appears. The touch alters the state of electrical charge on that part of the screen, and the change is transmitted to the computer as input. It is possible to attach a keyboard to the terminal in order to input responses or instructions which are not on the "menu."

Other methods of inputting data to a computer include magnetic ink printing (used for the numbers on bank cheques), mark sensing (marking in predetermined locations on a form with a soft lead pencil), hand printing, and voice recognition (at present still confined to a limited vocabulary). These methods have not been applied to bibliographic data yet, for the range of characters required in bibliographic records is a very broad one by the standards of the computer industry in general.

Once characters (letters, numbers, marks of punctuation, special symbols, etc.) have been input to the computer, it is not possible to determine which kind of input device was used. Within the computer, there is absolutely no difference between a word or number received from an online terminal and the same word or number received via an OCR sheet, a punched card, a magnetic tape cassette, or any other medium.

Output Devices

Machines that produce output from the computer form an array as varied as the different kinds of input devices. Some record the data onto a magnetic tape or disk, which can then be used by another computer program. In order to be useful to a human, the information must at some point be output in visible form on paper, film, or a display screen.

Machines that print on paper are by far the most common form of output device, and seem the most familiar to those unaccustomed to using computers. A *line printer* is a machine that can print pages and forms of various sizes, including 3 × 5 inch cards punched with a hole, the familiar continuous perforated roll of wide paper with sprocket holes along the edges, or any other opaque format. The line printer is so named because it prints a whole line virtually instantly, then moves the paper up and prints the next line. Most of these machines are impact printers; that is, like typewriters, they use metal type and an inked ribbon. Line printers are noisy, they produce print of variable quality (depending on the state of the ribbon, quality of the paper, age and condition of the printer, etc.), and they operate at speeds of roughly nine hundred to fourteen hundred lines per minute, depending on the range of characters to be printed. This may seem fast, but it is not uncommon for such a printer to be by far the slowest device in a computer system, and for the computer's other work to be held up waiting for a chance to produce output. Also, because impact printers have moving parts, they are far more prone to failure than electronic equipment, and so require more frequent service.

A *character printer,* as the name suggests, prints a single character at a time. Speeds range from twenty to two hundred characters per second. Some character printers are *impact printers,* typically using a metal or plastic sphere, cylinder, or disc to produce high-quality images. Others are *thermal printers,* using heated wires against heat-sensitive paper to form letters and numbers silently out of patterns of dots. Some impact printers show a character as a pattern of dots which may or may not not be visible to the naked eye.

Ink-jet and *laser printers* are more recently developed machines which avoid the complex mechanisms of older line and character printers with their many moving parts. Printouts from these are often indistinguishable from the product of a professional printing shop. A laser printer is capable of producing a number of different type fonts and sizes (chosen from among hundreds available), and draws graphs and diagrams as easily as it prints characters. It can print on a continuous roll of high-quality paper, or on single sheets or card stock, at speeds up to two pages per second! The visual image is made by a laser printer using the same technology as an electrostatic photocopier uses; hence the product has the appearance of a photocopier reproduction.

A *COM* (computer output microform) machine produces output from the computer directly as images onto microfilm or microfiche without an intermediate photographic stage. COM has become a popular form of computer output, especially for large amounts of data, because of the small size of the product. Miniaturization means that it is less expensive to produce and store than the equivalent information would be on paper. It is also far less expensive to reproduce in multiple copies. But it has its faults: it requires a projector for human reading, it is not immune to rising prices (the film base is a petroleum byproduct), and it is far from popular with those who must read it for long periods.

COM is thus an almost ideal replacement for the card or book as a physical form for conveying bibliographic information which is briefly consulted, but not read at length. Within a few recent years, a large range of bibliographic tools, including many library catalogues, have begun to appear on COM, sometimes instead of and sometimes in addition to previous physical formats.

The display tube has become a more common output device as prices of electronic equipment have fallen. A video terminal displays characters on the phosphorescent face of a tube virtually identical to a television tube, except that it can "hold" an image on the screen until the terminal is turned off or new input received. Along with the more recent liquid crystal and plasma panel displays, the speed and silence of electronic display tubes makes them valuable for use in public areas. As computer applications enter the home, the existing television screen is being turned into a computer output device for in-home personal computers and for remotely based *videotex* systems. The one disadvantage is that no permanent product is possible: consultation of a bibliographic database using only a display tube can be very frustrating as citations disappear off the screen.

Terminals

"Terminal" is used to denote a portable (or potentially portable) unit capable of input and/or output. Thus a terminal may consist of a bar code reader and a character printer, a keyboard and a display tube, a touch-sensitive display screen, or some other combination of input and/or output devices mounted into a single unit. Because both input and output are commonly provided by one physical unit, it is natural to think that as on a typewriter, the key (input) directly generates the visible character (output). In fact, in most instances, depressing a key causes a signal to be sent to the computer which then stores it and "echoes" it back to the output unit. This permits the user to know whether the message received by the computer was the same message as the one sent from the input section. Of course, the signal travelled at potentially the speed of light (300,000 km/sec).

Terminals come in two general types: dumb terminals and smart or intelligent terminals. A dumb terminal is one which acts as no more than an input/output device. An intelligent terminal is one which has either its own data storage or a microprocessor (or both) built in. The microprocessor might be programmed to produce special output characters, to prompt for the desired input by automatically generating questions or cues, to check and edit the input, to produce special error messages, etc.

Some intelligent terminals are programmed to permit the display, editing, and transmission of an entire screen of information at a time, rather than only a single character or line at a time. There may be "soft" keys: keys which produce one or another result, according to how the terminal is programmed. The intelligent terminal, therefore, is itself a programmable computer, usually one attached to another *host computer*. The direct transfer of programs from the host computer to the intelligent terminal's storage space is called *down loading*. This is just one example of multiple computers being connected to accomplish more than any one of the group could on its own, a topic covered more fully on pages 50–52 under Computer Networking.

The Central Processing Unit

The processor of a computer is often referred to as its central processing unit, or its CPU. A computer is generally referred to by the manufacturer's designation of its CPU, even though two examples of the same processor may have very different combinations of input, output, storage, and communication capabilities. Thus one IBM 3081 may have very little in common with another machine of the same number except for its CPU, and even that will not likely be equipped with exactly the same optional features. Like automobiles, computer hardware comes in stock models but can be modified and tailored closely to the individual requirements of the purchaser.

This central part of the computer consists of one or a number of microcircuits without moving parts, enclosed within a metal cabinet. It provides the computer's processing power, a power encompassed in only a few basic operations carried out one step at a time according to prior instructions. The CPU can (1) move data from one location to another (including accepting it from an input device and transmitting it to an output device), (2) compare one unit of data to another and carry out an instruction based on whether the two units are the same or not, (3) go to a specified location to get its next instruction, and (4) perform the basic arithmetic functions.

Programs

A program is a sequence of instructions. A computer program is a sequence of instructions stored in the computer (in internal storage) or accessible to the computer (in auxiliary storage). Without a program, the CPU is powerless to perform any function at all.

The instructions must be coded in a way intelligible to the particular computer which is to receive and act upon them. The concept of coded instructions is a very old one. Decimal digits constitute a code to represent mathematical quantities, and the codes of language (written symbols and sounds) represent thought and feelings. Numeric and alphabetic characters are used not only for these most basic of human codes, but also for other less widely known ones. Most chess players would recognize "Q-B6ch" as representing the movement of a piece in a chess game; some people who knit would recognize "P2, (K5, K2 tog, P2) 11 times, K2" as representing a series of stitches to be made with knitting needles. There are also non-alphanumeric codes. Telegraphers use Morse code, choreographers use Labanotation, the blind use Braille, composers use musical notation, and so on. Similarly, a computer programmer familiar with the language PL/I would find "GET EDIT(CARD) (A(80));" quite intelligible, and a programmer who knows FORTRAN would quickly recognize "READ (5,87) NUM1,NUM2,NUM3".

Computer programs are of two types: *operating systems* and *user programs*.

Taken together, they comprise the *software,* as distinguished from the hardware (the physical circuitry, cabinetry, etc.). The operating system, or *monitor* as it is sometimes called, is a large and complex program that determines how a particular computer's CPU accepts incoming signals, transmits outgoing signals, allocates storage space to individual users and programs, controls the various peripheral input and output devices, permits access to various files of data and computer functions, moves data internally for processing, and accomplishes other housekeeping tasks.

The operating system in a small computer may be quite simple, requiring the programmer to specify some details which a more sophisticated operating system (more likely to be found in a large computer) would take care of without further instruction. For example, the operating system transfers data from an input device to the CPU's internal storage, and ultimately from the CPU to an output device, but it must also allocate space for a file of records on an available storage device, and continue to find more space as the file grows to many times its original size. Its operating system is normally written by the computer's manufacturer, is provided with the computer, and normally cannot later be tampered with.

Algorithms

A user program is a set of instructions which tells the computer how to execute a specific process on the particular set of data provided. The instructions are based on a sequence of operations commonly referred to as an algorithm. An algorithm is very much like a formula or recipe, in that its application will always produce an identical result if it is followed precisely. Each computer program is based on one or more algorithms devised by the programmer to solve the problem at hand. The typical algorithm examines a piece of data to determine whether a certain condition exists. If it does, then one action will be taken; otherwise, another will.

Much of the programmer's time is spent in inventing, refining, and perfecting algorithms to solve specific problems, but without regard to the actual data involved. For example, any program written to look up a single item in an alphabetic or numeric list will be essentially the same regardless of whether the item sought (referred to as the key) is a number of any length or a word of any kind, provided it appears in the list in numeric or alphabetic order. One kind of algorithm that may be used to search the list (though not the only one) is shown in Figure 4.

Of course, this algorithm requires further refinement before it is a satisfactory basis for a computer program. For example, it is not evident how the computer is to determine which is the middle item (the item halfway between the top and the bottom of the part of the list being examined), nor how it is to determine whether the item being sought will be in the top half of the list or the bottom half. Neither is it apparent what is to be done either when the key is found or when every item has been examined without success. This algorithm also assumes that the key can occur only once in the list, since step 3 stops the operation as soon as the key is found. Nevertheless, a completed version of this simple algorithm will ultimately serve as the core of a program which can look up any item in a sequenced list of any length. This particular process is called a *binary search* because of its repeated division of the file into two parts.

It is common to express an algorithm in the form of a *flowchart,* using boxes of various shapes to denote various functions: a diamond for decisions, a rectangle for processes, and so on. Figure 5 is a flowchart illustrating the above algorithm for searching sequenced lists.

```
1. Repeat the following steps until the "key" is found
        or the entire list has been examined.
2. Locate the middle item of the remainder of the list.
3. If it is the correct item, then the search is finished.
4. Otherwise:
        a) If the key is in the top half of the list,
           then disregard the bottom half of the list
           and return to step 2.
5.      b) If the key is in the bottom half of the list,
           then disregard the top half of the list
           and return to step 2.
```

FIG. 4. An algorithm for searching a sequenced list.

Programming Languages

When the algorithm has been completed, it must be coded into a form recognizable to the circuits of a specific machine: the programmer must translate from any natural language used (English, French, etc.) to the machine's language. The degree to which the machine assists in this translation process depends on the type of programming language used. Programming languages may be divided broadly into three types: *machine language, assembler language,* and *higher-level languages*.

Machine Language: Binary Numbers

Within a computer, all information is contained on huge numbers of switches. These retain programs and data, and carry out instructions, by being turned on and off. All programs and data therefore efist within the computer in the form of binary numbers. Based on the power of 2 (rather than the more familiar 0-9, based on the power of 10), these are the only symbols that can be stored in circuits with just two possible states: ''on'' and ''off,'' or on a

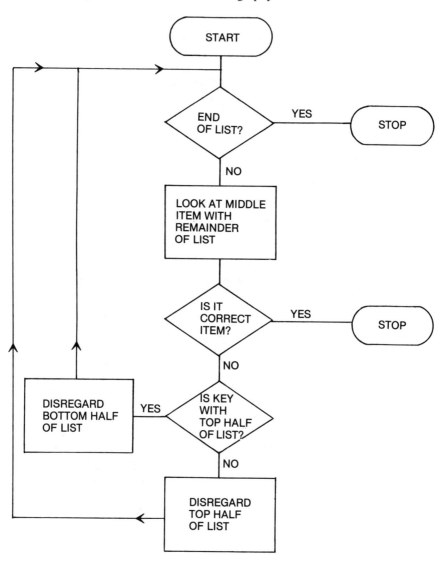

FIG. 5. A flowchart illustrating the algorithm in Figure 4 for searching a sequenced list.

magnetic medium where the two states are "positive" and "negative." One state in a switch is used to represent 0, while the other represents 1. Using binary numbers requires six switches to represent sixty-four characters, as shown in Figure 6. Because sixty-four choices provide room for individual coding of the ten decimal digits, one twenty-six character set of the roman alphabet, plus certain necessary auxiliary symbols (such as $? & ; : , .), such a system is satisfactory for representing language.

However, fifty-two characters are needed to reproduce both upper and lower case letters (A-Z and a-z). The sixty-four character system is therefore inadequate to handle the upper and lower case letters, ten digits, and necessary punctuation. Thus most computers use eight switches (vacuum tubes, transistors, sections of a microcircuit, etc.) to represent each letter, number, or other symbol input. They are called eight-bit machines, *bit* being a contraction of the words "binary digit." Eight-bit machines permit the encoding of 256 different characters, a sufficient number to handle a wide variety of alphanumeric characters and to leave room for codes which are not represented by any visible character.

000000	001000	010000	011000
000001	001001	010001	011001
000010	001010	010010	011010
000011	001011	010011	011011
000100	001100	010100	011100
000101	001101	010101	011101
000110	001110	010110	011110
000111	001111	010111	011111
100000	101000	110000	111000
100001	101001	110001	111001
100010	101010	110010	111010
100011	101011	110011	111011
100100	101100	110100	111100
100101	101101	110101	111101
100110	101110	110110	111110
100111	101111	110111	111111

FIG. 6. All possible combinations of six bits result in sixty-four unique codes. Each addition of one to the number of bits doubles the number of codes available.

A machine language consists entirely of numeric symbols and is designed for use by a computer directly, without translation. The machine language comprises the total set or repertoire of operations the machine can perform: perhaps a hundred different instructions, including input and output as well as arithmetical operations for handling numeric data and logical operations for handling alphanumeric data.

In machine language the instruction to clear out a section of internal storage and add the following number to it might be represented by the code 11. If the number 0193 provides the address or location of the area to be cleared and added to, the entire instruction would be 110193. This decimal number is converted into the corresponding binary number when the instruction is read into the CPU.

Computer users never see a binary number. It is extremely rare these days even for programmers to use machine language or to have to examine strings of binary digits. The translation of information from alphanumeric symbols to binary codes and back again is done by the computer itself. Computer programmers normally write their instructions using either assembler language or a higher level language.

Assembler Language

Most computers likely to be used in libraries come equipped by their manufacturers with their own assembler languages. This language is itself a computer program which translates instructions looking like parts of ordinary English words into the binary-number machine language. To continue the preceding example, an assembler language instruction to clear out a section of storage and add a number to it would likely be the mnemonic instruction ADD, or perhaps CLRAD (for "clear, add"), followed by the location that is to be cleared.

A program written for a computer in its assembler language would be unlikely to work on any other computer. Similarities might be obvious among the various models of a single manufacturer, but attempting to move an assembler program from one machine to an ostensibly identical machine might not work, for no two machines are likely to have all the same optional features, identical amounts of available internal storage, the same numbers and types of auxiliary storage devices, and so on.

Higher-Level Languages

The higher-level languages are the easiest to learn and master, and thus the most commonly used. FORTRAN, COBOL, PL/I, ALGOL, BASIC, SNOBOL, WATFOR, SPITBOL, PASCAL, and others are widely known and commonly taught in vocational schools and at computer centres. Some higher level languages were devised to make general programming easier to learn, while others were designed to deal with a particular kind of problem, such as solving equations or manipulating strings (sequences) of alphanumeric characters. A program written in one of these languages is passed through a *compiler,* a translation program which produces the set of machine-language instructions actually used by the computer. The computer will not be able to accept a program written in FORTRAN, for example, unless it has a FORTRAN compiler in internal storage or available to it in auxiliary storage. Because compilers must be purchased or leased, and because they occupy memory space that the computer could otherwise use for other programs and data, most computers are equipped with very few compilers, and many have only one or two.

Higher-level languages are not standardized: each of them comes in a number of versions, called dialects, in order to take maximum advantage of the capabilities of each general class of computer. The dialect of BASIC used on a large Amdahl mainframe computer may have a larger vocabulary, permitting more special operations, than the dialect written for a Radio Shack microcomputer. There are at present more than a dozen major dialects of BASIC, as well as many local variants, and many dialects of FORTRAN. Therefore, a program written in IBM BASIC will not necessarily be directly transferable from one computer to another without modification, and especially not from a larger machine to a smaller one.

In addition to their ease of use by humans, higher-level languages offer the advantages of (1) requiring fewer instructions to accomplish a task than assembler languages, (2) providing instructions specifically oriented toward the problem at hand, and (3) tending to be relatively "portable." Portability means that a program written in PASCAL for an IBM mainframe computer will likely also work on a DEC minicomputer (assuming that both have PASCAL compilers) and with only minor changes may work on an Apple microcomputer. The computer programmer hired today can be writing programs tomorrow, rather than starting to learn yet another assembler language.

Whether a given program is less expensive to produce and run in one language or in another will depend on such variables as the competence of the programmer, the suitability of the available higher level language to the problem at hand, how often the program will be used, and so on. The difference between two choices is often not trivial; it can take ten or even fifteen assembler instructions to equal a single instruction written in a higher-level language, and an instruction that takes a single line of code in one higher-level language may require four or five lines in another.

There are certain disadvantages to these languages, and in some cases they may be serious. Precisely because a higher-level language is not designed for any particular computer, it tends not to take advantage of the specific features of the computer it will be used on. In a perverse way, it can occasionally be difficult or even impossible to get a higher-level language to carry out instructions it was not designed for, even though it might be relatively easy to write those instructions in the machine's assembler language. Use of higher-level languages also removes some of the programmer's freedom to specify instructions or to tailor a program to the particular data configuration it is to handle. For these reasons, a program written in assembler language will usually take less computer time to run than the equivalent program written in a higher-level language.

Command Languages

Many computer programs are designed to permit options during their use. At the most simple level they provide for the interruption of a run to "ask" one or more questions which must be answered either YES or NO. In other cases, the user may be able to issue a series of commands which will operate as part of the program, such as to specify whether the desired record in a file must have one, two, or all three of the subject terms being searched for, whether an entire bibliographic citation should be printed or only the author and title, and so on. Such options are stated in a command language. A command language is not a programming language. When using a command language, the user is restricted to only those commands which the programmer has built into that particular program.

Programmers

The function of a computer program is to instruct the computer to carry out some process on the data it will receive. If it is to account for human error, the program should take account of every possible kind of data input at every point, including totally illogical input due to keying errors. For example, a program intended to add two numbers together must be able to handle (which in this case means guard against) data which erroneously includes a letter—and not only the obvious ones, such as a lower-case l for the figure one and an upper-case O for a zero. (Another example of this is shown on page 176.) Because it is not practicable to protect against all possible errors all the time, every program is ultimately limited by the perceptions, the ability, and often the creativity and imagination of its creator, the programmer. A program can only do what the programmer thought it should.

Programming is therefore a creative and in many ways a unique activity. It can be done as well (and occasionally better) by a tenth grade dropout as by a university professor. All that matters is that the programmer understand the problem to be solved and be able to analyze it into its smallest component parts. In the bibliographic context, the programmer's understanding of the function to be performed depends almost entirely on the ability of professional librarians, indexers, bibliographers, archivists, etc., to formulate and communicate their needs at an equally analytical level. Experience has shown that when automation fails in a library, the blame is as likely to lie with librarians as it is with programmers.

Storage

The capacity to store data is, not surprisingly, called memory. In order for a computer to function it must be able to "remember" data input to it, even if only for a small fraction of a second while the data are being operated upon. Computers often need to be able to store data for far longer than that. Virtually every computer has two kinds of storage, called internal (core, main) storage, and auxiliary (external) storage. Figure 7 is a conceptual diagram of a simple computer system showing the relationship among the CPU, the input/output device(s), and the two types of memory.

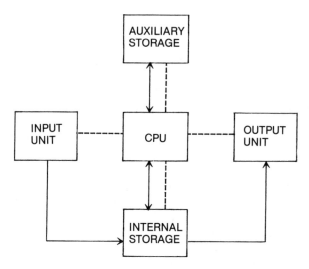

FIG. 7. A simple computing system. The solid line shows the flow of data; the dotted line shows the flow of control between the CPU and its peripheral devices.

Internal Storage

The speed of the computer's operation tends to be controlled by the rate at which it can get data into and out of its internal storage. In order to keep signal paths as short as possible, internal storage is physically located either within or immediately next to the CPU. "Next to" a mainframe means in the next cabinet; "next to" in a microcomputer means being on the same chip as the CPU. Internal storage is therefore limited, for enlarging it only succeeds in moving the newly added storage further and further from the CPU, thus slowing down operations. The size of internal storage is determined by what the CPU can handle and by the amount of money the computer's owner wishes to spend. Physically, internal storage consists of semiconductor microcircuits similar to those that form the CPU.

Internal storage is usually divided into *read-only memory* (ROM) and *random-access memory* (RAM). The information held in read-only memory cannot readily be changed by a user. It typically includes the operating system described on page 28 and other housekeeping programs. The random-access memory is where data for specific purposes is stored for brief periods while operations are being performed on it.

Auxiliary Storage

In addition to its necessarily limited amount of internal storage, a computer must have access to some medium where large amounts of data can be stored for long periods. All such equipment falls into the category of auxiliary or external storage, for the storage machines are located in their own cabinets, separate from the computer but connected to it by cables.

The storage of bibliographic data represents a challenge for the computer hardware industry. Individual bibliographic records consume more space than do typical business or scientific records, as is seen in Chapter 5. Bibliographic files typically grow without foreseeable limits, whereas in business applications a file is often in some balance, with new data constantly replacing old. In a single bibliography or library catalogue, each entry must be as readily accessible as each other one; a library rarely has one catalogue of frequently used or current materials and another of the more esoteric or outdated items, as is often true in scientific applications. In fact, all other factors being equal, the best file of bibliographic records is the biggest one, a factor whose administrative and technical consequences are discussed in Chapter 9.

The two major classes of auxiliary storage are those which preserve data magnetically and those which do not (see pages 22–24). Punched cards, bar code labels, OCR typed sheets, etc., are some nonmagnetic media for data in machine-readable form. For processing complete bibliographic records, the magnetic media are at present the most popular and efficient.

Magnetic Tape and Disk Storage. Computer signals can be recorded onto magnetic tape (in open reel and cassette formats) in virtually the same way as sounds or visual images are preserved in home recording equipment. Tape is a *sequential access medium,* for it is necessary to pass sequentially through a tape to get to the desired information, even though this can be done quickly. Despite this and some other disadvantages (see, for example, File Security, page 38), tapes are valued for their cheapness, the ease with which copies can be made, the simplicity of their transportation and shipment from one place to another, their relative permanence, and their huge capacity. A one-inch length of half-inch wide tape can hold up to 6,250 characters.

The speed with which data can be moved to and from disks is considerably faster than is possible with tapes. Disks come in singles and in stacks (much like phonograph records stacked on a record changer), on rigid aluminum plates or as floppy pieces of thin film, in sizes ranging from four to fourteen inches in diameter. The disk spins like a phonograph record, while a read/write head similar to the record/erase head of a tape recorder travels on the end of an arm across the surface of the rotating disk.

The speed of reading or recording data by this method is only a few thousandths of a second (even less in cases where there is a fixed read/write head for each track). Disk is a *random-access medium* since the head can be rapidly and specifically positioned to write or read a piece of information. Unlike a phonograph record stylus, the read-write head does not follow a single spiral groove or track sequentially until it reaches the desired location. Nor does it touch the surface of the disk, but rather it floats or "flies" on a cushion of moving air.

The data handling capacity of disks is constantly being increased. Billions of characters can now be recorded on a single rigid disk, about twelve hundred per inch of track and about a thousand tracks per inch of the disk's diameter. The smaller *floppy disks,* which are much less expensive, record far fewer tracks per inch, but a single surface still holds up to two and a half million characters.

It is true of both disk and tape storage that if one must wait for the right disk (tape) to be mounted on an available disk (tape) drive, a considerable delay can result. It has therefore become the norm in computing centres to use permanently mounted rigid disks for information which may be needed at any time and must be retrieved quickly. Budgetary considerations determine how much immediate-access disk storage can be provided in this way (see page 45).

Virtual Storage

Because many bibliographic functions require the computer to compare very large numbers of records in a single processing step, it is relevant to note the major method of increasing a computer's apparent memory capacity. Virtual storage systems are attempts to make internal storage appear larger than it really is through the use of an extremely fast auxiliary storage device located close to the CPU. This is often a large disk with one or more fixed read/write heads for each track. Multiple fixed heads eliminate the delay incurred in moving-head disks where the computer cannot start reading until the mechanically moved head has arrived at the right track.

When virtual storage is used, portions of data files and programs are moved back and forth between it and internal storage by the computer's operating system. Typically, all information is arbitrarily divided into "pages," each perhaps a few thousand characters long. When information is required in internal storage, space is made for it by shifting to virtual storage some pages of data which have not been used for a period of time. When the information that has been moved out is needed again, other inactive pages are moved out to make room for it. The period of time that an unused page will remain in internal storage is a function of the demand. At peak times it may be no more than a few milliseconds; at other times it may be many seconds, or the virtual storage area may not be used at all. The operating system thus becomes an extremely dynamic manager of space, changing the contents of internal storage in response to the users' needs.

Future Developments in Data Storage

In many ways, the use of virtual storage represents a stopgap measure. It is designed to make up for an insufficient amount of internal storage and the inadequate speed of accessing data from auxiliary storage. But new storage devices are being developed. Mechanical machines are starting to give way to far more sophisticated devices which are constantly changing the practical limits of storage.

Videodisk has yet to make a great impact on computer systems, but it seems likely that it, along with magnetic bubble memories, holograms, and other devices still in the laboratory stages, will offer far more compact forms of mass storage in the near future. They avoid the wear and occasional tear associated with moving-surface memories and provide greater potential for the storage and instant manipulation of the truly huge files involved in bibliographic operations. As computers grow smaller and faster, as storage grows smaller and cheaper, and as computers are linked in new and more efficient ways, new methods of employing networks of electronic components are perfected. Many of the methods briefly described here may soon be abandoned for others, which will no doubt be even more complex.

File Security

Librarians now recognize the need to be concerned about the security of any unique bibliographic file, whether a card catalogue or a machine-readable file. In particular, the magnetic media used at present for storing large bibliographic files are highly vulnerable to deterioration, accidental damage, and inadvertent destruction.

There are recognized security measures for the protection of the content of machine-readable files. Magnetic tapes are periodically taken from the tape library, physically inspected, and copied onto fresh tape. During the copying procedure, the computer "examines" the data to detect areas that may be faulty or damaged. The contents of disks are copied onto tape periodically, the period ranging from every few hours to every month depending on the value of the file and the rate at which it is changing. A duplicate copy of each tape may be made periodically for safekeeping either in a fireproof vault or in a separate physical location.

Because of the expense involved in these procedures, not every computing centre is as careful as it might be in protecting files, and accidents causing the loss of many thousands of bibliographic records occur occasionally. Librarians responsible for bibliographic files should participate in planning the security measures to be applied, and in checking periodically to be sure that the plans are followed.

Inter-Computer Communication

Computers are essentially machines that communicate. By accepting and transmitting signals, a computer moves programs and data from input devices, into and out of various kinds of storage, and ultimately to output devices. In a small machine this all takes place within a single physical unit. But even the addition of a single peripheral device (a small disk drive perhaps, or a line printer) means that it is necessary to establish communication links to carry the signals from one component to another, whether they are in the same room, in the same city, or in different countries.

For short-range communication the solution is to use wires as part of the computer system itself. Once the signals are required to travel from one building to another, from one region or country to another, or even from one continent to another, it is more common to take advantage of existing commercial communication facilities. Telephone companies, to give the major example, are already the possessors of huge amounts of communication equipment, and are always seeking paying customers who will lease their facilities for short periods of time. Those facilities include not only wires and microwave relay stations, but also fibre optics and satellites.

Fibre Optics

The reduction of sound waves to binary coded pulses has permitted research into completely new methods of data transmission, the most promising of which at present is the laser beam. To use lasers or *light emitting diodes* (LEDs) as practical communication devices, it was necessary to invent a "wire" that could carry light beams. These "light guides" are fine glass fibres which can carry beams of light for long distances with very little loss of signal.

The use of glass fibres offers major advantages over older methods. One is that silicon, the raw material for these fibres, is a plentiful resource. Once in mass production, silicon fibres will be far less expensive than copper wires. Being lighter, they require less expensive protection and supports. Since the signals they carry are not electrical, they are immune from disturbance by crosstalk, atmospheric electricity, faulty electrical equipment, sunspot activity, etc.

Fibres have immense potential for carrying signals. A three-quarter inch copper cable can carry about forty television channels, while a cable of just six fibres can carry a thousand channels. There are still some problems to be solved before fibre optics can replace copper wires, but the advantages seem sufficiently significant to permit the prediction that fibre optics will enable unprecedented amounts of information, including bibliographic records, to be transmitted cheaply between computers and television sets.

Satellite Communication

In transcontinental telephone systems, microwave relay stations are required every thirty kilometres or so because of the Earth's curvature. Each station in turn receives the signal, amplifies it, and retransmits it to the next. The multiplicity of stations can be eliminated by locating a single relay station in space above the Earth. As a result, the cost of communication is no longer strictly related to the distance involved.

Use of such a satellite for radio broadcasting was suggested in 1945 by the English author Arthur C. Clarke.[3] Although satellite communication technology was only begun in 1959 and is still in a period of rapid development, the satellites used for communication today are essentially as Clarke envisioned them. Their numbers grow annually as more and more nations and international groups launch their own. Data transmissions are sent by microwave from an originating station on Earth. The satellite receives them, amplifies them, and broadcasts them to another satellite or back to Earth. Depending on the power of transmission, satellite transmissions can be picked up by a small dish-shaped antenna, often only one to two metres in diameter.

Digital Transmission

Since the 1880s telephone companies have been engaged in efforts to transmit more than one conversation over a single telephone line. For many years these efforts met with only limited success. Although it was well known that a telephone line is used only part of the time even while a conversation is taking place, it was not until 1960 that it became possible to determine the exact instant when speech begins and to assign it to a vacant channel. An ordinary telephone line can now carry about a dozen voice communications simultaneously using this technique, which is generally known in the computer industry as *timesharing* and in the communication world as *time multiplexing*. Improvements in the basic technique were relatively minor until means of transmitting digital signals were perfected.

In digital transmission the continuously varying (analogue) sound wave that characterizes the human voice is not transmitted as such. Rather it is electronically measured, perhaps once every eight-thousandth of a second. Each such sample, called a *pulse*, is transmitted as a numeric representation of its frequency and amplitude. This is known as *analogue-to-digital conversion* or *modulation*. It is accomplished by a small and inexpensive device called a *modem*. At the receiving end, the numeric signal is reconverted to a sound frequency by another modem, recreating the original series of sound pulses. Although the human ear receives a pulse only once every eight thousandth of a

3. Arthur C. Clarke, "Extra-Terrestrial Relays," *Wireless World* 51 (October 1945):305–308.

second, the brain accepts these as continuous sound waves, just as the sight of a rapid sequence of still photographs projected on a screen is accepted by the brain as a moving picture.

By dealing only in exact numbers, digital transmission can result in relatively distortion-free reproduction of any information: sound, picture, and machine-readable. The importance of analogue-to-digital modulation to automation lies in the fact that the transmission of groups of binary digits can be accomplished reliably at extremely high speeds.

Packet Switching

Signals of various kinds require sampling less or more often. A keyboard input device, for example, may transmit a single character once every tenth of a second, or perhaps a whole line of data every fifteen seconds, with occasional time out while the keyboard operator stops to rest or do other tasks. An automated circulation system may transmit a number read from a bar code only once every few minutes at some times, but every second at others, taking a small fraction of a second to transmit any one transaction. There is plenty of free time between these momentary transmissions for many signals from various sources to be carried on the same line.

Packet switching is a transmission method in which groups of binary signals representing the data are put into blocks or "packets" of fixed maximum length by a computer at the transmitting end. Each packet includes information on where the packet is going, how large it is, and where it has come from. Packets are routed by computer-controlled switchboards over any available line (not necessarily the most direct one) until they reach their destination. There the destination and origin labels are removed, and the content is delivered to the computer or output device to which the packet was addressed.

This electronic activity is completely "transparent" to the user since all processing of packets is done automatically by computers. The user transmits/receives only the signals conveying the content and an "end of packet" code generated by the ENTER or SEND key.

Value-Added Networks

Because telephone companies still have a huge investment of capital in older equipment, it has not been easy for them to change quickly from analogue transmission of sound waves to high-speed digital transmission. The installation of new equipment at all of the many switchboards and transmitters of all the telephone companies will not be completed for many years, and until then transmission speed is greatly restricted. The demand for high-speed digital transmission has elicited different responses in different parts of the world. In countries where communication facilities are owned by the government (this includes all of Europe, Asia, Africa, and most of Latin America), digital communication services have become available slowly, and usually at a high price, as the governments have upgraded their equipment.

In the United States, the major country where communication facilities are in the hands of the private sector, the inability of telephone companies to react quickly permitted the growth of new commercial ventures, called value-added carriers. These companies lease existing telephone channels, add their own computers to carry out the analogue-to-digital conversion, and sell the resulting digital communication services. In the process, regulatory legislation has been abandoned for nonvoice communication in the United States, leaving free enterprise to determine developments and changes. This has already begun to increase the rate at which changes are occurring. Global networking is quickly becoming a reality, for it is already quite simple to communicate between the American value-added networks (Tymnet, Telenet, and Uninet), the Canadian systems (Datapac and Infoswitch), and the major European network (Euronet). By adopting the international standards for bibliographic description and for the formatting of bibliographic records described in Chapter 5, librarians are preparing to take advantage of this ability to communicate worldwide via computer.

Locally Owned Networks

As computers become more widely used in business, companies are building communication networks entirely in their own control in order to link computer hardware in various units of the organization: within a building, within a city, and even in different cities and countries. Although most still employ lines leased from the telephone and telegraph companies, wholly owned and maintained networks are appearing. These use not only every standard communication technology from wires to satellites, but also technologies uniquely suited to short-range communication such as coaxial cables and infra-red transmitters and receivers.

Like companies, individual multibranch libraries and groups of libraries use computers as concentrators, to send and receive messages digitally and thus make more efficient use of telephone lines. The future will likely bring library and bibliographic uses of the kinds of networks pioneered by private industry.

Combining the Components

The hardware (the CPU, terminals, other input and output devices, auxiliary storage, etc.) and the software (both the operating system and any other programs created for specific jobs) are major determinants of a computer's ability to handle information. Other less obvious determinants include whether the machine is being shared among a number of tasks, and whether the program is being run in *batch* or *online* mode. As is true of communication lines, computers may be dedicated to a single task, shared among a number of tasks, or timeshared among a number of tasks.

Dedication

A dedicated computer is one that is used only for a single task. Dedication is characteristic of a microprocessor built into another machine (for example, a calculator, chess-playing unit, translation device). It can perform no other function. It is not uncommon to use a general-purpose machine in a dedicated manner: that is, to decide to purchase a computer for a single task. For example, a library may purchase a minicomputer only to handle circulation for one or more locations. The circulation procedures may be varied and complex, but so long as that computer is used only for them it is said to be dedicated to circulation. When the library wishes to automate its acquisitions processes, it may purchase another machine or rent time on a computer owned by a commercial service bureau, or it may expand the capabilities of the computer formerly dedicated to circulation to use it for shared tasks.

Serial Sharing

The sharing of tasks on a computer may be done serially or simultaneously. When a computer is used for more than one task, but only one of them at any given time, it is said to be serially shared. Using the example above, when the library is closed and thus not circulating materials, the circulation computer could be used to produce batch catalogues, to print lists of periodicals received, or to accomplish any other occasional job. A computer might be used for monograph acquisitions in the mornings, periodical check-in in the afternoons, payroll at the end of each pay period, etc. A library may sell time it is not using on its computer to other libraries, a practice that is growing. In each case, while the computer is performing a particular task, it is dedicated to that task exclusively, giving that user access to all the internal and external storage, etc.

Timesharing

The apparently simultaneous sharing of tasks on a computer is called timesharing. In communication timesharing, it is not possible for two messages to travel along a single channel at the same moment, but it is possible to interleave them so closely that the channel is used zo maximum efficiency, each user remaining unaware of the others. Similarly, timesharing operating systems permit computer messages and functions to be interleaved in such a way that each user is usually unaware of other users. The various uses seem to be simultaneous, although for the most part they are not.

There are, of course, practical limits dictated by the capacity of the computer in relation to the complexity of the operations. When more and more users attempt to share a computer simultaneously, as frequently happens in bibliographic networks, there comes a point where its operating system can no longer fit each instruction from each user into the *job queue* for operation without some delay. The sequence of operations backs up, and users experience slow *response time* as they wait at their terminals for output or for the computer to accept further input. The methods described in the remaining sections of this chapter are all ways of attempting to enlarge the capacity of a system to accommodate increasingly large numbers of simultaneous users.

Batch Operation

Closely related to the issue of sharing computers is the matter of whether a given machine is used for batch work, for online work, or for both. The use of punched-card readers and paper-tape readers in the 1950s permitted the preparation of data on a keypunch or paper tape machine that was not in any way connected to, or dependent upon the immediate attention of, the computer. The cards or tape were gathered into a batch as described on pages 21–22, then carried to the computer when it was ready or required to act on the data.

Today one would use a magnetic medium rather than paper, but regardless of the storage medium used, batch operation still separates the functions of input and output from each other and from the function of processing the data. Batch operation offers the great advantage that the programs and data required may occupy the entire machine and all of its internal storage for a period of time, and that these operations may be relegated to periods of the day when the computer would otherwise be relatively inactive. The great disadvantage is that the processing time must be scheduled in advance. The job is not done *now*, and there is no immediate response from the computer.

Batch operation is especially efficient for functions which will result in permanent or hard-copy output when it is not required instantaneously. Printed or COM lists, indices, and catalogues may be produced annually, monthly, or even daily, along with statistical reports, purchase orders for acquisitions, circulation overdue notices, claim letters for missing periodical issues, and similar byproducts of the automation of library procedures.

When a huge file of bibliographic records is to be searched in order to extract a small number of items, batch operation may be the only economically efficient method. This is particularly true when more than one user may request a search of the same database during a period of, say, a day or a week, and it is possible to combine requests so that the database need be scanned only once during that period, rather than once for each request. The results are mailed, or are copied into computer storage for posting to the user's terminal at the next sign-on, or are simply held for the user to pick up later.

Online Operation

When a computer is used online, no significant delay in response is experienced. The request for information is input from a terminal linked to the computer. The required programs are immediately moved to internal storage from active auxiliary storage (disk or tape mounted on a drive and ready for reading at all times). The files of records to be searched must also be accessible in the same way. The searching is done and the results delivered to the output section of the terminal while the user waits. In the online mode, a process may take only part of a second or as much as a few minutes, but it will always start immediately following the individual request for service.

The online mode is also called the *interactive mode* of computer use because immediacy of response permits the user to conduct a "dialogue" with a computer program. This may merely involve the use of a command language (see pages 33–34) to modify a procedure on a preplanned basis; but it also means that a user can abort one procedure and initiate another, based on a judgement about how satisfactory the former proved to be. A manual search of a bibliographic file is always a holistic experience: the searching strategy is altered as results appear to be more relevant to the need, or less. This capacity is therefore also desirable in computerized searching, and is the greatest advantage of the online mode of access over the batch mode.

The ability and willingness of a computing centre to offer online access to its equipment and files depends to a great extent on economic considerations. Sufficient communication equipment to accommodate the number of potential simultaneous users, an operating system capable of managing the complex operations of an online computer, and fast-access storage devices must all be acquired and installed; none of these is inexpensive. Storage devices can be especially costly. It is typical of a batch operation to use a small number of tape drives even though thousands of reels of tape may be stored. But online access implies that the convenience of the user is more important than cost, and such access will be unsatisfactory if the user must wait for one of the many reels of tape to be mounted onto one of the few tape drives, assuming that one is immediately available.

Therefore, online systems commonly make use of disk storage devices, which are considerably faster and more expensive than tape drives. Although it is still possible to have more disks than disk drives, the criterion of user convenience will dictate that virtually any information which might be requested will be available immediately on a disk already mounted on a disk drive. Although the gradually falling cost of disks and disk drives is contributing to the replacement of batch systems with online systems, the immense amounts of data stored by libraries still require the expenditure of large sums for fast-access storage.

Online operations may take place on a dedicated computer or on a time-shared computer. An example of the former occurs in online circulation systems. Each time a book is checked out or in, the terminal at the circulation desk sends its message to the CPU, which in turn updates the files immediately. The program may also call for a search of the files at that instant to report to the circulation terminal information about the status of the borrower or of the item involved in the transaction.

Yet this same computer, dedicated to circulation functions, may also be described as timesharing, for the single computer is serving a number of terminals in a period of time sufficiently short to be considered simultaneous. Another kind of timesharing called _multitasking_ occurs when a single computer is used for a number of unrelated tasks by multiple users. Each user may ask the computer to operate on different sets of data using different programs. The computer's response time may become slower as the number of users rises, but apart from that each user is unaware of the others.

Partitioning

In addition to using a computer in batch mode or serial sharing part of the time and in timeshared mode part of the time, it is also possible to partition computers. When partitioning takes place, some part of the machine's internal and external storage may be set aside for batch use, while the remainder is available for online use; or two different groups of online users may each use a part of the computer (a partition), simultaneously or nearly so. Whether a computer is used in batch mode, online, or both, is a function of decisions made by the director of computing and the availability of a suitable operating system. Virtually any general-purpose minicomputer or mainframe can be used in any of these ways, providing it has sufficient communication ports and internal storage to support its potential users.

Stretching Computer Limits

Usually it is possible to add more communication equipment and more internal and external storage to a computer, but no computer can be expanded indefinitely. There are ultimately limits to the number of terminals that can be connected to a single CPU, to the amount of internal storage available for programs and data, and to the number of auxiliary storage devices the operating system can handle. Moreover, the operating system of a computer used for timesharing must be highly complex. Tasks must be assigned priorities by the operating system, for without this function the potential problem exists that when a sufficient number of jobs await execution, the computer will spend all of its time interrupting tasks and moving programs and data into and out of external storage, having no time left to complete tasks and produce output.

The quantity of bibliographic information stored and the complexity of operations required for more sophisticated bibliographic searches make overloading a real danger in larger library systems, particularly in bibliographic networks. A number of techniques have been developed to help computers cope with large numbers of simultaneous users and functions and to avoid overloading. These include the use of buffers, access by intelligent terminals, the use of front ends and back ends, computer networking, and distributed processing. These techniques are usually transparent to the user, who has no way of knowing whether any or all of the methods described below are being used.

Buffers

On page 26 it was implied that as each key on a terminal is pressed, a single character is transmitted to the CPU, where it is stored but also echoed back to assure the keyboard operator that the correct character was transmitted and received. In fact, in order not to involve the CPU in the receipt, storage, and retransmission of every individual character, a buffer is used. A buffer is usually an area of internal storage reserved for a series of incoming or outgoing characters; each peripheral device has its own buffer. Pressing the RETURN, ENTER, or SEND key of a terminal typically results in the contents of the input buffer being transmitted to the CPU. Only then is the CPU able to distinguish commands from data, instructions that are acceptable from those that are not, etc.

There is always some limit to the number of characters a buffer can hold before it must be emptied by transmitting its content to the CPU. When the buffer is full, further transmissions to it will be lost; an error message may or may not be generated. Obviously, the problem of exceeding the capacity can be overcome by using large buffers, but buffers, like so many useful computer features, require the allotment of space in internal storage, which is always limited.

Output buffers are also commonly used to act as intermediaries between the CPU and the printer, the display terminal, etc. In effect, the CPU transmits data to the buffer in batches, according to the latter's capacity. The buffer in turn feeds the data to the output device at whatever speed the device can accept them, while the CPU performs other functions. Input, output, and storage buffers help to overcome the mismatch of varying speeds at which computer components can operate. Because it is possible for a buffer to act in exactly the same manner whether it is physically located in the computer's internal storage or in the terminal itself, the terminal user need not be concerned about its location.

Front Ends and Back Ends

Despite the use of buffers, the pressures on a timeshared computer grow significantly as more terminals and other peripheral devices are added. It is not uncommon for a bibliographic network to have thousands of actual or potential terminal connections, and it may be prohibitively expensive to provide buffers for each within the central processor. One method of relieving this pressure is through the use of one or more additional computers (often micro- or minicomputers) whose purpose is to act as buffers and "traffic controllers" for the data to be channelled to and from the central processor. In such a configuration, the terminal deals with at least two computers. The *input-output processor,* or front end, is the auxiliary computer. The host computer executes programs, and it transfers data and programs between internal and external storage and between its own CPU and the front end. Figure 8 shows a typical configuration.

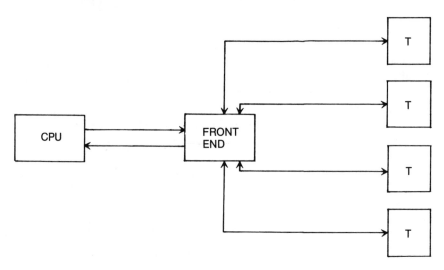

FIG. 8. The front-end processor is dedicated to the task of handling the flow of data to and/or from terminals, which may operate at varying speeds and deal with varying amounts of data. The CPU is left free to process the data.

The front end may be programmed to handle any number of tasks which otherwise would be the responsiblity of the host computer. These include providing and managing the input/output functions, handling sign-on and sign-off routines, and warning terminal users when a piece of peripheral equipment or the host CPU is malfunctioning. A front end may be programmed to re-interpret any designated key on the terminal keyboard, invoking a special preprogrammed routine or function with it. Front ends are especially useful when the terminals communicating with a host computer can easily be divided into a few categories. In such a case, one front end can manage all dumb terminals, another (or a partition of the first) can handle intelligent terminals which have their own buffers, another the intelligent terminals which can accommodate special character sets, and so on.

If the computer's input and output devices may be said to stand at its front end, the auxiliary storage devices stand at its back end. In order for the operating system to be able to locate a file, it must have access by file name to a directory indicating the file's physical location. There may also be one or more files of indices to the records within the major file. When there are only a few disk files, the directory occupies part of the disk storage and must be searched for each desired file. When there are many files, one or more disk surfaces may be given over exclusively to a directory of those files. The use of a separate *storage controller,* or back-end processor, permits more efficient indexing and management of huge amounts of stored data, relieving the host CPU of these tasks and allowing it to perform operations, as shown in Figure 9. A single computer system may include a virtually unlimited number of input and/or output processors and storage controllers.

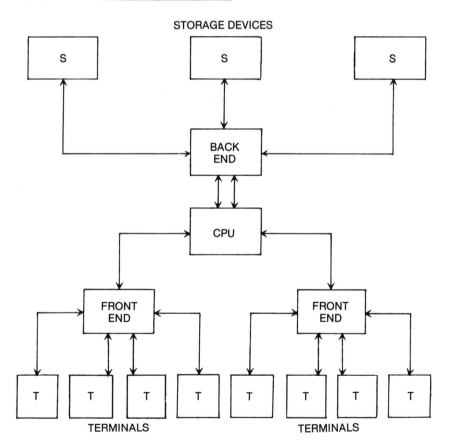

FIG. 9. There is virtually no limit to the number of front ends, back ends, peripheral devices, and CPUs which may be interconnected.

Computer Networking

By now it will be apparent that the computer used for a particular job may be not one computer but many. A person accessing a distant computer using telephone communication and an intelligent terminal (which is a computer) may be using a number of message-switching computers owned by value-added carriers and front-end and back-end processors, as well as the host computer. The combination of these constitutes a computer network. The variety of available components permits a huge number of possible combinations, especially when one considers such developments as intelligent modems, intelligent copier/printers with communication capability, microprocessor-controlled videodisks, etc.

Multiprocessing

The most powerful computer networks are those which combine more than one host processor. Called multiprocessing, this situation may involve two processors or many. When only two are involved they are usually said to be duplexed, though the term is a vague one. It is often used to signify the existence of two machines of the same general type, selected to ensure compatibility of the associated hardware and software. Each performs its own processing. They are linked by a communication line which permits the transfer of programs and data from one to another, as shown in Figure 10.

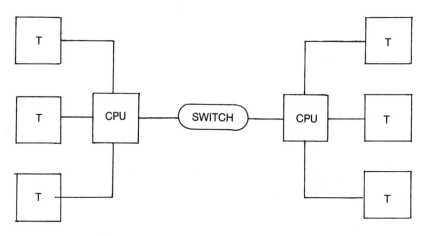

FIG. 10. Duplexing permits two machines to share the load. If one machine fails or must be taken out of service, the other can assume the entire load. Duplexed CPUs will often be identical computers.

The major advantage of such an arrangement is that the two computers share the total user load between them. If one machine is taken out of service because of malfunction, for regular maintenance, or when service demands are low, the other can handle all the traffic alone. But such a system presents certain inefficiencies, for two operating systems and their related software must be supported, and the group of users must be balanced between the two machines.

Distributed Processing

A different type of multiprocessing known as distributed processing has many possible configurations. One of these is a duplexed network that links the two CPUs in a master/slave relationship. The master is the general-purpose CPU; it both performs operations and handles input and output. The slave has no input or output capability, and is present only for executing instructions. When the master is forced by its operating system to interrupt execution to perform input or output, it passes the job to the slave to be continued. When the job is completed, the slave passes it back to the master for output.

Another type of distributed processing permits each of two or more CPUs to have access to a single shared operating system and a single shared internal storage area. The operating system maintains a single job queue. As soon as a CPU has available time, it takes the first job in the queue, recalls the required programs and data from storage, and carries out the task. Requests for output from or input to auxiliary storage are designated as separate jobs and passed via the job queue to a processor that has access to the particular device involved. Terminals may be attached directly to one of the processors, or may be handled by a front end. In such a system there is no one host computer. A single job may be worked on by a number of CPUs before it is completed.

These are only two of the many examples of distributed processing. The advantages of such systems are evident. The system is not dependent on any single machine, and is therefore relatively invulnerable to CPU failures; the several CPUs may all be of the same type, simplifying the selection of hardware and software as well as maintenance and servicing of the equipment; and the system's capabilities may be extended by merely adding another compatible machine rather than changing to something larger and therefore different. The use of high-speed digital communication means that the CPUs need not be physically close to one another. In fact, a distributed processing network may be set up among a number of separate organizations in different locations, permitting each to use its own computer when this is possible, but able to make use of other machines when the capacity of a single computer is insufficient.

Distributed processing, like any complex procedure, also has its drawbacks. The communication channel, or *bus,* can become a weak link, expensive, yet trouble prone. The large number of interconnections carry a correspondingly large cost and potential for failure. The operating systems for such complex networks are of necessity highly complex, difficult to design, and potential trouble spots. The control activity that takes place when processors spend time leaving messages for one another in internal storage (for example in the job queue) and attracting the attention of others by interrupting them, occupies part of the time that would otherwise be spent executing tasks. As the number of processors increases, each must spend more of its time talking to the others.

Despite these and other problems, the availability of cheap microprocessors and of silicon fibre light guides to pass large numbers of messages between programmable devices makes it inevitable that the large computers of the future will in fact be highly complex networks of microprocessors. In the past the high cost of hardware made it necessary to centralize program execution on a single processor. (The C in CPU stands for Central.) In multiprocessor distributed networks, each intelligent device has its own task, and each contributes to the execution of the program, so that it is no longer possible to say which part of the computer system actually performs a given program's instructions.

The use of distributed computer processing is likely to be a highly significant development for libraries since bibliographic resources are themselves distributed among a huge number and wide variety of libraries. As the number of publications held in many libraries expands rapidly, it becomes obvious that no single tool capable of describing and recording all of these holdings can even be imagined, unless that tool is a computer system linked in such a way that both the processors and the bibliographic records are widely distributed among the libraries of the nation, and of the world.

II *The Content and Format of the Bibliographic Record*

3

BIBLIOGRAPHIC
DATA

The building blocks of bibliographic control are bibliographic data: elements of information which help to identify a piece of recorded communication *as a physical object*. This includes any kind of document in one or in many pieces, for example a clay tablet, a reel of microfilm, a kit, a slide set, a motion picture, or a multivolume printed monograph. Bibliographic data are of three types: (1) data which uniquely identify a particular document to distinguish it from others (for example a date of publication or a count of the number of pages in a printed book), (2) data which reveal an association of two or more documents (for example common authorship or the fact that one is a continuation or reprint of the other), and (3) data which describe some characteristic of the intellectual content of a document (for example a statement of its subject or the fact that it is a Festschrift). No bibliographic record can claim to be adequate if it fails to provide the first kind of data, but many stop there. Libraries generally treat all three kinds as of equal importance and incur considerable expense in developing catalogues which display all of them.

Value judgements have no place in bibliographic control. The price of an item at the time of its publication is an element of bibliographic data since it can help identify a particular issue or format of the publication; but a judgement that the item is or is not worth the price is bibliographically irrelevant. A title is usually important to a user as an aid in making a value judgement whether or not to select that item for purchase or consultation. To the bibliographer, what makes it the title is not that it describes the content, but that it is the name which identifies the publication.

Expressing Bibliographic Statements

Bibliographic data are communicated by means of a language. The language of bibliography looks superficially like, for example, English or French. It does use the words of such natural languages, but it has a syntax of its own. In addition, a natural language as used in bibliographic records is always used very concisely and often elliptically. The wording of a title does not always connote the same thing to different people, and the same can be true of wording expressing publishing conditions, authorship, etc. Like any other language, the language of bibliography is nothing but a set of commonly accepted conventions, and like any other language, it is subject to both misunderstanding and misinterpretation. The study of the language of bibliography, whether expressed in words or in computer codes, is the purpose of much of this book. When a bibliographic situation arises for which the pattern of the conventions is not decisive, one must use judgement based on broad experience of similar bibliographic situations, on a sense of the bibliographic language, and on the purpose of the listing in question.

Thus a person who has no feel for the layout of modern title pages, and/or who does not know the English language, might look at the title pages illustrated in Figure 11, and say that the titles of the books are, respectively, *Harpooned* and *The Conversions of a Bishop,* or, conversely, that the titles are *The Story of Whaling Harpooned* and *Dom Helder Camara: the Conversions of a Bishop.* Anyone who knows either title-page layout or English style is in no doubt that the first title page is correctly read as *Harpooned: the Story of Whaling.* That there is a single "correct" reading of the other title page is more doubtful. If the title is *The Conversions of a Bishop,* what does one make of the preceding words "Dom Helder Camara"? Since an author's name often precedes the title on a title page, these words may be taken as the name of the principal author of the book rather than as its subject. The nature of the book's content makes the title-page presentation ambiguous, as shown by the two entries reproduced in Figure 11, both of which were based on the same title page. They show that even cataloguers in national bibliographic agencies may differ in their interpretations of the same evidence.[1]

No cataloguing or citation rule will help. Every rule merely expresses the words of the poet, "A title is a title is a title." In the final analysis, a title is something recognized as such by a person who has had much experience in noticing and using titles for bibliographic purposes. Thus subjective judgement may be exercised in determining which of various possible wordings is the title

---

1. This chapter is concerned only with data elements which might be incorporated into a bibliographic record. Whether or not any single element should also be an index entry, or access point, for that record is a matter taken up in Chapters 6 through 8. The different choices of title in this example result in part from the cataloguers' different decisions as to who should be considered the principal author of the work (see pages 217–220).

THE STORY OF WHALING

harpooned

by Bill Spence

CONWAY MARITIME PRESS
GREENWICH

Dom Helder Camara
THE CONVERSIONS
OF A BISHOP

an interview with
José de Broucker

Translated by Hilary Davies

Broucker, José de
  Dom Helder Camara, the conversions of a bishop : an interview
with José de Broucker / translated [from the French] by Hilary
Davies. — London [etc.] : Collins, 1979. — [1],222p ; 22cm.
Translation of: 'Dom Helder Camara'. Paris : Éditions du Seuil, 1977.
ISBN 0-00-216460-4 : £4.95
1.Ti 2.Camara, Helder 3.Conversions of a bishop
  (B79-17299)   COLLINS

Câmara, Hélder, 1909-
  The conversions of a bishop : an interview with José de
Broucker / Dom Helder Camara ; translated ₁from the French₁
by Hilary Davies. — London ; Cleveland : Collins, 1979.
  ₁1₎ 222 p. ; 22 cm.   GB79-17299
  Translation of Les conversions d'un évêque.
  ISBN 0-529-05624-0 (U.S.) : $9.95
    1. Câmara, Hélder, 1909-   . 2. Catholic Church—Bishops—Biography.
  3. Bishops—Brazil—Biography.   I. Broucker, José de. II. Title.
  BX4705.C2625A3313 1979   78-74858
              282'.092'4
              79   MARC

FIG. 11. Two different entries were prepared from one of these title pages: the upper
one is from the *British National Bibliography*, the lower one from the *National Union
Catalog*.

of an item. But bibliographic data are not simply made up at the whim of the bibliographer. Unless there exists no usable title for the document, in which case the bibliographer has to compose something to serve as its name, the title must originate with the document itself. The same is true of the other bibliographic data elements; bibliographic data are essentially objective, not subjective.

Only after one knows all the possible options in dealing with a bibliographic problem and can recognize the practical implications of each is it possible to formulate a useful bibliographic record or to search for one in a file. These options all stem from the interpretation of bibliographic data derived from the items in question. In the remainder of this chapter, therefore, the elements of bibliographic information are discussed by analyzing some aspects and examples of them and by noting the ways in which they help fulfil the purposes of bibliographic control. Formal definitions may be found in any of several glossaries, but the meanings and functions of most bibliographic terms cannot be understood by memorizing definitions. One must come to understand their nature and purpose through personal experience. (See also the section Terminology, pages 10–12.)

The following notes presuppose a minimal acquaintance with simple bibliographic data. They are intended to amplify the experience brought by a person who has already often tried to identify items in a library catalogue or bibliography.[2] A lengthy article could be written on each of these elements, and there is no intention of attempting to explore all the possible ramifications in depth here. The order of treatment below may look partly familiar, but the following is not to be taken as the definitive means of isolating the elements, or as their definitive arrangement in a standard citation. Chapter 5 deals with those matters.

Title(s)

The mythological force which gives one control over what one can name operates in bibliographic control as well. As noted already, a title is the name of a work or of a particular document. Just as two persons may have the same name, so may two different documents. In fact there are dozens which bear the title *Principles of Economics* and thousands which bear the title *Annual Report*. Over the whole range of existing documents, however, a title may be expected to distinguish any one from all others more often than can any other single element of bibliographic data. This is why for the five hundred years of the development of bibliographic practice for many different purposes, a title has been the one essential ingredient in every bibliographic citation.

2. The beginner must examine many more examples than can be provided with these notes. Many samples have been compiled to illustrate the application of cataloguing codes. A useful one, keyed to the current Anglo-American code and containing reproductions of a number of title pages, etc., is Eric J. Hunter and Nicholas J. Fox, *Examples Illustrating AACR2* (London: Library Association, 1980).

A title is a grammatical unit. It may incorporate words designating an author, publisher, date, or other information as well as what the average reader normally considers to be title words, as in the case of the titles *Shakespeare's Complete Works, The 1981 Proceedings of the Conference on Aging, The Barbara Kraus Calorie Guide,* and *Macmillan Bible Atlas.* Figure 12 reproduces the title page of a book which is essentially an anthology from the writings of Lowell. The wording "James Russell Lowell" is clearly intended to name the author, the person responsible for the content of this book. Therefore to say that the book's title begins with the words "Representative Selections . . ." is not unreasonable. The front cover bears the one word "Lowell" and the spine reads "Lowell * Clark and Foerster". After considering all these facts, but giving priority to those presented on the title page, virtually every cataloguer would transcribe the book's title as *James Russell Lowell* followed by "representative selections . . . " as a subtitle.

An item may have different title-like wording in more than one location: on the cover, on the spine, in running heads, etc. This situation is frequently encountered among nonprint items consisting of more than one physical piece.

James Russell Lowell

REPRESENTATIVE SELECTIONS, WITH
INTRODUCTION, BIBLIOGRAPHY, AND NOTES

BY
HARRY HAYDEN CLARK
Professor of English
University of Wisconsin

AND
NORMAN FOERSTER
Director of the School of Letters
University of Iowa, 1930–1944

AWS

AMERICAN BOOK COMPANY
New York · Cincinnati · Chicago
Boston · Atlanta · Dallas · San Francisco

FIG. 12. A title page whose typographic layout requires the use of an author's name as the title.

For example, in a particular kit the box container bears the title *Regional Geography of Canada, an Economic and Urban Study,* while the guide accompanying the filmstrip inside bears the title *Geography of Canada, a Regional Survey.* A title being so important an element of identification, one title must be chosen as any item's principal title. This is now called the *title proper* in library cataloguing terminology. Variant titles are of bibliographic value since a user may remember only one of those, but they are less significant in description than the title proper and are usually not even recorded in, for example, footnote citations. In the case of any printed material bearing a title page, it is a universally accepted bibliographic tenet that the title proper is the title appearing on the title page rather than one appearing elsewhere (see also page 85).

Where a title *ends* may be a matter of concern, for example when creating a title index. If title wording can be grammatically separated into units, the first such unit is the title proper, while succeeding ones are now called units of *other title information* (any *subtitle* is included here). Thus in the following title, only the first four words are the title proper, and there are two units of other title information: *Nuclear plant emergency plans, an administrative response to the alarm bell, a selected bibliography.*

A collection or anthology often does not have a *collective title,* a title which applies to the whole, as shown in Figure 13. If only a few individual works are named, the sequence of individual titles/authors may be transcribed as the title of the whole. However, where the number of named works is very great, a reluctance to do this is understandable. Long-playing sound recordings and tapes are frequent illustrations of this situation, as illustrated in Figure 14. If it seems undesirable to transcribe the whole series of composition titles, etc., as the title of this disc, perhaps it is reasonable to say that the title is *Riegger, Prokofiev, Copland,* by analogy with the Lowell book in Figure 12. Yet it is unlikely that any cataloguer has ever instinctively opted for such a solution, any more than one would instinctively decide to make *Clara Reeve—Horace Walpole* the title of the book illustrated in Figure 13.

The difference between these examples and the Lowell item is that here individual works are explicitly named. There are also some prejudices based on the medium itself. For sound recordings without collective titles, two alternatives have been sanctioned in the past by cataloguing rules: (1) a successive listing of the titles of the individual works (along with their respective composers) in a single bibliographic entry, or (2) the production of a separate entry for each different composition within the item. That the latter solution has been commonly applied in the case of sound recordings but not in the case of printed items is an inconsistency easy to explain historically, but almost impossible to explain on any rational grounds. Perhaps the musician has been more concerned with the identification of individual compositions because there have existed so few indices to anthologies of recorded music (see Chapter 4 for further implications of these observations).

CLARA REEVE—HORACE WALPOLE

THE

OLD ENGLISH BARON

A Gothic Story

By CLARA REEVE

ALSO

THE

CASTLE OF OTRANTO

A Gothic Story

By HORACE WALPOLE

With Two Portraits and Four Drawings by A. H. Courrier
Etched by Damman

LONDON
J. C. NIMMO AND BAIN
14, KING WILLIAM STREET, STRAND, W.C.
1883

FIG. 13. The title page of a book containing two independent works. There is no collective title.

FIG. 14. A label on a disc recording. Three works are named, but there is no collective title. If the label named only one composer and a much larger number of individual works, Library of Congress policy would consider it acceptable to transcribe the composer's name as a collective title.

Items which lack any acceptable title wording were mentioned on page 58. The need for the cataloguer to make up a *supplied title* is rare in the case of published materials, though it occurs where separately issued items are later brought together in one binding. In the case of unpublished unique materials such as manuscripts and homemade slide sets, videorecordings, or cassettes, it is almost inevitable that a title must be "invented." A supplied title has always been enclosed in square brackets to show that it is not transcribed from the document.

Serials

The display of title wording on a serial is often ambiguous. Two equally experienced cataloguers may well disagree on the title proper of the serial illustrated in Figure 15. No definition of title can resolve the problem. If experienced judgement varies, a flip of a coin may have to decide the issue, and references from the different possible interpretations of the title will be needed in any serials list.

FIG. 15. The publication statement on an inside page reads as follows: "The Dow Canadian, Insight Edition, is published . . . by Dow Chemical of Canada Limited. . . ." (The words Insight Edition are in bolder type than the rest of the statement.)

There are greater problems with serial titles than their ambiguous display. Too often, different serials bear the same (or almost the same) title, and there is a tendency among users to cite a serial not by its exact title but by some paraphrase or abbreviation thereof. The community of science/technology writers, who cite far more serials than monographs in their footnotes, have long sought a system of standardized, unique, and brief serial titling. Today, many journals themselves suggest a brief method of self-identification, for example "Int.j.cir.theor.appl." for the *International Journal of Circuit Theory and Applications.* An attempt to systematize and further compress abbreviated serial naming led in the 1950s to the introduction of the *coden* system, in which a serial is identified by a unique four-character (now a six-character) designation. "ICTACV" is the coden for the journal named above. The first four characters, at least, are usually related to the journal title. The application of the coden system has not grown much outside the scientific community. It has been overtaken, but not entirely replaced, since 1970 by the establishment of a master file of *key-titles* by the International Serials Data System. These are linked to the ISSN, the unique-numbering system described on page 83.[3] Many scientific serials still carry several kinds of titling: the bibliographic title or title proper, a coden, an ISSN and key-title, and a suggested citation title!

Responsibility for Intellectual Content

Information indicating all person(s) and/or corporate body(ies) responsible in any way for the intellectual content of an item was once very straightforward. In a simpler era, a bibliographic item was usually a printed monograph composed primarily of verbal content written by one person. Any additional credits were discreetly buried in a preface or statement of acknowledgements, safely away from bibliographic prominence. Today, authorship is often hard to define. More and more works are being created by combinations of persons interacting in varied ways, both as individuals and as members of corporate bodies (committees, societies, institutions, government agencies, etc. (see page 198). A listing of "authors" typically includes the names of writers, illustrators, performers, creators of related works, sponsoring agencies, publishers, and even institutions serving only as conference sites. Any rule for citation requires judgements to be made about which of these activities is relevant to each of the persons and/or bodies involved in creating the content of the work being described.

Corporate bodies are the authors of such things as their own annual reports, of course; increasingly, they also commission works on almost any topic. This

---

3. For the ISSN/key-title system, see UNISIST, International Serials Data System, *Guidelines for ISDS* (Paris: Unesco, 1973). CODEN assignments are now under the control of Chemical Abstracts Service of Columbus, Ohio.

usually involves little or no control over the writing itself, but the body some-times lays down policy concerning the content of sponsored material and/or uses staff writers anonymously, as for example in series such as the *Sunset Travel & Recreation Books,* in which a typical title claims to have been written "by the editors of Sunset Books and Sunset Magazine."

Corporate involvement is particularly evident in the case of reference works such as directories, and a production company is often the effective originator and controller of the content of an educational film or filmstrip. The degree of corporate versus personal responsibility for the content can rarely be ascer-tained objectively, especially when both person(s) and body(ies) are named in conjunction with a title, for example:

> *A College in the City: an Alternative,* "a report from Educational Facilities Laboratories. . . . The primary author . . . was Evans Clinchy"

> *Worldwide Directory of Computer Companies, 1973–1974,* "Marie B. Waters, editor, and the staff of Academic Media"

> *The City Fights Back, a Nation-Wide Survey . . . ,* "narrated and edited by Hal Burton from material developed by the Central Business District Council of the Urban Land Institute."

Words such as *editor* and *compiler* appear frequently in relation to authorship activity. A person so designated may perform any one or more of the following rather different functions:

1) cause a work to come into existence by conceiving its scope, general focus, and arrangement, then convincing others to do the actual writing
2) determine what a deceased author intended, and reconstruct an "ideal" text from corrupt evidences
3) add a commentary, glosses, footnotes, bibliography, etc. (together called critical apparatus) to an existing work by someone else
4) abridge, revise, paraphrase, bowdlerize, or otherwise modify a work by someone else
5) collaborate with an author in putting the latter's ideas into acceptable verbal/visual form for publication (when the editor has done most of the writing but is not named in the published work, the activity is called ghost writing)
6) select for inclusion in a new publication material which was created for other purposes by one or many persons or bodies (this is the activity often called compiling an anthology, but it may also be called editing as in the case of published conference proceedings)

7) go over a writer's work to ensure consistency and/or correctness of style, punctuation, orthography, etc., but without authority to make substantial changes (this function, known as copy editing, is normally not acknowledged in the publication or in any citation).

A person (or, rarely, body) undertaking one or more of the first six functions is usually prominently acknowledged in the publication, although the precise function is more often implied than specified. It can be useful for the cataloguer to attempt to determine which function is in fact at issue in a particular case, since most cataloguing rules make some practical distinctions among them.

In the case of sound recordings, motion pictures, videorecordings, and similar media, there is an added aspect of responsibility for content, namely the function of performance. In traditional theatre and music it is easy to distinguish the author/composer from the performer, even when there has been some "arrangement" of the original content. Many contemporary art forms have blurred these distinctions. In particular, a sufficiently different performance of a piece of contemporary popular music is often taken to be in fact a new work, no longer ascribed directly to the original composer(s).

The expression of the above facts on a title page, disc label, etc., ranges from the clear and explicit to the vague and ambiguous. An *author statement,* now called a *statement of responsibility,* is always subject to a degree of interpretation. Selection from the information provided may also be necessary, although library cataloguing practice is more likely than footnote practice to transcribe the wording as found on the item (see page 113). Still, it has been traditional to transcribe as bibliographic data only personal names relating to such functions as writing, illustrating, and collecting materials for a publication; or corporate names relating to sponsorship and authorization of the content.

A qualification, institutional address, or affiliation of a personal author is traditionally ignored in a library catalogue or footnote on the grounds that these are impermanent facts. Yet a science abstracting service may consider them to be very important bibliographic data, not only transcribing but even indexing them because of the significance of the location of research activity. Designers and typographers of print materials are normally ignored, even if prominently noted in the publication; but the nature of a visual medium may make it important to include such activities in its citation. Publishers are normally named only in the context of their publishing activity (see the next section), but in the case of noncommercial publishers the line between publishing and the sponsorship of content may be very hard to draw.

A multiplicity of names in a document is in itself not a problem as long as they all represent persons or bodies engaged in the same function, as in the case of five authors jointly writing a textbook. If there are too many, one can simply adopt a cutoff point, whether according to the cataloguer's traditional but arbitrary "rule of three" or at any other number. In briefer bibliographic citations only the names of primary contributors will be transcribed from the item, minor functions such as writing a foreword or introduction being ignored. In the case of nonprint materials, information concerning authors, etc., is usually much more voluminous and is often presented in arrangements and locations which makes judgement of its bibliographic value more difficult. In the visual media, this information is called the *credits*. Figure 16 is a typical example, the verso of the front cover of a guide accompanying a kit.

CREDITS

Produced by the National Education Association.

Based on "Femininity in American Women: The Influence of Education" by Dr. Ester Manning Westervelt, published in the Fall 1971 issue of the Journal of the National Association of Women Deans and Counselors.

Creative Supervision:	GORDON H. FELTON
	RICHARD E. NIELSEN
Script Adaptation:	ANN K. KURZIUS
	JANE POWER
Photography:	JOE DIDIO
	CAROLYN SALISBURY
Art:	TOM GLADDEN
Narration:	FLO AYRES
	WALT TEAS
Sound:	MIKE JONES
Production:	PAUL BERGMAN
Project Assistants:	ANN MARIE BOHAN
	CHARLES DENT
	THERESA FURYE
	ANTOINETTE K. WASHINGTON
Advisory Panel:	HAZEL BLAKEY
	KATHERINE COLE
	SAMUEL B. ETHRIDGE
	MARY FABER
	CHARLOTTE HALLAM
	SHIRLEY MCCUNE
	MARTHA MATTHEWS
	ADELE SWEDELIUS

Copyright © 1973
National Education Association
1201 Sixteenth Street, N.W.
Washington, D.C. 20036

FIG. 16. The credits page of a booklet accompanying an audiovisual item.

Where the name or names appear on a printed item has traditionally been significant, particularly in the case of corporate names. A person named at the top of a title page is almost always correctly understood to be the author. A corporate name in the same position may or may not have a close association with the content of the item; it is likely to designate a sponsor in some vague and unspecified way. A corporate name appearing at the bottom of a title page is automatically taken to be the item's publisher; but modern title pages do not necessarily follow traditional patterns, as is shown in Figure 17.

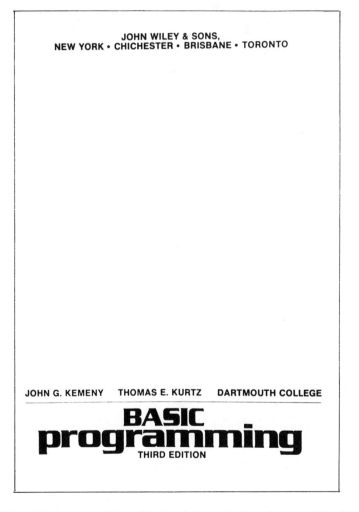

FIG. 17. A title page on which publication information is at the top and the title at the bottom.

Publication/Distribution/Manufacturing Data

In the world of printed materials, information concerning the place, agent, and date of publication and/or manufacture is known as the *imprint*. Its first appearance was as a *colophon,* a statement at the end of the work relating to its physical production. This information drifted from that position to the foot of the title page once title pages became common. Today the manufacturer may not be named anywhere on the item. Printing and publishing became separate business functions by the eighteenth century. Since then, identification of the publisher of an item has always taken precedence in bibliographic description over identification of its printer/manufacturer, but if the manufacturer is named and the publisher is not (or cannot be readily deduced), manufacturing information can be a useful substitute.

Since it names the agency which wants to sell or otherwise disseminate the document, publication information is usually displayed very prominently. However, it may be difficult to distinguish publishing from manufacturing functions. For example, there are firms which exist to make and sell single-copy photographic reproductions of out-of-print items, whether in hard copy or in microform, as these are ordered. Some consider such reprint houses to be publishers, but others consider them as merely manufacturers of additional copies of existing items.

Although many multinational publishing houses exist, publishing is still largely a nationally based business. Identifying the place of publication can therefore indicate to a reference librarian or selector a national or even regional bias of the content. Identifying the publisher also allows value judgements to be made, since the quality standards, subject specializations, etc., of a publishing house are likely to be identifiable. This dual purpose of publication/manufacturing information raises the intractable issue of whether identifying content or identifying the physical object in hand should be the primary bibliographic concern.

The names of publishers, manufacturers, and distributors are also of value to the acquisitions librarian beyond their primary bibliographic purpose of distinguishing two items. While an item is in print, such information is the most direct and useful indication of where to obtain it. Even a street address for a small firm may be essential for this purpose. But the value of data for acquisitions purposes is limited by several factors, the most obvious being that the publisher is the source of the item only in that firm's country and while the item is in print.

In this century, the function of *distribution* has assumed increasing independence from that of publishing to the degree that it is now often separately acknowledged in the item, particularly in the case of nonprint materials. Distribution is a business undertaken at the national or even regional level, and rarely has anything to do with the item's content. Distribution arrangements, especially foreign ones, are notoriously unstable. The information may therefore not be worth including in the permanent bibliographic record, even if it is of primary importance at the time of publication for acquisition purposes.

At one time a book published in both the United Kingdom and the United States would usually be set in type in the two countries separately, with consequent changes in spelling and sometimes even in vocabulary, style, the use of statistical measurement units, etc. Today, international publishing arrangements are increasingly common. Names of publishers in different countries sometimes appear on the same item, either with equal prominence or in primary and secondary positions. In such cases it is not unreasonable for, say, a Briton to cite a publication in a footnote naming only its British publisher, while an American cites the same physical item naming only the American one. This may seem harmless, or even useful in indicating where to acquire the item, but it can mislead the researcher into thinking there are two different editions. To avoid confusion, therefore, it is necessary always to indicate at least the first-named publisher in a citation if there is more than one.

Another common situation is that the same printed sheets are sold in the two countries, but with different title pages. Only the name of the British publisher appears on that firm's title page, while the American publisher's name appears alone on its title page. In every respect other than the publication information on the title leaf, the books are identical. Bibliographic tradition has always considered their different imprints to be sufficient reason for making wholly separate bibliographic records. Thus a Canadian library receiving both editions may feel it is a justifiable economy to treat the one received later as a copy of the first-received edition. The existence of the variant may or may not be noted.

An analogous situation exists in the case of paper or microform reproductions, the content being identical to that of the original except that a title page or other source naming the reprint publisher is added or substituted for the original one. Recent library practice has offered different solutions to the problem of how to identify, on one entry, both the reproduction and its relationship to the original from which it was reproduced. Yet is is clearly vital that both be identified. A number of bibliographic and administrative circumstances complicate the matter. Again, some argue that identification of the intellectual content of an item and its publishing origin should take precedence over identification of the physical object in hand; others argue the converse.

Date

At least three different kinds of dates are frequently incorporated into bibliographic records, as illustrated in the date information from the verso of a title leaf transcribed in Figure 18.

```
First published        1931
Second edition         1932
Third revised edition  1954
Fourth impression      1958
Fifth impression       1963
Fourth revised edition 1967
·Fifth revised edition  1981
      Copyright © 1981
```

FIG. 18. Date information from the verso of the title leaf of Roy Stokes, *Esdaile's Manual of Bibliography,* 5th rev. ed. (Metuchen: Scarecrow Press, 1981).

One kind is the *publication date,* the year in which the publisher named in the imprint first issued the work in the edition in hand. Another is the *manufacturing date* of the particular physical item, that is, the year in which the type image was actually inked and transferred to the paper in hand, the sound recording matrix was actually stamped into the vinyl, the magnetic impulse was actually copied onto the tape, or the image was actually transferred to the piece of microfiche. These two types of dates express purely bibliographic facts. The third type is the *copyright date,* designating the year or years in which legal title to the content as literary property was formally claimed. In addition to these three, a rarer type is the date when the writing of the work was completed (often found at the end of a preface), or when the work was first published anywhere (not merely in the edition or version in hand), that is, the "original" date (say 1850 in the case of Hawthorne's *The Scarlet Letter*).

A copyright date is the date most closely associated with the completion of the intellectual content of the work, or with its most recent substantial alteration. Thus a new edition of a work typically bears its own copyright date, but a new impression does not.[4] A document may show many copyright dates, particularly an anthology or a work of collective authorship, where a different date of copyright claim can exist for each separate contribution. Under some laws and conventions, no date need appear in the item for it to be legally protected. Thus while items published in the United States have typically shown a copyright date for more than a century, it was not common for such a date to appear in British publications before 1957 and in Canadian ones until 1962, the years in which these countries ratified an international convention prescribing formal notice. Copyright is a complex legal matter governed by ever-changing national laws and international agreements. Copyright dates therefore cannot be viewed primarily as aids to bibliographic identification and are rarely transcribed in citations unless no other dating is available.

---

4. Operating under their 1976 Copyright Act, many publishers in the United States have begun to record and date a fresh copyright claim for each impression of an edition. See *Cataloging Service Bulletin* no. 10 (fall 1980): 15–16 and no. 13 (summer 1981):73.

The publication date is likely to be valid for all copies of the item produced by the same publisher and having the same content, no matter when they were manufactured. It is the preferred date in a citation. A library usually does not wish to make a new bibliographic record for each new printing of an item as such, except in rare-book cataloguing where it is common to distinguish copies from different press runs. Hence the date of manufacture is typically ignored. This may seem inconsistent with the decision noted earlier that separate records are usually made if only the publisher's name differs, but a date is usually of much less significance than a publisher's name in the acquisition of an item, and a manufacturing date is of no consequence in dating the content for selection.

Terms of Availability

The value of such data as price, conditions of sale or distribution, etc., is likely to be temporary and is fairly restricted. Obviously, the price of an item on its first publication does not remain the current price for very long. In bygone years such data were included on bibliographic records because they were stable. Today they are included on entries intended to be used for selection and/or acquisitions purposes, which is the principal reason why national bibliographies include such data.

The Physical Makeup of the Item

An item's physical existence may be expressed in terms of its medium (paper, acetate, etc.), the number of its component parts (pages, frames, reels, pieces, etc.), and the method by which they are assembled (binding, container, etc.) The description and quantification of the physical pieces composing an item is the basis of bibliography as the study of the physical object. Printed books (particularly early ones) and manuscripts of all kinds have been subjected to the most detailed physical inspection. Whole treatises are devoted to an analysis of the paper composition, the watermarks, the chemical structure of the ink, etc., of a bibliographically interesting item in order to ascertain its origin and its relationship to other items.

The newer media have their own physical identities, often more technically complex, calling for an identification of the nature of the magnetic coating on a strip of plastic, the material of the frame in which a slide is mounted, the density of the image electronically produced from a videorecording, or the transfer process of the photographic emulsion on a Technicolor film. These data can distinguish one state from another of the same work, just as in the print media the physical description may distinguish, say, a hardback from a paperback of the same publication.

For items whose content cannot be perceived without the intervention of some mechanical or electronic reading device, the bibliographic record must contain information on the kind of machinery needed, such as the required turntable speed and cartridge/stylus type in the case of a disc recording or the required magnification in the case of a microform. In the case of electronic media it is possible for the same state of the same work to appear in many physical guises, for example a television programme on half-inch Beta-format cassette, one-inch Sony U-matic open reel tape, etc. These formats are more directly interchangeable than is the case with print or photographic images. Finally, how does one describe the physical state of a computer program which may exist momentarily in, be transferred to/from, or be stored on, tape, disk, core or auxiliary storage, etc.? Yet computer programs are also documents, and a means of citing them must be established.

It is impossible to prescribe in quantitative terms how much information about the physical identity of an item to record in a citation. In the case of traditional print materials, where both the examination and its result are called *collation,* there have been long-standing conventions for various purposes: one for footnote citations, another for library catalogues, etc. Only the fullest description suffices in rare-book cataloguing, for example:

> Demy 8° (227 x 142 mm. uncut). [A]² b⁸ (-B⁸+'B⁸') C-D⁸ E⁸ (+E2) F⁸ (-F6+'F6') G⁸ H⁸ (-H2,3+H2:3) I-Z⁸. Pp. [i] title, [iii]-iv preface, 1-356 text
>
> A complete collation by (1) format and size, (2) the separately sewn gatherings in the book, known as signatures, and (3) pagination. The complexities of the gatherings are noted in detail as to their signing, folding, and order.

Until about thirty years ago it was considered desirable for a general library catalogue to specify the existence of each leaf within a book, for example:

> 1 p. l., 5-401, [1] p. 18 cm.
>
> A collation by pagination and size, accounting for each leaf in the book.

Today, in the same catalogues it is common only to indicate major groups of paging, each identified by the final number in the group, for example:

> iv, 356 p. 24 cm.
>
> A simplified collation by pagination and size, which merely indicates the rough total of each separately numbered sequence.

> 356 p.
>
> A collation which ignores all irregularities and merely notes the number on the last numbered page.

The needs and practices also vary in the case of the nonprint media. In order to interpret the data in bibliographies, filmographies, discographies, etc., or to make reasonable decisions concerning what should be included and what may be omitted, one must acquire a detailed knowledge of the nature and functions of the physical characteristics of each medium likely to be encountered.

An Item's Relationships with Other Items

Information concerning an item's relationships with other bibliographic items can be almost endless. This is certainly the most complex type of bibliographic data, and that which most often requires the bibliographer to investigate sources of information outside the item in hand. If an item has any significant relationships with previously existing ones it does not always reveal them. Furthermore, it is impossible to indicate at the time of its publication how an item will be related to other future publications.

Two or more documents may be related in many different ways: (1) as the same work published under different titles, (2) as different editions of the same work, (3) as different physical formats (paper, microfilm, machine-readable tape) of the same content, (4) in the fact that they share some material in their content, whereas other parts of their content differ, (5) as items published in the same series, (6) one as a reprint of another, (7) one as a sequel (as in monographs), or a continuation (as in serials) of another, or (8) in only a physical relationship, such as ten pamphlets bound together years after their separate publication or a phonograph record slipped into the rear cover of a book it is intended to "illustrate."

Is the bibliographic record the place to attempt an identification of the inellectual relationships among versions of a work? Should it help distinguish, say, the various mediaeval Tristan legends? Should it trace the publishing history of the successive corrupted texts of *Moby Dick* by Melville? Can it begin to identify the bibliographic grounds for textual criticism? It can take lengthy bibliographic investigation to ascertain such information, and great skill to state it succinctly and intelligibly. To the degree that it identifies works as such, and not merely publications (see pages 215–217), the library catalogue does undertake such functions, but only minimally.

The most common bibliographic relationships, the easiest ones to determine and express concisely, are introduced briefly below. They are the ones normally revealed by the document itself: (1) the relationship among editions, (2) the series relationship, (3) sequels/continuations, (4) any separately identifiable contents, and (5) any physically separate item(s) published with and intended to accompany the main item. These are the relationships most likely to be expressed in citations or on catalogue entries.

Edition

The term "edition" probably has more numerous and significantly different uses than any other technical term in bibliography. It is usually taken to specify one of several different states of the content. Thus differences in the text are expected among an improved edition, a third edition, an illustrated edition, and of course a German edition. Figure 19 shows an example of a publisher's complete honesty about the bibliographic history of an item and of its content.

First Published 2 November 1922
Second Edition October 1937
Third Edition with an Appendix October 1946
Fourth Edition with further Appendix April 1950
Fifth Edition July 1951
Sixth Edition, revised, 1956
Reprinted 1960

This book, originally published in 1922, consisted of the text of Dr. Einstein's Stafford Little Lectures, delivered in May 1921 at Princeton University. For the third edition, Dr. Einstein added an appendix discussing certain advances in the theory of relativity since 1921. To the fourth edition, Dr. Einstein added Appendix II on his Generalized Theory of Gravitation. In the fifth edition the proof in Appendix II was revised.

In the present (sixth) edition Appendix II has been rewritten. This edition and the Princeton University Press fifth edition, revised (1955), are identical.

The text of the first edition was translated by Edwin Plimpton Adams, the first appendix by Ernst G. Straus and the second appendix by Sonja Bargmann.

FIG. 19. From the preliminaries of Albert Einstein, *The Meaning of Relativity,* 6th ed., rev. (London: Methuen, 1956).

However, the word "edition" is also used to describe the same content as published by a particular firm, in a particular physical format, or at a particular time. The Bantam edition of *Bleak House,* or the 1923 edition, or the Limited edition, may all be identical, word for word, in their textual content, their differences being only in paper, typography, binding, price, and perhaps publisher's name.

When editions are numbered or otherwise designated in a sequence, the title and author usually do not change. On seeing the third edition of *Basic Pro-*

gramming by Kemeny and Kurtz, it is reasonable to assume that there existed first and second editions of the same title by the same authors. But this is not always the case. The ninth edition of *Guide to Reference Books* is by Eugene P. Sheehy, whereas the eighth edition of the same title was by Constance M. Winchell. Earlier editions were compiled by by Isadore Gilbert Mudge and by Alice Bertha Kroeger, and bore slightly different titles. There is an *Introduction to Respiratory Physiology* by Harold A. Braun, Frederick W. Cheney, Jr., and C. Paul Loehnen, 2nd ed. (Boston: Little, Brown, 1980), but there is no "first edition" under that title. The preceding edition turns out to be *Physiologic Bases for Respiratory Care* by Cheryl E. Beall, Harold A. Braun, and Frederick W. Cheney (Missoula, Mont.: Mountain Press Publishing Co., 1974). Editions of *Reference Books for Elementary and Junior High School Libraries* by Carolyn Sue Peterson appeared in 1970 and 1975, the latter numbered as the "2nd edition." The subsequent 1981 revision of the same material bears a new title, *Reference Books for Children,* the name of an additional author, Ann D. Fenton, and no edition numbering at all.

A *reprint edition* is not simply one more *impression,* even if its content is only a photoreproduction of an earlier edition. Impressions emanate from the originating publisher, although the firm may have changed its name; a so-called reprint edition is issued by a different publishing house which has acquired the rights after the original publisher no longer exists or wishes to reissue the work. Such reprints are bibliographically problematic for several reasons. The content of a reprint is not always identical to that of the original. New material such as a critical introduction, bibliography, etc., is frequently added. It may be in the reprinter's interest not to state prominently that the company is really selling an old work, and it is possible to make a reprint appear to be a newly published item, or an edition with revised text, without actually telling a lie. Figure 20 shows a fairly complex reprint relationship honestly presented. Often only a comparison of all the available bibliographic evidence, both on the item and in lists citing earlier versions of the work, can ensure that one is not misled.

A critical scholar will go to some pains to determine what, if any, differences exist between two so-called editions, but almost no library administrator can afford to allow a cataloguer to engage in close textual examination for that purpose. In any but the most specialized bibliographies, it is common simply to transcribe statements of edition, publication, series, etc., as they appear on each item. Taken individually, these may be ambiguous and confusing, but taken together and interpreted in the context of the complete bibliographic citation, they will usually "place" the edition in question in its proper relationship with other versions and appearances of the work. Lest any possible ambiguity result from recording these facts, it is essential to follow closely the requirements of the format for a citation (see Chapter 5).

If a user brings a citation from another work or from a class reading list specifying an edition/imprint which the library does not have, the librarian

This Volume Was Reproduced
From A 1930 Edition
In The
North Carolina Collection
University of North Carolina
Chapel Hill

The Reprint Company
Post Office Box 5401
Spartanburg, South Carolina 29301

Reprinted: 1971
ISBN 0-87152-064-8
Library of Congress Catalog Card Number 70-149342

Manufactured in the United States of America on long-life paper

Studies in North Carolina History
Number 3

Ante-Bellum Builders of North Carolina

By R. D. W. CONNOR
Former Secretary North Carolina Historical Commission
KENAN PROFESSOR OF HISTORY, UNIVERSITY OF
NORTH CAROLINA

Issued under the Direction of the
Department of History

Published by
The North Carolina College for Women
Greensboro, N. C.
1930

First published, in 1914, as the North Carolina State Normal and Industrial
College Historical Publication

FIG. 20. These pages reveal that the same content was published first in 1914, second in 1930, and third in 1971, each time by a different publisher. Each of the 1914 and 1930 publications was issued in a different series; the 1971 publication was not issued in any series. They are, properly, *not* numbered as first, second, and third editions.

must always be aware that the collection may have exactly the desired material in a form bearing a different edition statement or publisher's name. It is important, therefore, to gain some experience of the many ways editions and impressions are designated by publishers, particularly the photographic reprint editions so common today.

Series

More and more nonfiction monographs bear at least two titles: a title proper and the title of a series in which the monograph is published. The connotation of the word "series" which normally comes first to mind is a unit like *Pelican Books* or *The World's Classics,* that is, a true serial comprising a theoretically unlimited number of separate parts numbered in sequence. However, a series is any larger unit that has its own title distinctive from the titles of the unit's individually published parts. If it is a unit of a finite number of items, such as the six-volume *Oxford Anthology of English Literature,* it may be called a set rather than a series, but the relationship between its *collective title* and the titles of its individual parts (part 1: *Medieval English Literature,* part 2: *The Literature of Renaissance England,* etc.) is the same. Figure 21 shows an example of two

TECHNIQUE OF ORGANIC CHEMISTRY
Volume III
Second Completely Revised and Augmented Edition

PART I
SEPARATION AND PURIFICATION

Editor: ARNOLD WEISSBERGER

Authors: Charles M. Ambler, A. Letcher Jones, Geoffrey Broughton, K. Kammermeyer, David Craig, Frederick W. Keith, Jr., Lyman C. Craig, E. MacWilliam, A. B. Cummins, Edward G. Scheibel, F. B. Hutto, Jr., R. Eliot Stauffer, R. Stuart Tipson

1956
INTERSCIENCE PUBLISHERS, INC., NEW YORK
INTERSCIENCE PUBLISHERS LTD., LONDON

TECHNIQUE OF ORGANIC CHEMISTRY
Volume III
Second Completely Revised and Augmented Edition

PART II
LABORATORY ENGINEERING

Editor: ARNOLD WEISSBERGER

Authors: John W. Axelson, Richard R. Kraybill, Richard S. Egly, Glenn H. Miller, Richard F. Eisenberg, J. H. Rushton, M. P. Hofmann, William C. Streib

1957
INTERSCIENCE PUBLISHERS, INC., NEW YORK
INTERSCIENCE PUBLISHERS LTD., LONDON

FIG. 21. The title pages of two works which together form one unit within a larger work.

works with different titles, which together comprise volume 3 of yet another work, the thirteen-volume series, or set, *Technique of Organic Chemistry*.

It is a publishing company which brings a series into existence by creating the common naming for a group of otherwise independently named publications. Normally, a noted person is named as series editor, and the publications are given uniform typographic and binding treatment. The number of series in existence is ever increasing; many, perhaps most, exist because of the publisher's hopes for automatic sales of successive items identified by a common series title. These hopes are encouraged by library acquisitions practices which in times of adequate collection budgets tend to encourage standing orders for series because of lower unit acquisitions costs for subscriptions. From the point of view of the publisher, advertising a series and servicing standing orders for it are probably the most cost-effective methods of promoting and distributing nonfiction works.

The degree of intellectual or even topical connection among items in a series is not bibliographically relevant. The bibliographer merely states the series relationship where it exists. The reason for doing so is not primarily to identify a particular version of one work. Most works published in a series are never again published in any different series; hence the series name in itself does not serve to distinguish different objects. Rather, in many instances a user will know the series name and not the name of the individual item. A citation may provide only the information *University of London Institute of Education. Studies in Education* when referring to the monograph whose title page is shown in Figure 22, although its title as a monograph is *The Arts and Current Tendencies in Education*.

Sequels and Continuations

That *The Empire Strikes Back* is a sequel to *Star Wars* is significant. The relationship works both ways, but of course at the time of release of *Star Wars* it was not known that there would be a sequel or what its title would be. Frequent changes of title among serial publications (periodicals, journals, etc.) such as that shown in Figure 23 make it necessary to note the relationship between one title of the serial and either a previous title, a succeeding title, or both.

Contents

Most longer writing is divided into chapters or parts; musical compositions into movements; plays into acts, etc. Such divisions have no bibliographic significance because they are not units separately identified or sought. But the names of parts which can or do have separate bibliographic identity can be very important pieces of bibliographic data. A separate bibliographic identity usually means different author/title data for the part than pertains to the whole. The most typical example is the anthology, which has a title and editor but is

UNIVERSITY OF LONDON INSTITUTE OF EDUCATION

STUDIES IN EDUCATION

**THE ARTS AND CURRENT
TENDENCIES IN EDUCATION**

Published for
the University of London Institute of Education
by Evans Brothers Limited, London

FIG. 22. A title page illustrating ambiguity as to which is the title of the work and which is the title of the series.

composed of a number of works each identifiable by its own author and title. "Anthology" and "collection" are very general terms used in a wide variety of print and nonprint media. Conference proceedings, symposia, Festschriften, record albums, and monographic series are some of the specialized types of the same kind of publication. Figure 24 shows a title page bearing both a collective title for an anthology and an identification of each individual work contained therein; the accompanying Library of Congress entry shows the use of a *contents note* to record the latter.

Accompanying Items

A teacher's manual accompanying a language text, statistical tables on a microfiche inserted in a pocket in the rear of a study of economics, a map in a folder tipped onto the flyleaf of a travel book: these are all examples of independent or quasi-independent items whose existence and identity should be noted in some way in association with items they accompany. It can be exceedingly difficult to decide which should be considered the main item and which the accompanying one. Sometimes they appear to be co-equal. If a filmstrip

CANADIAN LIBRARY ASSOCIATION
ASSOCIATION CANADIENNE DES BIBLIOTHEQUES

B U L L E T I N

Canadian
library   association bulletin
bulletin de l'association   canadienne des bibliothèques

CANADIAN
LIBRARY
ASSOCIATION   BULLETIN

CANADIAN LIBRARY

CANADIAN LIBRARY
JOURNAL

Canadian
Library
Journal

FIG. 23. Successive titles of the official journal of the Canadian Library Association; the numbering has continued in an unbroken sequence from its beginning to the present.

and a cassette sound recording are produced for use together in a synchronized carousel projector, is the combination to be considered as a sound recording accompanied by a filmstrip or as a filmstrip accompanied by a sound recording? Defenders of either view can easily be found among their users. A neutral solution would seem to be to treat the package as a single unit, a *kit,* but in fact this solution also has its adherents and detractors. Some feature of the description of one medium will inevitably take precedence over the other in any bibliographic identification of the pair.

Other Bibliographic Relationships

The following brief statements quoted from particular publications show something of the possible range of relationships other than those already described:

> The dictionary section was taken from Polygraph Woerterbuch der graphischen Industrie in 6 Sprachen.

```
"Text adapted from Of them he chose
twelve, by Clarence Macartney."

Supplement to Zulu ethnography, 1976.
```

Bibliographic relationships can be multidimensional. For example, the second edition of a work may be published in a different series than that in which the first edition appeared. A reissue of a recording of rock music may contain one new song replacing a single band of the original issue. A microform collection often assembles material from many previous publications. The implications of the relationships identified in this section occupy most of Chapter 4, while the

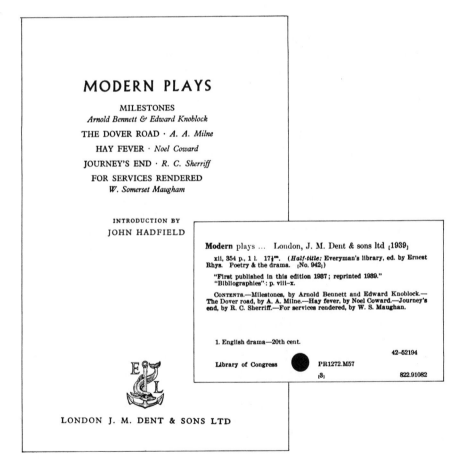

FIG. 24. A title page bearing both a collective title and the titles of the independent works contained in the item. The latter appear in a contents note on the bibliographic record.

section Describing Items at Various Bibliographic Levels on pages 121–126 in Chapter 5 deals with how some existing bibliographic formats provide for the description of these relationships. Finally, the use of access points to bring together the records for related items is analyzed in the section Works on pages 215–220.

Coding Intended to Identify an Item Uniquely

A combination of the bibliographic data already described should suffice to identify any item for retrieval. However, the computer era has brought with it increased attention to the value of numbers as unique identifiers. Telephone numbers, social insurance numbers, and bank account numbers have been used to identify persons and accounts for years. By adding prefixes such as the area code and the country code, the world's telephone companies have ensured that no two numbers in their combined networks are exactly the same.

Numbers with bibliographic significance are also not new: for example a serial number in the *Gesamtkatalog der Wiegendrucke* identifies an incunabulum, a Superintendent of Documents number identifies a United States government publication, a plate number identifies a particular state of the printing of a musical composition, and an LC Card Number identifies a catalogue entry created by the Library of Congress. To these and many others, publishers and librarians recently added the International Standard Book Number (ISBN) and the International Standard Serial Number (ISSN), the most universal of the numbering systems in the field of bibliographic control.

The ISBN system was devised by and for publishers for their own inventory control and accounting systems, not by librarians for cataloguing control. An ISBN therefore has a component which uniquely identifies a particular publisher, as well as one which uniquely identifies the item the publisher wishes to sell. The latter is not a work, but any separately invoiced manifestation of the work. Thus a "quality paperback," a "hardback," and a "limited autographed edition" of the same book each receives a different ISBN, even if they are simultaneously published and are printed from the same plates. Almost no library would create different catalogue entries for these if it acquired all three, but in a publisher's stock they are very different items. Similarly, each volume of a multivolume work receives a different ISBN if it can be sold separately, but there will likely also be a separate ISBN for the set; thus the same physical volume carries two different ISBNs.

The ISBN is always a ten-digit number, conventionally printed in four segments with separating hyphens. The last segment is always one character, the only one which may be a numeric digit or the letter X. It is a *check digit,* of use only to computer programs which can verify the validity of the number and help identify erroneous transcriptions of it. Each of the other three segments is of variable length, as in the following examples:

```
0-949946-29-X
3-7825-0052-0
92-67-10017-3
```

The first two segments uniquely identify the publisher. The first segment alone identifies a language/country area rather loosely. Thus a publishing house which normally issues items in the French language allots ISBNs beginning with the one-digit segment 2 whether the firm is in France, Quebec, or Switzerland.

The ISSN is always an eight-digit number, of which the final digit is the check digit, and may be an X. It is printed in two four-digit segments separated by a hyphen. ISSNs originated in librarians' desire for a more unambiguous identification of serial publications than could be provided by their often similar titles. An ISSN has no meaningful parts, two numbers in sequence have no necessary relationship to each other, and no unit designates a language or a publisher. Each ISSN simply identifies uniquely *one* serial publication for the period of *one* titling of that publication. When a serial publication changes title, the issues under the new title have a new ISSN. The title referred to here is not necessarily the item's title proper, but its key-title (see page 63).

The assigning of ISSNs and key-titles is administered ultimately as part of UNISIST's International Serials Data System in Paris; application of ISBNs is controlled by an independent publisher-sponsored agency, the International Standard Book Numbering Agency in Frankfurt. National agencies in each country supervise the local operation of the two systems; they are usually associated with, or are part of, the country's national library. International numbering schemes have been proposed for various nonprint formats; in fact, ISBNs are being applied by some publishers of such material.

Information Peculiar to an Individual Copy

A description incorporating the elements listed above identifies any one of the dozens, hundreds, or thousands of copies of a publication. Still, it may be desirable to specify data peculiar to a single one of those copies. Examples include a fore-edge painting, a hand binding, a gold-plating of one copy of a disc, the existence of an author's autograph, the number of the particular copy of a limited edition of a book or lithograph, or the fact that the copy was once owned by a famous person, which makes it an *association copy*. If the individual copy is anything other than a complete or perfect example of the item, mention may also be made of this, noting missing leaves, damage, etc. Which characteristics of this kind should be sought and recorded must be the decision of the individual library or bibliographer. Only rare and valuable items are likely to be accorded such detailed description.

Bibliographic Data for Unique Unpublished Items

A footnote citation or a library catalogue entry usually describes a published item; hence rules have always been based on factors relevant to multiple-copy publication. The description of a manuscript, or of some other unpublished item such as a locally made videorecording of an amateur show or a cassette tape of a lecture, necessarily relates to a single unique item. Data identifying such items are not necessarily the same as those for published items. For example, should information relating to the place, agent, and date of publication be simply omitted in the case of unique items, or should it be replaced by data concerning manufacturing or the production of the content? How can an acceptable title best be composed by the cataloguer if none is displayed on the item?

Although some patterns can be established, much has to be left to ad hoc decision in the identification of unique items. Archives, the traditional institutional repositories of unpublished material, have tended to establish their own criteria for the choice and display of identifying elements. The first five centuries of library catalogues consist entirely of lists of unique manuscripts, but only recently have librarians and archivists consciously attempted to systematize their practices. A coherent analysis of the bibliographic characteristics of the many types of unique nonprint items now in library collections has yet to be completed.[5]

Status within the Collection or List

Since it does not describe the item itself, information concerning the status of an item within its library collection or the listing in question is not bibliographic information, strictly speaking. Still, library catalogues and bibliographic lists must incorporate some housekeeping and inventory data for both the item and its catalogue entry. For circulation and shelving control systems, a unique number for each separate physical object in the collection, such as a *call number* (see page 265) or an *accession number,* is desirable. Even information on whether the item is in circulation, to whom, and when it is due to be returned may be considered temporary bibliographic data, generated and used by the library's circulation department. To date, this latter information has rarely been an integral part of the basic bibliographic record of an item, but systems which integrate catalogue searching with circulation control functions are now becoming operational in libraries so that a user may determine whether

5. A good example of such analysis is that undertaken by the Subcommittee on Rules for Cataloging Machine-Readable Data Files of the Catalog Code Revision Committee, Resources and Technical Services Division, American Library Association. Its work resulted in the rules in AACR2 for machine-readable data files, materials for which no rules had previously existed.

or not the item is "on the shelf" at the same time as discovering whether the library owns it. If an item is published in more than one physical part, it is possible (even likely, if it is a serial) that a collection does not have all the parts. A *holdings note* lists the parts actually in the collection.

There is also a need for some accounting system for the bibliographic record itself (as distinguished from the document it describes). In a multiple-entry card catalogue, for example, it is necessary to know where the various entries for the same item are in case they must be changed or deleted. The listing of their locations in the card catalogue is called the *tracing,* shown on the entry in Figure 2 on page 17. In a computer-based system a *control number* identifies a single bibliographic record in all its manifestations or parts within the system.

Sources of Bibliographic Data

What makes a title useful as the name of a publication is its location in a place where every user can expect to find it. In the case of a book printed since the late fifteenth century the expected location is at or near the top of a *title page,* a page early in the book on which are displayed many of the elements of bibliographic data analyzed in this chapter. By the eighteenth century a standard selection of these elements was being presented, usually in a standardized sequence, on every typical title page. These elements and that sequence have come to dominate the bibliographic formats analyzed in Chapter 5.

Some data elements have gradually drifted to locations other than the title page, particularly to the verso of the title leaf where it is now common to find date and edition information. The colophon, little used today in English-language books, is still a common location for date information in French publications, for author information in Russian books, etc. The *preliminaries* (the group of leaves up to and including the title leaf) and the colophon now constitute the expected locations of most bibliographic data for printed materials, though the title page is still pre-eminent. For printed items without a formal title page (notably most serial publications), a caption, masthead, cover, spine, or even running heads may have to supply some or all of the data normally taken from a title page. It is traditional to bracket data which do not come from the expected location for the type of data in question.

A particularly pressing issue today is the definition of sources of bibliographic data for nonprint media. Some display bibliographic data in ways closely analogous to a printed title page, such as in the cartouche of a map or the title frame of a filmstrip. Other nonprint media have not had a tradition of even twenty years to settle where the authoritative form of bibliographic data should be located. Nor is there a tradition of how those data elements may best be worded for unambiguous interpretation. In some media there exist several equally reasonable sources which seem at times perversely to contradict each other, as for example when the labels on a disc sound recording give only the titles of a dozen individual songs, while its slipjacket reads *Favourite Songs by Schubert,* and the textual insert providing the lyrics is headed *Excerpts from Die Schöne Müllerin and Die Winterreise.* An example of different title wording on parts of a kit is given on page 60. Just as a title proper is the chief title of an item, so it is necessary for rules to define one *chief source of information* for each physical medium of communication, so that the same basis for selecting its bibliographic data can be used by all cataloguers.

At all periods of bibliographic history there have been items which do not reveal one or another expected data element: the anonymous work, the undated film, the book issued by a clandestine publisher using a fictitious imprint, the serial whose ISSN does not appear anywhere on a given issue. Research, whether very easy or extremely time-consuming, can often identify the true facts of the situation. When it does, these facts are published in articles, encyclopaedias, and bibliographies. How much effort should be made to ascertain bibliographic facts not revealed in the item itself? How suspicious should one be of the truth of statements which do appear within the item? A bibliographer or cataloguer can only develop a sense of good judgement about these matters through experience and in the context of the purposes of the task. It is a cliché that a problem does not exist until it is recognized. Unrecognized problems do not vanish: they represent failings of the biblographic instinct and will return to haunt the cataloguer and confound the reference librarian.

How Complete Must a Bibliographic Record Be?

Very few data elements are required in a citation whose only purpose is to identify an item and to distinguish it from others. The surest identification is a unique code or number such as the ISBN. But it will be a long time before anyone suggests to a friend, "Read book number 0-226-81620-6." A serial is more likely to be referred to by its coden, which is at least mnemonic: "Get volume 28 of BAPS" (an early coden form for the *Bulletin of the American Physical Society).* Among the more meaningful designations possible, a title alone frequently suffices, as when the teacher tells students, "Read *Future Shock."* Still, it is possible that another book already bears the same title, or that one still to be written will be assigned the same title, since copyright cannot be claimed in a title alone. Common sense warns that it is not sufficient to tell a friend to look up *Principles of Chemistry* or *Statistical Report for 1981.* Misremembered and mistranscribed titles give every reference librarian a personal stock of humour, recalling the patron who asked for *Mice in the Beer* as "My Sin, the Beer."

Copies of works were not so readily available before the invention of printing to check the accuracy of a text, and in any case each copy, being a manuscript, was unique. There existed no concept of the value of an exact quotation which could be documented by item and page number. (The very few instances such as Scriptural texts, significant for salvation and memorized by "chapter and verse," are the exceptions which prove this rule.) Since a reference was more an allusion than a citation as we know it, it was common to give only the name of the author: for example, "Aristotle states that. . . . " Even today, one may be referred to an item by the author's name alone ("Read Herodotus."), but this is only satisfactory in the case of a writer of a single work.

Thus reference by title alone or by author alone is in general inadequate. Even when author and title together are used to cite a work, additional information such as an edition number, physical medium, date, or publisher's name is often required to distinguish the desired form of the work from any other. The user may, for example, only be interested in the second edition of the *Anglo-American Cataloguing Rules,* or only a recording in cassette form of Beethoven's *Fifth Symphony,* or only the Northwestern/Newberry edition of Melville's *Typee.*

One cannot predict when a citation which seemed satisfactory will be rendered too brief by the appearance of a new publication bearing the same title, a new edition or translation of the same work, another work by the same author, etc. An entry is adequate when it ensures that the user can unambiguously identify the one intended document, and is given sufficient information for the purposes for which the list was consulted.

Bibliographic records are used for many different purposes within libraries and in many nonlibrary contexts. Many people consult a library catalogue solely to find a call number so that they can browse among the shelves: a brief listing is probably sufficient for this purpose. A bookseller seeking to verify a first printing of a Ben Jonson play would know that it takes a very specialized bibliography to provide the necessary data.

There can be no one standard or universal rule to determine which data elements are just enough in a citation. Over the centuries a different standard combination of bibliographic data elements has come to be expected in each different type of tool: a footnote, a library catalogue, an author bibliography, etc. In addition to ensuring adequate identification of the items listed, each tool provides whatever additional information serves its specific purposes.

Figure 25 shows descriptions of the same item in six different bibliographies and catalogues. They differ in two ways: (1) the amount of information given, and (2) the arrangement of its presentation, this being the subject of Chapter 5. At the heart of every good bibliographic citation are at least a title, some statement of who is responsible for the content (when ascertainable), the name of the edition (if applicable), and rudimentary publication information. Any citation reduced beyond these, such as the following transcribed from actual publications, looks and probably is inadequate for any purpose other than to give unnecessary work to an interlibrary loan librarian:

```
Aristotle, New York, Columbia University Press

Quaternary Research. University of Washington, 1970
```

Nevertheless, some documents are so famous in themselves that the briefest verbal description is sufficient to elicit instant recognition. Thus most educated English-speaking people would recognize "The First Folio" or "Shakespeare. Folio. 1623" more immediately than they would recognize a description of the same book which follows the current library cataloguing standard:

```
Mr. William Shakespeares Comedies, histories, &
tragedies : published according to the true
originall copies. - London : Printed by Isaac
Jaggard, and Ed. Blount, 1623. - [18], 303, 100,
[2], 69-232, [30], 993 [i.e. 299] p. : ill.
(woodcuts) ; 33 cm. (fol.)
```

The latter is still not an adequate description for a Shakespeare scholar. The importance of the item in the establishment of the text of the plays and the vicissitudes of its printing have been the cause of a more thorough bibliographic study than of most books. That study, by Charlton Hinman, incorporates only bibliographic evidence, and resulted in nothing more than a thorough bibliographic description of the known copies of the First Folio. It is two volumes long, more than a thousand pages: rather too extensive to be contained on a 7.5 × 12.5 cm. card![6]

Economics and common sense restrain the cataloguer in the average library from spending hours of research effort and many lines of notes in describing a common item. A particular set of data elements has become accepted as sufficient in most cases to describe an item for ordinary library purposes, although the smallest libraries may still abridge more, and the largest may add a bit more detail. Beyond this, there must always be latitude for ad hoc adjustment as demanded by the bibliographic nature of a particular item.

It is in the area of recording the relationships described on pages 73–81 that different types of bibliographic endeavour differ most basically from each other. In a footnote citation it is rare to find any information drawn from outside the item being cited: edition and series statements found within the item are usually the only bibliographic relationships expressed. At the other extreme, a specialized critical bibliography explores all possible relationships, including authorship, publication history, and textual differences among the versions of a work. Library cataloguing practice falls somewhere between the two extremes, but leans toward the side of searching out and expressing rela-

6. Charlton Hinman, *The Printing and Proof-Reading of the First Folio of Shakespeare* (Oxford: Clarendon Press, 1963).

—— Report of the Tripartite Economic Survey of the Eastern
Caribbean. January–April 1966. [Leader, J. R. Sargent.]
pp. xxi. 278. *London, 1967.* 8°. B.S. 251/66.

Report of the Tripartite Economic Survey of the Eastern
Caribbean, Jan.-Apr. 1966. London, H. M. S. O., 1967.
xxi. 279 p. diagr., tables. 25 cm. £2/10/-
(B***)
At head of title: Ministry of Overseas Development.

Report of the tripartite economic survey of the
Eastern Caribbean [appointed by the governments
of the United Kingdom, Canada and the United
States of America, carried out] January-April
1960. London. H.M.S.O.. 50/-. [dFeb]1967.
xxi,279p. tables, diagrs. 24½cm. Pbk.

Report of the Tripartite Economic Survey of
the Eastern Caribbean, Jan.-Apr. 1966. London,
H.M. Stationery Off., 1967.

xxi, 278 p. 25 cm.

At head of title: Ministry of Overseas
Development.
"To the Governments of the United Kingdom
of Great Britain and Northern Ireland, of Canada
and of the United States of America".—p. iii.
50/- pa.

Report of the Tripartite Economic Survey of the Eastern Caribbean, January-
April 1966, Ministry of Overseas Development, H.M.S.O., London,
1967.

Tripartite Economic Survey of the Eastern Caribbean, January-April 1966.

FIG. 25. These entries are taken from the catalogue of the British Museum Department of Printed Books; the *National Union Catalog;* the *British National Bibliography; Canadiana;* Sir Harold Mitchell, *Caribbean Patterns* (Edinburgh: Chambers, 1967); and Aaron Segal, *The Politics of Caribbean Economic Integration,* Special Study no. 6 (Rio Piedras, P.R.: Institute of Caribbean Studies, University of Puerto Rico, 1968).

tionships so that the catalogue can be an organized bibliographic guide and not merely a finding tool for specific known items.

This can make a library catalogue entry look considerably different from a citation in a footnote or other source. It also makes library cataloguing essentially more expensive, a fact not necessarily reflected in the length or outward complexity of the entries. The hidden costs are those of checking reference sources for every item catalogued, in making the judgements required to verify relationships, and in maintaining records of these relationships.

If the variety of purposes prevents the establishment of any one rule for citation, so does the infinite variety of the presentation of data within individual documents. This is either the joy or the despair of bibliography, depending on one's point of view. It can seem to a beginner that almost every item presents a slightly different challenge in the selection and arrangement of its bibliographic data. Finally, individual bibliographers have been known to exercise particular whims in the compilation of data (rules tend to discourage the exercise of too much individuality by library cataloguers). For all these reasons, there will forever be a variety of presentations of the kinds of data described in this chapter for librarians to interpret to library users. However, when different bibliographies and catalogues are likely to be consulted in conjunction with each other, there are significant benefits in adopting a common (or at least compatible) treatment of bibliographic data, and the application of computers to bibliographic work has increased the desirability of greater standardization.

The development of rules adopted widely at the national and even the international level has largely been the work of librarians over the past hundred years. In the following chapters, attention is focused on the principles of the twentieth-century library cataloguing codes and subject analysis systems. The rules and purposes of other agencies such as the abstracting and indexing services are considered in their relationship to this principal focus.

4

BIBLIOGRAPHIC
RELATIONSHIPS

The student writing a term paper gives a *citation*. A reference librarian refers to an *entry* in the catalogue. The cataloguer distinguishes two separate functions: composing a *description* and establishing headings for it. The abstractor at an indexing company has appended the abstract to a *document surrogate*. The terms "citation," "entry," "description," and "document surrogate" all refer to what is essentially the same thing: an arrangement of bibliographic data elements concerning a single document and considered relevant for the purpose of the listing in question. "Bibliographic record" may be considered a neutral general term encompassing all the others. It has been so used in the title of this book and in previous chapters.[1]

Items, Titles, Documents, and Physical Units

Each entry identifies one bibliographic *item*. It is displayed with entries for other items in a file (catalogue, list of references, bibliography, etc.) in which the entries are organized according to some intelligible principle of arrangement. Rules are needed for the consistent compilation of entries into bibliographic files, but there are some questions no rule or manual even attempts to answer. The most basic of these is the question of what is the item that a single bibliographic record should attempt to describe.

1. "Entry" is still the term most frequently used by librarians. Unfortunately that term is something of a red herring for two reasons. Until 1981 the accepted North American cataloguing codes used the word in at least two quite different senses (see the Glossary in *Anglo-American Cataloging Rules,* North American Text (Chicago: American Library Association, 1967), pp. 344–345). Also, in the usage "index entry," the word implies only a single piece of bibliographic data, often a subject term. In this book, "entry" is used as a synonym for "bibliographic record," that is, "a record of an item in a catalogue or bibliography." (Cf. the Glossary in AACR2.)

One speaks of a bibliography of a thousand items, in which the twenty-two-volume *The World Book Encyclopedia* is one item, not twenty-two. But are the annual supplementary volumes, *The 1976* [etc.] *World Book Year Book,* also part of that one item? If not, do these yearbooks taken together constitute one additional item? Or is *each* annual supplementary volume a separate additional item? If an anthology of ten plays is one item, is each play included in it also an item? Any of these suppositions may be true, depending on the purposes of the particular list. No cataloguing code has ever defined what an item must consist of, but leaves the decision to common sense and the particular circumstances. A current standard defines the word in what is in fact a deliberate nondefinition chasing its own tail, in which the key clause is "considered as an entity":

> The term "item" used in this text means a document, group of documents, or part of a document, in any physical form, considered as an entity and forming the basis of a single bibliographic description. The term "document" is used here in its widest sense.[2]

Librarians often use the word "title" with the same meaning as "item" since a title is the principal distinguishing feature of an individual bibliographic record. If the 7,632-microfiche set entitled *European Official Statistical Serials on Microfiche* is only listed as a single anthology in the library's catalogue, it is one "title." But if each of the forty serials reproduced therein receives a separate bibliographic listing, as would be the case in many libraries, then it is forty titles. This is the basis for the expressions: "The collection has ten thousand titles," or "There are sixty thousand titles in our catalogue."

Intellectual versus Physical Entity

People looking for information are interested in (1) an intellectual creation, or *work,* but also, of course, in (2) the physical thing (whether in one piece or in many) which embodies the intellectual creation. Either is a reasonable focus for a bibliographic description. In a psychological critique of English drama, there is a footnote citing Shakespeare's *Hamlet,* that is, the play as such, not any one particular edition, translation, version, or printing of it. The user who comes to the library to borrow Thornton Wilder's play *Our Town* probably thinks only of the work in the abstract, and does not much care whether the library's copy of the text is in a British printing or an American, illustrated or unillustrated, a reading text or a promptbook version, a paperback or a hard-bound book, in a separate publication by itself, in an anthology of plays by

---

2. *ISBD(G): General International Standard Bibliographic Description: Annotated Text* (London: IFLA International Office for UBC, 1977), p. 2. "Document" in some contexts implies a single physical piece; at other times it is used with the same meaning as "item." It is among the least clearly definable words in bibliography.

many playwrights, or in a volume of the collected plays of Wilder. The reader may even want the play in a language other than English if it is so available.

A public or school library will be constantly losing or discarding and acquiring copies of a "classic" in various editions. It would be an economy to use one permanent entry instead of many more or less temporary ones, simplifying catalogue maintenance at the time of withdrawing and adding the books. Such an entry might simply read:

```
Fic      Dickens, Charles.
DIC        Bleak house.
           [Library has various editions.]
```

Where a work is revised in successive editions, and the library regularly discards a superseded edition, replacing it with the latest, a similar technique is possible:

```
Z 731    American library directory. - New York
A5         : Bowker.
           [Library has only current edition.]
```

Such an entry is not a bibliographic record, strictly speaking. A library does not buy *Hamlet* or shelve *Bleak House*. It buys or locates a particular edition of one of these works. It shelves and circulates a particular copy. More importantly, only by describing both the work and its physical embodiment can the bibliographer satisfy the reader who will accept only the Ford/Monod edition of *Bleak House* because it is based on the best textual criticism; only the Cambridge University Press reprint edition of Hume's *An Abstract of a Treatise of Human Nature* because it has a critical introduction by John Maynard Keynes; or only Burl Ives' recording of *Waltzing Matilda* by Cowan. For the same reasons, "work entries" are unsatisfactory in union catalogues, cooperative cataloguing projects, and even inventory control. Once popular, their use is now probably restricted to smaller isolated libraries.

A majority of all the works ever created exist in only one published form. They have never been subsequently reprinted, published elsewhere, put into an anthology, or converted to microform, sound recording, machine-readable form, etc. For these, it is not necessary to consider the distinction between the work and its physical manifestation; they are one and the same thing. A famous work, however, exists in many different physical forms and separate publications. It also exists in various versions of its content: varying editions, translations, abridgements, adaptations, etc. If a work exists in more than one published form, it is essential that bibliographic records distinguish the forms and versions from one another, but at the same time clearly show that the work contained in them is the same. The function of *description* (see Chapter 5) is to establish the identity of the physical forms, while name *access points* (see

Chapters 6 and 7) serve to identify the works. The entries for *Bleak House* and the *American Library Directory* on page 93 are essentially access points without descriptions.

Bibliographic Identity

Many documents suffer from a real "identity crisis," complicating the decision as to what to encompass on their bibliographic record(s). For example, what Sir Winston Churchill wrote about World War II was originally published over a period of six years as six separate pieces. Editions were published in several countries. Figure 26 shows the first and last title pages in the British and the American editions, which raise some questions:

1) Did Sir Winston write one work in six volumes, or six works? If the latter, do they constitute a "series" in the sense discussed on pages 77–78?

2) Is this history of the war more likely to be recognized, or sought in an alphabetically arranged catalogue, by the one common title or by each of the six separate titles? For example, would a search for the title of the first book focus more naturally on the letter G for Gathering, or on S for Second? (Note that searching under C for Churchill is not a complete solution since the subarrangement of the considerable number of entries under his name will be by the chosen title.)

3) How much influence does (or should) the wording, layout, and typography of the title page bring to bear on the above issues? Should the outcome be different for the American edition where the individual-volume titles are more prominent, than for the British edition where the common title is more prominent?

4) Should a library which intends to buy all six volumes view the situation differently from one which will only acquire, say, volume four and not the rest? (This is unlikely in the Churchill instance, but would not be at all unusual in many bibliographically similar cases.)

5) Should a catalogue in which the whole set is listed contain one bibliographic record (for the six volumes together), six records (one for each volume), or seven? Provision of a reference under each of the seven possible titles may be useful for the searcher, but begs the question of what the catalogue entry will look like: a description must begin with *one* title.

6) Would it be easier or more difficult to arrive at a decision in this matter in 1948 when only the first part existed and not the other five?

Figure 27 illustrates how the levels of title information may be ambiguously presented even between volumes of the same edition of a work. There can be no single objectively correct answer to the problems raised by these and the

The Second World War
★
THE
Gathering
Storm

Winston S. Churchill

Published in association with
The Cooperation Publishing Company, Inc.

HOUGHTON MIFFLIN COMPANY BOSTON
THOMAS ALLEN LIMITED
CANADA
1948

The Second World War
★ ★ ★ ★ ★
Triumph
and
Tragedy

Winston S. Churchill

HOUGHTON MIFFLIN COMPANY BOSTON
The Riverside Press Cambridge

WINSTON S. CHURCHILL

———•{✦}•———

THE
SECOND WORLD WAR

VOLUME I

THE GATHERING STORM

CASSELL & CO. LTD
LONDON · TORONTO · MELBOURNE · SYDNEY
WELLINGTON

WINSTON S. CHURCHILL

———•{✦}•———

THE
SECOND WORLD WAR

VOLUME VI

TRIUMPH AND TRAGEDY

CASSELL & CO. LTD
LONDON · TORONTO · MELBOURNE · SYDNEY
WELLINGTON

FIG. 26. Two pairs of title pages for the same works, showing the effect of typography in emphasizing titling at different levels.

Documents of
European Economic History

VOLUME ONE

The Process of Industrialization
1750–1870

S. Pollard
Professor of Economic History, University of Sheffield
C. Holmes
Lecturer in Economic History, University of Sheffield

Edward Arnold

Documents of
European Economic History

VOLUME TWO

Industrial Power
and National Rivalry

1870–1914

Sidney Pollard
Professor of Economic History, University of Sheffield
Colin Holmes
Lecturer in Economic History, University of Sheffield

Edward Arnold

FIG. 27. In volume 1, the series title appears prominently on the title page; in volume 2, the series title appears only on the half-title page.

Churchill volumes. To arrive at a reasonable decision one must discover and investigate the bibliographic relationships of the work in question in all its existing editions, and consider what each title page is trying to convey through its language and syntax. Having done that, one considers the local circumstances: how is the typical user of the catalogue in question most likely to identify the wanted item? Anyone looking up a publication of this kind in a catalogue or bibliography must always be aware that a situation involving bibliographic relationships may result in different possible methods of dealing with it. It was noted on pages 88–90 that library cataloging practice has always paid particular attention to such relationships. Not every bibliographic tool is as thorough: it is worthwhile to discover the degree to which particular bibliographies can be relied upon.

The bibliographer unfortunately has no control over how publishers and printers display bibliographic information. An increasing proportion of publications even in the print media are being produced by nontraditional techniques, and more persons unfamiliar with the tradition and the needs of bibliographic control are composing title pages, publicity, and other identifying information for them. It is therefore becoming more, not less, common to find the odd, the unexpected, and the ambiguous display of bibliographic data in publications. Even some traditional publishers have consistently shown a cavalier attitude toward acknowledging bibliographic relationships within their publications; others must be credited with always trying to give helpful and correct data.

In the nonprint media, where any attempt at bibliographic control is relatively recent, it is understandable that publishers are especially uncertain about what kind of information they must supply for the unambiguous identification of their products in catalogues. At the same time, multimedia nonprint items (kits, etc.) are notorious for often presenting problems like those illustrated above with the Churchill set. The experienced librarian has developed an instinct about when to be suspicious in the presence of potentially misleading information, and when to suspect that relevant data are lacking and must be sought elsewhere.

Levels of Identity within a Work or a Document

A single published item normally contains one, and only one, complete intellectual composition:

The Meaning of Relativity by Albert Einstein

However, it may contain (1) only a part of a work:

Anglo-American Cataloging Rules, North American text,
Chapter 14 revised, Sound Recordings

(2) a combination of related works:

> *Major Classification Systems: the Dewey Centennial, Papers*
> *Presented at the Allerton Park Institute . . .* edited by
> Kathryn Luther Henderson
> *The Philosophy of William James Selected from His Chief*
> *Works*

or (3) an agglomeration of works previously unrelated to each other:

> *Mantovani and His Orchestra Play Your Favorites*
> *London Mathematical Society Lecture Note Series*

As noted earlier, it has to be possible to produce a bibliographic record for Churchill's *The Second World War* as a single six-volume work *or* to produce one for *The Gathering Storm* as a one-volume work, depending on the context of the decision. In the same way, a paper delivered at a conference may be considered a work, but so may the published conference proceedings as a whole. *Hedda Gabler* is a work, but so is any anthology in which it has been published, whether only of works by Ibsen (*The Best Known Works of Ibsen*), or of works by many playwrights (*Twenty-five Modern Plays*).

The purpose of the bibliographic list in question has always been the most important determinant of which level of identity is emphasized. Many abstracting and indexing services produce more bibliographic records than most libraries do, but at a different level: for the *Social Sciences Index* the basis of each separate entry is the single article in a journal, whereas for *New Serial Titles* the basis is the journal itself, as shown in Figure 28.

In the *New Serial Titles* entry the individual article is not mentioned at all, whereas in *Social Sciences Index* the description of the journal is reduced to an abbreviated title (a fuller description is given once at the beginning of each cumulation). Similarly, the *Play Index* records the existence of each play in each of the anthologies indexed, whereas the *National Union Catalog* records only the existence of the anthology, sometimes with and sometimes without a contents note to reveal which specific plays it contains, as shown in Figure 29.

Although it is unusual today for a library to prepare a separate catalogue entry for a single article in a journal, it is not unusual to prepare one for a single issue of a journal if it has a separate distinctive title or editor and all its articles are on a single theme, as illustrated in Figure 30.

But is it feasible to create a separate entry for each issue of a journal as a usual practice? The answer is both "yes" and "no." Somewhere in the serials check-in unit of the library, the existence of each single issue must be recorded as it arrives. In the library's public catalogue, it is usual merely to describe on one unfinished entry the continuing journal as a whole: the many volumes

Zepelin, Harold and others
Evaluation of a yearlong reality orientation program. bibl J
Geront 36:70-7 Ja '81

Journal of gerontology.
v. 1-   Jan. 1946-
[Washington, etc., Gerontological Society]
    v.   ill., diagrs. 26 cm.
    Quarterly, 1946-   ; bimonthly
    Each issue, Jan. 1950-   includes "Index to current periodical litera-
ture."
    Vol. for 1946 includes Journal of gerontology, Non-technical supple-
ment, v. 1, no. 1-4, Jan.-Oct. 1946, paged separately and issued as pt. 2 of
the Journal of gerontology.
    Key title: Journal of gerontology (Kirkwood), ISSN 0022-1422.
    1. Gerontology—Periodicals.   I. Gerontological Society.   II. Key
Title.

HQ1060.J6   301.435   48-4536
Library of Congress

DLC

FIG. 28. Above, an entry for a single article in a journal; below, an entry for the
journal as a whole.

Odets, Clifford
    Awake and sing!
    Jewish family in Bronx during depression
    years endures frustrations of circumscribed
    lives. 3 acts 4 scenes 7m 2w 1 interior
        In Block, H. M. and Shedd, R. G. eds.
            Masters of modern drama
    ——▶ *In* Clurman, H. ed. Famous American
            plays of the 1930s
        In Gassner, J. ed. Best American plays;
            supplementary volume, 1918-1958

Clurman, Harold, 1901–   *ed.*
    Famous American plays of the 1930s. [New York, Dell
Pub. Co., °1959]

    480 p. 17 cm. (The Laurel drama series, LX117)

    1. American drama—20th cent. · I. Title.

PS634.C57   812.52082   60–412 ‡

Library of Congress   [2]

FIG. 29. Above, an entry for a single play in an anthology; below, an entry for the
anthology as a whole which does not reveal its contents.

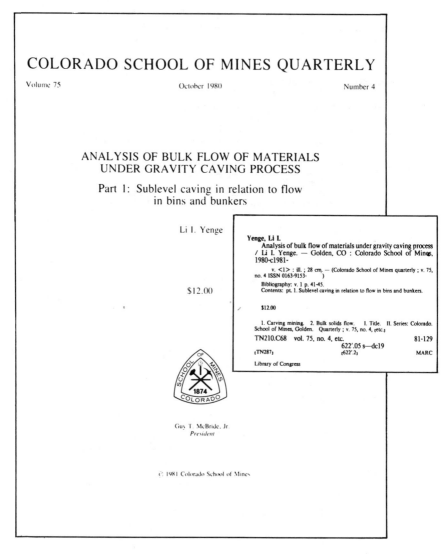

COLORADO SCHOOL OF MINES QUARTERLY

Volume 75   October 1980   Number 4

ANALYSIS OF BULK FLOW OF MATERIALS
UNDER GRAVITY CAVING PROCESS

Part 1: Sublevel caving in relation to flow
in bins and bunkers

Li I. Yenge

$12.00

Yenge, Li I.
    Analysis of bulk flow of materials under gravity caving process
/ Li I. Yenge. — Golden, CO : Colorado School of Mines,
1980-c1981-
    v. <1> : ill. ; 28 cm. — (Colorado School of Mines quarterly ; v. 75,
no. 4 ISSN 0163-9153-   )
    Bibliography: v. 1 p. 41-45.
    Contents: pt. 1. Sublevel caving in relation to flow in bins and bunkers.

    $12.00

    1. Carving mining.   2. Bulk solids flow.   I. Title.   II. Series: Colorado.
School of Mines, Golden.   Quarterly ; v. 75, no. 4, ¡etc.¡
TN210.C68   vol. 75, no. 4, etc.   81-129
                                    622'.05 s—dc19
¡TN287¡   ¡622'.2¡   MARC
Library of Congress

Guy T. McBride, Jr.
President

© 1981 Colorado School of Mines

FIG. 30. A title page for a single issue of a journal, and an entry for this issue.

which have already appeared as well as those which are yet to be published. Sometimes bound volumes are individually listed on this record, but it is more usual only to indicate when the library began subscribing to the title, leaving the user to assume that the collection contains every issue from then to the present.

The Basis for the Bibliographic Record
in a Library Catalogue

The catalogue of a public, school, college, university, or national library is the most general of all types of bibliographic lists, covering all published media and all subjects. It is impossible to adhere to a consistent policy concerning what units are to be described in it, particularly with respect to the cataloguing of those units at different levels. Almost every other type of bibliography or index, and often the catalogue of a special library, can state a fixed and clearly understood policy on its levels of listing. Many tools such as periodical indices, indices of papers delivered at conferences, etc., exist for the express purpose of dealing with one definable level of bibliographic unit or work.

In the case of a general library catalogue, a pragmatic attitude is necessary, and ad hoc decisions are frequent. Over the policy looms the budget: bibliographic work costs money, and there is always more work than money to pay for its completion. The most common starting point for a general library's policy is to call for a separate catalogue record for any monograph bearing a separate title page or other "chief source of information." This policy is then modified based on circumstances or type of material. For example, monographs in series may only get an entry for the series, government monographs may not be catalogued at all if they can be shelved by issuing agency and retrieved through specialized indices, and large amounts of report material may be relegated to vertical files arranged by subject without any concern for the identification of single items.

One of the most difficult problems in bibliographic control is how to deal with the work which sometimes appears as a separately published unit, but is (or may be) also published as a part of some other bibliographic unit. The user who finds one catalogue entry for Wilder's *Our Town,* but discovers that the book is in circulation, at the bindery, or missing, too easily concludes that the library does not have an available copy of the play, while six anthologies containing it sit on the shelves. What a user recognizes as a separate item may, in other words, be different from what the cataloguer or bibliographer chooses to consider an item for identification in the catalogue or bibliography.

For this reason it is not uncommon for a library to file a catalogue entry for each individual work reproduced in a microform set or for each composition recorded on a long-playing record. This is particularly true when the publisher makes available inexpensive standard catalogue entries ready to be filed into a manual catalogue, as has been the case with some publishers of microform sets. Whether or not the particular policy adopted seems consistent or adequate to users' needs, it should at least be definable so that users and reference librarians know when to search in the catalogue and when to search in some other type of bibliographic tool for a given kind of item.

Analysis

The practice of preparing *both* a bibliographic record for a larger unit and one or more records for units contained within it is called *analyzing* the contents of the larger work, or making *analytic entries* or *analytics* for it. This was routinely done in many library catalogues earlier in the century before abstracting and indexing services began to cover the field of journal and technical literature so thoroughly. Figure 1 on page 16 showed the separate listing of a single volume, as well as a listing for the multivolume set of which it is a part, in a public library catalogue. Figure 31 shows a group of entries from the catalogue of the United States Department of Labor Library, many of which are entries for single articles in journals, single papers read at conferences, single chapters of books, etc.

There now exist so many published indices to the contents of anthologies, conference proceedings, serials, microform sets, etc., that it is not considered necessary in most libraries to prepare separate catalogue entries for items contained in such collections—at least if the collection is indexed elsewhere. When the materials budget is meagre and each purchase must be fully utilizable, one factor in deciding whether to buy a magazine or anthology is whether or not its contents are indexed in a periodical index or a published bibliography acquired by the library.

Simple budgetary restraint is another reason for the decline in making analytic entries. In the face of other legitimate and pressing demands, many administrators simply cannot justify the expenditure of time and money on so labour-intensive an operation whose limits are almost impossible to define. Many "works" in a library's collection (contributions to collections, articles in journals, etc.) therefore remain undescribed on any bibliographic record readily available to the user since they appear as separate entries neither in the library's catalogue nor in any bibliographic index to which the library user has ready access.

The ecologist who comes to the catalogue with a citation for a paper given at the eighth International Conference on Water Pollution Research expects to find an entry for the proceedings of that conference; finding none, that patron submits an interlibrary loan request for them. But if the library subscribes to the journal *Progress in Water Technology,* it in fact has the proceedings of this conference; they were published as volume 9 number 1 of that journal. Thus perhaps the library should analyze this journal in its catalogue. A search of *Pollution Abstracts* (if the library subscribes to that tool) would reveal the location of the desired paper if its author or subject were known, but even it does not list conference papers under the names of conferences.

It is clearly desirable, but an unattainable ideal, to incorporate within every bibliography or catalogue all possible information concerning (1) the larger unit(s) of which the catalogued item may be considered a part (particularly series or serials), (2) the smaller units or works contained within it which might

INCOME - U.S.

HD
2775
A61
no.4

[Goldenthal, Adolph James, 1916-

... Concentration and composition of individual incomes, 1918-1937 ... Washington, U. S. Govt. print. off., 1940.

xv, 112 p. incl. tables, diagr. 23ᶜᵐ. (U. S., Temporary national economic committee. Investigation of concentration of economic power ... Monograph no. 4)

At head of title: 76th Congress } Senate committee print.
3d session

Running title: Concentration of economic power.

"A study made under the auspices of the Department of commerce for the Temporary national economic committee, Seventy-sixth Congress, third session, pursuant to Public resolution no. 113 (Seventy-fifth Con-

INCOME - U.S.

Goldsmith, Selma F
Income distribution in the United States, 1950-53.

(In Survey of current business, March 1955, v.35, no.3, p.15-27)

"Brings up-to-date the size distributions of family income that were initiated by the Office of Business Economics in a supplement to the Survey of current business, 'Income distribution in the United States, by size, 1944-50.'"

INCOME - U.S.

HB
601
C6
v.8

Haberler, Gottfried, 1900-
Taxes, government expenditures, and national income [by] Gottfried Haberler ... and Everett E. Hagen ...

HD
8055
N293
no.6

INCOME - U.S.

Franklin, William B
Discretionary income [by] William B. Franklin, assisted by Alfred Tella, New York, National Industrial Conference Board [1958]

45 p. diagrs. 28 cm. (National Industrial Conference Board. Technical paper no 6)

Cover title
Bibliographical footnotes

—— Supplement no 3— Sept. 1959-

1 Discretionary Income—U. S. For f[?]. c[?]. decision (Series: National Industrial Conference Board. Technical papers, no. 6)

HB
1
A5
1922

INCOME - U.S.

Friday, David
The course of agricultural income during the last twenty-five years.

(In American economic association. Papers and proceedings of the 35th annual meeting, December, 1922. p. 147-158)

Discussion: p. 179-184.

INCOME - U.S.

Friday, David.
Income during business depression.

New republic, June 20,1923,v.35:89-90.

see

Fig. 31. A group of entries reproduced from a library catalogue. Individual journal articles, reports, and chapters of books are separately catalogued, as well as monographs.

themselves reasonably be the subject of separate search, and (3) other forms of publication of the intellectual content of the catalogued item.

The first of these requirements is usually fulfilled since most bibliographic formats specifically call for such information. The other two are not necessary for the identification of the item as published, and they can be costly projects. Hence they are not commonly carried out thoroughly or consistently. The third, that of identifying other forms of publication of the same intellectual content, can in any case only be fulfilled retrospectively; one cannot know at the time of cataloguing a particular item what future forms the same work will take. As noted on page 93, to *describe* any of these relationships is a purpose of a bibliographic format (see Chapter 5), whereas to *group* works in a file so that the various manifestations of a single work may be found together is a purpose of name access points (see Chapter 7, particularly the section "Works" on pages 215–220).

Establishing Policy on What to Catalogue

A library's policy on the level of bibliographic control it will support must be influenced by local factors: the expectations and sophistication of its own clientele, the published bibliographies and the abstracting and indexing services it acquires, the expertise of its own staff, and the administrative and economic priorities established for its services. These factors change over the years, and policies are hard to formulate precisely. In default of a clear local policy on what to consider the "catalogable" unit, or in case of disagreement in a particular case, there is a natural tendency to "follow the leader." This promotes interlibrary consistency and common user expectations, and it can be less expensive than to establish and apply local decisions.

A leader in shaping decisions on all aspects of library cataloguing is the Library of Congress, whose practices are the most specifically explained and the most widely publicized in the whole library world.[3] In addition to the existence of its separately issued decisions, the descriptive cataloguing codes followed in most of the English-speaking world from 1908 through 1980 have embodied Library of Congress policies which go beyond merely interpeting and applying cataloguing principles, but which also reflect its application of the kind of judgements here under discussion. When it is discovered (or can reasonably be inferred) what stance the Library of Congress would take, at least most of the major academic libraries in Canada and the United States have followed suit. Larger libraries almost everywhere are conscious of the implications of Library of Congress practice on the bibliographic world at large.

3. The publication which announces Library of Congress decisions both on its cataloguing policies and on its detailed application of rules and standards is the quarterly *Cataloging Service Bulletin* (Washington: Processing Services, Library of Congress, 1978–) [formerly *Cataloging Service,* 1945–1978]. It is among the most widely distributed publications in librarianship.

However, the policies of the Library of Congress concerning such matters as series cataloguing, the provision of analytics and contents notes, etc., are those best suited to its own particular needs as a large research library with a huge array of bibliographic resources in addition to its own vast catalogue. They are not intended to represent the best policies for any other particular library. But because they are so often copied, all librarians do well to be aware of them.

It should be no surprise that the policies of the Library of Congress, like those of any other library, change from time to time. It has steadily reduced the production of analytic entries over the years as commercially published tools have moved into the field of providing them in almost all areas of knowledge. Other libraries which once acquired relevant Library of Congress analytics have not necessarily assumed the function of locally producing those which would still be desirable. However, groups of libraries are now undertaking cooperative ventures in analysis (see page 281).

As another example of policy change, Figure 32 illustrates a Library of Congress entry for a larger unit. Today, each edition would be considered a separate item for cataloguing purposes, with notes on each of the several entries to show the relationship. This situation illustrates the intractable problem of what to define as a serial for cataloguing purposes.[4]

For as long as a library's catalogue is maintained independently, local policies can be developed and explained to local users. When the practices of different libraries are brought together in a union catalogue or other common bibliographic database, any variant becomes a "sore thumb." If one library can contribute an entry shown in Figure 33 while another library is satisfied with the one in Figure 32 as a description of the same item, there is inevitably a potential for difficulty when a third party searches the common file to identify the item in question.

Investigatory skill and persistence are usually rewarded in the case of a search for a known item. Even with such an awareness, the search for a particular desired item can involve paging through the tables of contents and indices of individual volumes when no clearer clue has been given to the bibliographic identity of the desired item. The lack of separate bibliographic identification of works is likely to be a more serious handicap to the locating of relevant items in a subject search. There, expectations cannot be as precisely expressed and the search is therefore more likely to be given up before all avenues have been explored.

---

4. The *American Library Directory* used as an example on page 93 is another example. Since it makes economic sense not to have to produce a separate entry for each edition of a title when these are issued frequently, many libraries choose to adjust their working definition of a serial. Even defining a serial as a publication which appears annually or more frequently will not suit the purposes of many national bibliographic services which feel obliged to create separate listings for annuals and indeed for any item described as an edition rather than as an issue or volume.

THE READER'S ADVISER

AND BOOKMAN'S MANUAL

A Guide to the Best in Print in Literature,
Biographies, Dictionaries, Encyclopedias,
Bibles, Classics, Drama, Poetry, Fiction,
Science, Philosophy, Travel, History

9th Edition, Revised and Enlarged by

HESTER R. HOFFMAN

NEW YORK · R. R. BOWKER COMPANY · 1960

The **Reader's adviser.** ₍1st₎–   **ed.**
1921–
New York, R. R. Bowker Co.
    v. 22–27 cm.
    Title varies: 1921–41, 1958, Bookman's manual.—1948–54, Bessie
Graham's bookman's manual.—1960, Reader's adviser and bookman's
manual.
    Compilers: 1921–41, B. Graham; 1948–   H. R. Hoffman.
    1. Bibliography—Best books.   I. Graham, Bessie, 1883–
comp. II. Hoffman, Hester Rosalyn Jacoby, 1895–   comp. III.
Title: Bookman's manual. IV. Title: Bessie Graham's bookman's
manual.
Z1035.B7   57–13277 rev 3

FIG. 32. The Library of Congress entry shown here was intended to apply to all editions, existing and future. It was prepared from the information available up to the appearance of the ninth edition (whose title page is reproduced). In the Library of Congress's own catalogue, it replaced the eight separate entries previously prepared for each of the first eight editions. (See also Figure 33.)

The Reader's adviser; a guide to the best in literature. Edited by Winifred F. Courtney. 11th
ed. , rev. and enl.   New York, R. R. Bowker,
1968-69.
    2 v. 26 cm.
    Vol. 2 has subtitle: A layman's guide.
    1. Bibliography–Best books. 2. Literature–
Bio-bibliography. 3. Reference books–Bibliography.   I. Courtney, Winifred F.
NN   NUC77-38574

Courtney, Winifred F   ed.
    The Reader's adviser, a guide to the best in
literature, edited by ...   New York, R. R.
Bowker, 1968.
    xxvii, 1114 p. 26 cm.
    1. Literature–Bio-Bibliography.   I. Title.
OWorP Wa   NUC69-50892

FIG. 33. Non-Library-of-Congress entries from the *National Union Catalog* for an item which is also covered by the entry in Figure 32.

Summary

The argument that a library must have only a single catalogue of its holdings was once a psychologically persuasive one. It has less relevance today, when the bibliographic resources of any library are scattered throughout many catalogues, bibliographies, and indexing tools, both manual and computerized. But this means that the reference librarian must be the more aware of the scope and level of analysis of each tool.

Almost every original writer on library cataloguing has addressed the issue of the two types of unit discussed at the beginning of this chapter in the creation of bibliographic records: (1) the published unit (usually also the physical unit), and (2) the intellectual unit, or work.[5] What emerges clearly is that there are great problems in defining either type of unit, and that the two can only be usefully distinguished in the context of particular purposes and of particular bibliographic methods and formats.

The past decade has seen the development of networks based on large machine-readable databases composed of records contributed by many cataloguing agencies, each with its variant local policies. To decide and to define

---

5. The classic analysis of the dilemma is Eva Verona, "Literary Unit Versus Bibliographical Unit," *Libri* 9, no. 2 (1959):79–104.

what unit or level should be the basis for such contributed records is a very real problem in such networks. Until it is resolved, unrelated entries will continue to appear for the same item in the same database. Such entries mislead both cataloguers and reference librarians, even though each individual entry may be technically "correct."

One critic feels that it is possible to specify what unit should be the basis of the catalogue entry, berating the current English-language cataloguing code for its failure to take a stand on the matter.[6] Some method of coding the levels of series, unit, work, analytic, etc., would seem to be a more practical approach, particularly in a machine-readable system in which the codes could generate links for retrieval purposes.[7] Concern for improving the methods of item identification so that single bibliographic records can be exchanged and shared has been the first priority of cataloguers for years. The need for clearer methods of linking related records is becoming more obvious now that the computer must also "judge" relationships. Perhaps the most immediately practical solution is simple duplication, though of course clearly identified duplication. For example, the Canadian Task Group on Cataloguing Standards recommended a decade ago that

> Libraries report to the Canadian union lists of serials all series (including monographic series) under a covering series entry, if they intend to receive substantially all items in the series, even when they also report analytics to the Canadian Union Catalogue.[8]

6. J. A. Shinebourne, "A Critique of AACR," *Libri* 29 (October 1979):231–259.

7. Levels in bibliographic relationships are analyzed in detail in *Hierarchical Relationships in Bibliographic Descriptions;* INTERMARC Software-Subgroup Seminar 4, Library Systems Seminar Essen, 25 March–27 March 1981, Publications of Essen University Library, v. 2 (Essen: Gesamthochschulbibliothek Essen, 1981) [available without charge from Essen (Germany) University Library]. Several existing formats for distinguishing such levels in manual cataloguing are described on pages 121–125. Coding is also provided for that purpose in most of the machine-readable formats, but a more elaborate structure is proposed, for example, in Herbert H. Hoffman, "A Structure Code for Machine Readable Library Catalog Record Formats," *Journal of Library Automation* 14 (June 1981):112–116. Two very new formats, the ISBD(CP) (see pages 125–127) and the Common Communication Format (see pages 148–149) address the problem of levels specifically.

8. *Cataloguing Standards, the Report of the Canadian Task Group on Cataloguing Standards* (Ottawa: National Library of Canada, 1972), p. 50. The preceding and the following recommendations in the same report are also attempts to rationalize the treatment of levels of bibliographic indentification.

5

FORMATS FOR
BIBLIOGRAPHIC DATA

A bibliographic record consists of the bibliographic data concerning one item as assembled according to a particular *format*. A format is like a compartmentalized container, designed to fit the data in such a way that each data element is recognizable and can be separately recalled, correlated, sorted, printed, etc. Even if the user does not recognize the name of the publisher in a particular citation, the fact that a certain name is the publisher is clear from its position between a place name and a date in a three-part unit of information.

A bibliographic format is the grammatical structure, or syntax, of the language of bibliography referred to on page 56. Understanding the syntax is largely dependent upon correctly interpreting the significance of the order or arrangement of the elements. There are few connectors other than punctuation to help make the combination of elements intelligible, and the structure is a very condensed one. Experienced library users are not conscious of any special syntax in a bibliographic citation because they have become familiar with it in a simple form: author—title—edition—place—publisher—date. A cataloguer encounters the subtleties of this language, and must know it intimately in order to create unambiguous entries which concisely reveal the significant facts in an appropriate context.

The most important virtue of any collection of bibliographic records is not comprehensiveness, neatness, or other such subjective value, but consistency in the use of this syntax. For data expressed so concisely to be intelligible, it is essential that each entry within a given file follow a standard format. But the format must be applied to facts clearly understood and correctly interpreted. When a beginner creates a poor citation, it is usually not because its parts are wrong, but because they have been put together unthinkingly. ''Principles of Chemistry by John Smith. Fifth edition revised by Walter Jones'' implies a different kind of author/content relationship from "Principles of Chemistry by John Smith, revised by Walter Jones. Fifth edition," or "Principles of Chemistry. Fifth edition by John Smith, revised by Walter Jones." Only one of these three statements can be the "correct" way of describing the actual item, but in fact any one of the three types of relationship is possible. The use of a standard format does not mean that an edition number always follows an author's name; what it does mean is that the correct interpretation of the facts should be consistently displayed. As another example of this vital point, the statement "Terrorism, a bibliography. Supplement. Second edition. 1961" implies a different dating of the original content and the supplementary material from the statement "Terrorism, a bibliography. Second edition. 1961. Supplement," or "Terrorism, a bibliography. Second edition. Supplement. 1961."

It is not difficult to establish and maintain consistency in using a format when the number of records in a file is small, such as a few footnotes to a term paper. Rules for footnote citation and the compilation of brief reading lists are typically only a few pages long. They lay down basic principles, give examples to imitate, and attempt to solve only the simplest and most frequently encountered problems in applying the format to the data elements of actual documents. As the number of citations in a list grows larger, close attention to a very detailed rule may be needed to ensure consistency.

Who Sets the Standards for Manual Formats?

A small number of bibliographic formats have gained favour throughout the English-speaking world and its areas of cultural influence. Each one focuses on a particular broad area of application. A *style manual* dictates the form of bibliographic citation in the writing of scholarly articles, books, theses, etc. Pre-eminent among these is the relevant portion (notably Chapters 15 and 16) of the internationally used guide commonly known as the Chicago Style Manual.[1] A shorter manual, and probably the most frequently recommended one for academic use in North America, is Kate L. Turabian's *A Manual for Writers of Term Papers, Theses, and Dissertations.*[2] The aim of these and other such manuals is brevity and clarity in footnote citation and in the compilation of shorter reading lists.

The abstracting and indexing services have developed their own group of bibliographic style manuals in which the focus of attention is the technical document and the journal article. At first, almost every agency wrote its own

1. *A Manual of Style for Authors, Editors, and Copywriters,* 12th ed. rev. (Chicago: University of Chicago Press, 1969). The 13th edition is to be published in 1982 under the title *The Chicago Manual of Style for Authors, Editors, and Copywriters.*
2. 4th ed. (Chicago: University of Chicago Press, 1973). Turabian's closest contender in popularity appears to be the *MLA Handbook for Writers of Research Papers, Theses, and Dissertations* (New York: Modern Language Association of America, 1977).

rules, but practices have gradually coalesced. Turabian includes in her fourth edition a chapter with an alternative format for scientific papers which reflects some practices of the indexing services. The rule now most widely adopted for report citation in North America appears to be the current version of the manual known as the COSATI Manual. The American National Standards Institute has adopted a standard for citing journal articles.[3]

Rules for library cataloguing are the most complex and detailed of them all, because their scope is the entire world of recorded communication and a seemingly infinite variety of bibliographic problems. A library catalogue is created by many different persons over a long period of time, and different cataloguers are very likely to interpret a general principle in different ways at different times. Even though a very high proportion of the actual cases encountered are solved by a very small proportion of the rules in any style manual or cataloguing code, very detailed rules are needed for the more esoteric cases. In addition to the requirements which affect the intelligibility of the resulting entries, almost everyone would like some standards whose purpose is simply neatness: rules for capitalization, for indentations, for the physical placement of data on a card or sheet, etc.

Library cataloguing codes have the longest continuous history of development at the level of national and international cooperation. Through most of the twentieth century, librarians in the whole English-speaking world have spoken of, and for the most part used, *the* cataloguing code, rather than *a* cataloguing code; that is, a code commonly accepted as the Anglo-American standard, even if not every library applied it fully.

Development of this cataloguing code, through a sequence of editions and of interedition supplements and amendments, has been the responsibility of committees representing national library associations and national bibliographic agencies.[4] The effective initiator and most important contributor from the turn of the century until 1974 was the Library of Congress, in consultation with committees of the American Library Association, the Library Association, and after 1957 the Canadian Library Association. The process has become increas-

3. *Guidelines for Descriptive Cataloging of Reports: a Revision of COSATI Standard for Descriptive Cataloging of Government Scientific and Technical Reports* (Washington: Committee on Information Hang-ups, Working Group on Updating COSATI, 1978) [available through NTIS]; *American National Standard for Bibliographic References* (Washington: American National Standards Institute, 1977).

4. The principal publications in this sequence, briefly cited, are: Charles A. Cutter, *Rules for a Dictionary Catalog*, 1876; *Catalog Rules, Author and Title Entries* [the "Joint Code"], 1908; *A.L.A. Cataloging Rules, Author and Title Entries*, Preliminary 2nd ed., 1941; *Rules for Descriptive Cataloging in the Library of Congress*, 1949; *Anglo-American Cataloging Rules* [AACR1] in separate North American and British editions, 1967; and *Anglo-American Cataloguing Rules*, 2nd ed. [AACR2], 1978. (The 1949 *A.L.A. Cataloging Rules for Author and Title Entries*, 2nd ed. [that is, second edition of the 1908 code], deals only with name access points, not with bibliographic description. See page 192.)

ingly collegial over the past decade as national Canadian and Australian committees, other agencies in the library communities of the United Kingdom and the United States, the British Library, library associations elsewhere in the English-speaking world, and various IFLA committees have become formally or informally involved. The process of review and revision is now much slower, more expensive, and more cumbersome, but one result is that the current code (AACR2) commands the attention of a wider group of potential users than any previous one, and can claim to be an international standard in all but the strictest meaning of that term.

Older manuals and cataloguing rules are largely, or even exclusively, concerned with printed materials. As more and more nonprint items appeared in citations and particularly in school library catalogues, formal rules were required to deal with their particular bibliographic and physical characteristics. Various publications have appeared since the 1950s to fill the need. For example, Eugene B. Fleischer's *A Style Manual for Citing Microform and Nonprint Media* is directed at substantially the same audience as are Turabian's and the MLA handbook.[5] The "official" cataloguing code mentioned above paid scant attention until the 1970s to nonprint materials other than those likely to appear in research collections. This forced many school district cataloguing agencies, educational media associations, and individual authors to attempt the compilation of rules for educational teaching materials.[6] As a result of their efforts, the characteristics of nonprint materials have now been incorporated into the mainstream of cataloguing rules. In AACR2 the integration of print and nonprint characteristics is almost complete.

Arrangement of Data Elements

From the sixteenth century until the mid-twentieth, almost everything catalogued or listed in a bibliography was a printed item with a title page (or a substitute such as a caption or masthead). The value of a title page as a source both of bibliographic data and of its ideal arrangement was discussed on page 85. It is therefore no surprise that most rules for formatting bibliographic data were originally based on the principle that a proper description consists prima-

5. (Chicago: American Library Association, 1978).

6. Probably the most widely used of these is the one which first attempted conformity with the official cataloguing code, Jean Riddle Weihs, Shirley Lewis, and Janet Macdonald, *Nonbook Materials; The Organization of Integrated Collections,* 2nd ed. (Ottawa: Canadian Library Association, 1979). This and its 1973 edition include bibliographies of the many previous efforts at writing cataloguing rules for nonprint materials. The development of manuals for special types of material, but conforming with AACR2, is proceeding. See, for example, *Cartographic Materials; a Manual of Interpretation for AACR2,* prepared by the Anglo-American Cataloguing Committee for Cartographic Materials, ed. Hugo L. P. Stibbe (Chicago: American Library Association; Ottawa: Canadian Library Association; London: Library Association, 1982).

rily of a complete transcription, in sequence, of what appears on the item's title page. In other words, the individual title page itself creates the format for the citation.

The Library of Congress catalogue card shown in Figure 34 illustrates this close relationship between a bibliographic description prepared according to the rules used between 1898 and 1948 and the title page on which it is based. The paragraph between the boldface heading and the smaller-type collation/series paragraph is a transcription of the words of the title page in the order in which they appear there. In the rules of the day it was called the *body of the entry*. Additions deemed absolutely essential are made, but bracketted to show that they do not appear on the title page; omissions are permitted under stringent controls, but are signalled by use of the ellipsis.

This catalogue entry does not note line-endings, and does not necessarily preserve the capitalization and punctuation found on the title page. In more specialized bibliographic tools, these and even other refinements are preserved, as shown in Figure 35, a more detailed description of the same item. This level of detail, usually reserved for rare books and/or entries in critical bibliographies, is proper to what is sometimes loosely called *bibliographic cataloguing*.

Most style manuals depart readily from the requirement of complete title-page transcription in the interest of brevity. They do require accurate copying of titles, but allow other elements to be paraphrased or rearranged, for example allowing "comp. John Smith" where the title page reads "selected and arranged by John Smith." The data are formatted, though the rules for this are rarely extensive and leave much to ad hoc judgement in more complex cases. The arrangement typically begins with the name(s) of the author(s), even inverting the first one where alphabetizing by surname is intended. A citation for the item illustrated in Figure 34, composed according to the Chicago Style Manual, looks like this:

```
Gill, Eric. Art and a Changing Civilisation. The Twentieth
Century Library. London: J. Lane, 1934.
```

The International Standard Bibliographic Description

The location of bibliographic data in a publication and their arrangement on a title page are no longer as predictable as they once were. Because modern typographers are as conscious of the decorative aspects of a title page as of the informative ones, unusual arrangements of data are becoming more common, as shown in Figure 17 on page 67. Modern nonprint materials have neither title pages nor, in many instances, any single location for bibliographic data which could be considered analogous to one. As a result of such factors, and also of changes in the economics of cataloguing, the rules for formatting bibliographic

The Twentieth Century Library
Edited by V. K. Krishna Menon

ART

ART

and a changing civilisation

by

ERIC GILL

JOHN LANE THE BODLEY HEAD LTD.
LONDON

First published in 1934

Gill, Eric, 1882–
    Art and a changing civilisation, by Eric Gill. London,
John Lane ₁1934₁
    xi p., 1 l., 158 p. 19ᶜᵐ. (*Half-title:* The twentieth century library,
ed. by V. K. Krishna Menon)
    "Appendices: ɪ. The question of anonymity (by Rayner Heppenstall)—
ɪɪ. The school of Baudelaire (by G. M. Turnell)": p. 141–151.
    Bibliography: p. 152.

    1. Art. 2. Esthetics.   ɪ. Heppenstall, Rayner. ɪɪ. Turnell, G. M.
ɪɪɪ. Title.
                    ₁*Full name:* Arthur Eric Rowton Peter Joseph Gill₁
                                            35–4636
        Library of Congress   N70.G48
                            ₁5₁   701

PRINTED IN GREAT BRITAIN
BY WESTERN PRINTING SERVICES LTD., BRISTOL

FIG. 34. The half-title page, the title page, and the verso of the title leaf of a book, along with its Library of Congress entry, the latter prepared according to pre-1949 rules for description.

29. ART AND A CHANGING CIVILISATION

TITLE-PAGE: ART | AND A CHANGING CIVILISATION | BY | ERIC GILL |
JOHN LANE THE BODLEY HEAD LTD. | LONDON

SIZE: 7¼×4¼.   COLLATION: [A]⁸, B–L⁸.

PAGINATION AND CONTENTS: Pp. xiv+162; [i] [ii] half-title to series worded:
THE TWENTIETH CENTURY LIBRARY | EDITED BY V. K. KRISHNA MENON | ART,
verso blank; [iii] [iv] list of other volumes in the *Twentieth Century Library*, verso blank;
[v] [vi] title-page, verso printers' imprint worded: FIRST PUBLISHED IN 1934 | and,
at foot: PRINTED IN GREAT BRITAIN | BY WESTERN PRINTING SERVICES LTD.,
BRISTOL; vii–x Preliminary; xi–[xii] Contents, verso blank; [xiii] [xiv] half-title worded
ART, verso quotations from Ecclesiasticus and A. K. Coomaraswamy; 1–138 text;
[139] [140] blank, verso author's and publishers' acknowledgements; 141–5 Appendix I
The Question of Anonymity by Rayner Heppenstall; 146–51 Appendix II *The School of Baudelaire* by G. M. Turnell; 152 Bibliography; 153–8 Index; [159] [160] publishers' announce-
ments concerning the *Twentieth Century Library*; [161] [162] blank.

ILLUSTRATIONS: None.

BINDING: Red cloth, lettered on front, at top, in black: THE TWENTIETH
CENTURY LIBRARY with a design ('Laocoon'), specially made for the series by
Eric Gill, blocked in black. Lettered in black on spine: TWENTIETH | CENTURY |
LIBRARY | ART | ERIC | GILL | and, at foot: THE | BODLEY HEAD All edges
cut.

DATE OF PUBLICATION: 1934. MS. dated 8 December 1933–6 January 1934.
PRICE: 2s 6d.

NOTES: The following note appears on the flap of the wrapper: "The design on the cover
and wrapper of this book has been specially made for *The Twentieth Century Library* by
Mr Eric Gill, who writes: 'I can think of nothing more appropriate for a symbol for
The Twentieth Century Library than a version of Laocoon, that is Man, fighting with the
twin snakes of War and Usury. These are the powers of evil with which man in the
twentieth century will have to settle, or perish.'"

REVIEWS: By Wyndham Lewis, *The Listener*, 26 September 1934. By Harold Nicolson,
Daily Telegraph, September 1934.

SUBSEQUENT EDITIONS: A new edition, entirely re-set in a smaller format, was
published by John Lane, The Bodley Head under the title ART, in 1946, and again in
1949. Price 6s.

FIG. 35. A fuller description of the item illustrated in Figure 34, reproduced from
Evan R. Gill, *Bibliography of Eric Gill* (London: Cassell, 1953).

data for library catalogues have undergone a remarkable transformation since
the mid-1940s. Instead of transcribing a title page, the cataloguer now selects
from the appropriate sources the data elements relevant to the item and required
by an externally imposed format. Their arrangement in the entry is no longer
necessarily that of the title page or other chief source of information, and the
arrangement follows a standard order for all types of document, print and
nonprint.

The changes evolved in a number of stages, and the process was only carried
to its logical conclusion in the late 1970s: a four-hundred-year-old tradition
could not be broken overnight! A 1945 Library of Congress study written
chiefly by Seymour Lubetzky heralded the new method.[7] Efforts toward greater
standardization at the international level and the introduction of automation to
bibliographic control completed the process of transition from the pre-1949
mode of transcribing a title page. The format used in the current rules is known
as the International Standard Bibliographic Description (ISBD), developed

7. Library of Congress, Processing Department, *Studies of Descriptive Cataloging: a Report to
the Librarian of Congress* (Washington: U.S. Government Printing Office, 1946). The landmark
critique of the economics of library cataloguing which had led to the preparation of this report is
Andrew Osborn, "The Crisis in Cataloging," *Library Quarterly* 11 (October 1941):393–411.

since 1969 under the auspices of the International Federation of Library Associations and Institutions.

The purposes of ISBD are (1) to standardize national practices in the content and arrangement of a bibliographic record, (2) to make it easier to recognize data elements despite the language of their content, and (3) to facilitate the application of computer processes to the manipulation of bibliographic data. The latter two purposes are directly related to the abandonment of the individual title page as a self-generating format and its replacement with an externally determined format.

The elements called for and their prescribed order are not markedly different from what had appeared on the typical title page of the early twentieth century. Hence the introduction of ISBD did not radically change previous descriptive cataloguing practice, particularly in the Anglo-American community. (The one visible difference is in the ISBD punctuation pattern, discussed below.) What ISBD accomplished was to define and fix the existing components of a standard description so that they could apply more readily to all types of material. However, ISBD deals only with the *description* of an item. It has nothing whatever to say about access points, the headings under which a description may be located in a list. In most previous cataloguing and citation rules, description and access are inextricably linked.[8]

By 1977 the ISBD system had passed its trial period with some changes from first drafts, and it appeared in its most abstract form as ISBD(G) [G for general].[9] ISBD(G) is an outline format, not a detailed set of rules. For the beginner, it is perhaps less helpful than a style manual in solving specific questions. Its importance lies in the fact that it has been accepted in many countries and is already the basis for detailed rules in a number of new cataloguing codes, among them AACR2. Dozens of national bibliographies now use ISBD as the basis for their bibliographic description, including those of all the major English-speaking countries.

The essential format requirements of ISBD(G) are expressed in somewhat greater detail in a series of standards derived from it, of which the following

8. International agreement on details of a code involving the choice or the form of access points is still not possible; hence an international format which included these would have been doomed to failure. Many, including the present authors, also feel that in the automated mode a separation of the functions of description and of access is necessary (see Chapter 6).

9. The recent history of descriptive cataloguing, including the development of ISBD, is described in Ronald Hagler, "Changes in Cataloging Codes: Rules for Description," *Library Trends* 25 (January 1977):603–623. Earlier history is covered in Kathryn Luther Henderson, " 'Treated with a Degree of Uniformity and Common Sense' : Descriptive Cataloging in the United States, 1876–1975," *Library Trends* 24 (July 1976):227–271. The latter article deals with both bibliographic description and access points. The continuing development and application of ISBD is regularly reported in the journal *International Cataloguing*.

have been published, all by the IFLA International Office for Universal Biblio-graphic Control in London: ISBD(M) [monographs] (First standard edition revised, 1978); ISBD(CM) [cartographic materials] (1977); ISBD(NBM) [non-book materials] (1977); ISBD(PM) [printed music] (1980); ISBD(A) [antiquar-ian, or pre-1820 books] (1980); ISBD(CP) [component parts, or analytics] (due in late 1982 or in 1983); and ISBD(S) [serial publication in all formats, to be used in conjunction with other relevant ISBDs] (First standard edition, 1977).

Data are composed into a full ISBD-style description in up to eight segments called areas. Each area contains one or more elements, again in a fixed order of arrangement. Thus Area 5, the Physical Description Area, consists of up to four elements: (1) extent of the item (for example, number of physical pieces, number of pages, running time), (2) other physical details (for example, speed of rotation, existence of colour), (3) dimensions (for example, height, diame-ter, size of container), and (4) accompanying materials (for example, slides in a pocket attached to the back cover, a portfolio of maps). An element, or even a whole area, is ignored in the description of a particular document if the infor-mation called for is not pertinent to that document. For example, relatively few books have an edition statement of any kind, so most descriptions do not include an Edition Area at all. One of the areas, Area 3, is used at present only for cartographic items, serials, and printed music.

In writing ISBD, a deliberate attempt was made to use terms equally applica-ble to print and to nonprint materials, and to all types of bibliographic situation which might be encountered. Thus ISBD shuns the book-oriented term "colla-tion" in favour of "physical description," and expands the narrow term "au-thorship" to the more generalized one "responsibility."

Figure 36 is a slightly abridged outline of the ISBD(G) areas and elements. Seven of these eight areas comprise a formal structure for bibliographic data transcribed from objective sources. One of them, the Note Area, provides for the cataloguer or bibliographer to state in a relatively nonstructured way wha-tever cannot be put into the form or context of any of the other areas. The Note Area would more logically be placed after the Standard Number Area, but the latter was an "invention" of the 1960s and simply got tacked onto the end of what constituted the complete record at that time.

Punctuation as a Part of the ISBD Format

Punctuation has almost always been used as a part of the conscious format-ting of bibliographic records. In standard British practice, and according to the Chicago Style Manual, a place of publication is separated from the publisher's name by a colon. In library cataloguing practice, as well as in many style manuals, a series title is distinguished from the title of the item not only by its

1. Title and statement of responsibility area
       1.1   Title proper
       1.2   General material designation
       1.3   Parallel title(s)
       1.4   Other title information
       1.5   Statement(s) of responsibility

2. Edition area
       2.1   Edition statement
       2.2   Parallel edition statement(s)
       2.3   Statement(s) of responsibility relating to the edition
       2.4   Additional edition statement
       2.5   Statement(s) of responsibility following an additional
             edition statement

3. Material (or type-of-publication) specific area
       [Used only for cartographic items, printed music, and
             serials.]

4. Publication, distribution, etc. area
       4.1   Place(s) of publication, distribution, etc.
       4.2   Name(s) of publisher, distributor, etc.
       4.4   Date of publication, distribution, etc.

5. Physical description area
       5.1   Specific material designation and extent of item
       5.2   Other physical details
       5.3   Dimensions of item
       5.4   Identification of accompanying material

6. Series area
       6.1   Title proper of series
       6.2   Parallel title(s) of series
       6.3   Other title information of series
       6.4   Statement(s) of responsibility relating to the series
       6.5   International Standard Serial Number of series
       6.6   Numbering within the series
       6.7   Enumeration and/or title of sub-series
       6.8 - 6.12 Parallel title of sub-series, through Numbering
             within the sub-series, the same as for 6.2 through 6.6
       [The above sequence is repeatable within a single Area 6 if
             the item is published in two (or more) series.]

7. Note area (Repeatable, each note being a separate area)

8. Standard number ... area (Repeatable)
       8.1   Standard number (or alternative)
       8.2   Key-title
       8.3   Terms of availability and/or price
       8.4   Qualification(s) following 8.1 and/or 8.3

FIG. 36. Slightly abridged outline of the ISBD(G) Areas and Elements.

location, but also by its enclosure within a set of parentheses.[10] Such punctuation has always been a format indicator, not part of the content; the opening parenthesis is not part of the series title, but a signal that a series title is about to occur; the closing one is the signal that series information is finished.

When the ISBD system was first drafted in 1969, Michael Gorman suggested, and the IFLA Working Group concurred, that its purposes would be best served if marks of punctuation were used to demarcate the various elements systematically, rather than only in parts of the description as had previously been the case. As more and more persons are handling bibliographic data in languages which they do not understand or even recognize, it can be useful to know, for example, that ISBD prescribes a colon preceding a subtitle and a slash preceding a statement of responsibility in Area 1. The incorrect entry in Figure 37 would not have been possible if ISBD punctuation had been present, and one who cannot interpret the scripts in the entries in Figure 38 can at least point out where an author or an edition is named.

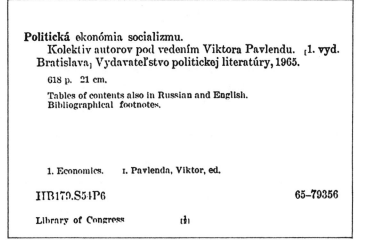

FIG. 37. This faulty entry, in which a statement of responsibility was formatted as if it were the title proper, was soon withdrawn and replaced by a correct one.

10. Since this data element does not derive from the title page, it had no fixed position in title page transcription according to earlier rules. Hence its position varies among codes more widely than any other element. Anglo-American practice has traditionally placed it after the physical description, where it remains in ISBD. The Chicago Style Manual places it immediately before the publication information (imprint), and does not use parentheses to delimit it. The pre-ISBD Swedish and some other cataloguing traditions place it following the imprint and before the collation.

ဒေတ်ဟောင်း ဒေတ်သစ် စာကြည့်တိုက်ခရီး, ၁၀၅၇–၁၉၇၇ / မောင်
ကောင်းမြင့်. — ရန်ကုန် : စာပေဗိမာန်, 1978.

264 p., [4] leaves of plates : ill. ; 20 cm. — (ပြည်သူ့လက်စွဲစာစဉ်)

ਭਾਈ ਵੀਰ ਸਿੰਘ, ਸੰਦਰਭ-ਕੋਸ਼ / ਸੰਪਾਦਕ ਵਿਸ਼ਵਾਨਾਥ ਤਿਵਾੜੀ, ਹਰਿੰਦਰ ਪੰਨੂੰ,
ਜਗਤਾਰ. — ਚੰਡੀਗੜ੍ਹ : ਪਬਲੀਕੇਸ਼ਨ ਬਿਊਰੋ, ਪੰਜਾਬ ਯੂਨੀਵਰਸਿਟੀ, 1974.

220 p. ; 23 cm.

Μιχαὴλ Περάνθης : εἰσαγωγή-βιβλιογραφίακρίσεις / 'Ι. Μ.
Χατζηφώτη ; μὲ τὴ συνεργασία τῆς Νίκης Πολίτη. — 'Αθήνα :
'Εκδόσεις τῶν Κριτικῶν Φύλλων, 1976.

524 p. ; 21 cm.

FIG. 38. ISBD descriptions in nonroman scripts, from Library of Congress entries. The access points are not reproduced.

These benefits of prescribed punctuation could only be fully realized if each different mark uniquely identifies a single data element. The resultant need for a fairly large number of different marks caused the introduction of some which were rarely before seen in bibliographic description. In addition, spacing conventions different from those of normal style ensure that the punctuation prescribed by ISBD as format signals is visibly different (both to the human eye and to the computer program) from any punctuation that could occur in the content of a data element. Thus the mark of punctuation which separates each area from the following one is a four-character mark: period, space, dash, space; a statement of responsibility is preceded by a three-character mark: space, slash, space. Early fears that the prescribed punctuation would slow down typing or appear odd to users proved unfounded. The basic features of the ISBD punctuation pattern appear in the following skeletal entry.

```
*Title proper [general material designation] =
Parallel title : other title information / first
statement of responsibility ; second statement of
responsibility. - Edition statement / statement of
responsibility relating to the edition. - Material
specific details. - First place of publication ;
second place of publication : publisher, date
(Place of manufacture : manufacturer, date of
manufacture). - *extent of item : other physical
```

```
details ; dimensions + accompanying material. -
(Series title proper = Parallel series title /
statement of responsibility for the series, ISSN ;
numbering within the series. Title of subseries ;
numbering within the subseries) (Second series
subarranged as the first). - *Note. - *Note. -
*ISBN : terms of availability (qualification). -
ISBN
```

Where an asterisk (*) appears, it is permissible to begin a new paragraph instead of using the period-space-dash-space as an area separator.

The book illustrated in Figure 34 on page 114 would be described as follows in accordance with ISBD:

```
Art and a changing civilisation / by Eric Gill. - London :
J. Lane, 1934. - xi, 158 p. ; 19 cm. - (The Twentieth
century library)
```

Describing Items at Various Bibliographic Levels

A principal use of the Note Area is to state bibliographic relationships other than those which it is possible to specify in, for example, the edition or series area. It therefore has strong connections with those areas. The nature of the relationships was introduced on pages 73–82. Their more detailed analysis throughout Chapter 4 assumed that any bibliographic format would contain provisions for (1) treating an item at any desired bibliographic level, (2) displaying formally the levels pertinent to the item, and (3) indicating the nature of the relationships among the levels.

"Level" is used here to describe the relationship existing between, for example, (1) a poem and the anthology which contains it, or conversely the anthology and the poem contained within it, (2) a song and the whole Broadway show of which it is a part, or vice versa, (3) an article and the journal in which it appears, or vice versa, or (4) a monograph and the series in which it is published, or vice versa. Each level bears its own title, hence it can form the basis for a bibliographic record according to any rules (Turabian, ISBD, etc.)

Figure 39 shows a fairly complex set of bibliographic levels in operation in the same physical object, all being shown on the same title page. *Water Resources Paper* is the most broadly ecompassing level. Within it are reports on sediment data, flood reports, etc., but one of its several component parts is the survey of the *Surface Water Supply of Canada*. That survey is itself divided into four parts, one of which is that of the *Pacific Drainage: British Columbia and Yukon Territory* (this is a single level, not two, since there are no other parts of Canada which drain into the Pacific Ocean). Finally, the *Water Year*

1958–59 is one of the physical volumes resulting from the annual publication of the Pacific drainage survey.

Common sense indicates that it would serve no useful purpose to produce a bibliographic record at the lowest level, with the title proper *Water Year 1958– 59*. However, any of the other three levels makes an entirely reasonable basis for description: any one of the titles *Pacific Drainage, Surface Water Supply of Canada,* or *Water Resources Paper* might well be the title which begins a footnote citation in a hydrological journal article. It would depend on the purposes for which the article's author intended to draw attention to the publication. Equally, any one of the three is an acceptable title proper in Area 1 of an ISBD description. (See Figure 30 on page 100 for another example, one with three levels on its title page.)

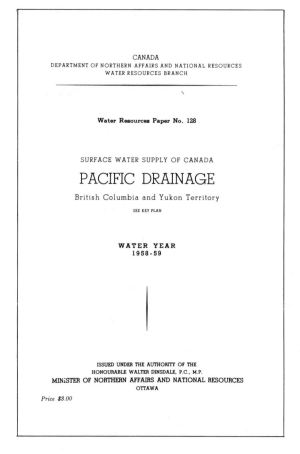

CANADA
DEPARTMENT OF NORTHERN AFFAIRS AND NATIONAL RESOURCES
WATER RESOURCES BRANCH

Water Resources Paper No. 128

SURFACE WATER SUPPLY OF CANADA

PACIFIC DRAINAGE

British Columbia and Yukon Territory

SEE KEY PLAN

WATER YEAR
1958-59

ISSUED UNDER THE AUTHORITY OF THE
HONOURABLE WALTER DINSDALE, P.C., M.P.
MINISTER OF NORTHERN AFFAIRS AND NATIONAL RESOURCES
OTTAWA

Price $3.00

FIG. 39. A title page bearing titles at four hierarchical levels.

The consequences for the rest of the description depend on which title is chosen for Area 1, since the levels are all relative to one another. If *Surface Water Supply of Canada* is chosen as the title proper (Area 1), then *Water Resources Paper* is the series (Area 6) in which that title appears, and *Pacific Drainage* is one item in the enumeration of its contents (Area 7). (ISBD(G) does not provide a separate area for the enumeration of contents, but includes this among the types of notes.) On the other hand, if *Pacific Drainage* is chosen as the Area 1 title proper, then both *Water Resources Paper* and *Surface Water Supply of Canada* fall within the scope of series statements (Area 6), the former being the title proper of the series (element 6.1), and the latter the title of the subseries (element 6.7). Thus a title proper, a series title, and the title of an item in a contents note are a hierarchy of titles associated with one another in the description of the same item, each having its proper place in the bibliographic format.

Bibliographic Links

Besides the series—item—contents relationship, there are other relationships which are not so predictable or do not fit a standard pattern. It is up to the cataloguer to phrase a note in Area 7 to convey the nature of the relationship as accurately and concisely as possible. Some examples were given on pages 80 and 81; others are shown in the entries in Figure 40. Brief citation practice would probably ignore these since they involve relationships not evident from formal bibliographic statements in the item in hand, but ascertainable only from its content or from outside sources.

In every instance where a relationship between bibliographic items is expressed in an entry, the entry in fact describes more than one item. The level whose title proper is recorded in Area 1 is described fully. Description(s) of related items whose titles appear in Area 6 or 7 are normally abbreviated, giving just enough detail (often only a title, or a title and author) so that the searcher can locate a fuller description of the related item if one is needed. For example, every series statement (Area 6) is a short description, containing neither imprint nor collation, and not even a statement of responsibility if the title is sufficient to identify the series. A note in Area 7 indicating that a serial was formed by the merger of two previous serials provides only the titles of the latter.

These abbreviated descriptions are links between one bibliographic record and another. Automated formats call some of them *linking entry fields*. Use of the series area and of contents and other notes for linking has long been common in formats for all purposes. Other linking methods exist for special purposes. For example, at one time supplements tended to bear "dependent" titles which made it convenient to include two *full* descriptions on the same

Heller, Jules.
Papermaking : the white art / Jules Heller. — Scottsdale, AZ : Scorpio Press, 1980.

[2], 216, [1] p., [13] leaves of plates : ill. (some col.), samples ; 29 cm.

———▶ Reissue of the New York, 1978 ed. with cancel t.p., additional half title, "Afterword." and sample papers mounted on plate leaves.
"Arabic numeral edition of 200 of which 15 are hors de commerce"—Afterword. LC has no. 119.
Bibliography: p. 205-211.
Includes index.

1. Papermaking and trade.   I. Title.

TS1105.H54   1980   676'.22—dc19   81-468104
                                                          AACR 2   MARC

Fodor, R. V.
Frozen earth : explaining the ice ages / R.V. Fodor. — Hillside, N.J. : Enslow Publishers, c1981.

64 p. : ill. ; 25 cm.

———▶ Adaptation of Ice ages, by J. Imbrie and K. P. Imbrie.
Bibliography: p. 61.
Includes index.
Summary: Discusses the evidence for the existence of ice ages, explains what glaciers are, and presents the many explanations offered for the causes of ice ages with emphasis on the astronomical theory. Also considers the effects of future climatic changes.
ISBN 0-89490-036-6 (lib. bdg.) : $6.95

1. Glacial epoch. 2. Glaciology. [1. Glacial epoch. 2. Glaciology]   I.
———▶ Imbrie, John. Ice ages. II. Title.

QE697.F6   551.7'92—dc19   80-21588
                                                          MARC

Library of Congress   AC

FIG. 40. Entries on which a note links the item being described to another item. On the lower entry, a name-title added entry for the related item is traced. The Library of Congress also provides a summary and alternate subject headings on its AC entries for children's materials.

catalogue card using a format called a *dash entry,* or a *dashed-on entry.* This method was abandoned partly because the format caused problems in computer manipulation, and partly because today fewer related items bear dependent titles. AACR2 prescribes a separate entry for a related work, either the title itself or a note showing the relationship. These conditions are illustrated in Figure 41.

ISBD provides another format for the linkage in specified circumstances. This is the *multilevel description,* the final section of ISBD(G) and of most of

Toronto Nutrition Committee.
Selected list of reliable and unreliable nutrition references. — ₍Toronto₎ : Toronto Nutrition Committee, 1973.

12, 3 leaves ; 28 cm.   C***

——————Supplement / compiled by the Toronto Nutrition
Committee. — ₍s. l.₎ : Ontario Hospital Association, 1974.

4, 10 leaves ; 28 cm.

                            Z663.N9T67   1973   Suppl.

1. Nutrition—Bibliography.   I. Title.

Z6663.N9T67   1973   016.6411   76–362603
[QP141]   (MARC)

Library of Congress   76

CATALOGING IN PUBLICATION 05/82

Sheehy, Eugene Paul, 1922-
Guide to reference books, 9th edition, Second supplement /
edited by Eugene P. Sheehy, with the assistance of Rita G.
Keckeissen, Eileen McIlvaine, Diane K. Goon ; pure and applied
sciences by Richard J. Dionne, Elizabeth E. Ferguson. —
Chicago : American Library Association, 1982.

        p.   cm.

Includes index.
ISBN 0-8389-0361-4 : $20.00 (est.)

1. Reference books—Bibliography.   I. Title.

Z1035.1.S43   1976 Suppl. 2   82-1719
                            011'.02—dc19
                                        AACR 2   MARC CIP
Library of Congress

FIG. 41. Above, an item and its supplement described interdependently. The latter is
said do be ''dashed'' onto the entry for the former. Below, an independent entry for a
supplement. (This example is a CIP entry: see pages 273–274.)

the specialized ISBDs. It is not at present used by the Library of Congress, but
is illustrated in the example of *centred contents notes* used in the three-part
entry shown in Figure 42.

ISBD(CP) is a complete format designed specifically for records where a
linkage is involved. It attempts to reconcile existing practices of the library and
the abstracting and indexing communities. It can be used for any item, at any
level, composed of component parts which are deemed worthy of the process of

Manitoba. Historic Resources Branch.
Final report - Historic Resources Branch. no. 1-   1976-
[Winnipeg] Dept. of Tourism, Recreation & Cultural Affairs,
Historic Resources Branch.
no. ill., maps. 26 cm.   (Papers in Manitoba archaeology)
Includes bibliographies.
ISSN 0706-0475 = Papers in Manitoba archeology. Final
report   : Historic Resources Branch, 1981 Portage Ave.,
Winnipeg, Man. R3J 0J9
I. Series.
CP76-83353-2
Contents.
no. 6.   Carmichael, Patrick H.   The Thunderbird Site,
EgKx-15 : a prehistoric petroform and habitation site in
Manitoba / by Patrick H. Carmichael. 1978, cover 1979. pa.
CP80-81654-4
no. 7.   Snortland-Coles, J. Signe   The Duck River of
Aschkibokahn Site of west-central Manitoba : the role of the
northern marsh in the subsistence of Late Woodland peoples
by J. Signe Snortland-Coles. 1979. pa.
CP80-81655-2

FIG. 42. One type of multilevel description, from *Canadiana*. Both the whole and the
parts are fully described.

analysis (see pages 102-104). Figure 43 shows the same relationship as formatted in (1) a contents note, (2) the multilevel description, and (3) an analytic entry according to a draft version of ISBD(CP).

Formatting Machine-Readable Records

Any manual format described above can be converted to machine-readable
form, but to keep the programming required to deal with the format within
reasonable and economic limits it is necessary to transform the human judgements involved in interpreting the nature and purpose of the information into
consistent and predictable patterns. Since bibliographic data and relationships
are so varied and complex, this is not easy. Even for human use, title-page
transcription alone has not sufficed, and ISBD was developed as a means of
systematizing the recognition of bibliographic data elements. But even in
ISBD, where a mark of prescribed punctuation designates the nature of the
following information, some human interpretation is needed. Although it is true
that every publisher's name is introduced by a three-character mark (space,
colon, space), other elements of bibliographic data in other parts of the record
also start with the same mark. In the title and statement of responsibility area,
other title information is introduced by space, colon, space, and in the physical
description area, other physical details are introduced by the same punctuation.
Although no person would ever confuse a publisher's name with a subtitle, a
machine could not be expected to "perceive" the difference. It is no help to
program the computer to count the occurrences of the area-separation punctua-

Tawow : a multi-media native studies kit [kit] / [prepared
by] D. Bruce Sealey ... [et al.]. - Agincourt, Ont. :
Book Society of Canada, c1975.
    50 study cards, 100 photo cards, 6 booklets,
1 teacher's guide, 2 cassettes, 1 filmstrip,
1 box of quiz cards, 5 books ; in container,
35 x 24 x 24 cm.
    "Prepared under the auspices of Project Canada
West."
    Partial contents: Indians without tipis / edited
by D. Bruce Sealey and Verna J. Kirkness - When the
morning stars sang together / John S. Morgan -
Indian / by George Ryga - Defeathering the
Indian / by Vernon LaRoque - For every North
American Indian who begins to disappear, I also
begin to disappear / by William A. Pelletier -
"Only yesterday" [sound recording] / Chief Dan
George.
    ISBN 0-7725-5250-9
_____

Tawow : a multi-media native studies kit [kit] / [prepared
by] D. Bruce Sealey ... [et al.]. - Agincourt, Ont. :
Book Society of Canada, c1975.
    50 study cards, 100 photo cards, 6 booklets,
1 teacher's guide, 2 cassettes, 1 filmstrip,
1 box of quiz cards, 5 books ; in container,
35 x 24 x 24 cm.
    "Prepared under the auspices of Project Canada
West."
    ISBN 0-7725-5250-9

    When the morning stars sang together / John S.
Morgan. - 1974.
    xvi, 201 p. : ill. (part col.) ; 22 cm.
    ISBN 0-7725-5079-4 (pbk.)
_____

    When the morning stars sang together / John S.
Morgan. - Agincourt [Ont.] : Book Society of Canada,
1974.
    xvi, 201 p. : ill. (part col.) ; 22 cm.
    ISBN 0-7725-5079-4 (pbk.)
    In: Tawow [kit] / [prepared by] D. Bruce Sealey ...
[et al.]. - Agincourt, Ont. : Book Society of
Canada, c1975.
    ISBN 0-7725-5250-9

FIG. 43. The book *When the Morning Stars Sang Together* was published in 1974. In 1975 it was used as part of a multimedia kit entitled *Tawow*. The relationship between the book and the kit is shown here in three ways. In the top record, the kit is described fully, and a contents note identifies its more significant parts briefly. The second is in the multilevel format (ISBD(G), section 9): both the kit and the book are fully described, but any element common to both (the place and publisher, in this instance) is not repeated. The third is an analytic entry: the book is described fully, the kit briefly. These descriptions may be filed under any applicable name or subject access point.

tion (period, space, dash, space) in order to determine which area it has arrived at, since a whole area may be lacking in a particular entry.

Computers do not make judgements: they only compare, count, calculate, and communicate. If one wants the computer to search through a number of records looking for publishers' names, it must be possible to identify precisely where in each record such names are to be found. Unique identification of data elements is the function of any computer format. Like ISBD, a computer bibliographic format must identify information at the level of the particular element since the variety of possible uses of bibliographic information can require the isolation of virtually any element.

To use a nonbibliographic example, one may wish to print paycheques from a file of payroll records. The computer program must know exactly where, within each record containing many facts, to find the employee's name, the rate of pay, and the number of hours worked. It can then cause the computer to print these facts on the final paycheque form, and also to multiply the rate and the number of hours. Other elements, such as the employee's tax status, are needed for the calculation of the total amount but will not be printed on the form. The fields which are printed will probably not appear in print in the order in which they appear in the computer record. The machine-readable record is likely to be organized in sequence by employee serial number, whereas the printed cheques are probably wanted in alphabetic order by name, in postal code order, or in order by the department or section in which the employee works. If in the latter order, subarrangement by the employee's name may be desirable. Certain designated employees' cheques may have the home address printed under the name for mailing in a window envelope; others, printed from the same original computer file, might have the company department printed in that position. Each cheque requires a date. This is not needed as part of each employee's permanent record, but is a *print constant,* generated on every cheque from a single instruction in the computer. The date will likely appear in the program as 820703, while it is printed out as July 3, 1982.

All of these variations, seemingly arising from human judgements, are possible for the computer provided the format in which the data are stored permits a program to find any required data element. Calculations can then be made involving two or more data elements, or a data element and an element fixed in the program itself. The manipulation of bibliographic data in libraries using computers is in no way essentially different from that suggested in this payroll example. The requirements of a bibliographic format are, if anything, more complex than for any other kind of information because of the unpredictability of bibliographic data.

Fixed-Length Formats

A fixed-length format is one in which each field is allowed a certain number of characters. In many cases that number is easily determined by the nature of the data to be included in it. A year can always be represented by four digits, or three if a code is used for the century, or even two if all possible dates in the file occur in the same century. All Canadian postal codes fit into a six-character field, and American zip codes into nine characters. All social insurance numbers, international standard book and serial numbers, and universal product codes will fit into fields of fixed length, often called *fixed fields*.

In other cases the data element itself is not of predictable or uniform length, but for convenience in computer handling, a fixed-length field is allocated, long enough to encompass the maximum size foreseen for the data. The field for annual salary in any payroll file could be fixed at nine digits, for surely nobody's annual salary exceeds $9,999,999.99. The dollar sign, commas, and period are not stored: they appear in fixed places and can therefore be supplied as print constants by the program which produces the output. Salaries of less than nine digits will be moved to the right part of the field, with zeroes filling in the unused spaces on the left. A fixed-length format for names and addresses will be more of a procrustean bed. Someone must decide what length of field is economic to store and manipulate in the system, and after that, compromises are required. Longer names and street addresses are chopped off or abbreviated; shorter ones are moved to the left with blanks filling the remaining spaces on the right.

A fixed-length format arranges a fixed number of fixed fields in a fixed order. For example, in a mailing list each record might contain a 22-character field for name, always followed by a 22-character field for house and/or apartment number and street, always followed by a 12-character field for the city, then 4 for the province, and 6 for the postal code. Other fields for serial numbers, subscription expiry dates, etc., are also fixed in length and sequence. Every record in the file must adhere to the same format even though the data within that format may vary from one record to the next.

A Sample Bibliographic Record

An example of a format used to contain bibliographic data might be taken from any library subsystem. The example used here is a typical bibliographic record for an automated system to control the acquisition of monographs. The purposes of the system are (1) to store and maintain a file of information about items on order, (2) to permit the searching of this file by various access points, (3) to permit the production of various kinds of printed outputs, one of which is the purchase order, and (4) to control the financial aspects of acquisitions, including the debiting of accounts as payments are made and the periodic production of financial statements. The existing manual file of copies of purchase orders is to be maintained; therefore the system has been programmed to produce printed purchase orders looking like the one in Figure 44.

An analysis of this purchase order reveals the existence of at least eleven fields of data. There will be additional fields in the machine-readable record but not shown here, such as the person or department requesting the item, where

```
┌─────────────────────────────┬──────────────────────────┐
│ LIBRARY NAME                │ PURCHASE ORDER           │
│ STREET ADDRESS              │ PO# 00000141             │
│ CITY AND COUNTRY            │ DATE 17.06.82            │
├─────────────────────────────┴──────────────────────────┤
│ AUTHOR: Wolfe, Tom                                      │
│                                                         │
│ TITLE:   THE RIGHT STUFF.                               │
│ IMPRINT: NY: Farrar, Straus, Giroux, 1979               │
│ SERIES:                                                 │
│ COPIES:  5          ISBN: 0374250324                    │
│                                                         │
│       PRICE: $12.95                      RUSH           │
│                                                         │
│ TO:   LIBRARY WHOLESALE INC.                            │
└─────────────────────────────────────────────────────────┘
```

FIG. 44. A completed purchase order form, one of the desired output formats from an automated bibliographic file.

the item will be housed in the library system, whether it is an added copy or volume, and the fund to be debited. These will appear on other lists and reports produced by the system, using the same records. The above purchase order shows fields for (1) purchase order number, (2) date, (3) author, (4) title, (5) imprint, (6) series, (7) number of copies requested, (8) ISBN, (9) price, (10) notes, and (11) vendor. RUSH appears in field 10 (notes) in this example. For other items, the notes field might include such words as PAPERBACK, SEND ONLY THIS EDITION, etc.

The name and address of the library, such label words as PO#, DATE, and AUTHOR, the dollar sign before the price, the word COPIES, etc., will either be preprinted on a form or stored in the output program as print constants. Anything intended to appear as part of each printed product therefore does not need to be repetitively stored as part of every separate record in the database.

Using Fixed-Length Fields

A fixed-length field format to contain these acquisitions records might look like this:

ELEMENT	CHARACTERS	LOCATION IN RECORD
Purchase order number	8	0 - 7
Date	6	8 - 13
Author	20	14 - 33
Title	40	34 - 73
Imprint	40	74 - 113
Series	30	114 - 143
Number of copies	2	144 - 145

ISBN	10	146 - 155
Price	6	156 - 161
Notes	20	162 - 181
Vendor	30	182 - 211

Space must be reserved for every field in the format. A missing ISBN will occupy the same space (ten blanks) as an existing ISBN (ten digits). (The convention of beginning "location in record" at 0 is explained on page 296.) The data for the purchase order using this fixed-field format would look like this to the computer:

00000141	170682	Wolfe, Tom	THE RIGHT STUFF

	NY: Farrar, Straus, Giroux,

1979		05	037425

0324	001295	RUSH	LIBRARY WHOLESALE IN

c.

This format provides identification for each element of data by placing it in a fixed location. The person who must write a computer program to print, for example, a list of items on order sorted by title, knows that every single record in the file is 212 characters long, and within that the title always starts at character position 34 and ends at 73.

There are relatively few cases where it is very difficult to use data in fixed field formats, but bibliographic records constitute one of them. The length of a title of a book is impossible to predict, but even though some are extremely long, librarians do not accept the idea of truncating a title proper at some arbitrary point. In fact, there are very few elements of data within bibliographic records which can easily be fixed in length. It would obviously be unreasonable to truncate a call number in a library catalogue, but who would care to predict with complete accuracy what the longest call number in a file could ever be? To choose a cautiously high number (perhaps 75 characters) is to incur a high price, for call numbers probably *average* no more than 20 characters, even in a large library. In a fixed-field format leaving 75 spaces for a call number, an average of 55 blank spaces would exist in the call number field of every record, as well as hundreds of blank spaces in the various other unpredictable fields. These blanks would permanently occupy valuable storage space which is ultimately limited and which, in some computing environments, must be paid for directly by the user. Each time a call number is operated upon by a computer program, 75 characters of data, two-thirds of them on the average "blanks," would need to be communicated and manipulated. Thus it is inescapable that where bibliographic data must be complete and accurate, and where the length of the data is extremely variable, fixed-length formats are not suitable. Instead, variable-length formats are used.

Variable-Length Formats

A variable-length format is one in which each field or element is allotted exactly and only as much space as it requires. The only blanks are meaningful ones: spaces between words, or blanks as codes. Any field, and of course a complete record, can be as long or as short as it needs to be. The problem is how to identify the parts since a computer program cannot instruct the computer to "look for a date," but must say, "The date is in the following place." The solution to this problem lies in the use of *content designators*. These correspond roughly to the prescribed punctuation in the ISBD system: they exist to announce what kind of data is about to follow. Content designators fall into at least two categories: (1) identifiers, including *tags, indicators*, and *subfield codes*, which identify specific types of data; and (2) *delimiters*, the separators which act as location markers at the end of a subfield, a field, or a record.

Using Tags

A tag identifies a field and may consist of any number of letters or digits or a combination of both. Using the same example as for the fixed-length format above, a variable-length format using three-letter tags might look like this:

SEQUENCE IN RECORD	ELEMENT	TAG
1	Purchase order number	PON
2	Date	DAT
3	Author	AUT
4	Title	TIL
5	Imprint	IMP
6	Series	SER
7	Number of copies	NUM
8	ISBN	SBN
9	Price	PRI
10	Notes	NOT
11	Vendor	VEN

Because each field is, at least in theory, variable in length, "sequence in record" indicates only the order in which the fields appear in the record, if they are present. If a field is not relevant, for example if there is no series or the price is unknown at the time of ordering, it is simply omitted. In fact, the use of tags makes it unnecessary to preseve the original arrangement of the fields in the machine-readable record since the computer can be programmed to identify and locate a given field wherever it occurs, and to manipulate it for ouput in any desired arrangement or location (see page 150). Thus, unlike the fixed-length format, each record is only as long as it needs to be. The stored data for this sample purchase order would be as follows:

```
PON 00000141 F
DAT 170682 F
AUT Wolfe,*Tom F
TIL THE*RIGHT*STUFF. F
IMP NY:*Farrar,*Straus,*Giroux,*1979 F
NUM 5 F
SBN 0374250324 F
PRI 1295 F
NOT RUSH F
VEN LIBRARY*WHOLESALE*INC. R
```

Of course, the fields are not laid out in this tabular form within the computer or in any machine-readable medium. If it were possible to see the data as it appears on a continuous length of magnetic tape, it would look like this:

```
PON00000141FDAT170682FAUTWolfe,*TomFTILTHE*RIGHT*STUF
```

```
F.FIMPNY:*Farrar,*Straus,*Giroux,*1979FNUM5FSBN037425
```

```
0324FPRI1295FNOTRUSHFVENLIBRARY*WHOLESALE*INC.R
```

An asterisk denotes a blank space; an underlined F (F) is used here as an end-of-field delimiter and an underlined R (R) as an end-of-record delimiter. These are merely conventions for the purpose of printing these delimiters. In fact, the *field separator* and *record terminator* may be input using any keys on the input keyboard not required for data; a pound sign (£) and a double amper-sand (&&) are often used. A program converts these into the appropriate delimiters, characters recognizable by the computer but which do not represent any printed character. An eight-bit computer offers 256 unique codes; since few printers can produce this many unique characters, a number of codes are left free for special uses. When displaying or printing a record for proofreading purposes, the F and R can be used. In a finished product (a purchase order, claim, or listing) the tags and delimiters are of course not printed.

The structure of this format is simple. Each field follows this pattern:

TAG	DATA	DELIMITER
3 characters	variable	1 character

A count of this variable-length record reveals that data can be stored compactly in comparison with fixed-length fields, without necessitating any short-cuts. Although four additional characters are now a part of each field used, the total length of the record has dropped to 153 characters in the variable-length format from 212 in the fixed-length format, besides allowing unlimited flexibility. The program written to handle these records will "know" (that is, be instructed) that the first three characters are a tag identifying the data to follow. When a field separator (F) is encountered, it denotes that the preceding character is the end of the data. It is followed in turn by another three-character tag signifying a new data field. When a record terminator (R) is found, this marks the end of the record. It is not necessary to mark the end of any tag itself, for all tags are fixed in length at three characters, and the computer can be relied upon to count to three following each field or record terminator.

Using Subfields

One of the fields used in the example is unlike the others in that it contains more than one data element. The field tagged IMP includes a place, a publisher, and a date. Although this is the only such field in this record, there are many other examples of fields which could potentially hold more than one data element. For example, a single item might have more than one author, more than one title, more than one place, date, or ISBN, or it may be necessary to print more than one note on the purchase order, such as PAPERBACK and RUSH.

A field, like an ISBD area, may thus consist of several elements, called subfields in computer terminology. In the two formats shown above the fields are identified so that they can be handled individually for a variety of purposes. It is easy to imagine reasons for wanting to manipulate not the entire field, but only one subfield. If there are two authors, for example, it might be necessary for the item to appear under each of them in an alphabetic author list of items on order. If the item is in two series, it should appear under both in a list of standing orders for series. If statistics are needed showing how many items are on order by publication year, it must be possible to identify the year, which in the above example is buried in the imprint, its location not identifiable to the computer with certainty since the preceding data in the same field may be of any length.

Just as a tag is used to identify a field, so a subfield code is the content designator used to identify a subfield. For an in-house format any device may be used, but a common convention for subfield codes is to use a dollar sign ($), or in Britain a pound sign (£), followed by a letter or number, for a total of two characters. The dollar (pound) sign serves as a delimiter; it alerts the computer to the fact that the following character is a subfield code. It also marks the end of the previous subfield except, of course, in the case of the first subfield of each field. As with the F and the R, the use of the dollar or other sign is a convention for proofreading and instruction purposes. The code reserved in the computer for the subfield delimiter is another of the "nonvisible" 256 possible stored characters, one which is input/output in North America as "$" or sometimes "‡", but in Britain as "£".

A typical pattern is to label the subfields within a field $1, $2, $3, or $a, $b, $c, etc. Using subfields, the variable-field format now looks like this:

SEQUENCE IN RECORD	ELEMENT	TAG
1	PURCHASE ORDER NUMBER	PON
2	DATE	DAT
3	AUTHOR	AUT
4	TITLE	TIL
5	IMPRINT	IMP
	Subfields:	
	$a Place	
	$b Publisher	
	$c First date	
	$d Second date	
6	SERIES	SER
7	NUMBER OF COPIES	NUM
8	ISBN	SBN
9	PRICE	PRI
10	NOTES	NOT
	Subfields:	
	$a First note	
	$b Second note	
	$c Third note	
11	VENDOR	VEN
	Subfields:	
	$a Vendor name	
	$b Vendor address	

Each field containing a single subfield automatically receives the subfield code $a for uniformity in identifying the location of the starting character of the data. Using this format the data for the purchase order will look like this:

```
PON $a 00000141 F
DAT $a 170682 F
AUT $a Wolfe,*Tom F
TIL $a THE*RIGHT*STUFF. F
IMP $a NY: $b Farrar,*Straus,*Giroux, $c 1979 F
NUM $a 5 F
SBN $a 0374250324 F
PRI $a 1295 F
NOT $a RUSH F
VEN $a LIBRARY*WHOLESALE*INC. R
```

Although there is only one field in this particular record that has benefitted from adding subfield codes, programs now have access to those separate data elements. A different solution, to put place, publisher, and date each into a separate field, would work equally well, but the problem of unpredictable repetitions of elements still suggests the use of subfields. Moreover, the formatting of bibliographic data for information retrieval and catalogue production purposes suggests that within a seemingly simple field such as "author" there will be benefits in separating personal from corporate authors. Within a personal-author field it can be useful for filing or identifying to separate the name from such qualifications as honorific titles, roman numerals which may follow a forename, dates of birth and/or death, and terms like "editor" which describe the author's relationship to the work. Within titles, subfield codes are useful to distinguish between the title proper and other titles. Analysis of the uses of bibliographic data has shown such widespread need for subfields that they are commonly employed.

The format has become difficult to describe exactly in a schematic diagram, for the number of subfields will vary from one field to the next within a record, and from one record to the next, according to the characteristics of the data. However, the basic structure of each field is as follows:

TAG	SUBFIELD CODE	DATA	SUBFIELD CODE	DATA	DELIMITER
3 char.	2 char.	variable	2 char.	variable	1 character

Using Indicators

If this format has one obvious weakness, it is that the tag does not always give enough information for satisfactory computer manipulation of entire fields. For this reason, additional characters called indicators are commonly used in bibliographic formats. Indicators can be used (1) to provide additional information about a field, (2) to facilitate specific methods of data manipulation, and (3) to show relationships between one field and another. In Canadian MARC, a bibliographic format used by the National Library of Canada, one indicator in each subject field is used to show whether the data in the field is from a French or an English list of terms. In this way a Canadian MARC record can contain subject headings in two languages, and libraries using these records can program their computers to select either language or both.

An indicator may be used to show whether the author is a person, a conference, or any other type of corporate body. This would permit separate lists of these types of authors to be produced. In the title field, an indicator can be used to control a filing program. Since the accepted location of the title *The Right Stuff* is under R, not under T, a filing indicator 4 in the title field can be used to suppress the first four characters of the data in sorting (that is, the letters T, H, E, and the space). This is more direct and efficient than comparing the start of every title with a prepared list of every nonfiling article, etc., in many languages. An indicator in the vendor field might be used to show whether the vendor is in North America, Europe, Asia, etc. This would permit the library to write a program to print letters of inquiry automatically if no response had been received within a certain period after the purchase order was sent. The time period might be 60 days for vendors in North America, 120 days for vendors in Latin America, 90 days for Europe, and so on.

As was the case with subfield codes, if indicators are used in some fields, they must now be added to (or at least a space must be left in) all fields for consistency in the format. As a result, the format now looks like this:

SEQUENCE IN RECORD	ELEMENT	TAG
1	PURCHASE ORDER NUMBER	PON
	Indicator not used	
2	DATE	DAT
	Indicator not used	
3	AUTHOR	AUT
	Indicator shows type of Author:	
	1 Personal Author	
	2 Conference Author	
	3 Other corporate body	
4	TITLE	TIL
	Indicator shows number of characters to be skipped in filing	
5	IMPRINT	IMP
	Indicator not used	
	Subfields:	
	$a Place	
	$b Publisher	
	$c First date	
	$d Second date	
6	SERIES	SER
	Indicator not used	
7	NUMBER OF COPIES	NUM
	Indicator not used	
8	ISBN	SBN
	Indicator not used	
9	PRICE	PRI
	Indicator not used	
10	NOTES	NOT
	Indicator not used	
	Subfields:	
	$a First note	
	$b Second note	
	$c Third note	

```
11       VENDOR                                        VEN
         Indicator shows location of Vendor
            1 North America
            2 Latin America
            3 Western Europe
            4 Eastern Europe
            5 Asia
            6 Africa
         Subfields:
            $a Vendor name
            $b Vendor address
```

With the addition of indicators, the data stored in the format look like this (indicators not used are set at ''0''):

```
PON 0 $a 00000141 F
DAT 0 $a 170682 F
AUT 1 $a Wolfe,*Tom F
TIL 4 $a THE*RIGHT*STUFF. F
IMP 0 $a NY: $b Farrar,*Straus,*Giroux, $c 1979 F
NUM 0 $a 5 F
SBN 0 $a 0374250324 F
PRI 0 $a 1295 F
NOT 0 $a RUSH F
VEN 1 $a LIBRARY*WHOLESALE*INC. R
```

Each field in the format now has this structure:

TAG	INDICATOR	SUBFIELD CODE	DATA	SUBFIELD CODE	DATA	DELIMITER
3 char.	1 character	2 char.	variable	2 char.	variable	1 character

It might appear that the amount of overhead in the format is beginning to result in records that are far too large. Yet the record as it is now formatted occupies a total of 185 characters. Even though the fields in the original fixed-field format were kept small, and would probably prove inadequate in actual use for many libraries, the same record occupied 212 characters in that format.

Using Control Fields

Since each new field added must carry its overhead of at least seven characters (tag, three; indicator, one; at least one subfield identifier, two; and field terminator, one), it might be worth using a technique to save some space. Examination of the data shows that the record contains a number of fields which are naturally of fixed length, even though the field is declared to be variable. The elements which seem to suggest themselves for this treatment are the purchase order number, date, ISBN, price, and number of copies. It seems logical to combine them into a single control field at the start of the record, each element occupying a fixed amount of space, just as it did in the original fixed-length format. Because it is clear that no additional information will be required for this field (it is the elements within the field that are significant, rather than the field itself), it need not start with an indicator. Also, subfield coding is unnecessary since each element is in a fixed position with relationship to the beginning of the field; the computer can find any specified element by counting.

Here is how the format now looks, with the control field given the tag FFD (for "fixed fields," even though they are here used in a variable-length format):

```
SEQUENCE
IN RECORD       ELEMENT                                      TAG

                CONTROL FIELD
    1             FIXED FIELDS (No indicator)              FFD
                    Purchase order number (8 characters)
                    Date (6 characters)
                    ISBN (10 characters)
                    Price (6 characters)
                    Copies (2 characters)
                    Delimiter (1 character)

                VARIABLE FIELDS
    2             AUTHOR                                    AUT
                    Indicator shows type of Author:
                      1 Personal Author
                      2 Conference Author
                      3 Other corporate body
    3             TITLE                                     TIL
                    Indicator shows number of characters
                    to be skipped in filing
    4             IMPRINT                                   IMP
                    Indicator not used
                    Subfields:
                      $a Place
                      $b Publisher
                      $c First date
                      $d Second date
    5             SERIES                                    SER
                    Indicator not used
    6             NOTES                                     NOT
                    Indicator not used
                    Subfields:
                      $a First note
                      $b Second note
                      $c Third note
```

```
7            VENDOR                                    VEN
             Indicator shows location of Vendor
                1 North America
                2 Latin America
                3 Western Europe
                4 Eastern Europe
                5 Asia
                6 Africa
             Subfields:
                $a Vendor name
                $b Vendor address
```

As a result of the concatenation of fixed-length data elements, the sample record would appear as follows:

```
FFD 00000141170682037425032400129505 F
AUT 1 $a Wolfe,*Tom F
TIL 4 $a THE*RIGHT*STUFF. F
IMP O $a NY: $b Farrar,*Straus,*Giroux, $c 1979 F
NOT O $a RUSH F
VEN 1 $a LIBRARY*WHOLESALE*INC. R
```

Thus the entire record with all its content designators now occupies only 157 characters. If one could see it in linear fashion as it would exist in any magnetic storage medium, it would look like this:

```
FFD00000141170682037425032400129505FAUT1$aWolfe,*TomF
TIL4$aTHE*RIGHT*STUFF.FIMPO$aNY:$bFarrar,*Straus,*Gir
oux,$c1979FNOTO$aRUSHFVEN1$aLIBRARY*WHOLESALE*INC.R
```

This section has shown some of the techniques devised to build variable-length bibliographic formats. A computer programmer can write the systems needed to handle such a format no matter how complex it becomes, provided it has been clearly thought out and consistently applied. Format design in a particular situation is dependent to some degree on specific features of the computer hardware available, on the limitations imposed by available storage and by demands for specific types of output, and on a host of other details, but in theory the application of a format is limited only by the inventiveness of those responsible for its design.

National and International Formats

The formats shown here, even the very simple ones, are perfectly practical formats and might well be used to contain bibliographic data for a variety of library purposes. None of them is unconditionally superior to any other; each is designed to perform certain functions and has certain limitations. So long as the format is to be used within a single institution, a designer (or even better, a group of librarians and systems analysts acting as a team of designers) is free to invent any format desired. Each computer system (including its local data format) is designed and implemented in a different environment (different time constraints, funds, personnel resources, etc.) and to serve a different group of end users. Even if the data they are handling are the same, therefore, the physical systems are unlikely to be identical and the processing formats designed for them may also differ from institution to institution.

Who Sets the Standards for Automated Formats?

A more complex situation arises when one institution wishes to exchange data with another. Just as the desirability for manual exchange of bibliographic records once fostered the acceptance of the standard medium of the 7.5 × 12.5 cm. card and the standard format of the data it contained, so for communication of machine-readable data to take place there must be some agreement as to the format and organization of the information to be exchanged. It is the purpose of an *exchange format,* or a *communication format,* to embody such an agreement. These interlibrary, or standard, formats are designed as vehicles for the transmission of data between one national bibliographic agency and another, between national bibliographic agencies and individual libraries, between libraries and commercial agencies (including bibliographic utilities, for which see pages 276–277), among individual libraries and consortia, etc. This makes it unnecessary for any organization to keep track of the local formats used by the many other organizations from which it might receive records and to which it might send them.

The development of the manual formats which have gained national or international acceptance was briefly sketched earlier in this chapter. In the case of communication formats for machine-readable data, the first steps were taken in the mid-1960s by the Library of Congress. Its version, now known as LC MARC or U.S. MARC, constituted an acceptable basis for development in the United States and was soon imitated by national agencies and committees in other countries. As was the case with manual formats, automated communication formats have developed somewhat independently for the abstracting and indexing services and for the library community. The two types of exchange format which have had the most international acceptance are the numerous MARC formats derived from the original one, and the UNISIST Reference Manual. However, these are themselves compatible to a great extent because both conform to an internationally agreed *structure* for machine-readable communication formats. This structure is the result of international cooperation under the auspices of the International Organization for Standardization (ISO).

ISO 2709

In the examples of variable-length formats above, such a format was shown to be composed of three elements:

1) the *structure* of the record, which is the physical organization of information on the machine—readable medium; for example, TAG—DATA or TAG—INDICATOR—SUBFIELD—DATA

2) the *content designators* for the record, which are the means of identifying the data elements or providing additional information about a data element; for example the tags, indicators, subfield codes, and delimiters

3) the *contents* of the record, which are the data fields themselves; for wexample, "THE RIGHT STUFF." and "Wolfe, Tom."

Structure

In 1973, ISO adopted the standard known as ISO 2709, which is not a complete format but a format structure for the exchange of bibliographic data from one system to another.[11] This structure is divided into three distinct areas: (1) a *record label* (called a *leader* in some formats), (2) a *directory,* and (3) the *bibliographic fields,* or *data fields.*

The label is fixed in length at 24 characters. These consist of pieces of information relating to the record itself (for example, the total number of characters in it), codes relating this record to other records, and codes which instruct the computer where within the record to find certain specific kinds of data. The purpose of the label is to ensure that every program written to accommodate any ISO 2709 format can identify to a computer the structure and relationships of the entry which follows the label.

The directory comprises a number of separate units plus a field separator. Each of the units identifies for the computer the identity, the quantity, and the location within the complete record, of each field of bibliographic data following the directory. The identity of each field is denoted by its tag. Its quantity is shown as the number of characters comprising the field. The location of the field is denoted by an *address,* that is, the number of the first character in the field relative to the first character of the first field. ISO 2709 permits a fourth element within each directory entry to accommodate local practice. The purpose of the directory is to locate, in computer terms, each of the areas of data in the record. By this means, the computer can "get at" any desired piece of

11. This, and other ISO standards for manual and automated information handling, may be found most conveniently in *Information Transfer,* 2nd ed., ISO Standards Handbook, 1 (Geneva: ISO Central Secretariat, 1982) [available without charge from General Information Programme and UNISIST, Unesco, Paris].

information without looking sequentially at every character in the entire record until it finds the specified tag. Thus there are as many units in the directory as there are fields of data, and each unit consists of the following:

TAG	LENGTH	STARTING POSITION

A field separator appears at the end of the entire directory. It is the first field separator encountered in the record, and conveniently introduces the location of the fields of bibliographic data.

The bibliographic data fields constitute a variable number of variable-length fields of data. ISO 2709 permits the use of some further codes within each field, such as indicators to describe the nature of the data and subfield codes to identify elements within the field. Each data field ends with a field separator.

The entire record ends with a record terminator in order to separate it from the start of the next record. Thus the entire record appears as follows in the ISO 2709 format structure:

LABEL	DIRECTORY	FIELDS OF DATA

Content Designators

Because ISO 2709 constitutes only a framework for a format, it is left to each designer of an actual format to decide what content designators will be used. This makes it possible for a particular format to use a subfield code one or two or ten characters in length, tags consisting of letters or numbers or both, and such other variants as seem best suited to the nature of the data for which the format was devised. The field and record separators have, however, become standardized: they consist of a single character each, whose computer designation in binary form is specified in another standard (ISO 646, also reproduced in the handbook of standards cited on page 142).

Data Fields

The structure laid out in ISO 2709 is thus seen to be a very flexible one, amenable to the control of any kind of variable-length data. Each individual format has its own list of fields with their associated tags, subfields and subfield codes, and indicators.[12] Bibliographic records of various levels of completeness (skeletal, brief, and complete), containing descriptions of any medium (maps, music, phonorecords, computer tapes, books, manuscripts, motion pictures, etc.), incorporating the practices of many different cataloguing rules and classification systems, and created by a variety of sources (national libraries and bibliographic agencies, local libraries, abstracting and indexing services, government agencies at the national and international levels) are all now communicated in formats designed in conformity with this standard. So are records for the purposes of name and subject authority control (see Chapters 7 and 8).

Not only do the data vary with the type of bibliographic record, they also vary with the set of characters used. The 256 unique codes available in eight-bit computers are usually used to cover the roman alphabet including all possible diacritics, digits, punctuation, etc. But romanization is obviously not always acceptable. Bibliographic agencies which issue records in Arabic, Chinese, Cyrillic, Hebrew, Korean, or Sanskrit characters need to use the same 256 binary codes to denote their different characters. Thus there will be great variety in content between records in one ISO 2709-based format and those in another. Despite the great amount of freedom that the designers of individual formats have, their adherence to ISO 2709 means that the various formats currently in use by different information-handling communities share the common structure described here.

The MARC Formats

The name MARC, an acronym for machine-readable cataloging, originally described the single pioneering format developed in the mid-1960s. In a pilot project which lasted more than a year, The Library of Congress experimented with encoding its new bibliographic records using a very simple variable-length format. The records were distributed weekly on magnetic tapes across North America to sixteen libraries which agreed to participate in the project by devising programs to use the records in a variety of experimental ways. As a result of this pilot project a new format named MARC II was published in January 1968. This is the format now known as LC MARC, the historical forerunner of ISO 2709 and of the other computer formats discussed in this chapter.[13]

---

12. Appendix I (pages 295–322) is a practical detailed illustration of a complete format for library purposes in which a fuller explanation is attempted of many of the technical concepts in this chapter.

13. LC MARC is documented in a number of publications, notably *MARC Formats for Bibliographic Data* (Washington: Automated Systems Office, Library of Congress, 1980– [looseleaf]) and *Authorities: a MARC Format,* 1st ed. (Washington: Library of Congress, 1981). These are supplemented by separate publications of code lists, a history of the format, and several editing guides. For the current status of these publications, see the sales catalogue of the Cataloging Distribution Service, the Library of Congress.

The International MARC Format

Although the first MARC format was produced by the Library of Congress, MARC-like formats have been issued elsewhere with such modifications as would accommodate special bibliographic problems and different cataloguing codes. There are MARC formats in approximately twenty countries to date, including Canada, Mexico, Britain, France, Sweden, Malaysia, Japan, and Italy. In addition, UNIMARC was developed as a universal MARC format by IFLA to facilitate the exchange of bibliographic records among the national agencies.[14]

UNIMARC, like most of the national MARC formats, follows the structure set out in ISO 2709. Since it is a product of the IFLA Programme for Universal Bibliographic Control, it attempts to set standards for content designators based on the various ISBDs, which are also part of the IFLA UBC programme. This marks a significant difference between it and the UNISIST Reference Manual described below, since the latter includes its own somewhat differing rules for description. However, even among the users of the ISBDs, variations in national formats occur because of differences in systems of access points, and because of the effects of language differences. It is assumed that a national bibliographic agency will convert records from its own national MARC format into UNIMARC before transmitting them to another country, and will convert records received from another country from UNIMARC to its own MARC format.

National MARC Formats

There are too many national MARC formats to try to categorize them in any significant way. In Appendix I, a single one, Canadian MARC, is used as an example and analyzed in detail. These national formats share a number of similarities which are worth noting. In almost every case, their structure is that of ISO 2709, their tags consist of three digits, two indicators are used within each field, and subfield codes consist of two characters. On the other hand, there are some marked dissimilarities. For example INTERMARC, the French format, uses six indicators, and the West German Maschinelles Austauschformat für Bibliotheken (MAB) has a structure varying somewhat from the requirements of ISO 2709.

The MARC formats of the different countries are also presented somewhat differently in print, a fact which may appear to magnify the actual differences

14. *UNIMARC: Universal MARC Format,* Recommended by the IFLA Working Group on Content Designators, 2nd ed. rev. (London: IFLA International Office for UBC, 1980). For a comment on the value of UNIMARC both as a translation format and as a model for future MARC formats, see Henriette D. Avram and Sally H. McCallum, "UNIMARC," *IFLA Journal* 8, no. 1 (1982):50–54.

between them. Canadian MARC, for example, appears in three separate loose-leaf parts: monographs, serials, and authority records.[15] Treatment of the different media (recordings, kits, films, etc.) is incorporated into the monographs format as applicable. The LC MARC format, originally published as a separate pamphlet for each medium, is now a looseleaf service with a columnar presentation of the media to which each particular tag relates.

A comparison of the various treatments accorded one of the more common fields quickly reveals a number of minor differences among the MARC formats. For example, in both the LC and the Canadian MARC formats, tag 260 identifies the field relating to the publication and/or release of the work described in the record. In both formats, the first indicator is set at 0 if this field includes the name of the publisher, distributor, etc., and at 1 if it does not. The second indicator is left blank, for no use has yet been determined for it. The subfields within this field vary somewhat with the type of material being described, but for books there are six subfields:

```
$a    Place of publication, distribution, etc.
$b    Name of publisher, distributor, etc.
$c    Date of publication, distribution, etc.
$e    Place of manufacture
$f    Name of manufacturer
$g    Date of manufacture
```

The UK MARC format also uses tag 260 to identify the same data, but it provides for twelve subfields, as follows:[16]

```
$a    Place of publication
$b    Name of publisher
$c    Date of publication
$d    Full address of publisher
$e    Function of publisher, distributor, etc.
$f    Place of distribution
$g    Name of distributor
$h    Date of distribution
$i    Place of manufacture
$j    Name of manufacturer
$k    Date of manufacture
$l    Full address of distributor
```

Other national MARC formats tend to follow one or the other of these practices, but many contain variations which, though minor, necessitate a certain

---

15. *Canadian MARC Communication Format: Monographs,* 3rd ed. (Ottawa: National Library of Canada, 1979– [looseleaf]); *Canadian MARC Communication Format: Serials,* 2nd ed. (Ottawa: National Library of Canada, 1979– [looseleaf]); and *Canadian MARC Communication Format: Authorities* (Ottawa: National Library of Canada, 1980– [looseleaf]). All three are also published in French-language versions.

16. *UK MARC Manual,* 2nd ed. (London: British Library, 1980– [looseleaf]).

amount of complex computer programming when national libraries exchange bibliographic records in machine readable form.

In UNIMARC, the format developed for the express purpose of overcoming varying national practices, the tag used to denote publication, distribution, etc. data is tag 210. Neither of the two indicators is used; both are left blank. Subfields $a, $b, $c, and $d denote respectively the place, address, name, and date of the publisher or distributor of the item, and subfields $e, $f, $g, and $h denote the place, address, and name of the manufacturer, and the date of manufacture. A ninth subfield, $j, is used exclusively to identify the subscription address for serial items. No doubt an analysis of the Dutch, the Mexican, and many other national MARC formats would reveal even more differences in this field, as in other fields, but the differences are minor. The formats are compatible and can be "translated" into one another either directly on a one-to-one basis or via UNIMARC.

The adoption of ISBD in a number of countries can be expected to result in gradual changes to the MARC formats in those countries in order to match the fields and subfields specified in the ISBDs. This suggests that the MARC formats in countries where ISBD has been adopted will tend to look more alike, whereas the MARC formats in other countries will continue to reflect their variant descriptive practices. In the data fields containing access points (main entry headings, other name headings, subject headings, classification numbers, etc.) there is once again a basically similar pattern, but because there exists less international agreement on these matters there will always be considerably more variation among different countries as reflected in the choice of tags, subfielding, etc.

The UNISIST Reference Manual

The UNISIST Reference Manual is also a communication format designed as a medium for the exchange of data from one organization to another.[17] It was conceived by representatives of various abstracting and indexing services who hoped that it would be widely adopted by organizations involved in information processing and exchange, including most kinds of libraries. This widespread use has not yet occurred. The Reference Manual contains its own rules for the description of monographs, serials, and other media; hence it is of broader scope than the MARC formats, which rest on the basis of ISBD and other pre-existing cataloguing rules. The Reference Manual rules were not meant to supplant other cataloguing codes, but to be available to agencies around the

17. *Reference Manual for Machine-Readable Bibliographic Descriptions,* 2nd rev. ed., ed. H. Dierickx and A. Hopkinson [for the] Unisist International Centre for Bibliographic Descriptions (UNIBID) (Paris: General Information Programme and UNISIST, Unesco, 1981) (PGI–81/WS;22) [available without charge from the publishers].

world which would otherwise not follow any established set of rules. Thus it "competes" with other rules for description such as the ISBDs.

The structure of the Reference Manual follows ISO 2709. The tags consist of a single letter followed by two digits, such as A02 and B19. The subfield codes consist of two characters, of which the first is usually shown (but not stored) as "@" and the second may be a number or letter, though it is usually the former. Each field uses two indicators; indicators not used are usually set at zero, rather than blank as in the MARC formats.

The Reference Manual's closest equivalent to UNIMARC's field 210 is its field A25, Publisher: Name & Location. In this field there are only two sub-fields: (1) publisher's name, and (2) location or address. No provision is made in the Reference Manual for the names and addresses of distributors or manu-facturers, although any two organizations using this format could agree to use field A25 for these. There is no subfield for date of publication in A25; that element occupies a separate field, A21, Date of Publication.

These differences in methods of identifying data elements may seem to be only slightly more important than those that exist among the various MARC formats, but more significant variations can be found when the data in records formulated under the Reference Manual are compared with library-produced MARC records. Librarians shun some practices permitted in the Reference Manual; for example in field A09, Title of a Monograph, the second indicator has five possible settings. If set at 2, it signifies that the title has been trans-cribed from the title page (or an equivalent source) in its original language and alphabet, but has been enriched or modified during the cataloguing process. An indicator set at 3 means that the title has either been transliterated or translated as part of the cataloguing process.

In contrast, the MARC formats do not include rules for formatting titles since such rules appear as part of the cataloguing code used in the country where the record was created. Those libraries using AACR2 will have followed rule 1.1B1 which instructs the cataloguer to "transcribe the title page exactly as to wording, order, and spelling. . . ." An organization creating records accord-ing to AACR2 would therefore not wish to accept records from one using the Reference Manual unless it programs its computer to separate out any records where the second indicator in field A09 is set at 2 or 3.

The Common Communication Format

If this were the only point of significant difference between MARC and the UNISIST Reference Manual, such a remedy might be possible, but there are many others, which raise the danger of creating files of incompatible records. For this reason among others, there has been to date virtually no exchange of records between the abstracting and indexing services and the community of libraries which use one or another of the MARC formats. Nevertheless, a number of agencies, many of them in developing countries, have expressed the desire to receive, for storage in a single database, records from both abstracting and indexing services and from libraries. This has led to the development of the Common Communication Format (CCF), to be published by UNESCO's General Information Programme in 1983.

This new format defines data elements that are identical with elements in both the UNIMARC and Reference Manual formats, although not every element in the two established formats is duplicated in the CCF. Thus it will be possible to create a satisfactory CCF record by direct transfer from UNIMARC or from the Reference Manual by omitting certain elements or content designators or by using a general tag in place of a specific one, to achieve a less specific level of identification. Although it will not be possible in all cases to create a fully designated UNIMARC or Reference Manual record by direct transfer from the CCF, the Common Communication Format provides a useful bridge between the potentially incompatible practices of abstracting and indexing services on the one hand and libraries on the other.

Processing Formats versus Exchange Formats

The standard formats described above were earlier described as communication formats, or exchange formats. Processing formats are the formats for in-house processing systems. A library's computer will be programmed to receive bibliographic data in a communication format, whether online or via tape or disk. The librarians determine what uses are to be made of those data in any aspect of the library's operations. Programs are then written which take apart the record as received and store the desired elements in the local processing format. Manipulation according to local program specifications results in the output of any products called for (purchase orders, accessions lists, catalogue entries, individual user notification of new titles, etc.) in whatever physical medium is specified (paper, cards, COM, or a display screen). Computer programs are required to convert records from one format to another: from an input format to a storage format, from a storage format to an output format, from an exchange format to a processing format, and vice versa.

Format Compatibility

It was suggested on page 141 that one library's processing format may be very different from another's. So long as it is designed to be compatible with the exchange format, however, the library can automatically accept and use records supplied by many national and regional organizations which create and share data in that format. If the local system is not compatible with a recognized exchange format, then data must be keyed locally by hand, usually at greater cost and with lower accuracy, and can probably not easily be shared with other libraries. "MARC" is the password to cooperative bibliographic control among libraries today.

Compatibility is sometimes defined merely as the ability to *accept* data from a recognized exchange format, whatever the data might come to look like in the library's processing format. For example, the exchange format might have separate subfields for the place, the publisher, and the date of publication. The receiving library may choose to eliminate these content designators and store the three elements in its processing format in a single field, separated only by punctuation. Moreover, the library may choose to ignore certain fields or subfields contained in the standard format, deleting them in the transfer of the data to its processing format. Obviously, this kind of compatibility works only in one direction. The library's processing format may be said to be compatible for the purpose of receiving data, but it will certainly not be compatible for the purpose of contributing data to a database using the exchange format. In the above example, place, publisher, and date could not be transferred from the library's processing format to their correct fields or subfields in the exchange format, because content designators isolating them as separate elements do not exist in the former. Fields not used by the contributing library cannot appear at all in the exchange-format version of the library's data. The term "compatibility" is often used very loosely among bibliographic organizations; without some further qualification it is not particularly helpful in advancing discussions on cooperation. (See also the section Compatibility of Systems and Standards on pages 286–288 in Chapter 9.)

Output

The output programs which manipulate records for any specified purpose differ from library to library depending on the products wanted locally. In fact, the many different uses any library has for bibliographic data (for acquisitions, cataloguing, reference search, etc.) will inevitably require a variety of formats, and hence of output programs. The latter must all share certain characteristics. An output program uses, but then strips out the content designators in the record. It adds some information which does not appear in the exchange or the processing format through the use of print constants (see page 128), including such housekeeping information as that day's date (larger computers have built-in clocks and calendars). Finally, the output program controls the selection of data to be displayed and the order and visual arangement of that display.

For example, the sequential numbering of tracings (whether in arabic for subject headings or in roman for added entry headings) is not part of the MARC format. If a library wants a visible display of them in the traditional manner, it must invoke an output program capable of inserting an arabic numeral (in sequence) before each term tagged as a subject heading and a roman numeral before one tagged as an added entry heading. Since paragraphing is optional in ISBD, the local output program governs whether to put a paragraph indentation or an area separator before any data identified as (1) title proper, (2) collation, (3) any note, and (4) the ISBN or ISSN. To do so produces a result in the format of the Library of Congress printed entry.

Typical input conventions used in conjunction with Canadian MARC and LC MARC are given more fully on pages 300–301. On the other hand, output formats are becoming less, not more, standardized. The existence of a variety of different physical forms of catalogues and other bibliographic listings means that the once almost universal card format no longer dominates. To depart from it has been made easy because the same database can be used to produce paragraphed, blocked, or columnar presentation incorporating full data or any selection of fields/elements from it.

Updating and Revising the Exchange Formats

Even an in-house processing format is unlikely to prove entirely satisfactory on its first test. When it does work, it is highly likely that new applications and refinements not originally foreseen will be considered desirable. Debugging and design changes are almost inevitable. Any format as complex as the variable-field formats for international communication cannot be considered complete and immutable for a long time, if ever; yet most are still less than ten years old. During these same ten years, a major worldwide change in descriptive cataloguing has taken place with the introduction of ISBD, requiring revisions to the first versions of many machine-readable formats. In the English-speaking world, the adoption of AACR2 in 1981 also occasioned many additions and some major changes to the tags and subfield codes used in various national MARC formats.

Considerable time and expense are required in writing the complex *file definitions* to describe to any computer what it can expect to encounter in a formatted record. Whenever the format is changed in even the slightest detail, some of that work needs to be redone. Descriptions in visual form on cards can be interfiled even if their formats vary somewhat; descriptions in differing machine-readable formats cannot be processed in common by the same computer program. For these reasons there is a tendency for a computer format to be viewed even more conservatively than a manual format. The work of revising them is cautiously undertaken.

The committees which have written and which revise these formats are generally not the same ones as revise cataloguing rules, although usually the same overall bodies are involved: IFLA, Unesco (for example through its UNISIST programme), national libraries, and national library associations. In-house library committees review their own processing formats, national committees and committees of user-bodies review the MARC formats, and international committees meet to try to find common ground for a greater degree of standardization and cooperation. A great deal of turmoil has been caused in the bibliographic world by its having to face automation, internationalization, and a vastly greater degree of cooperation almost simultaneously in the 1960s and 1970s. This turmoil has been the greatest in the field of computer format definition. Whether or not a period of greater stability in this area lies ahead remains to be seen. So many separate committees exist in various organizations to review and update both manual and computer formats, and to explore new methods of computer-to-computer communication, that long-term stability may be elusive. Constant change appears a more likely possibility, perhaps in the form of short periods of great upheaval followed by more lengthy periods of minor revision.

III *Using Files of Bibliographic Records*

6

ACCESS TO
BIBLIOGRAPHIC DATA
IN FILES

Bibliographic Files

A bibliographic record serves little purpose in isolation: its value derives from its association with other records in a file. Such files are almost as varied in their forms and arrangements as in their content. The physical forms of bibliographic files (typed or printed cards, printed sheets, edge-notched or punched cards, magnetic tape or disk, microfiche or reel microfilm) were a focus of Chapter 2. The focus here is the arrangement of the records within in the file. This arrangement must facilitate the easy location of any desired personal or corporate name, title, identification number, term identifying a subject, subject classification symbol, or almost any combination of these.

There is no single term used widely to describe a collection of bibliographic records in general. The awkward terms "bibliographic file" and "bibliographic list" have already been used in this book as abstract terms referring to any or all of the following:

1) a *catalogue*—a list of the items available in or from a particular source: a publisher, a library, etc. A *union catalogue* is a composite list of the items held in a number of separate locations or institutions.

2) an *index*—for example a periodical index like the *Education Index*. Something called an index may or may not be a bibliographic list. The subject index at the back of a book is not since it does not cite separate bibliographic items.

3) a *bibliography* (more precisely an enumerative bibliography)—this is the most general but the vaguest of the commonly used terms, embodying almost any kind of grouping of bibliographic records. The term is not usually applied to a list of either of the above types, but it

is used to describe such diverse tools as a teacher's reading list, the references cited at the end of a book, or a list of materials by a person or on a subject. The ongoing listing of the materials published in a country is called a *national bibliography,* although if it is produced by the commercial publishing industry (the "book trade") of the country, and is largely restricted to its products, it may be called a *trade bibliography.*

4) a *machine-readable bibliographic database* —any assemblage of bibliographic data which must be displayed or printed out by an electro-mechanical or electronic device (now usually a computer) before a human being can use the data. Synonymous terms are *machine-readable data file* (MRDF), *computer database, bibliographic databank,* etc. Its content can be of any of the above types, and once a permanent physical product (COM, full-size paper copy, etc.) is produced from it, that product is customarily referred to as a catalogue, a bibliography, or an index, as above.

It is not surprising that these many types of bibliographic files, created for varied purposes, differ so markedly from one another in internal organization, just as they differ in their methods of updating, cumulating, supplementing, etc., as described on pages 15–18. Nevertheless, good models are imitated in this as in other fields, and there is a tendency for lists which serve similar purposes to become more like each other. Widespread acceptance of the computer-based communication formats described in Chapter 5 is increasing the force of this tendency as bibliographic files of both commercial and institutional origin are being established in, or converted to, machine-readable form. Cooperation in the construction of a single list or database by many organizations, as discussed in Chapter 9, is an even stronger force toward uniformity of practice.

File Structures

Whatever its type, a bibliographic file is valuable only to the degree that one can efficiently locate within it a particular record or group of records, based on a specified characteristic of one or more data elements. There are many ways of organizing files for efficient information retrieval. Some are best for small files, others for large ones. Some are more practical for manual files, others for computer-based ones. Some are more efficient for the retrieval of whole records, others for the retrieval of individual data elements within those records. Most of all, the nature of user demands for access to particular file information determines what configurations might best meet those demands.

For example, the most obvious structural feature of a bibliographic file is the number of sequences in it. Among card files, the *dictionary catalogue* in which authors, titles, and subjects are interfiled in a single sequence predominated in North American libraries for a long time. Yet many libraries now find that their users prefer the *divided catalogue,* in which names and concepts (or authors, titles, and subjects) are separated into two or more alphanumeric sequences in one of a number of possible ways. Among printed bibliographies, file structures are even less standardized. Not long ago, the national bibliography *Canadiana* was printed in eleven separate sequences; eight contained entries for different types of publication (theses, sound recordings, serials, federal government publications, etc.), and there were three separate indices to these eight parts. Today the print version of *Canadiana* is presented in two sequences of entries plus five indices.

In the case of a computer-based file, the file structure is probably "invisible" to the human searcher; but the hardware, operating system, and storage devices of the computer which stores and manipulates the file exert their own influence on what is the best and most cost-efficient file structure for any given data retrieval purpose. For example, the use of a computer on which processing time must be minimized, regardless of how much storage space this demands, will require a different file structure than the use of one where storage space is at a premium with respect to processing time.

These superficial examples show that there are few absolutes in determining advantageous file structures in either the manual or the machine mode: there are only trade-offs in terms of both user service and economics. The issue of a structure for a bibliographic file is a very complex one because (1) these files tend to be very large, (2) the average record is consulted very infrequently yet is expected always to be instantly accessible, (3) each record contains an assortment of data elements whose interrelationships can be very complex, and (4) users have been trained to expect a high degree of organization in which works and subjects are intelligibly collocated, and persons and bodies easily identified. Cost-efficient file structures to meet all these demands simultaneously are probably nonexistent. However, librarians have produced good (if expensive) results to date with manual files and are in the process of perfecting computerized techniques for better service at lower cost.

Random versus Indexed Files; Access Points

Both the human brain and the computer are frequently used for the simple purpose of matching a character string no matter where it occurs in a file or in a part of a file. If one wants only items published during 1980 or later, the eye scans a reading list quickly to pick them out even if the list is not chronologically arranged. Many programming languages also make it easy to instruct a computer to locate, in the date area of a format, every instance of a 1 followed by a 9 followed by an 8 followed by any fourth digit, no matter in what sequence the records appear on the linear tape or the rotating disk being searched.

Combination matching, or the *coordination* of search terms, is another frequent occurrence only a little more sophisticated than matching a single character string. One scans the current issue of a periodical index to see whether it lists any illustrated articles on solar energy in Mexican publications. A computer can also search for the terms which it is told relate to solar energy, matching them with given values in the code for illustrations and in the code for country of origin. Citations in which all three characteristics match the request are retrieved. In either case, the format must ensure that each desired characteristic is expressed and can be isolated. The computer-based format must carry explicit coding for some characteristics which the human searcher would locate through the use of judgement (for example, by knowing from their titles or places of publication which journals are published in Mexico).

A random file is a group of entries not arranged according to a particular characteristic significant for a given search (in this case a Mexican place of publication or the existence of illustrations). All the entries in a larger group must therefore be scanned, item by item, before it is certain whether or not an item displaying that characteristic appears. Small bibliographic files are often random in this sense, even if they are sequential in some other sense. A manual file is usually in sequence by *some* desirable characteristic, usually authors' names or subject terms. A machine-readable file is likely to be in sequence only by arbitrarily assigned control numbers.

If more than a few dozen entries are involved, a human being must be highly motivated to go through an entire file, or even through a subgroup of a larger file, looking for a characteristic other than that of the filing arrangement. It is a well-known phenomenon in card catalogues that if there are more than perhaps fifty cards filed under the same name or subject heading, those at the beginning of the group always get dog-eared from use long before those at the rear. It is also frequently observed that a user overlooks a wanted item in a card catalogue although the desired entry is only two or three cards removed from the location expected by that user. The computer does not get tired or bored, nor can it "overlook" an item if it has been properly programmed. It searches each item with equal thoroughness, and the speed of its operation makes a comprehensive search of a random file less uneconomic than one might at first imagine, even in the case of quite large files.

Nevertheless, this kind of searching is probably never the most cost-efficient or desirable way of isolating the information desired. The solution is the "indexing" of files in some predictable arrangement, usually alphanumeric. Terms or codes called *index entries, filing elements, headings, search keys,* or *access points* are assigned to lead the searcher to relevant records. The first three of these nearly synonymous terms are traditionally used when describing manual files. The fourth is generally applied to machine-based files. The final one is the most abstract, and being new, the most neutral. It is coming into common use and is the preferred term in this book. An access point is what makes an element of bibliographic information searchable within a file.

Single versus Multiple Access

Smaller bibliographic lists typically identify each item only once, the arrangement following the characteristic most likely to be sought. That characteristic may be a subject word, an author's surname, or the date of publication of the item. Some very large manual files, usually older ones, are also basically or entirely single-entry files for economic reasons; examples of such files are the Mansell catalogue of pre-1956 imprints and the old British Museum catalogues.[1] The searcher looking up an item in such a bibliography must be very sure to have both accurate bibliographic information about the item and a knowledge of which type of access point is the one used in that particular list.[2]

One can make efficient use of a single-entry list provided one knows the principles on which its access points have been chosen. However, if the searcher comes to the list with too few relevant facts about the desired item, even the most detailed knowledge of the structure of the single-entry list will not lead to the desired item. For this reason most larger bibliographic lists today are of the multiple-entry (or multiple-access) type. The searcher has a better chance of finding an item which appears under more than one access point, since if an author is not accurately remembered, perhaps a title or something else will be.

Some serial bibliographies which for economic reasons began as single-entry lists have become multiple-access lists in their supplements, at least to a limited degree. The published catalogues of the Library of Congress are noteworthy in this respect. The original publication, *A Catalog of Books Represented by Library of Congress Printed Cards Issued to July 31, 1942* (Ann Arbor: Edwards, 1942–1946) was strictly a single-entry list. Gradually its continuations, the *Supplement,* the 1948–1952 *Library of Congress Author Catalog,* and now the serial *National Union Catalog,* have seen the addition of more name added entries and cross-references to the basic single-entry structure. Verbal subject access to the entries created by the Library of Congress was added in 1950 in

1. *National Union Catalog, pre-1956 Imprints* (London: Mansell, 1968–1981); British Museum, Department of Printed Btoks, *General Catalogue of Printed Books,* Photolithographic edition to 1955 (London: B.M. Trustees, 1959–1966). A separately published quinquennial *Subject Index of Modern Books Acquired* has been produced by the British Museum since the late nineteenth century.

2. The preferred access point in a single-entry author-title list is called the main entry heading by librarians (see pages 217–220).

the publication now entitled *Library of Congress Catalogs: Subject Catalog.* Access to series titles in the entries created by the Library of Congress began in 1974 with the appearance of *Library of Congress Catalogs: Monographic Series.* Access by title proper is offered for all entries in the *Library of Congress Catalogs: Audio-Visual Materials,* but in the other publications mentioned above a title proper is an access point only if it is the main entry heading.[3]

The unit-entry system was illustrated in Figure 2 on page 17. The reproduction of a single complete entry on each separate card or slip was shown there to be the best manual method for updating a file as well as for displaying its information fully. It is, however, a wastefully redundant method of organizing a multiple-access file. In any book, fiche, or other noncard system, attaching an access point to a *briefer* item description significantly decreases the size of the file and saves printing costs. A complete description must of course be provided somewhere. At one time this was called the *main entry,* but it is now more often called the *full bibliographic record* or "fbr" in order not to confuse it with a *main entry heading,* which is only an access point. Multiple-access printed bibliographies and catalogues have typically adopted this kind of file structure with one fuller and other briefer entries, as exemplified in Figure 1 on page 16 in an older example, and in Figure 45 in two newer ones.

If an abbreviated description is so short as to require reference to the full description, the user thinks of it as an index entry, and the search has required two steps: (1) discovering the access point, then (2) referring to the fuller description. On the other hand, if the abbreviated record provides sufficient information for the purpose at hand, it will not even occur to the user to think that there might be a fuller entry elsewhere in the list. Libraries are finding unit multiple entries too expensive to maintain in newer catalogue formats, and the value of each data element as it relates to particular access points is being reassessed.

Selection of Access Points

Interlibrary loan librarians look with dismay on their daily quota of unverified citations, which have typically come from many different bibliographic sources compiled according to many different rules (or worse, personal whims). The challenge of the job is to match something in the citation with an access point in a bibliographic tool. The compiler of each bibliographic list decides which data elements are to be included in its individual entries and

---

3. To date (mid-1982) it has been left to commercial agencies to provide systematic title and classification-number access to Library of Congress entries. They do this by creating a title index automatically by computer from LC MARC records, which are only available, of course, for cataloguing done since 1968. They also index by ISBN and LC Card Number, and use COM as the only output format.

Contemporary portraits and other stories → Bail, M.
Contemporary pottery in South Africa → Nilant, F.G.E.
Contemporary primatology. Proceedings of the 5th
International Congress of Primatology, Nagoya, August 1974.
Ed. by S. Kondo / M. Kawai / A. Ehara. 1975. x,522p. Basel/
München, Karger, bd Sfr285.00 ⟨3-8055-2165-0⟩ CH/D
Contemporary problems of Pakistan. Ed. by Korson.
1974. Leiden, E.J. Brill (International studies in sociology and
social anthropology, XV) Dfl40.00 NL

Kawai, K. / H. Tanaka: Differential diagnosis of gastric
diseases. 1974. vi,262p. Berlin/Heidelberg, Springer, cl
DM168.00 $68.90 ⟨3-540-06579-2⟩ D
Kawai, Keiichi / Hiromichi Tanaka: Differential diagnosis
of gastric diseases. 1974. 268p. Tokyo, Igaku Shoin Y17400.00
J
Kawai, M. → Contemporary primatology
Kawai, T.: Clinical aspects of the plasma proteins. 1973.
xvi,466p. Berlin/Heidelberg, Springer, cl DM148.00 $60.70
⟨3-540-06523-7⟩ D
Kawai, T.: Plecoptera (Insecta). 1967. 218p. Tokyo, Keigaku
Publishing (Series of Fauna Japonica), hb $16.10 J

**International Congress of Primatology, 4th, 1972,
Portland**: Primatology, symposia of the 4th International
Congress of Primatology, Portland, Oreg., August 1972. V.4:
Nonhuman primates and human diseases. Ed. by W.P.
McNulty. 1973. xii,149p. Basel/München, Karger, bd Sfr68.00
⟨3-8055-1497-2⟩. V1-4 Sfr320.00 ⟨3-8055-1498-0⟩ CH/D
International Congress of Primatology, 5th, 1974, Nagoya
→ Contemporary primatology
**International Congress of Psychopathology of
Expression, 6th, 1970, Istanbul**: Proceedings of the 6th
International Congress of Psychopathology of Expression,
Istanbul, 1970. Selected lectures. In Eng. & Fr. Ed. by R.
Volmat / T. Spoerri. 1972. 100p. Basel/München, Karger
(Confinia psychiatrica, vol. 15, no. 1 (1972)), pb Sfr21.00 CH/D

346.7104'34
Rhodes, F. W.
Williams' The Canadian law of landlord and
tenant. Second supplement to the fourth edition /
F.W. Rhodes with Peter R. O'Brien, author of the
Quebec chapter. — Toronto : Carswell, 1980.
xii, 468 p. ; 23 cm.
Title on spine: Williams' landlord and tenant.
2nd supplement.
Running title: Canadian law of landlord and
tenant. 1980 supplement.
Supplement to: Williams, Esten Kenneth, 1889-
Williams' The Canadian law of landlord and
tenant. 4th ed.
ISBN 0-459-33300-3 : $38.75
1. Landlord and tenant—Canada.
1. Propriétaires et locataires—Canada.
I. O'Brien, Peter R. II. Williams, Esten
Kenneth, 1889- Williams' The Canadian law of
landlord and tenant. 4th ed. III. Title. IV. Title:
Williams' landlord and tenant. 2nd supplement.
V. Title: Canadian law of landlord and tenant.
1980 supplement.
KE690   C81-1427-0
                         MRDS

O'Brien, Peter R.
Rhodes, F. W.
Williams' The Canadian law of landlord and
tenant. Second supplement to the fourth
edition. — Toronto : Carswell, 1980. —
ISBN 0-459-33300-3 : $38.75 C81-1427-0
MRDS **Pt. 1 346.7104'34**

FIG. 45. Above, a single full description and two index entries referring to it, reproduced from *International Books in Print, 1979*. Below, fuller and briefer descriptions under different access points, reproduced from *Canadiana*.

what the access points should be. The latter are determined by the purposes for which the list is likely to be consulted and are therefore different for different types of lists.

The user wanting to know what editions of Dickens' *Bleak House* a particular library owns consults the part of that library's catalogue in which authors and/or titles are access points. The collection development librarian who wants to know what books are being issued this year by a particular American publisher looks in the current edition of *The Publishers' Trade List Annual,* which lists items under the names of their publishers. A serials librarian checking an invoice who wants to know what serial publication has the ISSN 1234-5678 may consult manually the *Bulletin de l'ISDS* since it lists key title assignments in the numerical order of their ISSNs; or may access the CONSER database by computer using the ISSN as a search key since that database holds the ISSN in a separate searchable field. A user who wants to know what items are available on fly-fishing searches a bibliography with subject access, that is, one in which a term for this concept, expressed in words or in classification symbols, can be located.

Every possible data element is of some conceivable value in searching a bibliography or catalogue—if not in itself, then in combination with others. However, few if any bibliographies make it possible to find books with green covers together, or list books in ascending order of the number of pages in them, although one can find booksellers' catalogues which list only books with coloured illustrations or only items bearing authors' autographs. Author, subject, and first-word-of-title access points are those traditionally provided in the multiple-access library catalogue. These extend to the name of any person or corporate body associated with the intellectual content of the publication in hand or of any closely related publication; performer(s) if a performance medium is involved; title(s), including series titles, whether of the item itself or of the work it embodies; and subject headings/classification symbols according to any of several schemes. During the twentieth century, bibliographic control has seen the increasingly frequent preparation of keyword indices, citation indices, chronologic indices, and a host of indices of report, grant, and other code and numbering systems. This is a clear indication that the more traditional access points are far from sufficient, although they are still the most frequently used, the most intellectually rewarding for the searcher, and the most cost-beneficial to compose carefully for a bibliographic file.

Coordination of Access Points

Filing Rules as Determinants of Coordination

The compiler of a list also determines which access points should be made to operate in coordination with one another in response to a single search. Even in a single-entry list, at least two access points usually operate simultaneously. One must take precedence over the other(s). In a file arranged by authors' surnames, the problem of what to do with ten different works by the same author is commonly solved by subarranging them either by their titles or by their publication dates. That is, either the author's name and the title, or the author's name and the date, are *pre-coordinated*. They form a single filing unit. Either title or date is a reasonable subfiling element within this unit, but for obvious economic reasons no significant manual catalogue or bibliography has ever duplicated the two different pre-coordinate units: author-title and author-date. Therefore if the subarrangement is by title, one must scan every entry in the group to find the latest item by the author; if it is by date, one must scan every entry to find a particular title.

This is no real disadvantage in a small catalogue, or under a heading (like an author's name) where there is unlikely to be a large number of entries. It is, however, a significant problem in the subject catalogue of a general library of any size. Within the same subject heading, traditional subarrangement is by the names of persons and bodies deemed to be authors (technically, by main entry heading). That is, the subject heading and the main entry heading are pre-coordinated. This is the most reasonable arrangement in dealing with creative works since authorship is a more significant feature of such a work than any other characteristic. The file of items within the heading PSYCHOL-OGY begins with Abbott's book and ends with Zigfeld's.[4] But it is demonstrable in the case of scientific works that more users are better served if a subject heading is pre-coordinated with the date of publication, so that the file under PSYCHOLOGY begins with a 1982 publication and ends with a 1753 one (or vice versa). Some libraries so arrange their subject catalogues. What no general (that is, all-subject) library can do is establish one arrangement for humanities-related material and another for science-related material because of the difficulty of defining the line of demarcation between them. Psychology may be viewed as a subject on either side of that line.

Thus multiple access means only the provision of different access points for the same item, *not* the provision of various coordinations of elements within the same access point. It has traditionally been left to the filing rules of each single library or bibliographic list to determine in what order different elements on a single entry are coordinated. These issues are analyzed in greater depth in Appendix II.

Pre-Coordination of Subject Concepts

The term ''coordination'' has been used in the literature of information handling much more frequently in dealing with concept-concept coordination

---

4. In keeping with traditional practice in library technical services writings, a subject access point from a standard list (the *Library of Congress Subject Headings* in this case) is given in small capitals.

than with name-title, subject-date, etc., coordination. In all cases the problems are the same. For example, two different concepts are related in a fixed way in the pre-coordinate subject heading RELIGION AND SCIENCE. The other possible way of filing the pre-coordination, SCIENCE AND RELIGION, is traditionally relegated to the status of a cross-reference so that the file is not duplicated: SCIENCE AND RELIGION *see* RELIGION AND SCIENCE.

Similarly, the subject heading WATER CONSERVATION—COLORADO RIVER is a pre-coordination of a two-part concept with a geographic location. A hundred years ago, Charles Ammi Cutter recommended that a relationship of this kind be displayed under both terms, as WATER CONSERVATION—COLORADO RIVER and as COLORADO RIVER—WATER CONSERVATION. Still, he admitted that "as this profusion of entry would make the catalog very long, we are generally obliged to choose between country and scientific subject."[5] For the same economic reasons noted earlier, current practice in manual catalogues follows Cutter's reluctant suggestion: only one pre-coordinated version of such a combination of terms is provided. In fact, when one of the terms is a form aspect (for example, "History," "Collections," "Bibliography") or a geographic name (for example, "Colorado River," "Australia," "Asia"), not even a cross-reference is provided from this term to the chosen pre-coordinate form because of the huge number of cross-references which would thereby be required. An interdisciplinary search for material related to the Colorado River is therefore rendered very difficult indeed.

It is characteristic of all manually searched files that limitations are placed on the number of access points per item listed, and stringent limits are placed on the coordination of access points. This is because each access point, and therefore also each coordination of two elements into a filing or display unit, constitutes a separate physical entity, whether it be a card in a drawer or lines of text on a page or a microfiche. To maintain each of these units permanently in a growing file is very costly, and can even become inconvenient for the user as the file grows larger and more unmanageable. To permute each access point in combination with each other possible one in a multiple-access unit-entry card catalogue has never even been attempted since it is almost a physical impossibility. In summary, in a manual catalogue system the cataloguer is discouraged from adding "too many" entries for a given item, from providing permutations of concepts as multiple access points, and from making "excessive" cross-references.

The Computer and Searching Techniques

The computer did not cause an immediate revolution in either file structure or access techniques. It was at first used both in libraries and by the abstracting

5. *Rules for a Dictionary Catalog,* p. 68.

and indexing services principally in batch mode to automate the physical production of the existing types of manually searched files (catalogues, periodical indices, acquisitions files, serials lists, abstracting journals, etc.) As shown in Appendix I, the MARC formats clearly reveal their origins in the format and uses of the unit-entry card catalogue.

This use of a machine-readable bibliographic database will not soon die out. Most still serve in part as storage media from which to produce traditional printed bibliographies and indices to be searched manually. Thus much of what has already been said in this chapter regarding manual file structures, access points, and searching techniques applies also to machine-readable databases used to produce batch products. Even if the product has been miniaturized and the "space" argument against the cost of expansion is no longer so valid, the economic argument against displaying large numbers of redundant entries, and the psychology of human search methods, enforce the same constraints described above for manual lists.

Post-Coordination

That the computer could revolutionize the process of searching itself, and not merely that of printing, was foreseen in the earliest application of automation to information retrieval in the late 1940s. Subject indexing then, as now, was the weak link in bibliographic control. It seemed particularly weak to such investigators as C. Dake Gull, Calvin Mooers, Ralph Shaw, and Mortimer Taube, who concerned themselves particularly with the quick retrieval of scientific and technical data from reports of experiments—an area in which the need to match processes, techniques, materials, etc., in different ways is almost inevitable.

In this field one cannot easily predict what combination of concepts will be useful: for any particular search it is likely to be different. Therefore a limited number of pre-coordinations is not particularly helpful since these would represent only the indexer's notion of what might be sought. To elaborate on the same example as was used above, it would be desirable to be able *separately* to locate all instances of the concept "water conservation," all instances of mention of "recycling," and all instances of mention of the area of the "Colorado River," so that the three concepts could be coordinated with each other in a particular search without affecting the availability of those same concepts for searches in different contexts.

This technique is known as *post-coordinate searching*. Possible search terms are kept separate as individual concepts until they are combined in response to a single request. In other words, terms are coordinated not before they are sought in a request for information (pre-), but only at the time of such a request (post-). Each concept remains available for searching in combination with any other, and is not linked as a single filing unit with another concept. *Post-coordinate indexing* for such a searching process must therefore index the most specific separate concepts reasonable for the subject in hand. The early experimenters named above attached such terms as *descriptors* and *uniterms* to the access points suited to their post-coordinate systems, precisely to distinguish them from pre-coordinate headings which had come to be known as subject headings in library terminology.[6] The effectiveness of post-coordinate searching is, of course, dependent on a willingness to have a document indexed under many more, and probably more specific, terms than had hitherto been traditional in general bibliographic services.

However, an index entry which isolates only a single process, material, place, etc., would have to display such a large number of references (a high proportion of them irrelevant to any one search) that the process of manual searching becomes frustrating. This is why post-coordination is not suited to manual search routines. It is a process dependent on the availability of a mechanical method of sorting and comparing large numbers of terms quickly, accurately, and tirelessly. A human being is simply not normally willing to go through a file of hundreds of items under a general term like "conservation" to see which of them share the common secondary characteristics "water," "recycling," and "Colorado River." In the 1950s the pioneers of post-coordinate indexing applied or invented technologies ranging from some akin to manual ones (edge-notched cards sorted with a knitting needle) to forward-looking mechanical devices such as the patented Rapid Selector which applied optical scanning to coded microform.

It was soon evident that only the modern electronic computer used in the full context of the technology described in Chapter 2 could provide the storage, the flexibility, and the speed of operation which would make post-coordinate searching a practical reality. Computer applications of post-coordinate searching were at first merely byproducts of the computerization of bibliographic lists for printing purposes, but they now represent the computer's most significant contribution to information handling, far surpassing its value in lowering the cost and raising the accuracy of other clerical operations.

Post-coordinate computer searching on a significant database began with the inauguration of the MEDLARS service for medical literature in 1964, but only since the 1970s has the technique come into the range of everyday practice in general librarianship. By then, (1) significantly large machine-readable bibliographic databases had been built up, (2) the storage and processing costs for handling these databases were coming within reason (or could be charged directly to the user), (3) libraries were beginning to acquire the communication capability of accessing them, and (4) professional training in the efficient use of the new type of indexing terminology and searching techniques was becoming readily available.

6. The distinction is only relevant, of course, when there is more than one concept in a subject heading. An access point like pollution is equally a subject heading in a pre-coordinate system and a descriptor in a post-coordinate one. This and other issues in the structure of subject access points are analyzed in Chapter 8.

Boolean Logic

The greatest benefits are derived from post-coordinate indexing when searching is done in the online mode (as distinguished from the batch mode: see page 45). Today, post-coordinate searching is virtually synonymous with online searching, since the online or interactive access mode makes it possible while a search is in progress to add or change the elements to be coordinated, in response to the results presented on a printer or display screen. The commands which post-coordinate the desired search keys are known as *boolean operators,* and applying them is known as using *boolean logic*. It is now almost essential for a computer-based information retrieval system to have the capacity to apply boolean logic. Its more elementary uses are illustrated below.

Venn Diagrams. The diagram shown in Figure 46, called a Venn diagram, shows a situation in which the command to find items identified by the search key TELECOMMUNICATION retrieves 50 items, and the command to find items identified by the search key SATELLITES retrieves 22 items, for a total of 72 items. In this and the following examples, the search term TELECOMMUNICATION is symbolized by the letter A, and the search term SATELLITES by the letter B.

```
find subject telecommunication

RESULT A: 50 ITEM(S)

find subject satellites

RESULT B: 22 ITEM(S)
```

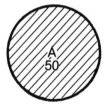 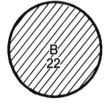

FIG. 46. A simple Venn diagram involving only two terms.

Combining Terms with AND. The use of AND to combine A with B retrieves only those records which have been assigned *both* index terms. Such a combination narrows the search, since it excludes records where the search terms do not occur together. As shown in Figure 47, only 12 records in the file had been assigned both terms.

```
combine A and B

RESULT: 12 ITEM(S)
```

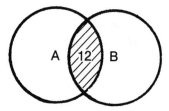

FIG. 47. Combining terms with AND.

Combining Terms with OR. The use of OR to combine A with B retrieves all records which have been assigned *either* of the two index terms. The result is illustrated in Figure 48. Sixty-three items are retrieved, showing that 9 of the 72 retrieved by the separate searches shown in Figure 46 were in fact duplicates. This elimination of duplicate items makes a search using the logical operator OR more effective (as well as more efficient) than two separate searches.

```
combine A or B

RESULT: 63 ITEM(S)
```

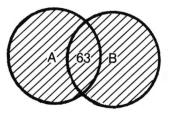

FIG. 48. Combining terms with OR.

Combining Terms with NOT. Like AND, the NOT operator serves to restrict the scope of the search. In the search illustrated in Figure 49, the searcher wishes to retrieve all records assigned the index term A *except* those which also contain B. That is, the searcher is interested in all forms of telecommunication except those which use satellites. As a result, 38 items are retrieved.

combine A not B

RESULT: 38 ITEM(S)

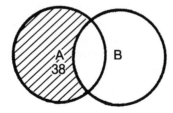

FIG. 49. Combining terms with NOT

Multiple Combinations. Most information retrieval systems permit the use of more than one boolean operator in a single search command. The computer follows a fixed order of precedence when it carries out the commands, though the exact sequence is not the same in every system. Therefore it is unwise to use a command such as FIND A AND B OR C before reading the instructions for the particular system to discover which of the pairings shown in Figure 50 will result.

combine A and B or C

RESULT: 22 ITEM(S)

combine A and B or C

RESULT: 30 ITEM(S)

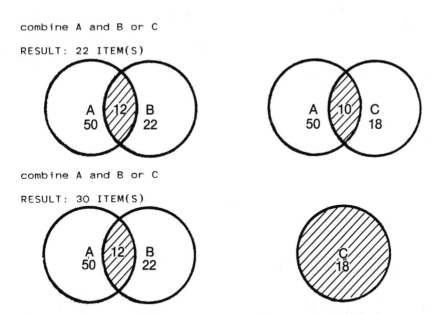

FIG. 50. The upper illustration shows the situation where "A AND B OR C" is interpreted by the system's computer programs to mean "A AND (B OR C)". This system retrieves every record to which either "A AND B" or "A AND C" applies, a total of 22 items. The lower illustration shows the situation where "A AND B OR C" is interpreted as "(A AND B) OR C". This system therefore retrieves every record to which either "A AND B" or "C" applies, a total of 30 items.

File Structures for Post-Coordinate Machine Searching

A manual file structure in which full document descriptions are located in one place and an index or indices to them in another is as common a structure for machine readable databases as for printed bibliographies in book form. This structure was illustrated in Figure 45 on page 161. In the terminology of those who work with computer files, this is the *indexed sequential access method.* Complete entries are stored in a single sequence in the *document file,* and one or more indices called *access point files* contain the search keys pointing to the complete entries.

If only machine searching is intended, the order of the entries in the document file is immaterial; since no human accesses the file visually, the order need not be alphabetic. It is much more efficient simply to put each new record at the end of the sequence as it is entered into the file. Sequential or even random numbering, usually assigned by the computer at the time of input, provides the link between the document file and the access point file(s) or indices.[7] This method tends to require large amounts of storage space because many data elements are stored twice: once as part of the entry in the document file, and again as access points in an access point file.

In a machine-readable database it is not only unnecessary, but in fact inefficient, to pre-coordinate elements. An efficient machine system ensures minimal or no redundancy of stored data by eliminating from the document file those elements which are also access points. This is possible because of the computer's ability quickly and cheaply to post-coordinate: it can select and display together various elements stored in several files, which together make up a complete entry. In this system each different document and each different access point is identified to the computer by a code number. Each document description contains the code number for each access point applicable to it. Conversely, each access point has attached to it the code number for each document description indexed under it. These code numbers are called *pointers.* A simple file of this type, known as a *nonredundant indexed file,* is shown in Figure 51.

---

7. Files are now sometimes arranged in this "random" way when printed on paper or reproduced on COM. Such a file is called a *register catalogue.* Its disadvantage is that the user cannot locate a complete entry except by first consulting an index. The advantage is that the document file is updated by merely adding entries (fiche, pages) at the end of the existing ones. Only the access point file(s) need to be cumulated and reissued periodically; this is much less expensive than cumulating the entire multiple-entry list, and more convenient for the user than requiring consultation of many separately contained supplements. With many bibliographies and catalogues now being issued on COM for visual consultation, the register format is gaining in popularity. For example, the CONSER microfiche listing is a register catalogue, and the COM version of *Canadiana* became a register catalogue in 1981.

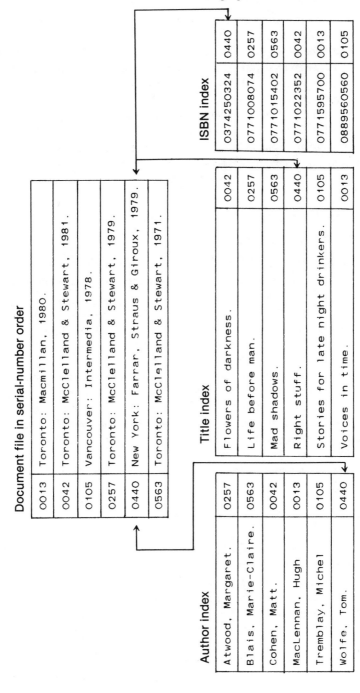

Fig. 51. Excerpts from a simple nonredundant indexed file.

If every element in a record were desired as a search key, and therefore existed in an access point file, the document description would have no material existence at all except as a series of pointers in the access point file(s). It would be assembled from these separately stored fragments only if a searcher specifically requested all the data elements making up a specific record number. However, a bibliographic record typically includes some elements which it makes no sense to index (collation, some notes, etc.) and some elements which require different forms as access points (Smith, John) than as elements of description (by John Smith). Therefore, some data must be in document files and some in access point files. Such a structure is increasingly common in machine-readable bibliographic databases.

Access Points for Post-Coordinate Machine Searching

In a machine-readable file, the decision on how to format the data and the decision on what should be the access points are not separate decisions, but the same decision. Every separately tagged, subfielded, or otherwise coded element within a format is a potential access point since a program can be written to locate it and compare it either with a specified character string in a request, or in post-coordination with any other element in the same or a different record.

In fact, it is possible to search for any separate word or number, for example to inquire whether in the description of an item the title contains the word chemistry and at the same time the arabic numeral in the pagination element is greater than 500. However, only in the most unusual circumstances could one afford to write a separate program tailored in this way for each individual search. Searching techniques and access points may have been made more flexible by the computer's capabilities, but standard practices have inevitably developed. The most common of these are described in this and the next section.

Assigned Search Keys

Access points were soon being called search keys in computer applications, but in many instances they have remained the familiar headings established for manual files: names of persons, bodies, subject concepts, etc., including cross-references and classification numbers. Because of the expense of storing and searching large files of access points, early mechanized information services did not always make each of these available for machine searching, but chose only the types which would give the best overall results for the purposes for which each system was used. Number codes are much cheaper to store and easier to search; the ISBN, ISSN, LC Card Number, Superintendent of Documents number, and other such search keys were almost immediately added to the familiar names and subject headings as access points in machine systems. All the above types of access points are called assigned search keys when they are established by applying recognized cataloguing rules and *controlled vocabularies*. Because they are established by the efforts of cataloguers and indexers whose purpose is uniquely to identify and distinguish names, concepts, and works, assigned search keys will always be the access points which inspire greatest confidence in use. Name and subject access points of this type are analyzed in Chapters 7 and 8.

Natural Search Keys

As computer storage and processing costs have declined while human labour costs have risen rapidly, it has become more and more attractive to let the computer create the access points by automatically placing into the access point file terms or words taken from the bibliographic description as it is keyed into the database. This is the equivalent of the making of a concordance, something only rarely produced manually, but which is easy and inexpensive for a computer to produce. The fields chosen for such automatic keyword indexing are commonly author and/or title fields. Many of the abstracting and indexing services add an abstract to each bibligraphic description, and it is common for it to be automatically indexed as well. (A professional abstractor usually employs something close to a controlled vocabulary, thus enhancing the value of the automatic indexing considerably; when the author writes the abstract, it is a little less likely to contain the standard terms for its field.)

Terms accepted for indexing as found in the data are called *keywords,* or *natural search keys,* to distinguish them from the "assigned" search keys of a controlled vocabulary. A computer-generated index of keywords is often printed out in batch mode, and the term *permuted keyword index* is sometimes applied to such a product because a single document appears under as many keywords as are indexed. Two formats are common and particularly useful for smaller files: (1) the *keyword-in-context* (KWIC) index, and (2) the *keyword-out-of-context* (KWOC) index. The distinguishing features of the two are illustrated in Figure 52.

The automatic indexing of keywords must be governed by quite sophisticated programs in order for the resulting index to be an effective searching tool. Punctuation and even spacing are most likely eliminated so that only alphanumeric characters are considered. Almost certainly, all alphabetic characters are stored in upper case only, and terms input at the time of searching are also converted automatically to upper case, so that for example the access point "Wolfe" is not rejected by the system simply because the searcher keyed in "wolfe" or "WOLFE".

```
6OO Users Meet the COM  Catalog
Two Years with a Closed  Catalog
         Closing the Card  Catalog:    the New York Experience
Card Catalog to On-Line  Catalog:    the Transitional Process
                   Card  Catalog     to On-Line Catalog: the T
     Living amid Closed  Catalogs
  The Effect of Closed  Catalogs    on Public Access
                         Catalogue   Use Survey
     Alternative Forms of  Catalogues   in Large Research Librari
```

```
Catalog     6OO Users Meet the COM Catalog
Catalog     Card Catalog to On-Line Catalog: the Transitional Pr
Catalog     Closing the Card Catalog: the New York Experience
Catalog     Two Years with a Closed Catalog
Catalogs    The Effect of Closed Catalogs on Public Access
Catalogs    Living amid Closed Catalogs
Catalogue   Catalogue Use Survey
Catalogues  Alternative Forms of Catalogues in Large Research Li
```

FIG. 52. Above, a portion of a KWIC index; below, a KWOC index covering the same items. In the former, the entries are arranged by the keyword and the following term(s). In the latter, subarrangement under a keyword is by the first nonarticle word of the title (or sometimes by the author's surname).

It is almost never considered practicable to index every word; some, such as articles, are simply not worth isolating as access points. Research has led to the development of complex algorithms to avoid the worst inconsistencies and inadequacies of automatic indexing. The program which governs the choice of words to index is probably designed to handle each field in a different manner. In the case of corporate names, for example, a _stop list_ is normally used to prevent the indexing of insignificant words so that the file is not choked with huge numbers of entries under "company," "association," "conference," "society," "incorporated," etc. Similarly, titles and abstracts are scanned to reject punctuation, articles, words of one or two letters, prepositions, nondistinctive words like "report" or "proceedings," etc. Part of a typical stop list for use in title indexing is shown in Figure 53.

ABOUT	BESIDE	IF	SINCE	UNTIL
ABOVE	BESIDES	IN	SO	UP
ACROSS	BETWEEN	INTO	STILL	UPON
AFTER	BEYOND	LA	SUCH	WHAT
AGAINST	BOTH	LE	THAN	WHEN
ALONG	BUT	LES	THAT	WHERE

FIG. 53. Part of a typical stop list for automated title indexing. This entire list contains eighty-seven terms.

To index personal names automatically is more difficult since only surnames, and not given names, are likely to be wanted as access points. Algorithms have been developed to eliminate most, if not all, given names.

An index of natural search keys is particularly helpful in retrieving material based on the rather common occurrence of incomplete recollection of a known item by the user. The advantage of being able to search all keywords in corporate names and titles is obvious. However, the resulting index file is much larger than a file of carefully selected assigned search keys. Although relatively cheap to create, it is relatively expensive to store and maintain, and is of course predictably inconsistent. It may offer many more opportunities for a "hit" with a requested term, but it also illustrates the law of diminishing returns: a fivefold increase in the number of access points available for a document has never been shown to achieve a fivefold increase in the effective accessibility of that document.

In order to have the best of all possible worlds in a computer system where data storage costs are not an overriding consideration, one may consider using both some natural and some assigned search keys for the same document. This practice is often found in commercial databases. Redundancy in file structures is usually a symptom of design flaws, but redundancy in the provision of access points can be useful.

Techniques of Using Computer Searching Systems

From the point of view of searching strategy, a manual file is passive. Different searchers can use it in many different ways: browsing, combining search terms, judging interim results, altering the strategy as the searching proceeds, etc. To a degree this is also possible in online searching, but only within the constraints of how the programs governing the system have been written. It is possible, but now highly unusual, for the searcher to write a computer program to accommodate the circumstances of a particular query. Rather, complex programs are written for use on a particular computer facility to accommodate those searching strategies which the system designers feel will be applicable to any query of any database in that system. The same bibliographic records are now sometimes loaded into each of several different systems, with the result that different searching strategies and/or output formats are available depending on which system is used.

Following are brief descriptions of the more usual features of machine searching systems at the present time. Most of them are particularly applicable to online searching. Many employ subroutines using a command language (see pages 33–34) so that the user can refine the search online. Any particular feature may or may not be offered in one or another individual system, and it is typical for somewhat different commands to be used to invoke the same specific feature in different systems.

Menu Screens

When an automated system is designed to be used by the general public, it is common to use the menu screen as an access method in order to limit the kinds of responses the user may send to the system. A typical menu screen is like a multiple-choice examination question. It displays a question along with all the permissible responses. Each response is accompanied by a number or mnemonic symbol, and the searcher is asked to key in the appropriate symbol. For example, a menu screen may say:

```
        DO YOU WANT TO SEARCH BY
          A - AUTHOR?
          T - TITLE?
          S - SUBJECT?
      PLEASE KEY IN A, T, or S
```

(When a touch-sensitive screen (see page 24) is used, the searcher is asked to touch the appropriate choice.) In response, the computer shows a subsequent menu screen, for example:

```
    DO YOU WANT TO LOOK AT SUBJECTS BEGINNING
              1 - A-E?
              2 - F-M?
              3 - N-S?
              4 - T-Z?
```

In order to conduct a search on a complex database or even a large single file, it may be necessary for the user to respond to a lengthy series of menu screens before "coming to the point." For this reason, and because the experienced searcher quickly becomes frustrated at having to respond to an all too familiar sequence of menus with no possibility of shortcutting the process, such systems are more popular with the general public (for whom they are designed) than with staff members or professional searchers. From the programmer's point of view, however, menu screens are an attractive possibility. It is far simpler to program a system which allows only predictable responses than to program one to deal with a response which might consist of YES, Yes, yes, Y, y, OK, ok, O.K., o.k., O K, o k, NO, No, no, or any miskeyed or intended "nonsense" which the user might input.

Multiplicity of Indices

Whether natural or assigned search keys are used, it is common to store them in separate access point files depending on their type, rather like dividing a manual catalogue into author/title and subject parts. Thus there may be one or more keyword indices (to titles, to abstracts, etc.) and one or more assigned search key indices (to names, to concept terms, etc.). Virtually all information retrieval systems permit the searcher to indicate which index is to be searched for the specified term(s). If no particular index is requested, the system may be programmed to select the largest index automatically. Some systems permit terms to be searched in more than one index with a single command.

Occurrence Counters

When searching is done online, the searcher cannot "see" the file to know how many bibliographic entries are associated with the access point in question. Because the number can be very large indeed, especially when natural search keys are included, the searcher must be protected from an unwanted avalanche of information. Most systems accomplish this by incorporating an occurrence counter which is kept up to date as new documents are indexed into the file. When the system searches the index for the desired term, the index file contains not only the term and the addresses of records containing that term, but also a count of the number of records containing the term, as shown in Figure 54. In some systems the count is not preserved in the record, but is calculated at the time of the search. In either case, the system reports to the searcher the number of items retrievable by using the specified term.

```
Index-term                             Items
MICROCOMPONENTS  ....................      13
MICROCOMPOSED  ......................       2
MICROCOMPUTER  ......................     129
MICROCOMPUTERIZED  ..................       5
MICROCOMPUTING  .....................       1
```

FIG. 54. A search key index containing occurrence counters.

Browsing

In a manually searched file, the user can scan many entries and/or headings to determine which are relevant. The online searcher also profits from being able to review more than a single index entry offered in response to a query. This is particularly necessary when there are natural (hence unpredictable and probably inconsistent) search keys in the indices. A good retrieval system displays several index entries on either side of the one keyed in by the searcher. Most access point files are maintained in the computer so that they are automatically output in alphabetic order. Thus a search can to a certain degree reveal grammatically related terms as well as alternate spellings, as shown in Figure 55.

```
┌─────────────────────────────────────────────────┐
│ ENTER SEARCH TERM                               │
│                                                 │
│ browse photography                              │
│                                                 │
│ Index-term                               Items  │
│ 1. PHOTOGRAPHIC EQUIPMENT .........        39   │
│ 2. PHOTOGRAPHS ....................        46   │
│ 3.*PHOTOGRAPHY ....................       113   │
│ 4. PHOTOSINTHESIS .................         3   │
│ 5. PHOTOSYNTHESIS .................        62   │
└─────────────────────────────────────────────────┘
```

FIG. 55. A sample interaction showing the browsing of an alphabetic index. The term requested is term number 3, signalled by a preceding asterisk. A number of terms on either side of it in the alphabet are automatically displayed when the command to browse is used. Term number 4 is a misspelled word occurring in three keyword index entries. The error probably occurred at the time of keying in the data, since it is unlikely that it appeared on the indexed documents themselves. In this and the following examples, the user has keyed the request in lower case, but the system has converted it to upper case for searching and responding (see page 173).

Truncation

Many systems permit the searcher to truncate a search term in order to retrieve all terms with a common root. Assuming that the symbol # denotes truncation (the actual symbol used varies from one system to another), LIBRAR# will retrieve all items having the search keys LIBRARY, LIBRARIES, LIBRARIAN, LIBRARIANS, and LIBRARIANSHIP. Using front truncation, #GLICERIDE retrieves items containing the terms GLICERIDE, MONOGLICERIDE, DIGLICERIDE, etc.

Truncation is a particularly helpful technique when applied to natural search keys, such as abstract and title keywords, since it makes possible the retrieval of both singular and plural forms of a word (COUNTR# retrieves COUNTRY and COUNTRIES), American and British spellings (BEHAVIO#R retrieves BEHAVIOR and BEHAVIOUR), and words with more than one standard spelling (HI#JACK# for HIJACKING, HI-JACKING, HIGHJACKING, HIJACKERS, etc.) But the power of truncation can corrupt the search if it is used carelessly. LAB# will retrieve not only LABOR and LABOUR, but also LABEL, LABIA, LABORATORY, LABRADOR, LABURNUM, LABYRINTH, and many other unrelated terms. Some systems attempt to guard against unexpected results by incorporating occurrence counters for truncated requests, as shown in Figure 56.

Compression Codes

The term "compression code" describes an access point created from either assigned or natural terms by a computer program for the sole purpose of assisting the searcher. These codes do not contribute to a description of the items retrieved. The best known examples of compression codes are those first used by the Online Computer Library Center (OCLC) for its huge file of bibliographic descriptions.

```
ENTER SEARCH TERM

find title lib#

"LIB#" RETRIEVES 87 TERMS.
DO YOU WISH TO CONTINUE? ANSWER Y OR N

n

ENTER SEARCH TERM
```

FIG. 56. A dialogue with a system which responds to a truncation search with an occurrence count and a request for confirmation.

As each new item is entered into the document file, a computer program creates a search key consisting, for example, of the first four letters of the author's last name, followed by the first four letters in the title excluding an initial article. This particular compression code would be known as a "4,4 key" or a "4,4 author-title key." Like all such codes, it is designed to permit known-item searches with a minimum number of keystrokes. Using the "4,4 key," a search for "WOLF,RIGH" might produce the result shown in Figure 57.

```
ENTER SEARCH TERM

wolf,righ

RESULT: 1 ITEM(S) AS FOLLOWS
1. WOLFE, TOM. THE RIGHT STUFF. NEW YORK, 1979.
```

FIG. 57. A typical interactive search using a compression-code search key.

Another common compression code is the "3,1,1,1 title key," which uses the first three letters in the first nonarticle word of the title, then the first letter in the second word, the first letter in the third word, and the first letter in the fourth word. Thus the code for the title *The Spy Who Came In from the Cold* is "SPY,W,C,I".

When this system is applied to a growing file, some codes will eventually retrieve a large number of items, as shown in Figure 58.

```
ENTER SEARCH TERM

boor,amer

RESULT: 8 ITEM(S) AS FOLLOWS
1. BOORSTIN, DANIEL JOSEPH. AMERICA AND THE IMAGE
       OF EUROPE. NEW YORK, 1960.
2. BOORSTIN, DANIEL JOSEPH. AMERICAN CIVILIZATION.
       NEW YORK, 1972.
3. BOORSTIN, DANIEL JOSEPH. AN AMERICAN PRIMER.
       CHICAGO, 1966.
4. BOORSTIN, DANIEL JOSEPH. THE AMERICANS. NEW
       YORK, 1965.
5. BOORSTIN, DANIEL JOSEPH. THE AMERICANS.
       HARMONDSWORTH, ENG., 1965.
6. BOORSTIN, DANIEL JOSEPH. AMERICANS THE COLONIAL
       EXPERIENCE. NEW YORK, 1958.
7. BOORSTIN, DANIEL JOSEPH. AMERICANS THE
       DEMOCRATIC EXPERIENCE. NEW YORK, 1973.
8. BOORSTIN, DANIEL JOSEPH. AMERICANS THE NATIONAL
       EXPERIENCE. NEW YORK, 1965.
```

FIG. 58. An example of a larger number of entries resulting from a compression-code search. A search for ANN,R,O,T using the 3,1,1,1 title key would result in hundreds of titles, *Annual Report of the*. . . .

The searcher must scan all the items retrieved to reject any unwanted or irrelevant ones. When the number of retrieved items becomes too large for convenient use much of the time, a more specific code must be substituted, probably incorporating a larger number of characters. This is an expensive operation because it requires a new index which can only be created by re-processing every record in the file.

The advantages of coded search keys are particularly great for the untrained user. To retrieve the items shown in Figure 58 the searcher only needs to know how to pronounce Daniel Boorstin's name (but not necessarily how to spell it) and vaguely how the title begins (but not the exact wording). This is typical of many users who search for a specific item, but begin with only brief and inaccurate information.

Controlling the Vocabulary of Access Points

The computer has greatly enhanced the access possible when a database is searched online, but it has also made it economical to reproduce more access points and indices in bibliographic tools which are now batch products from computerized operations, whether the output is print or COM. Fortunately, single-entry files of any size are almost a thing of the past. Still, regardless of how extensive are the indices or search keys, searching in any file, whether manually or online, is made easier when care has been taken in the creation and use of a controlled vocabulary for its access points. In such a vocabulary, each separate name or concept is identified by a single *established heading*. Having reached that heading, the searcher is confident of having found everything in the file relevant to the name or concept in question.

A person looking for general material about library science in a list which has only natural access points must take care to look under LIBRARIANSHIP, LIBRARY SCIENCE, INFORMATION SCIENCE, and other possible terms. Even then, documents may still have been overlooked because the use of index terms has depended on the chance of what wording was on the item or in the mind of the abstractor at the time the record was added to the file. Without established headings, most users would still be able to discover most of the works of the famous American humourist issued under the names "Clemens" and "Twain," since both are often cited in biographical material. They would, however, probably miss the works of the same humourist issued under more obscure pseudonyms such as "Sieur Louis de Conte."

Numbers

The only kinds of access points which do not cause such a problem are numbers. One is certain of being able efficiently to retrieve an item if one knows, and is able to use as the access point, an accurately transcribed ISBN, or Superintendent of Documents number, or LC Card Number, or grant number under which a project was undertaken, or record label number, etc. A search for the same item using the name of an author, performer, corporate sponsor, etc., may have desirable side effects, principally that of showing the item in relation to other possibly useful items. It cannot be as fast or reliable a means of discovering any single known item in isolation. Unique-number identifiers are therefore being incorporated as access points in more and more bibliographic files.

Authority Control

This is the name given to the function of discovering all available evidence relative to the naming of a person, body, topic, etc., and then establishing an access point and cross-references according to some rule. Being labour-intensive and dependent on professional investigation and judgement, it is extremely expensive. In fact, it is by far the most expensive function in all of bibliographic control. To be consistent, it must be carried out on all names, because until the research part of it has been carried out, it is not known whether or not the name or concept involves a problem of any kind.

Most bibliographic style manuals, even detailed ones like the Chicago Style Manual, say little about the need for, or techniques of, establishing standardized forms. This is because it is usually not their intention to facilitate the finding of items within large lists. Their purpose is simply to fix a consistent format and an alphabetic location for each isolated item cited. Many published indices to current journal and report literature do not take the trouble to standardize names as access points. Clerks are instructed to type what they see on the article into the list or index, not worrying about whether the "J.L. Smith" encountered today is or is not the same person as the "John L. Smith" encountered yesterday. Thus the same writer may appear under each of the several variant forms used in that person's different articles or papers, as shown in Figure 59.

John S.
Six is Fatal. A Case Study of Inter-Institutional Cost Comparison.
ED 136 703

Johnson, Cecil H.
The Identification of Opinion Leaders Among Teachers of Vocational Agriculture. Final Report. Research 40.
ED 030 764

Johnson, Cecil Heyward
The Identification of Teacher Opinion Leaders: An Element in a Change Strategy for Agricultural Education.
ED 023 858

Johnson, Charles
A Practical Management System for Performance-Based Teacher Education. PBTE Series No. 15.
ED 087 742

Johnson, Charles E.
Georgia Educational Model Specifications for the Preparation of Elementary Teachers. Final Report.
ED 025 491

Johnson, Charles Eugene
A Study of the Scholastic Achievement of Junior College Transfer Students at the University of Missouri.
ED 022 464

FIG. 59. Entries excerpted from *Resources in Education,* the ERIC abstracting journal. "John S." was obviously not verified, and may be an error resulting from the misapplication of a stop list. Cecil H. Johnson and Cecil Heyward Johnson are almost certainly the same person; but is it possible to be reasonably sure how many different Charles Johnsons there are?

A broad background of general education and considerable bibliographic experience are desirable for authority work. It requires (1) a thorough search of bibliographic, directory, and/or subject reference sources for information which may or may not exist, in order to establish the identity of the name or concept in question, (2) the ability to recognize the implications of any information discovered in relation to the name or topic, and (3) the making of professional judgements concerning relationships among different possible terms and/or name forms.

Cross-references. The products of authority work are twofold: (1) the standardized forms themselves, and (2) linkages relating one heading to another, whether they be visible cross-references alphabetically interfiled with headings, or invisible links in a machine-readable database. Any cross-reference is of course an access point, and a very important one. A searcher would consider a file to be well indexed only if it includes the reference "Canadian Pacific Airlines *see* CP Air" or vice versa, depending on which form was chosen as the established heading. Perhaps it is considered desirable for both forms to be allowed as access points, for one reason or another. In that case, one must still determine that these two names refer to what is essentially the same body, and provide two cross-references: "Canadian Pacific Airlines *see also* CP Air" and "CP Air *see also* Canadian Pacific Airlines."[8]

In a manually searched file, any cross-reference is a second-best alternative since it does not provide the information the user really wants, namely bibliographic entries relevant to the sought name or concept. A cross-reference is not attached to any item description, but is only an access point leading to another access point. Even so, any reference librarian is likely to claim that almost no bibliographic list or catalogue has enough cross-references to satisfy the needs of the lay user.

Automated Authority Control: Changing and Linking Search Keys

In a machine searching system, internal links make it possible to eliminate the concept of the cross-reference. The user can be led automatically to the established term or the desired bibliographic record without knowing whether the initial request was in the "correct" form or not. A very important advantage of the nonredundant indexed file structure described on pages 170–172 is that changing any search key in access point file(s) is relatively simple. The

---

8. Cataloguing rules do not normally countenance the establishment of two forms of name for the same person. Modern codes do, however, permit a corporate body to appear under two forms if it has changed its name, as in this example (see page 200).

code number of each relevant document description is "posted" to each appropriate heading in the access point file, as shown there in Figure 51. The terminology of any access point can therefore be changed more efficiently than in any other type of system. It is not necessary to change each bibliographic record in the file. Thus when the country's name was changed from Ceylon to Sri Lanka, only one record had to be altered, and presumably a cross-reference added, as shown in Figure 60.

Access point file before change

CESIUM	9587				
CEYLON	0018	0056	0392	2704	3195
CEZANNE	0519	1372			
– – – – – – – – –					
– – – – – – – – –					
SQUIRRELS	0250	5163	7421	8936	
STABILITY	0084	0729	6013		

Access point file after change

CESIUM	9587				
CEYLON	GO TO "SRI LANKA"				
CEZANNE	0519	1372			
– – – – – – – – –					
– – – – – – – – –					
SQUIRRELS	0250	5163	7421	8936	
SRI LANKA	0018	0056	0392	2704	3195
STABILITY	0084	0729	6013		

FIG. 60. The change from "Ceylon" to "Sri Lanka" can be accomplished by means of a simple change to the access point file, relocating the pointers and incorporating a cross-reference.

Alternatively, both names can be fully maintained in the access point file, as shown in Figure 61. The additional storage cost is minimal and the searching cost is the same no matter which form of name is accessed. If the circumstances make it desirable, any two or more terms can be linked in the access point file, as are "Ceylon" and "Sri Lanka" in Figure 62. For that matter, two or more bibliographic records can be linked in the document file, for example a directory and its supplement(s). The computer will then automatically retrieve all references no matter which of the search keys the user has employed, and no matter under which of the search keys a particular document has been indexed.

The development of automated authority control systems for large bibliographic databases is a very active field of interest in bibliographic control today. Canadian MARC and LC MARC, cited on pages 146 and 144, respectively, now incorporate formats for automated authority records, as do many other computer formats. This makes it possible for authority control information, like bibliographic information, to be exchanged among agencies in the standard ISO 2709-based communication formats.

Access point file

CESIUM	9587				
CEYLON	0018	0056	0392	2704	3195
CEZANNE	0519	1372			
- - - - - - - - -					
SQUIRRELS	0250	5163	7421	8936	
SRI LANKA	0018	0056	0392	2704	3195
STABILITY	0084	0729	6013		

FIG. 61. An attempt to search either "Ceylon" or "Sri Lanka" will retrieve the same records, since they are fully indexed under both terms.

Access point file

A0809	CESIUM	9587				
A0810	CEYLON	A7254				
A0811	CEZANNE	0519	1372			
	- - - - - - - - -					
A7253	SQUIRRELS	0250	5163	7421	8936	
A7254	SRI LANKA	0018	0056	0392	2704	3195
A7255	STABILITY	0084	0729	6013		

FIG. 62. In this situation, each access point has its own alphanumeric identification, separate from that assigned to documents. These are shown here with "A" numbers. Internal automatic links among the access points are therefore possible.

Authority Work in Libraries

Library catalogues and national bibliographies are carefully compiled on the premise that authority control is worth all the effort and expense involved in doing research, establishing standard forms, and providing cross-references. The specific criteria and rules used by libraries in standardizing name access points are analyzed in Chapter 7, and Chapter 8 analyzes controlled-vocabulary subject access points. Where other bibliographic tools adopt some kind of authority control, some use library-based standards, others create their own.

National bibliographic agencies and larger libraries tend to spend far more, proportionately, than smaller institutions on authority work. It requires more stringent efforts to control the larger number of names and subject headings in their databases, but they also accept a greater responsibility for authority work because their entries are the principal component of "derived cataloguing" used by others (see pages 271–275).

The adoption of authority control does not mean that the result is necessarily a simple tool, since what needs to be expressed is not always simple. It does mean that the searcher can have more confidence in its use. No computer program, however sophisticated, can supply terms or state relationships which are not explicit in the data input to it. In using natural search keys, the creator of the file deliberately bypasses authority control, hoping that its lack will be mitigated by the sheer abundance of access points for each document.

The question is whether it is preferable to bear the greater expense of authority control at the time a document is indexed, or to bear the greater expense and uncertainty at the time of each individual search for information from the whole file. Unfortunately, when the creator of the file is not also its principal searcher, it is all too tempting to shift the cost into the searcher's pocket. In the case of libraries, the catalogue is created primarily for the use of the trained searcher (including the reference librarian) who knows how to use it. Under these circumstances, it is usually considered a false economy to skimp on authority work since the result is only to make the process of using the catalogue slower and more inefficient.

Computer Searching versus Manual Searching

The user who is best served by a manual catalogue or bibliography has come to it with a knowledge of the subject in question, of the structure and limitations of the tool being searched, and of the nature of specialized searching procedures such as coordination. The introduction of machine-readable databases and automated searching techniques has not eliminated the need for this awareness. Rather, it has created a need for a different type of training in the use of new vocabularies, systems, and technologies.

The analysis of manual and computer-based searching techniques in this chapter merely scratches the surface of a complex subject which lies at the core of professional information handling. It is clear that "multiple-access file" means something radically different in the case of a machine-readable file searched online than in the case of a manually searched file. The great expansion of search capability introduced by the computer, particularly when used online, has its price. Although a larger average number of citations results from a given search when more sophisticated techniques and greater depth of indexing are used, there is also an increased risk both of retrieving documents irrelevant to the exact purposes of the search and of missing documents which are highly relevant.

The cliché "garbage in, garbage out" was applied early to the unthinking use of computer techniques for information processing, and is still a timely warning. New searching techniques for online data retrieval are the computer's most significant contribution to the practice of librarianship, but like all powerful technologies, they must be used with judgement and caution. The ability of the machine to search *efficiently* is trivial when compared with the ability of a competent information professional to search *effectively,* even in a manual file.

7

NAMES AS ACCESS POINTS

No matter how many or how few access points are made available for searching an item in a bibliographic file, a search for a single known item will always differ essentially from a search for anything in the file relevant to a particular person, body, subject, etc. An item which has already been partially identified by a citation, a verbal reference from a colleague, or a recollection of having previously seen it, is most easily and surely located in a list which provides natural search keys: access points taken directly from the wording in the item itself. On the other hand, a search for anything related to a given person, subject, etc., can only be accomplished with confidence in a list where "authority control," whether manual or automated, is in effect.

In the manual library catalogue composed in accordance with a cataloguing code, subject headings list, and classification scheme, there is only one type of natural access point, namely titles, filed under their first word not an article. All other access points are of the controlled-vocabulary type. Authority work for an online system does not simply consist of discovering every variant and linking them. It is still usually desirable to establish consistent forms so that the computer can most efficiently be programmed to find and alphabetize filing elements (surnames, etc.) for output display, and can most efficiently link any variant forms to a predictable base form of name for each person, body, work, etc.

This and the next chapter analyze the general problems in arriving at rules for controlled name and subject vocabularies. They also describe the criteria applied in solving these problems by twentieth-century library practices in the English-speaking world.

Name Authorities

A name is something which uniquely identifies (1) a person, (2) a nongovernment corporate body, (3) a location or geographic feature, (4) a government or an agency thereof, (5) a physical document, or (6) a work. Names are divided into these six categories for detailed examination in this chapter since they pose somewhat different problems. A name may be used as an access point for various purposes. A person may be an author, compiler, editor, illustrator, etc., of a work, or the subject of a work. A corporate body may be a sponsor, publisher, granting agency, authorizing body, or a subject. A work may be the subject of another work. Whether the access point is intended for an author/title catalogue or for a subject catalogue, the problems of naming and their solutions are exactly the same. It would be inadvisable to allow a name to appear in one form as, say, an author and in a different form as a subject.

Like the numbers (ISBNs, etc.) now often used to identify bibliographic items, names are in themselves *objective* data. A user may or may not know how to spell the surname of a particular "Smith" (Smythe?, Smithe?, Smyth?), or recall the precise name of the corporate body wanted (is it the "Department of Education," the "Ministry of Education," or the "Education Department"?), but in fact the particular name wanted has a determinable spelling or form, either in the legal sense or in the sense of what is preferred by the person or body.

The problems of using names as access points can be analyzed as follows:

1) *determining* what name or names have been used to identify a particular person, body, place, etc.
2) if there is more than one such name, *selecting* one to act as a principal identifier
3) *formulating* the characters of the chosen name in such a way that it can most readily be distinguished from other names and alphabetized in a file which includes many names
4) *linking* the selected name or form with other names or forms which might reasonably be sought by users looking for the same person, body, etc.)

Scope of the Problem

The names of most persons and works need never offer the user or the librarian any trouble. Statistical counts have consistently shown that more than sixty percent of the persons whose names appear in a catalogue as authors are so represented for only *one* work each. Similarly, the vast majority of all works never appear in more than *one* publication or edition, with *one* title. It is only a very small percentage of the individual persons or works which give rise to any difficulty. On the other hand, corporate bodies, serial publications, and "world classics" attract bibliographic chaos by their very nature. Special precautions are wisely taken when dealing with any of these, and library cataloguing rules have always required them.

Unfortunately, it is never possible to predict on first encounter whether any given person, location, body, work, or publication will later prove to be a problem case or not. A self-contained one-shot bibliography can ignore potential future problems. A library catalogue cannot since new entries are always being incorporated. Any library catalogue is also larger than most bibliographies, contains many times the number of potentially conflicting name headings, includes names of all periods and cultures, and is compiled over an indefinite time period by many different cataloguers. Not only is every newly established heading inevitably affected by every heading already in the catalogue, it is also linked to every heading yet to be established.

Searching for the Facts about a Name

The most difficult part of authority work is not the actual application of the cataloguing rules, but the prior reference work: the search for all the ways in which a given person, etc., has ever been identified. Only then can a particular cataloguing rule be applied to the remaining three steps of selecting, formulating, and linking the established access point. The reference search is ideally exhaustive, but its extent must be tempered in practice by pragmatic considerations. The reasonable cataloguer searches bibliographic, biographic, and directory sources in order to determine whether or not a problem exists with the name in question, but also knows when to give up if no problem surfaces. One of the sources searched will inevitably be bibliographic lists prepared by other agencies, particularly those which follow the same cataloguing code. After all, libraries adhere to standard cataloguing codes in part so that name access points will be the same in their catalogues. This is an economy for the cataloguing staffs and a benefit for searchers who use many different libraries.

The Library of Congress has been not only the principal author of the codes most widely used in the English-speaking world, but also the principal applier of these rules to real situations. It is to that institution that others tend to look for the accomplishment of the reference search which must precede rule application. One does not have to go to Washington D.C. to discover what decision the cataloguers at the Library of Congress have made with regard to a given name. These decisions are evident in the heading(s) on its bibliographic records, which are so readily accessible. However, the entries do not show the reasons for, or all the sources of, the decision in favour of the established form. Nor do they reveal in any one place all the cross-references which were considered desirable. In 1974 the Library of Congress began to publish its complete name authority decisions and accompanying cross-references, as recorded in its own Descriptive Cataloging Division processing files. Since then, the National Library of Canada and the British Library also began publication of their name authority files, in whole or in part.[1]

It is a principal tenet of the programme of Universal Bibliographic Control that a national bibliographic agency in the country of origin of the name is the ideal locale for conducting that reference search and then establishing the catalogue heading.[2] The three institutions named above are working toward a common authority control system in which the Canadian and British agencies will be entirely responsible for the forms of names originating in their countries. Part of the system has been functioning for some time already; the National Library of Canada has since 1976 established every name form for a Canadian corporate body in the Library of Congress database.

Cataloguing Rules for Name Headings

Although cataloguing codes exist precisely to standardize access points, there are many different codes, hence practices will vary a little, or a lot, among them. The English-speaking world has been fairly closely knit in following a common code, but that code has not remained unchanged. The period from 1967 to 1981 was a period of major transition—from rules based on one philosophy of how names should be formulated as access points to rules based on a radically different philosophy. The results of the "old" practices will forever remain embodied in published bibliographies and in many library catalogues, and a knowledge of these practices is essential for any reference librarian. A cataloguer, too, must recognize old practices so that in applying the "new" rules any conflicts can be taken into account. The approach throughout this chapter is therefore as follows: (1) each type of problem is identified, (2) examples show something of the range of situations which the reference search might reveal, (3) valid criteria on which to base a solution are evaluated, and finally (4) the old and the new library cataloguing rules related to the problem

1. *Library of Congress Name Headings with References* (Washington: Library of Congress, 1974–), produced since 1979 in a cumulating microfiche version as *Name Authorities; CAN-MARC Authorities. Vedettes d'authorité CAN/MARC* (Ottawa: National Library of Canada, 1978–), cumulating microfiche format only; *BL/BSD Name Authority List* (London: British Library, Bibliographic Services Division, 1981–), cumulating microfiche format only. All three services are now computer-based, and therefore record decisions on a name established long ago only if it has been reconverted to machine-readable form.

2. Cf. Dorothy Anderson, *Universal Bibliographic Control, a Long Term Policy, a Plan for Action* (Pullach: Verlag Dokumentation, 1974), p. 57: "The solution to the problems of authors' names can only be found nationally not internationally"; also p. 59: "As with personal authors' names it is recommended that responsibility for establishing the authoritative form of names of corporate bodies rests with national bibliographic agencies."

are briefly described. Fuller details of application and subtleties of interpretation of these rules must be left to other texts.

The old rules are the rules for name headings in Cutter's *Rules for a Dictionary Catalog,* and in all the cataloguing codes which stand in direct descent from Cutter. In the English-speaking world, these are (1) the so-called Joint Code of 1908, (2) its 1941 preliminary second edition, and (3) the 1949 second edition. The first of these was published and widely adopted in both North America and the United Kingdom. The last was published and widely adopted only in North America. The first two also incorporated rules for description (see Chapter 5); the last did not.[3]

The new rules are those which derive from the twelve principles subscribed to by the International Conference on Cataloguing Principles held in Paris in October 1961.[4] The general English-language codes whose rules for name headings follow the Paris Principles are the two editions of the *Anglo-American Cataloguing Rules,* published in 1967 (AACR1) and 1978 (AACR2).[5] Both editions have been widely translated and imitated in non-English-speaking areas, and other cataloguing codes conforming to the Paris Principles have been written. Committees of IFLA have also issued a number of both general and more specific guidelines for the formulation of name headings conforming to the Paris Principles in the hope that they will foster increasing international standardization.[6] Conformity to the Paris Principles is thus the cornerstone of reasonable conformity among the various current codes and guidelines for name access points.

3. *Catalog Rules, Author and Title Entries,* compiled by committees of the American Library Association and the (British) Library Association (Chicago: American Library Association, 1908) [also published as *Catalogue Rules . . .* (London: Library Association, 1908)]; *A.L.A. Cataloging Rules, Author and Title Entries,* prepared by the Catalog Code Revision Committee, American Library Association, and a committee of the (British) Library Association, Preliminary American 2nd ed. (Chicago: American Library Association, 1941); and *A.L.A. Cataloging Rules for Author and Title Entries,* prepared by the Division of Cataloging and Classification of the American Library Association, 2nd ed. (Chicago: American Library Association, 1949).

4. International Conference on Cataloguing Principles, Paris, 9th–18th October, 1961, *Report* (London: 1963), pp. 91–96. (This report was republished in 1981 by the IFLA International Office for UBC in London.) Useful interpretations are found in *Statement of Principles Adopted at the International Conference on Cataloguing Principles, Paris, October, 1961,* Annotated edition with commentary and examples by Eva Verona [et al.] (London: IFLA Committee on Cataloguing, 1971).

5. AACR1 was published separately in a "North American Text" by the American Library Association and a "British Text" by the Library Association. The two are not identical. The North American text departed deliberately from the Paris Principles by including some "exceptions" designed to mitigate the economic problems of fully adopting the principles embodied in that code. Both editions of AACR include rules for description as well as for access points.

6. For example, *List of Uniform Titles for Liturgical Works of the Latin Rites of the Catholic Church,* 2nd ed., 1981; *Form and Structure of Corporate Headings,* 1980; *List of Uniform Headings for Higher Legislative and Ministerial Bodies in European Countries,* 2nd ed. rev., 1979; *Anonymous Classics, a List of Uniform Headings for European Literatures,* 1978. All are published in London by the IFLA International Office for UBC.

Persons

A person may be identified by any one, or any combination, of the following:

1) the complete personal name as given by the parents and legally registered in an office of vital statistics (Mary Roberta Smith)
2) one or more titles (The Marchioness of Bucktooth; Prime Minister of Lower Slobbovia)
3) any kind of abbreviation of any of the above (Mary R. Smith; M. Roberta Smith; M.R. Smith; Lady Bucktooth; The P.M.)
4) one or more nicknames, known to many or to few (Bobbie; Buckie; Cuddles)
5) one or more pseudonyms (names designed to conceal identity) (Agent 009; M.R.S.; Jane Doe)
6) any name which represents a formal change from a previous name (Mrs. John Young; The Duchess of Worcester).

In the course of an ordinary lifetime, any person is almost certain to use and/or to be known by quite a number of different names. There is a time and an occasion for each. A significant number of persons identified in bibliographic lists appear in their own works or in reference sources under various names and/or under various forms of name. Many women still change name on marriage. Legal changes of name are announced in some numbers in every newspaper. In a number of countries, people still acquire and renounce titles of nobility, or receive terms of honorific address. Many writers and performers use pseudonyms, sometimes more than one simultaneously. But the unstandardized use by a person of forms involving initials and other abbreviations has always constituted the most common problem area by far.

Choice of Name

Either of the following criteria for choosing a name from among the different names or name forms available (including fuller or abbreviated forms) is reasonable under certain circumstances:

1) Use the full official personal name as it would appear on the person's birth certificate or the person's most recent passport, preferring the latter if there has been any official change of name. However, if the person possesses a title conferred by legal authority, use the most recent title along with the personal name.

The principal advantages of the above solution are stability and objectivity. A heading once established is unlikely to be rendered obsolete, since a full official name is changed more rarely than any other form. There can be no doubt as to what the real name is once it has been found.

The principal disadvantages are that it can be time-consuming to discover the full official name of, say, "Dr. X.," or "J.L. Smith," and that the average searcher may not even readily recognize a person by the full official name, for example "Thomas Edward Lawrence" or "Samuel Langhorne Clemens."

> 2) Use the name found commonly, or most frequently, in publications by
> and/or about the person.

The advantages and disadvantages of this solution are of course the exact converse of the above. The average user approaching a list of names is most likely to remember what appears in a footnote citation, on a title page of a publication, or in a newspaper article or magazine story about the person sought. Such a form is also the one most likely to reflect the preferences of the person (T.E. Lawrence, Mark Twain), and therefore to be perpetuated in general usage.

The principal disadvantage of this approach is the instability of the resultant headings in the case of living persons whose "common identification" may continue to change. A person known by one name may come to be known by another, even though no official name change has occurred, particularly with respect to the use of initials as against full forms of given names.

The pattern of pre-Paris Principles (old) rules was to stipulate use of the full official name or title most recently held by the person, for example:

```
Sir Pelham Grenville Wodehouse
George Herman Ruth
Friedrich Hardenberg
```

The new rules, those conforming to the Paris Principles, require the heading to be based on the name, in the degree of fullness, which the person appears to prefer. This may be a name given at birth or acquired later, a title, a pseudonym, etc. For authors, principal evidences of such preference are statements of responsibility (see page 65) in publications by them issued in their own language. For others, the cumulative evidence of reference sources in their own language is the determinant. Thus, in the case of the three persons exemplified above:

```
P.G. Wodehouse
Babe Ruth
Novalis
```

The following represents a possible, if fortunately infrequent, situation: A first work of an author identifies the author as "John L. Smith." It is followed by two more works which represent the same author as "J.L. Smith." The person's fourth and fifth publications once again identify him as "John L. Smith," while four succeeding ones give the author's name as "John Llewellyn Smith." If a library acquires each of these publications in sequence and follows the new rule requiring the use of "most common form of name" in its strict mathematical force, then three successive and different forms of name must be established for the same person. The first book generates the heading "Smith, John L." After the third book has arrived, this must be changed to "Smith, J.L." The form "Smith, John L." is once again the correct form on the arrival of the fifth book. Finally "Smith, John Llewellyn" is required after the arrival of the ninth. If the library does not acquire all nine books, it is still necessary to discover what form of name appeared on the ones not acquired in order to apply this criterion adequately.

This possibility of unstable headings was one (but only one) of the reasons why the "full official name" criterion prevailed for so long in cataloguing rules. Lest a concern over this kind of situation counterbalance the advantages of the "common name" criterion, it must be remembered that most persons identified in bibliographic lists are not famous writers of many works whose lives have been well documented in common biographical sources. Most persons named in library catalogues are obscure authors of a single work, persons not readily found in biographical sources. Hence if the common-name criterion is followed, the form of name found in the item in hand at the time of cataloguing is normally permanently acceptable as a heading, and only a brief biographical search is needed to uncover possible pseudonyms, etc.[7] Thus from a practical point of view, it requires, on the average, a smaller reference effort to search for a commonly used form of name than for an official form.

Change of Name. A deliberate change of name is another matter. Common sense indicates that an immediate change of heading is desirable when, for example, Karol Wojtyła decides that his name will henceforth be Joannes Paulus Secundus. No matter how well known the name "Karol Wojtyła" has been, and even if it continues in occasional use, the later name will quickly replace it for most purposes. The same is normally also true when a married woman assumes a husband's surname, in cases of legal name change, acquisition of a title, etc.

Both old and new rules require the heading to be changed immediately on a formal change of name (for example, from Cassius Clay to Muhammad Ali). Either apathy or ignorance may delay implementation of such a change in a particular catalogue. Rules have always left some latitude for judgement, providing for the retention of an earlier name if it appears likely to remain the

7. This premise and its implications are explored in William Gray Potter, "When Names Collide: Conflict in the Catalog and AACR2," *Library Resources & Technical Services* 24 (winter 1980):3–16.

common identification of the person. Thus John Buchan's later name "Lord Tweedsmuir" would not be adopted as the heading under either old or new rules since he continued to write using the former name. Hindsight is the best instructor in this matter.

Language. When the European scholarly community was more international, an entire personal name was often translated. The seventeenth-century Flemish Scripture commentator Cornelius van den Steen published principally under the Latin form of his name (Cornelius a Lapide), but is also known by the Greek one (Cornelios Petros) and the French one (Corneille de la Pierre). Old rules never allowed translation of any element of a personal name, but required use of the name in the person's vernacular:

```
Juan de la Cruz
Quintus Horatius Flaccus
```

New rules make exception for a classical Roman and for a person who is not identified by a surname. If such a person commonly appears in English-language writings under an English form of name, then the English form is preferred as an access point:

```
John of the Cross
Horace
```

The language-related problem of romanization, or transliteration, may occur in any kind of name heading. It is discussed on pages 220–223.

Choice of Entry Element

In names of modern times, it is an almost universal convention that the *entry element* (the filing term in an alphabetic list) is the surname, or family name. This is followed by a mark of punctuation and the given name(s) (Smith, John Llewellyn). However,

1) once a name has been chosen according to the above criteria, it may prove not to contain a surname (Saint Catherine of Siena)
2) even if a surname exists, it is not necessarily the last separate unit of a name written in direct order (Hary Janos, Mao Tse-tung)
3) compound and/or prefixed surnames consist of more than one unit, leading to uncertainty as to which should serve as the entry element (Richard Dennis Hilton Smith, Karel ten Hoope).

An acquaintance with national usages is needed in order to recognize a surname as such. If the surname is in several separate parts, or does not exist, old and new practices are almost identical. Entry is under the first name, whatever its type, if there is no surname. In the case of compound surnames and surnames involving prefixes, the entry element is that under which the person's name would normally be alphabetized in formal lists in the person's own language. Again, one must know the standard usage in various languages, although the rules provide a brief guide by language.[8] Finally, when a title is the chosen name, the proper word in the title is the entry element, and the personal name is also included:

```
Halifax, E.F.L. Wood, 1st Earl of
```

Qualifier(s)

When two or more persons bear, or are known by, exactly the same name, cataloguing rules are based on the assumption that works by or about each separate person should not be mingled with works by or about the others. Therefore the heading for each person must be unique. There are several possible types of qualifiers which might be added to a name in order to effect this distinction: birth/death dates, occupation, place of residence, academic degrees, a qualification accompanying the name on title pages, etc. The qualifier which has always prevailed in cataloguing rules is the most objective and stable one, namely birth/death date(s), but the type of name heading may make another kind of qualifier a more obvious choice. When it is known what the initials in a name stand for, new rules allow these to be added as a qualifier:

```
predominant name:      J.L. Smith
heading (new rules):   Smith, J.L. (John Louis)
```

> Under old rules requiring the heading to be based on the full official name, such a heading was impossible. Any known full forms were incorporated within the heading as follows: Smith, John Louis. There is a considerable filing difference between this and the form above established under the new rules.

Since names not containing a surname are very likely to be common ones, both old and new rules prescribe the addition in every case of one or more of the following: an office, epithet, rank, status, etc.

```
John, King of England
John, of the Cross, Saint
```

8. National usages are analyzed in some detail in a publication which is in harmony with current cataloguing rules: *Names of Persons: National Usages for Entry in Catalogues,* 3rd ed. (London: IFLA Office for UBC, 1977); also a 1980 *Supplement.*

Nongovernment Corporate Bodies

A corporate body is a person or group of persons choosing to act as an entity under a name and identity other than that of a person. A modern-day corporate body which has been legally incorporated is easily recognizable. A government agency has approved the name of the body (having ascertained that it is distinctive and unambiguous for its purpose), and has caused it to be registered and published in an official gazette. However, for purposes of bibliographic control it is not possible to restrict the notion of a corporate name to one which is thus legally authorized, in at least two areas:

1) Corporate bodies breed separately identifiable subordinate units. A single sequence of all the material produced by the American Library Association, without subgrouping the material which emanates from each separate committee, division, round table, discussion group, etc., would not be a useful file for the knowledgeable user who identifies a topic or report with some named subunit of the association. Even if the "Subject Analysis Committee" is not a separate legal entity, it must be identifiable in an access point. Similarly, in referring to a publication by or about the Library of Vancouver Community College, the library must be identified, not the college as a whole, and not the college's hierarchical superior, the Ministry of Education of the provincial government.

2) Since access points exist to make material available under names which searchers use naturally and recognize, a cataloguing code must provide for the naming of quasi-corporate ad hoc bodies such as conferences, fairs, projects, etc., despite the problems of doing so. Was the world's fair "Expo 67" a different corporate body than that which signed contracts and paid bills on behalf of the fair, the "Canadian Corporation for the 1967 World Exhibition?" Whether it was or not, it must be possible to name the two separately in a catalogue since each is responsible for its own quite different kind of publication.

What Is a Corporate Name?

The key to whether a corporate body exists for cataloguing purposes is therefore not what the body can do or what its legal status is, but simply whether or not it bears something which can be considered a name. Recognizing a name as such on a title page, etc., is a matter of interpreting linguistic style and intent, much like recognizing a title as such, a problem discussed on pages 56–62.

Names of corporate bodies commonly consist of a mixture of subject words, generic terms, proper words (often including one or more words designating some geographic location), grammatical links, articles, etc., such as 5th Annual Symposium on the Effects of Air Pollution in Coastal Areas; College of Physicians and Surgeons of British Columbia; National Council for Educational Technology. The casual searcher may not be conscious of where a corporate name begins and where it ends, particularly when it contains no proper words, but only common-word elements. Even title-page presentations of corporate names are not always unequivocal. Today, a name is often presented within a typographic design or a grammatical construction which obscures its elements or even its identity.

Formal presentation in isolation, and the use of full or initial capital letters, definite articles, etc., are aids to identifying a name as such. By definition, a name is a *specifying* appellation, in contrast to a generic reference to the existence of something. It need not, of course, be unique to be a specifying appellation. "Mary Smith" is a name, but "the girl who lives next door" is not. "Californians for Lower Taxes" is a corporate name, but "Citizens of California" is not. "Bureau of the Budget" is a name, but "the office that looks after budget preparation" is not. The dividing line becomes very subtle in the case of conferences, meetings, etc. The formally presented wording "Conference on the Analysis of Brain Waves" is accepted by the new cataloguing rules as a name, but the wording "a conference on . . .," especially if presented in grammatical connection with other elements, is not.

An individual corporate body may be identified by one or more of the following types of name:

1) the name under which it is officially incorporated by letters patent or other legal means (The Canadian-American Railway Corporation)
2) any abbreviation thereof, including any acronym however fanciful (CanAmRail; CANARY)—some of these have legal or quasi-legal status; others are only used informally
3) any translation of one of the above types of name, whether it has legal status (as of an officially bilingual body: La Société internationale des chemins-de-fer; SIC), or is merely used for convenience in referring to the body in foreign places (Kanadisch-amerikanische Bahnlinie)
4) one or more names which represent changes from previous names, as distinct from variant forms used simultaneously (International Transportation Inc.; Intrans).

Choice of Name

Cataloguing rules have always attempted to apply roughly the same criteria to the choice of name for a corporate body as to the choice of name for a person. Thus the old rules called for the heading "European Atomic Energy Community" (the full official form), while the new require "Euratom" (the form commonly found in publications of the body and reference sources). The names of corporate bodies cannot, however, be treated entirely the same as those of persons: corporate names which are changed, which exist in more than one language, or which appear in the abbreviated form called an acronym are special problems.

Change of Name. Changes of corporate names are increasingly frequent. When a person changes name, there is no doubt that it is the same person before and after the change, and consequently that only one name should represent that person in a controlled vocabulary. However, when a corporate body changes its name, it is often because the body has become something different and/or wishes to project a new image. Many name changes result from a change of purpose or constitution, from a merger with another body or a split from one, etc.

When a name change occurs, should continuity of the body be preserved in the list, with a single heading representing the body before and after the change? Or is it more reasonable to say arbitrarily that any change in a body's name means that a different corporate body has come into existence, with the result that the old and the new name are both established (linked of course by cross-references in both directions)? If the first choice is adopted, is it better to change all existing headings to the new name (a time-consuming operation) or to continue the use of the old heading for new material? There is no way of judging objectively how much change has taken place in the nature of the body, or quantitatively how much the name has changed; hence such judgements are not valid criteria in deciding whether one heading or two should be used.

Old rules required use of the *most recent* name of a body. Thus when the name of Long Beach State College was changed to California State University, Long Beach, all access points to it were to be revised. This proved on the whole to be so impracticable that the old rule was breached perhaps more than observed long before it was officially changed. Major institutions like the Library of Congress attempted to follow the rule to the letter. Even then, when a body did more than merely change its name (for example splitting or merging in a complex way), an ad hoc judgement was necessarily made as to whether old headings should be retained.

New rules require that *any* corporate name change be considered as the termination of a former body and the creation of a new one. Thus both "Long Beach State College" and "California State University, Long Beach" are acceptable headings, linked by "see also" cross-references (see page 183). This is not, of course, a trouble-free solution. Works *about* corporate bodies typically deal with a body both before and after a name change. The subject heading applied is therefore logically the latest name borne by the body during the coverage of the work in hand.

Language. The official existence of two or more language-forms of the same corporate name is frequent as international bodies proliferate, and as bilingual and multilingual countries encourage or even enforce the practice. Which name should take precedence? A name in the language of the jurisdiction where the body is incorporated? An English name, if one exists? The name which happens to occur first, or most frequently, in the body's publications or in other sources?

Another problem is that the use of semi-official or even unauthorized translations of a corporate name is endemic as bodies produce, and are referred to in, publications around the world. Should translation be allowed? That is, should a name which is found commonly in the body's publications in one language form (Deutsche Bundesbahn) be translated (German National Railways) in a catalogue to be used by English-speaking people? Should a body of international nature (for example the United Nations or the Catholic Church) be treated differently from a national or local body?

Neither old nor new rules allow translation of a corporate name, except as an alternative for small nonscholarly libraries used by a largely unilingual clientele. However, if a body officially has and displays a name in English, as well as one or more in other languages, the English name has always been preferred for use in an English-language catalogue.

Acronyms. Many would say that the use of acronyms and other abbreviated forms has gone entirely out of control. The acronym is a relatively modern phenomenon, but already names are frequently chosen solely as a basis for catchy acronyms. Cataloguing rules have only recently caught up with such practices and treated them as part of the mainstream of naming. Old rules generally ignored any brief form of a corporate name, preferring the full form. The first edition of AACR preferred most brief forms, but only permitted the use of an acronym if it could be found in print in upper/lower case letters ("Unesco" was acceptable as a heading, but not "AFL/CIO"). AACR2 treats an acronym as it does any other name, prescribing its use whatever its form, if it is the common or predominant identification of the body.

Choice of Entry Element

The selection of the element under which to file a corporate name has been the single most troublesome problem in the entire history of cataloguing. Attempt after attempt has been made to find a solution which would apply over the whole range of corporate names, would be easily grasped by catalogue users, and might become as instinctive as the location of personal headings under surnames. This has proved to be an impossible dream. There are simply too many complexities and different patterns found among the names themselves. In fact these complexities are multiplying rather than disappearing as corporate naming patterns continue to change. The result both of bibliographers' theorizing and of the many pragmatic solutions adopted since the mid-nineteenth century has unfortunately been a number of conflicting methods, each of which is now entrenched in various major bibliographic services.

The reasonable possibilities for choosing an entry element for a corporate name include (1) direct entry, (2) entry under the name of a hierarchically superior body, and (3) entry under a place name. Each of these must be separately examined.

Direct Entry. This would seem the only possible criterion since a corporate body has no "surname." Both old and new rules enter most independent corporate bodies in this way:

```
Council on Library Resources
American Association for the Advancement
    of Science
```

This is entirely in keeping with natural catalogue inquiry approaches, provided the body has a distinctive name and is not connected with a government.

Many a corporate name includes as its first element a personal name in direct order, for example "The R.J. Young Tractor Co." Rules before AACR2 required the personal surname to be the filing element: "Young (R.J.) Tractor Co." AACR2 abandoned this exceptional treatment of a corporate name as if it were a personal name. It requires the direct form.

Entry under the Name of a Higher Body in the Hierarchy. As noted on page 198, hierarchically subordinate bodies must be identified in bibliographic lists separately from their superior bodies. Corporate bodies at higher levels in hierarchies usually have names which include some uniquely distinguishing feature. At a subordinate level, the body's name may also be entirely distinctive, not implying in itself any hierarchical relationship. For example, the Vancouver Vocational Institute is a part of Vancouver Community College, and the Canadian Association of College and University Libraries is a part of the Canadian Library Association. More frequently, however, the name of a body at a lower hierarchical level is nondistinctive, often only a string of generic terms. For example, "The Library" is another part of Vancouver Community College. Such naming tends to imply dependence; it has the linguistic effect of focusing attention less on the lower-level body with such a name, than on some higher-level body whose name might help give it identity. Anyone would suspect from the nature of the name "The Library" that a subordinate unit of that same name is a part of any number of educational institutions. Similarly, a body named "Department of Finance" is a part of The University of British Columbia; but such a body is also a part of the federal government of Canada, of many other governments, and of myriad private companies.

A very high proportion of all corporate bodies are in some way subordinate. Fortunately, the problem of indistinctive naming only occurs in the private sector when the subordination is total (that is, when the higher body entirely controls the lower), and not always even then. There are innumerable bodies which are partly owned and controlled by each of several higher bodies, but in these cases the subordinate body invariably has a distinctive name. For example, Kelly, Douglas & Co. Ltd. is two-thirds controlled by Loblaw Companies Ltd., almost all the remainder being in the hands of Miss F.M. Douglas. A searcher looking for a Kelly, Douglas annual report would not be likely to go to "Loblaw Companies Ltd." in an alphabetically arranged file. Nor is it likely that a search for a policy statement of the Library and Information Technology Association would begin under the heading "American Library Association," even though LITA is wholly a part of ALA and can legally bind the parent body through some of its actions. Both these names are distinctive.

On the other hand, who would look for "Faculty of Law" or for "Friends of the Library" under F? The instinctive reaction is which university's "Faculty of Law?" the "Friends" of which library? Such a reaction leads to a first search under the name of the university or of the library, not under the name of the faculty or the friends group. If this quite reasonable strategy is to be rewarded, a two- (or more-) part heading is needed. The first part, the *main heading,* is not the name of the body in question, but rather that of a hierarchically superior body. The last part, the *subheading,* names the body for which the entire access point is being established:[9]

> Queen's University. Faculty of Law

The major difficulty posed by considering subordination as a factor is that of deciding how to define subordination for cataloguing purposes. One can consider

1) whether the body *is* subordinate on some organizational chart (but is it reasonable to expect that users should discover that Loblaw Companies Ltd. is itself a part of George Weston Ltd.?)
2) whether the body's *activity* is typically a subordinate activity, for example the activity of a teaching faculty, of a research and development division, etc. (but how does one define a subordinate activity?)
3) whether the *name* of the body has in itself some linguistic element of dependency, for example "Division," "Section," etc. (but some subordinate bodies have dependent names, for example "University Library," while others of the same kind have entirely distinctive and nondependent names, for example "Widener Library").

9. A main heading is simply the first part of a heading which includes a subheading, as shown in the examples here. This term has nothing to do with the concept of a main entry heading, for which see pages 217–220.

In dealing with subordinate bodies, old rules required one to consider the type or function of the body, rather than the name in itself, that is, the first two criteria immediately above. In some specified types of hierarchy, the name of a subordinate body automatically became a subheading; in others, subordinate units were entered independently. For example, subsidiary business firms were entered directly, but units of educational institutions generally were not. The heading for the "Widener Library" was

```
Harvard University. Widener Library
```

despite the distinctiveness of the library's name. Over the years, many ad hoc exceptions were made to the original old rule.

The new rules ask the cataloguer to judge whether a subordinate body's name is distinctive enough to be approached in isolation from the name of any higher body (the third criterion above). If so, it is entered directly, as is the name of any independent body:

```
Widener Library
Canadian Association of College and University
    Libraries
```

If, on the other hand, the name of the subordinate body *as a name* contains some element of dependency on the name of a higher body, the name of that higher body is established as the main heading, with the name of the subordinate body as a subheading, as shown in the following four examples in slightly differing applications:

```
1) name of subordinate body:  School of Librarianship
   higher bodies:  1) Faculty of Arts
                   2) The University of British Columbia
   heading:  University of British Columbia. School of
             Librarianship
```

The middle element of the hierarchy does not figure in the heading. It cannot be the entry element itself, and it is not needed to identify or to distinguish the school's name as a part of the university.

```
2) name of subordinate body:  Admissions Committee
   higher bodies:  1) Faculty of Law
                   2) Queen's University
   heading:  Queen's University. Faculty of Law.
             Admissions Committee
```

In this case the middle element of the hierarchy is required since there are many Admissions Committees within Queen's University.

```
3) name of subordinate body:  Yale University Library
   higher body:  Yale University
   heading:  Yale University. Library
```

The name of this subordinate body contains within itself the whole name of the higher body. Its heading takes the form of a main heading naming that higher body formally, plus a subheading naming the subordinate body, that is, "Yale University. Yale University Library," but with the redundancy eliminated. The rules suppose that this kind of name is more likely to be sought as a subordinate name within the group of entries naming the higher body. The period before "Library" accomplishes this grouping under most older filing rules and also the current Library of Congress rules (see page 331). If the list is alphabetized according to a rule such as the 1980 American Library Association rule, however (see page 330), the period will be ignored in filing, and the grouping will not occur.

```
4) name of subordinate body:  35th General Meeting of the
                                 Bibliographic Society
   higher body:  The Bibliographic Society
   heading:  Bibliographic Society. General Meeting[10]
```

This condition is the same as that in item 3 above; the name of the higher-level body is contained within the name of the lower-level body for which the heading is being established. One cannot logically have one rule for establishing the heading when the higher body's name is at the beginning of the name of the subordinate body, and another when it is within or at the end of that name. Either positioning is possible in various languages.

Fortunately, the way subordinate bodies are named in reality ensures that the great majority of nongovernment subordinate bodies receive the same headings whether old or new rules are used.

Entry under a Place Name. Certain types of corporate body are closely identified with the locality within which they render a service. For example, the following are all names of public libraries in the predominant forms found in their own publications:

> The Borough of Etobicoke Public Library
> Carnegie Library of Pittsburgh
> The Fraser-Hickson Institute
> The Free Library of Philadelphia
> Greenwich Library
> Indianapolis-Marion County Public Library
> Kirn Memorial Library
> The Library Association of Portland
> Portage La Prairie City Library
> Prairie Crocus Regional Library
> War Memorial Library

10. The name of any conference or meeting is further structured to indicate its number, place, and date following the name. See Qualifiers, page 208.

One of these names has no apparent keyword likely to stand out in memory, and one of them does not designate the type of institution. But the others, the more traditional types, contain some proper term, a geographic or personal name to remember. Some contain more than one.

It has often been argued that a person searching a directory or catalogue for one of these bodies is unlikely to remember, or even to know, the precise name of the body accurately, but does remember the place named and the type of institution. How certain is the average user whether the name of any given art gallery is "[Place] Art Gallery," or "Art Gallery of [Place]," or even "[Name] Art Gallery of [Place]?" As with the naming of subordinate units, linguistic patterns strongly influence the structuring of such a name, though without ensuring a completely uniform sequence of elements. For example, the first of the three structures in the art gallery example is more common in English, the second in French. In any case, it is the keyword which is memorable.

Old rules divided corporate bodies into two types: societies, and institutions. Societies offered few problems. Their names were established directly, as they are under new rules:

> Vancouver Opera Association

Institutions were defined as bodies dependent upon a physical plant and therefore likely to be permanently fixed in location (educational institutions, galleries, theatres, museums, churches, hospitals, prisons, libraries, laboratories, radio and television stations, etc.). The old-rule heading for an "institution" was its name, in direct order, if the name begins with a proper word other than a place name:

> Yale University
> Enoch Pratt Free Library
> Mendel Art Gallery

Otherwise, the name of the institution was filed as a subheading of the name of the place (municipality) where it functions:

> London, Ont. University of Western Ontario
> Paris. Musée nationale du Louvre
> Akron, Ohio. Public Library[11]

When Cutter prescribed that such a corporate body be entered under the name of the municipality in which it is located, the rule was fairly simple and made good sense. "Local place name" had a meaning uncomplicated by modern jurisdictional patterns; it was possible to define a place-oriented body both

---

11. Like "Yale University. Library" above, this is actually "Akron, Ohio. Akron Public Library," but with the redundancy removed.

by the nature of its operations and the nature of its usual naming. Significant problems arose only gradually, but the following eventually led to the realization that the whole basis for entry under a place name was less and less relevant to newly established corporate names:

1) "place," which in the old rules clearly meant "city," "town," or "village," might now mean a region, a taxation district, a metropolitan area, or even a very vaguely defined geographic territory (Cariboo-Thompson Nicola Regional Library)
2) the service area of many institutions is less rigidly defined by a single geographic or political unit whatever its name (Greater Victoria Public Library)
3) a body of the kind in question is no longer so likely to have a name consisting only of a place name plus a description of the kind of body it is (Prairie Crocus Regional Library).

As these complexities arose, the original rule was successively patched up with more and more exceptions intended to ensure that the basic premise would still operate, while minimizing its most undesirable side effects. By the time rules for place entry disappeared from active use, the basic rule had been modified by exceptions, exceptions to exceptions, and even one exception to an exception to an exception![12]

Under new rules, no nongovernment body is entered under the name of the place in which it exists. All are entered directly under the body's name unless a question of subordination to another body (see pages 202–205) is at issue:

```
University of Western Ontario
Musée nationale du Louvre
Akron Public Library
```

This means that any heading formulated according to AACR2 which consists of a subheading following a place name must represent a government agency (see pages 210–213).

Qualifier(s)

As in the case of headings for persons, headings for corporate bodies must be made unique. When more than one body bears the same name, added qualifiers distinguish them. The most usual are (1) the place where the body functions and (2) an institutional or other affiliation.

```
Loyola University (Chicago)
Loyola University (Montreal)
Newman Club (University of British Columbia)
Newman Club (York University)
```

12. See the analysis in Leonard Jolley, *The Principles of Cataloguing* (London: Crosby, Lockwood, 1960), pp. 72–97.

Qualifiers are often used with corporate names for an additional reason, namely to help identify the body. Thus rules have always permitted the option of including a place or other qualifier whether or not uniqueness of the heading is at issue. In some cases, a qualifier is useful simply to clarify that it is a corporate body being named:

Guess Who (Musical group)

Conferences. In the case of conference names, a qualifier is always required by the rules. Many such names are unique, but this cannot be predicted: a successful "Symposium on XX" is quite likely to be followed by a "Second Symposium on XX." It is also true that many users are as likely to "recognize" a conference by its place and/or date as by its name alone. For these reasons, both old and new rules require the formulation of a heading including, as relevant, the number, date, and place of the conference:

Ferring Symposium on Brain and Pituitary
Peptides (1979 : Munich)

> Old rules used different punctuation, and put the date after the place.

Locations and Geographic Features

A geographic name is used as an access point (1) to identify a location per se, and (2) in most cases to identify the government which holds jurisdiction over the geographic territory so named. A particular geographic location or feature may be identified by any one, or any combination, of the following:

1) a name assigned to it by tradition or by an official agency in the jurisdiction in which it is located (for example by the Canadian Permanent Committee on Geographic Names in the case of a Canadian place)
2) a name assigned to it by an official agency in some other jurisdiction (for example by the United States' Board on Geographic Names, which prescribes geographic names for locations the world over for use in the United States civil service)
3) one or more translations of an official or traditional name, as found in a gazetteer or other reference source in any language (Londres, Munich)
4) any name which represents a formal change from a previous name (Ho Chi-Minh City, formerly Saigon).

The problem of differing language-forms is particularly troublesome in the case of locations and geographic features. If it is wholly within a unilingual political jurisdiction, a place normally has only one official or traditional form of name, but all or part of it may be translated in reference sources in other places. The Chinese call it "Huanghe" (黄河), but in many English-language gazetteers it is found only under "Yellow River." The word "Bay" appears in gazetteers as "anse," "Bahia," "chong," "Haff," "juras licis," "ko," "vuopio," "wan," etc.

In bilingual jurisdictions there may be two or more equally official forms, for example "Svizzera," "Schweiz," "Suisse," and "Confoederatio Helvetica;" or "Louvain" and "Leuven." A large proportion of the best-known geographic features do not belong to any single jurisdiction; hence the name "Atlantisches Meer" is just as legitimate as "Océan atlantique," "Mar atlantico," or even "大西洋." Increased travel and familiarity with foreign place names mean that fewer geographic names are translated now than in the past, but the problem will long remain.

Both old and new English-language cataloguing rules prescribe the use of an English form of a geographic name if a common one is found in English-language reference sources. This is a principal area where international uniformity of headings can never be achieved, and where links in machine searching systems can be particularly helpful.

Governments and Government Agencies

In the 1850s, Charles Coffin Jewett firmly entrenched both the practice of considering a government agency as a corporate body for the purposes of establishing access points, and the practice of formulating its name in most instances as a subheading under a geographic name representing the jurisdiction. For example, "France," "Rhode Island," "Paso Robles, California," and "West Vancouver" are the names commonly used in catalogues for the governments whose official names are, respectively, "République française," "State of Rhode Island and Providence Plantations," "City of El Paso de Robles," and "Corporation of the Municipal District of West Vancouver." To prefer the geographic name to the formal one as the most convenient access point is to solve only half the problem. The other half is to decide what *is* the government in question. Wars between countries change boundaries, and civil wars change governmental forms. Even within peaceful states, the geographic extent and the naming of local jurisdictions are not as stable as they once were.

Counties and municipalities are fairly autonomous units in the United States. There have been few changes in two centuries which would radically affect headings for such jurisdictions, though of course there have been many additions. The need for regional and other larger-base services has largely been met by the establishment of single-purpose corporate bodies responsible to two or more jurisdictions, for example the "Twin Cities Metropolitan Planning Commission" composed of members from St. Paul and from Minneapolis.

In the United Kingdom and Canada, on the contrary, municipalities are the creatures of a higher level of government, which has not hesitated in recent years to change municipal structures, functions, naming, and boundaries. Total municipal reorganization in the United Kingdom in the early 1970s led to the abolition of many local governments and their replacement by others with different names and boundaries. For example, the new Dyfed County covers much but not all of the territory of the old Cardiganshire plus some territory formerly in other counties.

Municipalities in Canada are under the control of provincial governments, some of which have sporadically moved to impose an additional level of government upon those already existing. In some instances all the previous jurisdictions have remained intact (though with changed powers) within the new framework; in others, previous jurisdictions have disappeared as they did in the United Kingdom. For example, the Municipality of Metropolitan Toronto was originally a level of government additional to the cities, townships, and counties previously existing; but when the city of Mississauga was created, it obliterated the political existence of the former villages of Malton, Streetsville, etc.

As new jurisdictions have come into existence in any country, they are not always assigned familiar types of geographic names. "Mississauga" is an unequivocal geographic/jurisdiction name; but "Metropolitan Toronto" may be understood either as a specific political unit with clear boundaries and powers, or merely as a vaguely defined market- or population-area (as such a term implies in the United States).

New rules governing headings for jurisdictions rely on the usage of the locality and the evidence of local gazetteers. This is another good argument for the principle that name authority work is best done in the jurisdiction where the name occurs (see page 191). As might be expected, geographic gazetteers are compiled for the purpose of naming places, not governments, and have been slow to recognize new kinds of jurisdiction naming. Metropolitan Toronto is now listed under M in the Ontario volume of the *Gazetteer of Canada,* but Capital Regional District is still not to be found under C, or anywhere, in the British Columbia volume.

Government Agencies

In governments at all levels, everything is hierarchically organized. Name and function changes are even more frequent than in the private sector. Many governments restructure bureaucracies regularly and are ready to capitalize on the image fostered by new and progressive-sounding names. There has also occurred during the past decade a gradual abandonment of dependent types of name such as "Department of Cultural Affairs" and "Law Reform Commission.'' Many of these are giving way to distinctive names which incorporate the name of the government in one way or another, such as ''Alberta Culture,'' ''Statistics Canada,'' ''Connecticut Real Estate Commission.'' As this practice becomes the norm in more and more jurisdictions, it is having a profound influence in changing the way the average user identifies and refers to government agencies since acronyms and keyword identification are following this trend to include a specifying element.

Locating a government agency in an alphabetic list has always proved very difficult for the average untrained searcher. Many lists other than library catalogues provide an entirely separate index of government agency names. For example, telephone directories routinely list them on differently coloured paper at the beginning or end of the alphabet, or all under G for ''Government,'' or all under the proper name of the jurisdiction. This focuses attention on the problem of defining whether or not a body *is* a government agency. For example, is a government-owned airline to be included in the section of the directory containing other government agencies or not? Differences in attitudes and expectations will be obvious between free enterprise societies and more socialized systems, but a deep penetration of government into perhaps unexpected areas of corporate activity is a fact of modern life everywhere.

The major problems associated with entering government bodies as subheadings under the names of jurisdictions (countries, provinces, cities, etc.) are:

1) Should every government agency be entered subordinately or only some? If the latter, where is the line to be drawn?
2) Should the entire hierarchy be shown in the heading, so that agencies are grouped according to their bureaucratic organization, or should the heading be kept as brief as possible? That is, in the following hypothetical hierarchy:

```
Canada
Department of Agriculture
Production and Marketing Branch
Poultry Division
Turkey Section
Egg Unit
```

how many levels should be named in the heading for the Egg Unit? The filing order is very much affected by this decision since there are normally many entries under the name of a jurisdiction.

In response to both issues, the searcher or cataloguer must first consult the relevant government organization manual as a guide to the existence and naming of agencies. Most modern governments at every level publish and frequently revise such a directory. Both old and new rules treat governments and their agencies according to roughly the same principles as they treat other subordinate bodies. This means that under old rules the function of the body was the usual determinant of the heading, whereas under new rules the nature of the name is intended to be the usual determinant.

Old rules routinely entered executive functions of a government subordinately, for example:

> United States. Southern Forest Experiment Station
> Canada. Royal Canadian Mounted Police

As government activity has proliferated, cataloguing rules have increasingly restricted what is to be entered as subdivisions of a government, the intent being to disperse agencies with distinctive names throughout the alphabet and to limit what is to be filed under the geographic name. Government bodies which carry out the legislative, judicial, military, and highest-level executive functions are still always established subordinately, no matter how distinctive are their names:

> Alberta. Alberta Culture

> This is a major cabinet-level agency.

> Israel. Knesset
> Canada. Royal Canadian Air Force

However, under AACR2 any other government agency is only established as a subheading under the name of the government if its name is indistinctive in character:

> United States. Federal Bureau of Investigation

> However well known the body, the name is defined as not distinctive, since it contains a word implying subordination (Bureau), and no proper element.

> Royal Canadian Mounted Police

> This name is considered distinctive because it contains a proper word (Canadian).

With regard to how much of the hierarchy should appear in the heading, old rules tended to include more than new rules permit:

> old: United States. Dept. of Agriculture. Dairy Division
> new: United States. Dairy Division

> There is only one body named "Dairy Division" in the United States federal government.

The former practice of establishing the names of many nongovernment institutions as subheadings under place names was described on pages 205–207. It caused increasing confusion vis-à-vis the appearance of government agencies under the same local place names, or in patterns which *looked* like examples of entry under a place name. In theory, the heading "Michigan. University," established under old rules for the University of Michigan located in Ann Arbor, was an instance of entry under the name of the controlling government (the state of Michigan). However, the similarly structured former heading "Oxford. University" for the University of Oxford (a private institution at the time) is an instance of entry under the name of the municipality in which the institution is located.

These two examples only scratch the surface of an exceedingly complex situation in the history of post-Cutter, pre-AACR2 cataloguing rules. It is impossible to explain briefly the reasoning behind a long sequence of practices arising out of these two principles. In the aftermath of the Paris Principles, the attempt to preserve a keyword approach to corporate names persisted in North American practice for a time. In addition, the practice of superimposition (see pages 224–225), almost universal in North America until 1980, further confused matters. Perhaps it suffices to repeat that according to AACR2 the only subheadings which may appear under a place name are the names of some of the agencies of the government of that place.

Documents, or Publications

A document is, simply, an "item" as defined for cataloguing purposes (see pages 91–92). A published item existing in many copies is a document, but so is a unique manuscript. The primary name of any individual document is its title proper, the beginning of Area 1 of its description according to ISBD. The document may bear additional titles recorded in Area 1, Area 6, or Area 7; for example a parallel title, a series title, or a cover title. Traditional practice in both library catalogues and printed bibliographies which provide multiple access is to trace each such title (that is, to make it an access point) but normally only under its first word other than an article.

The casual user often fails to recognize that any such title access point is intended only to identify the one particular document. It is not intended as a guide to the subject of the document, although occasionally the first word of a title is a subject word, as for example in the title *Classification in the 1970s*. In a dictionary catalogue, titles and subject access points sometimes get confused in a user's search. A divided catalogue is more successful in separating the two functions. The section of Chapter 8 on pages 242–243 deals with the use of titles as access points. Of significance here is the fact that an access point under a title borne by an *item* is not necessarily a standard identifier of the *work* it embodies (for that, see the following section). It is a "natural" search key, not an element of controlled vocabulary.

Although cataloguing rules have always permitted liberal use of title access points, older practice tended to prevent many titles from being so used. A stop list is designed for KWIC/KWOC indices (see page 174) to prevent the overloading of access files with terms of limited search value. For the same reason, it was once the accepted practice to reject as an access point any title beginning with, or consisting solely of, a common or generic word such as "Proceedings" or "Introduction," a title which duplicates the subject heading under which the item appears in the same listing (for example, the one-word title *Chemistry*), or a title beginning with a word considered unlikely to be sought (for example, the title *Charles Dickens, a Biography*). The present trend, largely resulting from the increased popularity of the divided catalogue over the dictionary catalogue, is to include as access points all titles without exception. This tendency is evident from decisions shown on Library of Congress entries since that institution divided its catalogues.

Whether or not to make every *series* title an access point for a monograph within the series has been a particularly contentious issue. Series which are only publishers' series (for example the series entitled *Pelican Books*) have not traditionally received access points, but it is increasingly hard to define what is "only" a publisher's series. Acquisitions librarians tend to favour series-title access to all series because series identification is often the only one which comes to their attention. It is particularly important that all the libraries contributing to a multiple-entry union catalogue follow the same policy in what is traced. Responding to the demand for improved series identification, the Library of Congress began the publication in 1974 of *Library of Congress Catalogs: Monographic Series,* in which all series appearing in Area 6 of the ISBD description on Library of Congress entries are identified in access points.

Despite the general rule that a title is not altered in any way for use as a heading, the temptation to do a little tampering in order to increase the likelihood of retrieval has sometimes proved irresistible. Numerals and symbols have been a frequent cause of the temptation because problems in their alphanumeric arrangement are evident. At one time, a foreign-language title might appear on a catalogue entry as follows to ensure its correct filing: "50 [i.e. Fünfzig] Jahre Deutsche Buch-Gemeinschaft."

Accepting the computer filing conventions described on pages 329–331 does not entirely solve the problem, because the user who has heard but not seen the title-page wording cannot be certain whether letters or numerals appear on the item, and hence in the bibliographic description. Today, it is relatively common to file the "same" title in more than one location, assuming that the user would not necessarily know or realize precisely how it is transcribed in reality. Numerals, initials, symbols, and titles beginning with a form of the author's name are instances of this situation, as shown in the examples in Figure 63.

Olney, Judith.
Judith Olney's entertainments : a cookbook to delight the mind and senses / foreword by George Lang ; photographs by Matthew Klein ; design by Milton Glaser. — Woodbury, N.Y. : Barron's, c1981.

xii, 307 p. : ill. ; 27 cm.

Includes index.
ISBN 0-8120-5410-5 : $24.95

1. Entertaining.   I. Title.   II. Title: Entertainments.

TX731.O44   642'.4—dc19   81-14892
                                                          AACR 2   MARC

Library of Congress

1981 IEEE Region 6 conference : electrical engineering applications in the Pacific : April 1, 2 & 3, 1981, Honolulu, Hawaii / sponsored by the Institute of Electrical and Electronic Engineers, IEEE Hawaii. — New York, N.Y. (345 E. 47th St., New York 10017) : IEEE, c1981.

634 p. : ill. ; 28 cm.

Spine title: 1981 Region 6 conference.
Includes bibliographical references.
"81CH1664-2."

1. Electric engineering—Congresses.   I. Institute of Electrical and Electronics Engineers. Region 6.   II. IEEE Hawaii.   III. Title: Nineteen eighty-one IEEE Region 6 conference.   IV. Title: 1981 I.E.E.E. Region 6 conference. V. Title: Nineteen eighty-one I.E.E.E. Region 6 conference.   VI. Title: 1981 Region 6 conference.   VII. Title: Nineteen eighty-one Region 6 conference.   VIII. Title: Electrical engineering applications in the Pacific.

TK5.A16   621.3—dc19   81-81136
                                                          AACR 2   MARC

Library of Congress

Fig. 63. These Library of Congress entries show tracings designed to reveal the title proper at any point at which a user might reasonably search for it. The lower one, involving numerals, takes into account the new 1980 Library of Congress filing rules (see page 331).

Works

A document is a single bibliographic item, but the same work may exist in dozens or hundreds of different documents in various languages and physical formats. As described on pages 92–93, a work is a creative/intellectual entity conceived as a unit by its creator. It may be identified by any one, or any combination, of the following:

1) the title proper assigned to its first published form by its author and/or original publisher (*Ten Little Niggers*)
2) any title appearing on any subsequent publication of the work, whether in the original language or in any other (*And Then There Were None; Dix petits nègres; . . . e poi non rimase nessuno; Letztes Weekend*), or even on an adaptation or other modification of the work (*Ten Little Indians* [the dramatization])
3) any wording by which the work is referred to in reference sources, whether this be the title proper of any particular publication of it or not (this is more likely to be an issue in the case of obscure ancient and mediaeval works).

Like a corporate body, a work may have parts (arias, chapters, sections) known by more-or-less formal titles of their own; an individual separately created work may also be thought of as part of a larger work, for example "The Acts of the Apostles," also known as part of "The Bible."

The preceding are examples of vagaries in the *publication* of a work or its parts. Significant relationships may also be drawn between versions of the *intellectual content* of a work. A work can later be re-created or otherwise modified. If its original author does this, what results is normally supplied with a prominent edition statement. If someone else does it, what results may or may not bear an edition statement. An "edition" is likely to have the same title proper as the original; an adaptation is more likely not to; a translation rarely does. However, no fixed rules are followed by publishers in this matter. As examples, there are the "9th edition" of *Guide to Reference Books* by Eugene P. Sheehy (though successive previous "editions" were prepared by three different authors), and *The Wrath of Achilles* by Ivor A. Richards (Homer's *Iliad* in an adapted translation but its chief source of information does not mention its origins). See page 75 for other examples.

Finally, works may be excerpted for publication, and shorter ones (and parts of longer ones) are frequently incorporated into anthologies along with other works to which they have no essential content relationship. Excerpts from a work may appear under a title which identifies both the work and the fact of selection, abridgment, etc. (*Highlights from My Fair Lady*). Whole works or excerpts from them, whether of one author or more, appear in anthologies (*Agatha Christie's Crime Reader; Favourite Suspense Yarns*).

The result of all the above factors is that there is no guarantee that any title borne by a physical document will correspond to a particular user's title approach to the work sought. The cataloguer or reference librarian must discover and interpret all the available facts, often from sources other than the document in hand, and then decide, with the help of accepted rules, which of the available techniques for showing the relationship is best. If all available manifestations of a work are to be identified for a searcher who might know any one of the titles under which it has appeared, using a standardized title identifier of the work is one possibility. This is called a *uniform title*, a title chosen or constructed by the cataloguer for the same purpose as any other name heading: to identify uniquely and to distinguish.

A uniform title is not like other titles in the bibliographic record. It is not a part of the description of a document, hence it is not governed by ISBD. It is a standardized access point (or part of one) for a work. Perhaps only larger libraries need to be consistent in their application of uniform titles to all works which might appear under more than one title-page title. Smaller libraries have tended to adopt ad hoc filing arrangements under "voluminous" authors such as Shakespeare in order to group editions of individual works. Leaving the matter to a filing subroutine means, however, that the filer must exercise judgement about the relationships of works and documents as they are encountered in the catalogue. This is not likely to be effective if part-time clerks do the filing; it will never be done if left to the computer's "judgement."

The use of uniform titles has long been accepted in at least two areas in even the smallest libraries: (1) anonymous classics (for example the Bible, the Arabian Nights), and (2) "classical" music compositions whether in scores or on sound recordings. In these situations a single work is highly likely to be dispersed in any file unless it is grouped by means of a uniform title. In 1981 the Library of Congress began to print all applicable uniform titles in its card- and book-form entries, so it is likely that more libraries will now routinely apply them locally. Figure 64 shows two examples.

The basis for a uniform title can only be some title applied to the work in one of its editions or in some other published source. In practice, the choice is between (1) the title given to the work on its first published appearance and (2) the title by which the work is most frequently identified in modern reference tools. In the case of modern works, cataloguing rules have always included some combination of both principles, with a leaning in favour of the first. Obviously, only the second principle is relevant in the case of works created before the invention of printing and the title page. For such older works, and for musical works designated by a generic title such as "symphony" or "quartet," English-language cataloguing rules have preferred a titling found in English-language reference sources.

Main Entry Heading

The title of a publication or work, and/or the name of the person or body responsible for its content, are the data elements most frequently remembered

Chemierohstoffe aus Kohle.   English.
Chemical feedstocks from coal / edited by Jürgen Falbe ;
[authors] E. Ahland ... [et al.] ; translated by Alexander Mullen.
— New York : Wiley, c1982.

xii, 647 p. : ill. ; 24 cm.

Translation of: Chemierohstoffe aus Kohle.
"A Wiley-Interscience publication.
Includes bibliographical references and index.
Contents: Introduction / G. Kölling and F. Schnur — Low temperature
carbonization and coking / E. Ahland ... [et al.] — Acetylene from calcium
carbide / G. Strauss — Hydrogenation of coal / W. Krönig — Gasification of

---

Ager, Stanley.
[Way to easy elegance]
The butler's guide to clothes care, managing the table, running
the home, and other graces / Stanley Ager and Fiona St. Aubyn
; produced by James Wagenvoord. — 1st Fireside ed. — New
York : Simon and Schuster, 1981, c1980.

191 p. : ill. ; 24 cm. — (A Fireside book)

Previously published as: Way to easy elegance. 1980.
Includes index.
ISBN 0-671-43642-2 (pbk.) : $8.95

1. Home economics—Handbooks, manuals, etc.   I. St. Aubyn, Fiona. II.
Title.

TX159.A35   1981   640—dc19   81-5679
                                                    AACR 2   MARC

Library of Congress

FIG. 64. In the top example, the uniform title is the main entry heading. According to
Library of Congress typographic style, therefore, it is displayed in boldface type. A
uniform title following a name heading is displayed in Library of Congress style in
roman type smaller than that used for the title proper, and enclosed within brackets.
These conventions prevent a uniform title from being confused with a title transcribed
from the item.

in a search for a known item.[13] All citation rules require these two elements to
appear first, and to appear together. In Western culture the name of the author
always takes precedence over the title as the filing element in a single-entry list
even though it is less often a unique identifier in itself than is the title. Because
the single-entry list makes the choice of a predictable filing element vital,
cataloguing rules have always focused attention on criteria for choosing it, and

13. See Josefa B. Abrera, "Bibliographic Structure Possibility Set: a Quantitative Approach for
Identifying Users' Bibliographic Information Needs," *Library Resources & Technical Services* 26
(January/March 1982):21–36, for a summary of research on the use of data elements of various
kinds in bibliographic searches.

theories of authorship were developed so that a predictable author heading could always serve the purpose. The history of modern library cataloguing codes is the history of the attempt to define the functions of authorship and to establish an order of priority among them so that a principal author, like a title proper, could always be chosen for a particular work.[14]

In the absence of a principal author acceptable under the rules, a work must appear in a single-entry list under some other element, the most usual being its title proper or uniform title. (In addition, old rules sometimes allowed constructions such as "form headings" to be chosen, as in the heading "France. Laws, statutes, etc.") Thus a person, a body, or a title is chosen as the main entry heading for each item listed. In a multiple-entry list, the overriding purpose of choosing a main entry heading is not to ensure that the item can be found in the list since that is the purpose of using multiple access points. Rather, use of the main entry heading serves to collocate all versions of the same work under a single predictable access point.[15] This is accomplished by old-style filing rules which always treat a personal/corporate-name main entry heading and the following title (whether uniform title or title proper) as a pre-coordinate unit for filing (see page 327). Thus the title *Theory of Relativity* remains linked with the author's name "Einstein, Albert" at every appearance of the work in the list. One effect of this predictable linking is that it simplifies referral to a work, whether in citation practice or in a multiple-entry list. A critique of Shakespeare's *Hamlet* is to be found in the subject catalogue under SHAKESPEARE, WILLIAM. HAMLET, and not under HAMLET; a reference to the directory of the Library Association leads the searcher to "Library Association. *Directory,*" not to "*Directory.*"

As with all pre-coordinate linkages, the link of a name heading with a title has not survived automation unscathed. Post-coordinate searching techniques make it possible for the individual searcher to decide to post-coordinate the author with the title or not to do so, depending on the purposes and the foreseen results of the search. They do not need to be pre-coordinated in the machine-readable file, and are not pre-coordinated in the MARC format any more than any two other data elements are. Each is separately tagged or subfielded for whatever manipulation may be required by a particular search or output pro-

14. A concise history of the concept of authorship in cataloguing is in Ruth French Strout, "The Development of the Catalog and Cataloging Codes," *Library Quarterly* 26 (October 1956):254–275 [also published in a monograph: *Toward a Better Cataloging Code,* University of Chicago Studies in Library Science (Chicago: University of Chicago Graduate Library School, 1957), pp. 4–25].

15. Three working papers prepared for the 1961 Paris conference explore the implications of main entry headings. They are by Seymour Lubetzky, Eva Verona, and Leonard Jolley, and may be found in the *Report [of the] International Conference on Cataloguing Principles, Paris, 9th–18th October, 1961* (London: Conference Organizing Committee, 1963), pp. 139–163. (This report was republished in 1981 by the IFLA International Office for UBC in London.)

gram. The potential problem, of course, is that the untrained user will fail to remember the value of linking a name with a title in a search for a work, and will retrieve only a single publication relating to the work sought, not *all* the evidences of the work in the list. The problem is even greater when the database cannot be visually scanned and one accepts what the computer has generated in response to the imperfectly formulated request.

Even in manual systems using old-style filing rules, it has been hard to maintain the theory of authorship as it came to be practiced under old cataloguing rules. Those rules much preferred a personal- or corporate-name main entry heading to main entry under a title. It has never been particularly difficult to formulate relatively simple rules for the choice of one person among many as the basis for the main entry heading. The choice of a principal corporate author, however, became more and more subjective as "corporate author," "sponsor," and merely "publisher" are increasingly difficult to distinguish from one another and, in fact, from some kinds of personal authorship. Examples of the problem are shown on page 64.

If choice of a main entry heading is difficult and subjective for a cataloguer, would the user benefit from the agony of the decision? AACR2 preserves the values of choosing a main entry heading in the clear instances of personal authorship, recognizing that "Dickens, Charles. Our Mutual Friend" is still the most helpful way of designating that work for many purposes. It also continues to prescribe corporate-name main entry heading for a large number of works, including some close to the focus of corporate authorship as it was once defined (annual reports, laws, etc.) and some rather distant from it (proceedings of conferences). However, it abolished the theory of corporate authorship and considerably increased the incidence of title main entry at the expense of corporate main entry. Added entry is, on the other hand, prescribed more liberally than before under the name of any corporate body associated with the intellectual content of a work.

Romanization

Research libraries in Europe commonly keep entries for material in nonroman scripts (Cyrillic, Arabic, Japanese, etc.) in separate catalogues without romanizing either the bibliographic data or the access points. File arrangement is governed by conventional usage in the script in question. Most North American libraries, even the largest, have preferred to maintain a single catalogue of all holdings. At least the access points in such a catalogue must be in roman characters for filing purposes, even if the descriptive data are transcribed in a nonroman form. The process of changing nonroman characters into roman-alphabet ones is called *romanization,* or more loosely, *transliteration.* The expense of developing and maintaining many nonroman character sets for computer applications has forced many libraries (including the Library of Congress) to romanize all the data on a bibliographic record when it is incorporated into a machine-readable database. The problem of romanizing is not merely one for large, academic, or computerized libraries. A rapidly increasing number of names of nonroman-script origin are being used in everyday library work in English in even the smallest libraries, for example the following:

Peter Tchaikovsky	Пётр Ильич Чайковский
Anton Chekhov	А. П. Чехов
Sholem Asch	שלום אש
Yukio Mishima	三 島 由 紀 夫

All romanization is basically phonetic: it attempts to reproduce in the roman alphabet the sound of the foreign word as pronounced by a native speaker of the language in question. Unfortunately, this approach involves phonetics and orthography, both very imprecise arts. The "proper" sound of a single roman character or of a combination of them may seem quite different to speakers of different languages. Many individual languages are internally inconsistent in how they render roman characters in sound, English being notoriously so. Thus all romanization is a distortion of the sounds of both the original language and the language of the person who chooses the romanized form. For example a German, an Irishman, and an American may each "see" something differently spelled when they listen to the same native Israeli speak a Hebrew word.

The surname of the author of *The Cherry Orchard* (shown above in its original Cyrillic form) has appeared in at least the romanized forms shown below. All are copied from title pages of works printed in roman script, the language of the title page being indicated in brackets.

Anton Čechov [English, German, Italian]
Anton Čechow [German]
Anton Čexov [English]
Anton Chehov [English]
Anton Chekhov [English]
Anton Czechow [Polish]
Anton Tchehov [English]
Anton Tchekhoff [English]
Anton Tchekhov [English, French]
Anton Tchékhov [French]
Anton Tchekoff [English]
Anton Tschechov [German]
Anton Tschechow [German]
Anton Tsjechov [Dutch]

Each of these fourteen forms is an *existing romanization* because it "exists" in roman script in print. If a library collects materials in several languages, some variation among existing romanizations of the same name is fairly likely. Fortunately, Chekhov is an unusual case in having so many, but names originally in the Cyrillic script do cause the most problems for users of bibliographies and catalogues. Cultural exchanges between Russia and Western Europe began early enough that speakers of each Western European language romanized Russian names according to a native sense of how they should be spelled, before international standardization was of any concern. In German words, the "ch" sound is still normally spelled "tsch" or "tch." Because the English-speaking world got its nineteenth-century musical tradition through Germany, where most of the scores were printed for the West, English speakers took over the composer's name as Tschaikowsky (now usually anglicized somewhat to Tchaikovsky). Because the literary tradition came directly from Russia to Great Britain, Chekhov rarely starts with a T in English-language publications, unless the publication emanates from a German or German-influenced scholar or publisher.

Seeking and applying existing romanization is therefore bound to lead to international incompatibility. A more stable solution is to seek agreement on equating any given nonroman character or group of characters with a specific roman character(s), and to display the agreed equivalents in a table which can be mechanically applied. The use of such a transliteration table is called *systematic romanization*. Figure 65 shows part of the table for a romanization of the Thai script.

Vowels				**Consonants**		
					Initial and medial	**Final**
อะ, อั	a	อัวะ	ua	ก	k	k
อา	ā	อัว, ว	ūa	ข, ฃ, ค, ฅ, ฆ	kh	k
อำ	am	ไอ,ใอ,อัย,ไอย	ai	ง	ng	ng
อิ	i	อาย	āi	จ	čh	t
อี	ī	เอา	ao	ฉ, ช, ฌ	ch	t
อึ	ư	อาว	āo	ญ	y	n
อื	ư̄	อุย	ui	ฎ, ฑ, ท¹	d	t
อุ	u	โอย	ōi	ฏ, ฐ	t	t

FIG. 65. Part of the Thai transliteration table, from *Cataloging Service,* bulletin 120 (winter 1977).

As shown in the examples above, the name of the famous musical composer and that of the famous writer both begin with the same Cyrillic character: Ч. The use of any romanization table therefore requires that the *same* roman letter(s) be used to begin both names. Since English-language users are more accustomed to finding the above-mentioned musical composer under T in reference tools and the author under C, it is evident that applying systematic romanization can lead to results not readily recognizable by a generally educated library user. Systematic romanization as a solution is also plagued by the existence of conflicting romanization tables for the same script. ISO standards exist for Cyrillic, Arabic, and Hebrew, but are not widely accepted as yet and may never be. In most North American libraries, and to a degree in the international English-language library community, the tables applied when systematic romanization is required are those proposed by the Library of Congress and sanctioned by the American Library Association.[16]

These tables formed a de facto part of old cataloguing rules, and ensured a measure of consistency at least in North America. AACR2 prescribes both existing and systematic romanization in different situations although sometimes allowing the other as an option. When existing romanization is adopted, the heading is in the form most frequently found in English-language reference sources. When systematic romanization is adopted, AACR2 does not prescribe particular tables, but gives examples using the LC/ALA tables cited above. With the adoption of existing romanization by the Library of Congress in many instances, the musical composer is taking his place among the Ts.

Perhaps the only real solution to the intractable problems involved is to allow the originator of the nonroman-script message, and not the receiver, to determine the acceptable romanization. Not many years ago, the government of the People's Republic of China decreed the use of a particular system for romanizing Mandarin Chinese in all romanized publications issued in that country. It also applied cultural and diplomatic pressures to have that system adopted elsewhere. Although Pinyin differs substantially from the Wade-Giles system hitherto prevalent among English-language sinologists, journalists, etc., it has already been widely accepted as the standard in the West. The pronunciation by a native Mandarin speaker of the name of the imperial capital has not changed, but "Beijing" is slowly but surely becoming the accepted romanization.

Reasons for the Changes

Once a pattern of rules, or even a specific name access point, is established in an existing catalogue, its users' habits become ingrained and are not easily altered. Interlibrary cooperation and the economic benefits of sharing access points and whole records are additional reasons to maintain the status quo.

---

16. A cumulation of the tables then in force appeared in the Library of Congress' *Cataloging Service,* bulletins 118 (summer 1976), 119 (fall 1976), and 120 (winter 1977). Additions and amendments continue to be promulgated in that publication under its current title, *Cataloging Service Bulletin.*

Change as significant as that implied above between old and new rules is of traumatic consequence for a living tool like a catalogue, and never to be taken lightly. That it took over twenty-seven years between the first effective and organized challenge to the old practices until the new were put firmly and fully into place in the Anglo-American world on January 2, 1981, is clear indication that the profession has thought deeply about the consequences, and that there was healthy resistance offered all through the process.[17] The principal reasons why the changes were eventually effected are the following:

1) old rules fostered practices which were often less beneficial to the user than to the librarian trained in bibliographic research, or to the library (stability of headings is economically efficient)

2) names themselves, particularly corporate names, have undergone changes in patterns and usage: rules for old situations do not necessarily apply as well to new ones

3) a greater degree of international cooperation, hence of economic benefits in sharing records, is possible if varying national practices can be more closely merged

4) automation has given to bibliography a tool for the easier changing and updating of files, and their more effective searching; but this tool can only be used effectively if rules are internally consistent. Old rules were not.

Superimposition

There is no "right" moment for the institution of major changes in a continuing catalogue or bibliography. The "best" moment was undoubtedly during the period of the 1970s when automation was turning so much of the bibliographic world upside down anyway. The real problem is not how to institute new practices, but what to do with bibliographic records bearing access points in conflict with those called for by the new rules. No library can afford to revise even the estimated ten to fifteen percent of access points in an average catalogue which have been rendered obsolete by AACR2.

The "new" rules described throughout this chapter first arrived in 1967. Perhaps that was a truly "wrong" moment since automation was hardly on the scene anywhere at that time. The choices for a library in that year seemed to be the following: (1) closing one manual catalogue and beginning another in the same (usually card) format, or (2) coping with a possibility of two established forms for any name in the same catalogue (cross-referenced at some considera-

17. That first shot was fired by Seymour Lubetzky in *Cataloging Rules and Principles, a Critique of the A.L.A. Rules for Entry and a Proposed Design for Their Revision* (Washington: Library of Congress Processing Department, 1953). The original and very strong resistance came from the reference divisions of the same Library of Congress.

ble additional expense). Neither solution was acceptable to the larger libraries, including the Library of Congress. There were two results: (1) the first edition of AACR, particularly in its North American Text, included internal compromises with its basic principles in order to minimize the effects of change, and (2) libraries following the lead of the Library of Congress adopted a policy called superimposition as a practical means of incorporating old and new practices.

Superimposition may be explained briefly as follows: If a name heading existed in the catalogue before the date when AACR1 was implemented (March 20, 1967, at the Library of Congress), that same form continued to be used as the access point for all new materials referred to that name until December 31, 1980. Any person, body, etc., whose name was not previously established as an access point received a heading established according to the new rules. However, when a corporate body changed its name, the new rules were always followed and a new heading created for the new name. The net effect was that "familiar" names were retained in their old-rule form in catalogues where Library of Congress practices prevail.

The results of fourteen years of superimposition have not been beneficial to bibliography. Not only have existing catalogues displayed a mixture of possible searching patterns to confuse users, but a large number of access points in old-rule style have become part of machine-readable databases and networks. File maintenance techniques and automated authority systems described on pages 183–186 made it possible to revise many of these machine-readable databases in 1981, but the manual products formerly produced from them remain, with their old-style access points. Thus any reference librarian consulting bibliographic tools based on library cataloguing rules must be cautious about approaching entries created during the 1967–1980 period. They may contain old-style or new-style access points in any mixture.

Computer Searching and Name Headings

Machine searching techniques have in theory an almost unlimited capability for searching single elements in text. Yet for a human being to pattern a search and organize what the computer is to look for produces a more effective and probably cheaper search. This is very true for searches of name headings; it would not be very efficient to ask the computer to show all persons with the surname "Smith" if the searcher knew any other element.

Applying the methods of online searching described throughout Chapter 6 opens a powerful avenue of approach to name access points, though each technique has its own special area of greatest impact. The use of compression codes, for example, is probably best restricted to titles and personal-name/title combinations such as those illustrated on pages 179–180. A combination of truncation and post-coordination has unique potential for unravelling the mysteries of corporate naming since the searcher can request display of, for example, any access point which includes "Canad#" plus "Environ#" without having to know whether the desired agency is higher or lower in the hierarchy or the order or full complement of words in the name. As a final example, boolean logic might well be applied to problems of conference identification, for example: FIND ("Confer#" OR "Sympos#" OR "Workshop") AND ("Astronom#" OR "Astrophys#") AND any year greater than "1975." The implications of subjecting traditionally formulated name access points to such online searching techniques are only just beginning to be explored.

8

SUBJECT ACCESS POINTS

The user looking for the fifth edition of John L. Smith's *Principles of Chemistry* is not concerned about what other chemistry texts exist, nor about what other editions of Smith's can be identified. The application of the formats for description outlined in Chapter 5 and the rules for access points analyzed in Chapter 7 provides an exact and predictable formulation by which to identify a known item. Known-item searches are important uses of bibliographies and catalogues of all types. They predominate when a searcher familiar with a discipline or field of study looks for materials in that discipline, because such a searcher is most likely to come to hitherto unfamiliar material through bibliographic citations and the names of other experts in the field. It is no accident that the catalogues of some very important research libraries (for example the Widener, the Bodleian, the former British Museum Department of Printed Books) are considered very reliable for accurate and consistent name/title approaches, even if their cataloguing rules do not conform to present-day standards, but are considered weak in their provision of subject approaches.

What Is a Subject Search?

The following represent more typical queries, at least in school, public, and undergraduate college libraries: "Do you have anything about. . . . ?" "I'd like some examples of good after-dinner speeches." "Do you have any punk rock records?" "Where are the fairy tales for preschoolers?" Even some known-item searches must be approached in this way because the user cannot accurately recall any searchable bibliographic data about the item: "Where's that red chemistry book that used to be on the top shelf? Oh, I'd recognize its author's name if I saw it." The query is often entirely tentative: "I'm not sure what I want, but it's in the general area of. . . ."

Such searches for information begin without a particular name or known item in mind. The user wants items relevant to a given subject, or items presented in a specified form, or items pertinent to a particular audience level. Librarians commonly use the term ''subject,'' as in *subject analysis, subject search key, subject classification,* and *subject heading,* to denote not only the true subject approach, but also form and audience approaches. These all relate to the intellectual content of a document rather than to its objective bibliographic data elements. The same convention is adopted in this chapter except where it is intended to distinguish them (see pages 239–240).

Since a name heading can uniquely identify a single person and a bibliographic description can uniquely identify an item, one may expect that a given subject can also be described precisely using a term or symbol for it. ''Metal fatigue'' has a simple definition in an engineering dictionary, ''due process before the law'' is a concept clearly described in a legal lexicon, and a social sciences encyclopaedia leaves one in no doubt about the meaning of ''social welfare policy.'' Thus any document whose subject can be defined should be unambiguously retrievable by some designation of that subject used as an access point.

Bibliographic practice gives the lie to this simple statement of theory, however. No practising reference librarian expects a subject search to be conducted with the same degree of precision or assurance characteristic of a known-item search. The reason is not that subject access points are necessarily imprecise, though it is admittedly more difficult to isolate and to name a concept than a person. Rather, a subject search is imprecise by the very nature of the process. Such a search originates at some focus of interest within a context which is best represented as a continuum or spectrum. The search is therefore necessarily open-ended until enough of that context, in any direction from the originally sought focus, has been unveiled to satisfy the individual searcher. ''A book about abortion'' may appear to be a simple and precise expression of a subject query, but from one point of view this is actually a meaningless statement. No single item ever covers a subject (even a subject less controversial than this one) in all its ramifications and from all possible points of view.

Point of View

To express what a particular document does cover is the other aspect of the problem of subject definition. Subject access points representing concepts may be precisely definable, but they can only be applied to a particular document subjectively, to a greater or lesser degree. The points of view of the writer of a work, of the person who classifies and indexes it for retrieval, and of the work's ultimate user are not necessarily the same. The author of *Social Change in Tribal Society* conceived the work around one focus, but any given user will see its value in a different context, perhaps a radically different one. To one, it is a study in the discipline of anthropology; to another, in the discipline of political science; to a third, in the discipline of ethnology. These are only the disciplines to which the work as a whole might be particularly relevant; one cannot deny the likelihood that an historian, a musicologist, a theologian, and a philosopher would each be likely to find in the same work some sections of great interest and value.

One who has never read the work, and has taken no interest in any subject other than, say, physical chemistry, would probably find it easy to say what this work is about. Its title and table of contents show that it is a work about "primitive peoples' way of life." But the more one knows about ethnology, political science, etc., the more one is reluctant to pin any such superficial label on it. In fact, the person least prepared to specify concisely what is a work's subject is usually one who has read and understood it; perhaps the worst possible person to ask what the work is about is its author. The author knows what intentions motivated the creation of the work, but the resultant publication will be used to answer the questions of other people, not the author's.

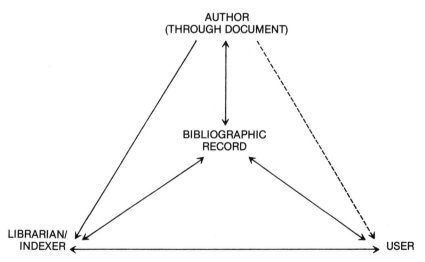

FIG. 66. A schematic display of the interrelationships between author, user, and librarian showing the central importance of the bibliographic record.

The Bibliographic Record as Author-User Link

The interrelationships between author, user, and librarian are illustrated in Figure 66. The author has created a work. The user comes to the library with a need for informational, recreational, or cultural material. The librarian as selector has decided to acquire the work for the collection, the librarian as cataloguer/indexer has created a description and access points for it, and the librarian as readers' advisor tries to relate it to the perceived needs of a given user. Whether the user approaches the librarian as a person, or only approaches the catalogue or shelf arrangement which express the librarian's perception of the work, that user cannot make contact with the mind of the author except through the librarian's bibliographic rules and conventions. If the user does not know the author or title of the work, author-user communication can only be initiated through the medium of a subject catalogue or bibliography, or through a subject arrangement on the library's shelves. It is possible for both the author and each particular user to have quite individualistic intentions in creating or using the work, but the librarian's approach must remain flexible enough to facilitate any reasonable use of the work. This is the "impossible task" of subject analysis.

Subject Groupings; Classes

Subject groupings do not just happen: they are deliberately created by people who have thought about the implications and ramifications of the subjects in question, have analyzed the literature of those subjects, and have decided on the best means of bringing that literature together for information seekers. A subject group, or class, is by its very nature a unit in some controlled vocabulary. A natural search term, as defined on page 173, may be useful to place a document within a class or retrieve it from the class, and it may serve as a help in deciding what to call the class, but it cannot of itself define the class.

A class is a group of individual items which share a characteristic, whatever that characteristic is called. The term "class" and its derivatives have frequently been used to refer to only one kind of such grouping, namely subject grouping as expressed in the notation of a classification scheme (for example a Dewey number) and intended for the physical shelving of documents. The process and purpose of defining a class is, however, the same whether the class consists of items having a common author or sharing a series title, or whether some subject characteristic is identified verbally or by assigning the item to a physical location.

In reality, of course, the bibliography or collection may contain many, few, or none of the possible items within a specified class. A collection may have no items on chemistry or by Shakespeare; it may have one of each, or a thousand. The class remains the same, regardless of the quantity involved. This chapter deals only with subject classes, but these classes may be expressed as subject entries in a catalogue or bibliography or as groups of items physically shelved according to a classification scheme.

Relevance versus Recall

It was suggested on page 228 that the expression "something about abortion" is simplistic. What is meant by these words may be either (1) items whose central focus is the topic of abortion, or (2) items which can contribute to a discussion of abortion. There exist many of the former; but there are far, far more of the latter, including many items whose authors did not intend to raise this issue consciously at all. The distinction between these two meanings may appear subtle, and does not generally occur to the casual searcher making a first inquiry on the subject. It is, however, the very basis of the problems of identifying subject classes and providing subject access points identifying these classes in bibliographic lists.

In even a small general collection, *all* the material falling into the second category above would encompass more items than the average enquirer foresees or in fact wants. But the indexer/cataloguer, who works in the abstract without a particular user in mind, cannot determine how much of the total possible context will be enough on this or any topic to satisfy any given individual. The public services librarian, though in direct personal contact with a single searcher, is also incapable of determining the extent of what that user needs. The only person who can do so is the individual seeking the material, and for that person the scope of interest typically alters as the searching progresses and the ramifications of the topic become more apparent. Even the original focus of interest is likely to shift in the holistic process of discovery.

The problem is therefore how, in the absence of feedback from individual users, to maximize the relevance of what is displayed as a single subject class under its specific access point without initially overwhelming every user with (that is, recalling) too large a number of documents. For any topic there are always some users whose approach is, "Any one item on the subject will do, thanks," while others require the *exhaustive search,* asking for "everything you have." The best retrieval system isolates the material of highest relevance, but at the same time permits expansion of any search toward greater exhaustivity if more information is required either because the user's interest has expanded or because the original request was incorrectly focused.

Relevance and recall may be illustrated in the example of a student required to write a term paper on "The Meaning of Light in the Imagery of William Blake." The obvious places to search are under BLAKE, WILLIAM in the alphabetic catalogue or in an index of literary criticism, or at the library shelves under the principal location for Blake among the "English poetry" material. The result of these approaches will daunt any but the most assiduous student. Recall is too high and relevance too low for the student trying to locate the few best sources for the special topic in hand. Reacting instinctively to the recall/relevance balance, the student may look for a different subject heading or shelf location in order to narrow the search: perhaps looking under BLAKE, WIL-

LIAM—IMAGERY in the catalogue, or looking in the classification area of symbolism in art. Here begins the problem of matching the thought processes of the searcher with the controlled vocabulary of the subject analysis system; there was no problem matching the name "Blake" to the system, precisely because it is a name; but concept terms are more uncertain.[1]

Specificity

As a rule the most relevant information exists in the smallest number of different documents. These must be culled both from the less relevant ones and from those unsuitable for other reasons (wrong intellectual level, poor quality, etc.). This raises the question of how broad or narrow the groupings isolated by a subject analysis system should be. At one extreme, material specifically about Blake can be visualized randomly scattered throughout a more general grouping of material about ENGLISH POETS (whether in an alphabetic subject catalogue or on the shelves), and not differentiated by any more specific characteristic. The user looking for anything about Blake, even just a biography, would be hopelessly frustrated by such a system. A high proportion of the items in any group dealing with English poets contains something about Blake, but because the most specific grouping available is still quite general, any search for Blake material would inevitably become an exhaustive one; recall would be unmanageably high, and the degree of topical relevance within the group as a whole would be very low except in response to the most generalized inquiries on English poets. The cataloguer would also be frustrated. How to decide whether the grouping in which Blake is to be included should be ENGLISH POETRY, or LITERATURE, or GRAPHIC ARTS, or ENGRAVING, or whatever? Almost any subject can be viewed as part of many larger ones.

At the other extreme, one can imagine the most specific possible index, one in which all the entries in the indices within every item in the collection are collected and interfiled into one alphabet. (This technique would of course be impossible for shelving the materials; one would have to shelve each chapter of a book separately!) It is unlikely that this would serve the user any better. In addition to the obvious difficulties of reconciling terminology, the system would lose the ability to display the relevance of any actual document as a whole to a particular search. Materials would not be revealed as unified items, but only as disjointed fragments of information out of context. Quick-reference tools exist and have an important place in satisfying this approach to knowledge, but the majority of items in any general collection are used for the context in which they treat ideas as much as for the ideas themselves. This

1. The use of small capitals designates a term to be understood as a hypothetical or actual subject access point. Names used as subject access points are not a principal concern in this chapter since they are treated according to the practices analyzed in Chapter 7.

enormous hypothetical collected subject index would not be cost-effective. It might conceivably aid in exhaustive searches, but not in searches aiming at high relevance within a specified context.

It takes less effort to expand a search toward greater exhaustivity (more recall) than to weed out the irrelevant when too much information has been retrieved. Thus the average user, who rarely requires an exhaustive search, is better served by low-recall/high-relevance techniques than by high-recall/low-relevance ones. Subject analysis in controlled-vocabulary bibliographic applications is always designed principally for the former type of retrieval.

A general library obtains materials on many subjects at all possible levels of specificity. It also serves users' questions of every possible degree of generality or specificity. Levels of specificity are relative, not absolute. There is no such thing as a specific query, only a query more specific than another one. The person who wants a textbook on science is making a specific request, since "science" is the exact topic that person is interested in. One reason for not expecting many documents to be highly relevant to the Blake investigation illustrated above is that the topic is relatively specific. More people write books on dog care in general than on the care of poodles in particular, or on Blake in general than on his imagery. But if "Light in the Imagery of Blake" seems an extremely specific topic to someone who knows little about Blake or eighteenth-century English culture, the Blake scholar immediately perceives possibilites for greater specificity yet, for example "The Interplay of Light and Shadow as a Model of Heaven and Hell in Blake."

Document format has a considerable bearing on specificity, and vice versa. The more specific the topic, the more likely it is that journal articles rather than books will be the most highly relevant items. The type and level of publication best suited to answering a given type of query will vary, along with the indexing language most pertinent to the situation. This is one reason why the subject analysis of journal articles, of books as a whole, of technical reports, of government documents, etc., is often deliberately kept in separate files or publications employing slightly different subject indexing vocabularies. Thus, although the kind of analytics we now expect to find in a periodical index were once interfiled with entries for monographs in many library catalogues (see pages 102–104), it is perhaps better that they be separated. The student working on the Blake topic checks the indices within the general books about Blake for any incidence of the word "light"; to search for that word in the library catalogue would obviously be fruitless, and should be in this case.

Specificity is therefore a desirable characteristic of any subject analysis system, though its meaning in any case is conditioned by the nature of the material analyzed and the expected level of searching. If any material on "light" in Blake, or on poodle care, is available, subject analysis in an index or catalogue which attempts to deal with requests at this level of knowledge must reveal it as a separate class and not scatter it among general material on poets or animals.

The only way of ensuring this is by letting the level of specificity of the *document* decide what should be the level of specificity of its indexing or coding, not the level of any particular *request* (which in any case cannot be known in advance), and certainly not the level of the indexer's personal knowledge of the subject if that is limited.

Ideally, the person who applies or interprets controlled-vocabulary search keys must know at least as much about the topic of any document being indexed as the person able to read it intelligently. This can be a real problem, especially in subject areas from which qualified persons are not easily attracted into information work or librarianship. Libraries operate on the assumption that general monographic material in any field, and any items whose use is peculiar to that library's clientele, can be satisfactorily analyzed by the library's own cataloguing staff (in a special library this may include some specialized subject indexing). It is still desirable, however, to purchase many subject analysis tools from agencies which can employ subject specialists. Chapter 9 describes trends leading to the greater use of integrated bibliographic searching on databases cooperatively created, as a means of making the most widespread and efficient use of indexing skills wherever they may be.

Methods of Designating Subject Classes

The processes of subject analysis may be defined as follows in terms of the concepts thus far introduced:

1) *foreseeing* any probable focus of a searcher's interest in any topic represented in the materials being analyzed
2) *defining*, in the light of those foreseen needs, subject classes of sufficiently precise focus that a search may begin at a limited range of highly relevant material
3) *identifying*, or naming, each defined class by means of a search key which is
   a) readily understandable to the average anticipated user of the material, and
   b) appropriate to the searching technology of the system
4) *linking* logically related classes, whether by proximate arrangement in a classification, by cross-references in a manual alphabetic list, or by suitable links in an automated system, so that the user can expand or contract the scope or context of the search as desired, and
5) *reinforcing* the chances for successful retrieval by using as many of the different available techniques as the sophistication of the users and the budget available for the purpose permit.

For greatest relevance to any particular search for information, a class would have to be defined and named specifically in the light of that one request. This is impracticable in manual systems where the number of terms and pre-coordinations is limited as described on pages 18 and 164. Automation facilitates a closer approach to this ideal by making it possible to post-coordinate concepts in response to an individual query. In an online automated system, defining classes and linking them are processes undertaken both at the time of analyzing incoming materials *and* at the time of answering queries.

The name access points described in Chapter 7, the most efficient ones for known-item searches, can only be presented in one way, namely in an alphabetic arrangement. On the contrary, at least two different methods of arranging subject search keys are provided simultaneously in almost every modern library catalogue and in a significant proportion of other bibliographic tools. They are:

1) *subject headings, subject indexing terms, uniterms,* or *descriptors;* that is, alphabetically arranged words (this is in fact not one technique but many, since there are many different indexing languages available)

2) *classification numbers,* which are a symbolic *notation* serving to arrange classes logically or "systematically" according to any of several available subject classification schemes; *or* words arranged not alphabetically, but in a table-of-contents fashion which displays related concepts together the way a classification scheme does.

Variations on these techniques which were not feasible in manual systems are now frequently offered in computer-based ones. These include *citation indexing,* the use of *relevance weighting* in word-counting, keyword indexing, and the employment of boolean logic. The last two of these were introduced on pages 173–175 and 167–169, respectively. Indexing using relevance weighting is a sophistication of keyword indexing. A search key is automatically created from any character string (other than one on a stop list) which occurs more than a given number of times in the complete text of a document or abstract. The assumption is that terms used more frequently in a piece of writing are more likely to express highly relevant concepts: an assumption with some validity in technical writing. The value of citation indexing is based on the fact that most published research acknowledges in footnotes and bibliographic references items considered relevant by the author, but which may not have a superficially evident subject connection with the ideas developed from them. It provides a ready-made context for any given search. If it is the right context for the particular user, both the relevance and the comprehensiveness of the search are greatly enhanced.[2]

2. The quantitative analysis of citations and of language usage in documents is part of the broad field of which an extensive bibliography in process is Alan Pritchard, *Bibliometrics, a Bibliography and Index* (Watford, Herts.: ALLM Books, 1981–   ). An older survey appears in *Annual Review of Information Science and Technology* 12 (1977):35–58. Eugene Garfield, the principal exponent of citation indexing, has written much on that subject. Karen Sparck Jones is a principal writer on linguistic analysis as it applies to information retrieval.

Alphabetic versus Systematic Arrangement of Classes

The techniques of both verbal and logical subject analysis are familiar to the average library user. The former appears in the alphabetic subject catalogue (or the subject headings forming part of the dictionary catalogue), in many of the abstracting and indexing tools including the most familiar periodical and news-paper indices, and in the indices appearing at the end of most nonfiction books. Systematic arrangement is evident in the shelf classification adopted for much of the collection in most libraries, in the classified *shelf list* of bibliographic records maintained by every library for inventory purposes and increasingly made available to the public for subject searching, in most national bibliographies, in many specialized subject bibliographies (particularly those originating outside North America), and in the tables of contents of most nonfiction books (see the second, detailed, table of contents at the front of this book). Thus the two techniques are used side by side at almost every level of subject control from the "macro" (a library full of ideas) to the "micro" (the ideas in a single document). The multiplicity of available subject indices parallels the multiplicity of bibliographic tools in which name/title access is provided, but the redundancy of using more than one technique simultaneously is peculiar to subject analysis.

If either one of the two traditional techniques, or any one of their computer-based offshoots, seemed even basically adequate for a high proportion of subject searches, bibliographers and librarians would not duplicate their efforts, providing subject access in different ways in an obvious attempt to make each one patch over some of the inadequacies of another. The duplication increases the cost to the institution maintaining the several systems, and adds to the time spent by every searcher attempting a subject investigation. Economy moves in library cataloguing have frequently resulted in the decision to dispense with either classification or subject headings (if not both!) at least for some types of material. Items in microform, for example, are often provided with verbal subject headings in a catalogue, but are physically arranged by form and a serial number.

That the two techniques serve quite different searching processes is shown in an example:

DAMS	DINOSAURS	DRAGONS
DANCING	DISASTERS	DRESSMAKING
DEAFNESS	DIVORCE	DRUGS
DEER	DOGS	DYES
DEMOCRACY	DOLLS	DYNAMITE
DETERGENTS	DONKEYS	

The alphabetic arrangement of these concept words facilitates quick retrieval of specific information on any one of the topics in isolation, but only coincidentally do any two terms found adjacent to one another have a conceptual relationship. It is therefore practical to display specific terms alphabetically in directories and encyclopaedias, in book and journal indices, and in the subject catalogue of a library. These are tools principally used for quick access to particular bits of information rather than for browsing or for trying to grasp contexts.

Systematic arrangement, or classification, is the process of relating concepts according to rationally detected similarities rather than according to how the concepts are named in any particular language. Used in thesauri, shelf arrangement, and many abstracting tools, it requires the user to be logical and to comprehend the classifier's reason for grouping certain topics together, but it also presents the searcher with a breadth of related information greater than is possible in any kind of alphabetic display. It is a tool for expanding and altering a search rather than for focusing it. Classification would show DEER, DINOSAURS, DOGS, and DONKEYS (possibly also DRAGONS?) in conjunction both with one another and with their animal relatives ELK, MOOSE, etc. DIVORCE and DYNAMITE would be distant from these animals, and displayed within their own sociological and technological contexts.

Neither the verbal nor the classified approach is intrinsically superior to the other. In fact it is hard to separate language and reason, for they are equally basic functions of human intelligence, but operate differently. Subject headings are language-dependent, with all the virtues and drawbacks that implies. The greatest virtue is that language is direct communication, and can bypass both the uncertain process of rationalization and the inevitable differences of opinion about subject relationships.

The greatest drawback was well expressed by Sansom: ". . . it is absurd to expect words to behave more logically than the people who use them."[3] Even in the same language a word easily connotes different things to different people or in different contexts.

The greatest advantage of classification is that it produces a sequence which can be browsed meaningfully. The person who has a choice does not search a classified arrangement in the sense of looking for a specific item. If a verbal index is available, one "searches" it, whereas one "browses" a table of contents, however detailed it may be. "Search key" is not a term commonly applied to a notation in a classification scheme, although technically it is valid to do so.

The Classified Catalogue

An item can only be placed in one physical location, whereas its content may be highly relevant to more than one concept. The use of classification for

3. G. B. Sansom, *An Historical Grammar of Japanese* (Oxford: Clarendon Press, 1928), p. 293.

shelving items is therefore a very limited use of its potential for information retrieval. Yet in North American libraries, where the open stack collection has long been in vogue, classification is used primarily for the physical arrangement of items. It is no wonder that some administrators of large libraries question the value of classification if they see so expensive a process serving principally for shelf location. There are cheaper ways of accomplishing that. In the larger academic library it is common in any case for the principal subject-classified sequence to contain a minority of the items in the collection.

Significant advantages of any subject catalogue are that it can be a multiple-entry listing, allowing the same item to be displayed under many subject access points, and that it displays all the catalogued items in the collection in one tool. If the chosen format of a bibliography or catalogue is the dictionary arrangement, subjects *must* be expressed as words so they can interfile with authors and titles. If it is divided into separate author/title and subject parts, it is possible to arrange the subject portion in systematic or classified order, bringing dogs and wolves together but separating dogs from doges. Such a subject catalogue is called a classified catalogue. Any classification scheme may be used as its basis. A classified catalogue offers browsability and multiple access as well as specificity. Persons with some awareness of the classification arrangement employed are well served by it. Those who must approach it each time through its verbal index are probably annoyed by the need to look in two places before any document is located.

The classified catalogue has not found much favour in North America, but its independence from language makes classification in bibliographic tools particularly useful in multilingual applications. It is no accident that research into classification as a primary method of subject analysis is pursued much more vigorously in Europe, where equally important languages claim attention in bibliographic tools, than in North America, a basically self-sufficient unilingual area. In general, classification has diminished in favour over time compared with verbal indexing. Books of the nineteenth century typically contain elaborate classified tables of contents but poor or no subject indices. Today a nonfiction book without a subject index is an anomaly, while tables of contents are rarely more than lists of chapter headings.[4]

Increasing computerization of information retrieval functions holds promise for expanding the practical uses of classification. Since the purpose of subject classification is to link concepts expressed in alphanumeric symbols, it is ideally suited to computerization where links are fairly effortlessly manipulated and where symbols are the most efficiently used designators. Many of the

---

4. Chapter 1 of Julia Pettee's old but classic study *Subject Headings, the History and Theory of the Alphabetical Subject Approach to Books* (New York: Wilson, 1946) explores these developments well. Both the table of contents and the alphabetic index of her book are models of their kind.

facetted classification schemes in particular subject areas developed during the past twenty years were designed with post-coordinate manipulation in mind.

Subject, Form, Audience

The distinction among the three types of subject query mentioned on pages 227–228 is illustrated in the example of a request for "a nineteenth-century children's fantasy." This request is satisfied neither by a history of such fantasies, nor by items on the technique of writing them, nor by critiques of their literary qualities. It is not a subject request, but a form request. The desired fantasy has a subject—magic mushrooms, perhaps, or life on the moon, or dwarfs—but the subject is irrelevant to the request.

Form and subject requests are often combined into one, for example, "a dictionary of the French language," "an encyclopaedia of gardening," "a collection of interviews on abortion," "statistics of grain transport in Canada." Many subjects lend themselves naturally to form treatment, resulting in documents so different from one another that a good retrieval system must be able to display the different forms separately. The user interested in political arguments about the Crowsnest freight rates for grain would not find statistics of grain transport in Canada of highest relevance, nor a history of those rates, even though the subject (the transport of grain in Canada) is the same. The form in which the subject is treated is what makes the different items more relevant or less to the particular request.

In the above examples, form is a secondary though important consideration. "Dictionary" or "statistics" would not be a very useful primary access point for the items. But form is the primary reason for the use of some kinds of library materials, particularly general reference works such as encyclopaedias. It is so difficult to describe the subject of much writing that for many purposes librarians call it creative, abandon any attempt to identify its subject, and group it solely by its literary or artistic form (short story, sonata, etching, etc.). Novels, which are mostly on the subject of interpersonal relationships, may be used for the study of such relationships. A sociologist may even wish to see them classified and itemized in the catalogue with related nonfiction writing on this same subject, but its form and/or author, not its subject, is at least as likely to be the principal reason for choosing a particular novel to read.

The "nineteenth-century children's fantasy" is an example of an item whose intended audience is also specified. Whether or not that fantasy is appreciated by adults is not the issue. Although subject, form, and intended audience are quite different ways of approaching an item, each defines classes of items differently. Every library classification scheme and subject headings list makes some provision for designating form and/or audience as separate classes or subclasses. Public libraries pay particular attention to the audience factor in the tripartite division of collection and services into children's, young people's, and adult. Often these three levels are given entirely separate catalogues and shelf arrangements. Universities often divide material between a graduate library and an undergraduate one.

The post-coordination of one or both of the form and audience characteristics with subject characteristics is therefore highly desirable. The MARC formats provide many codes designating form and audience level in a control field for post-coordinate searching (see field 008 in Appendix I, pages 303–307). IFLA has made proposals for a standardized audience-level code in bibliographic records.[5] Facetted classification schemes such as the *Univeral Decimal Classification,* the *Colon Classification,* and to an extent the *Dewey Decimal Classification* also make possible the coordination of subject/form/audience characteristics in a search since their notations provide separate identifiable codes for these characteristics. Pre-coordinate subject headings also incorporate generous provision for form treatment (see page 252), and to a lesser degree audience or level designation.

Literary Warrant; Change

There is an obvious temptation simply to use a dictionary or an outline of all of human knowledge in the abstract as the basis for a subject headings list or a classification scheme. However, works are not created to conform with dictionary definitions or trees of knowledge; hence to classify them and assign subject headings for retrieval purposes cannot be philosophical or linguistic exercises. They are intensely pragmatic occupations, based on real documents which warrant the creation of the subject vocabularies used to deal with them. Not to establish a class or authorize a term which validly describes the specific content of some existing material in the collection is almost the same as to censor the material itself (a topic beyond the scope of this book).[6] Conversely, to include provision for concepts before they are much evident in actual documents is a waste of effort. It will probably have to be redone when the topics in question do rise to significance and when their relationships with other topics have become stabilized.

To apply literary warrant is not merely to authorize new subject groupings as new topics arise. Chapter 7 explored the consequences of change for a controlled vocabulary of name headings, showing that cataloguing rules have changed from time to time, and that this has in some cases been the result of

---

5. Russell Sweeney, *International Target Audience Code (ITAC): a Proposal and Report on its Development and Testing,* Occasional Papers, no. 1 (London: IFLA International Office for UBC, 1977).

6. This is not to demean the efforts of those who ask that offensive terms and juxtapositions be eliminated when others are available to describe the existing material. Although it may not be easy to reach agreement on what is offensive, Sanford Berman's writings have certainly had a beneficial effect on current United States practice in this respect.

changes in naming patterns themselves. In the application of the subject headings lists and the classification schemes principally used in libraries, the basic "rules" have changed little since the beginning of this century. They are described in the following sections of this chapter. However, the perception of subject concepts themselves constantly changes according to the fashions of the times and the advance of knowledge. The growth of the literature on an established topic inevitably reveals fresh aspects and relationships of that topic, requiring change and/or expansion of the subject headings and classification arrangements provided for it.

A work is created through the rambling of a human mind among the ramifications of a topic of interest. The most significant writers and artists do not create new works about existing topics; they create extensions of topics not previously known, and even entirely new topics. Marshall McLuhan's *The Gutenberg Galaxy* was the culmination of a decade of his thinking about the effects of mass-media communication, but when it appeared in 1962 it was shelved and listed in the subject catalogues of most libraries among the works on the history of printing, a topic quite remote from its author's intent or the book's subsequent use by most readers. Even among standard works on established topics, the connotations of terminology and the context are constantly shifting. Yesterday's DOMESTIC ECONOMY is today's HOUSEHOLD SCIENCE, and has become a rather different topic in the process. MOVING PICTURES have become MOTION PICTURES, CINEMA, or just FILM (though the latter might be too ambiguous as a subject heading), and at least in the United States, NEGROES became COLORED PEOPLE, then BLACKS or AFRO-AMERICANS.

Natural-language (keyword) indexing systems can reflect changes in terminology as quickly as titles begin to appear incorporating new terms. Changes in any controlled-vocabulary subject headings list must follow sooner or later. Of far more consequence is the gradual but constant change in the logical relationships among branches of knowledge. Astrophysics, once clearly a branch of astronomy, is now as close to cosmology as to any other field. Communism, originally thought of as a branch of social economics, has long had less to do with economics than with political science. International law, once a branch of diplomacy, is coming into its own as an independent field. A mere change in the naming of a topic need not affect its location in a classified sequence, but the arrangement of topics within a classification scheme must be changeable as the common perception of subject relationships changes, even if the words used to express the affected subjects remain the same.

It is difficult enough to incorporate additions for new topics into a subject headings list or classification scheme. To show altered relationships with cross-references and new shelf locations is particularly difficult because concepts are so intertwined with one another. Furthermore, changes in subject terms and relationships do not come about suddenly and tangibly as name changes do; they insinuate themselves gradually through the cumulative efforts of writers, social groups, performers, etc. In practical terms, if inertia is the typical response to new descriptive cataloguing codes or to changing name headings, there is positive resistance to the need to change classification symbols and subject headings. The computer can do little to change a spine label on a book, even if the refiling of a catalogue entry is made easy by an automated authority system and a COM or online catalogue. Yet to keep the subject analysis systems up-to-date by making the changes required by current thinking is perhaps more important than altering name headings: subject headings and classification tend to condition the very way in which the less scholarly user learns about the concepts contained in documents.

The Verbal Approach

Natural Language (Title Keywords) versus Controlled Vocabulary

If no context is given for the term "dog," one is assumed, the obvious assumption being the animal. That "dog" is not an unequivocal term as a keyword is illustrated in the following list of actual book titles:

```
Dog Corner papers [about a hypothetical place]
Dog days [a novel]
The dog exercising machine [a book about problem-solving]
Dog ghosts, and other texas Negro folk tales
Dog sled to airplane
Dog soldiers, Bear men, and Buffalo women; a study of
        the societies and cults of the Plains Indians
```

Except in creative writing, titles are normally composed to reveal subject content, but the need to keep a title brief often prompts the use of elliptical and allusive, rather than direct, language. No term in a title can be relied upon to define a subject class, but only to help isolate a particular publication. Still, titles have always been of some use as the basis for subject access points. Keywords in titles are sometimes the only subject access points displayed in a bibliography, as is the case in the one illustrated in Figure 67.

The indexing of subject-significant title words, whether in or out of context (see pages 173–174) is once again in favour, not because it is so effective or sophisticated an information retrieval technique, but because the computer has made it inexpensive. In the older use of keywords for subject access, the indexer selected those of most value. Today, the computer only rejects those words programmed into a stop list; it indexes all others.

For the past hundred years almost all manual library catalogues and the majority of printed bibliographies limited title-based access points to the first

FERRIER, C. (Ed), Hecate's Daughters : Anthology of Contemporary Australian
   Women's Writing, 142p C8 1980 p $4.50 Lit, (0 959 468 8), Hecate
➤ Ferries, Across the Harbour : Story of Sydney's, J. GUNTER, $14.95, Rig
➤ Ferries, Western Port, A.E. WOODLEY, p $4.95, Hill
FERRY, J., Kamilaroi, 32p D4 1978 $5.95 Abor, (0 340 23242 0), Hodder
Fertility and Family Formation : Australasian Bibliography and Essays 1972 (Aus
   Family Formation 1), H. WARE, ix/349p D4 1973 p $5.95 Soc, (0 7081 0819 9
   ), ANUP
➤ Fertility, Immunological Influence on Human, B. BOETTCHER (Ed), $19.95, Harc
➤ Fertility : Papers on the Yoruba Society of Nigeria (Changing African Family 1),
   Socio-economic Explanation of High, J.C. CALDWELL, p $4.95, ANUP
Fertility without Drugs or Devices, Billing Method : Controlling, E. BILLINGS & A.
   WESTMORE. $12.95, O'Don

FIG. 67. The arrows identify permuted title entries in this excerpt from *Australian Books in Print, 1981*. As in a KWIC index, a keyword is brought into filing position. Here, the keywords are selected by an indexer and the title is rotated around it. The titles in question are, respectively, *Across the Harbour: Story of Sydney's Ferries, Western Port Ferries, Immunological Influence on Human Fertility*, and *Socio-economic Explanation of High Fertility: Papers on the Yoruba Society of Nigeria*.

word of a title not an article. Because this first word is not necessarily of much value as a subject indicator, the temptation frequently arises to supplement it with additional keywords from within the title. Forty years ago, Seymour Lubetzky argued cogently against this practice as being confusing when a controlled subject authority system is also in effect in the same dictionary catalogue.[7] The practice is certainly not tenable in a divided catalogue, where title catchwords do not appear in the subject part at all, but in the author/title part. Nevertheless, it still surfaces occasionally, as shown in the entry in Figure 68.

Biology of conidial fungi / edited by Garry T. Cole, Bryce Kendrick. — New York : Academic Press, 1981.

> 2 v. : ill. ; 24 cm.
>
> Includes bibliographies and indexes.
> ISBN 0-12-179501-2 (v. 1)

1. Fungi.   2. Conidia.   I. Cole, Garry T., 1941-   II. Kendrick,
➤ Bryce.   III. Title: Conidial fungi.

QK603.B5   589.2'3—dc19   80-1679
                                                            MARC

Library of Congress

FIG. 68. A Library of Congress entry showing a "partial title" tracing for filing under a subject keyword.

7. "Titles: Fifth Column of the Catalog," *Library Quarterly* 11 (October 1941):412–430.

The user approaches any subject index or librarian using natural language, just as the author or publisher has used natural language in composing a title. In the case of the user, that one person's habitual linguistic usage is based on many individual factors of knowledge and environment, and may or may not coincide with the usage of any given author, of another user, or of the librarian who receives the request or who indexed the item. In the attempt to match these various natural languages, the traditional solution is to translate all of them into terms in a controlled vocabulary, which becomes in effect a *switching language*.

Subject Headings following Cutter[8]

A controlled subject vocabulary not only matches the vocabulary of the user with that of the author; it also supplies a context for each term, defines each subject class or group, and fixes its relationships. In taking some of the guess-work out of locating material on a defined topic, this inspires a measure of confidence in searching. The application of any controlled subject vocabulary is costly, since it requires an indexer to determine that the context and topic of each of the following books is, specifically, DOGS:

```
An artist's models [they are all dogs]
The Canadian Kennel Club stud book
Canine pediatrics
De canibus Britannicis
Lassie come home
Man's best fiend [sic]
Mongrel mettle
The new puppy
Of English dogges
Wag-tail
```

Just over a hundred years ago Charles Ammi Cutter developed principles for controlled-vocabulary verbal subject access by means of "direct, alphabetic, and specific" terms in a basically pre-coordinate system.[9] These principles, although originally developed for library catalogues of monographic holdings, have been applied with complete success to every kind of manually searched subject index. In the context of their principal library applications today, Cutter's principles may be paraphrased and illustrated as follows:

8. The term "subject heading" almost invariably denotes the use of a controlled vocabulary. "Descriptor" usually, but less certainly, means the same thing; the term is sometimes used of natural access points. "Keyword" is used only of natural language terms.

9. *Rules for a Dictionary Catalog,* pp. 66–77 (rules 161–180). In addition, rules 150–153 (pp. 63–64) are rules for the use of title keywords for subject access.

1) An item should be listed under the one or more subject terms applicable to the intellectual content of the item as a whole, not merely to a part of it; that is, levels of specificity more appropriate to an index *within* an item are not appropriate to the subject listing for the *whole* item. For example, a book on technical services in libraries should appear under only one subject heading, PROCESSING (LIBRARIES), not under four (or more): ACQUISITIONS (LIBRARIES) and CATALOGING and SERIALS CONTROL SYSTEMS and LIBRARIES—CIRCULATION, LOANS.

2) Any term used should be one designating the specific subject of the item, not a broader class of which that subject is only a part. For example, a book on coal mining should appear under COAL MINING, not COAL, or MINES AND MINERAL RESOURCES, or NATURAL RESOURCES. This principle is the basis for pre-coordination in subject headings. It is not, however, pushed to the extreme of requiring a single subject heading for each item, tailored specifically to that item's content (see Pre-Coordinate and Post-Coordinate Headings, pages 247–250).

3) If the term designating the topic has more than one word, the entry word should be the one most likely to be naturally sought by users of the catalogue; for example, FRENCH BULLDOGS, not BULLDOGS, FRENCH. This principle is sometimes modified in favour of using the word which will best group like subjects together (see Changes in Subject Headings Practice, pages 253–254).

4) Subheadings may be added to a term to designate aspects, viewpoints, or parts of the topic which have no specific distinguishing names of their own, as well as a form or audience level; for example, CLASSICAL ANTIQUITIES—DESTRUCTION AND PILLAGE, CHEMISTRY—YEARBOOKS, and PRINTING—JUVENILE LITERATURE.

5) If terms are, for practical purposes, synonymous (that is, more than one term applies to what might reasonably be considered the same concept), only one of them should be chosen as a heading, preferably the one most likely to be familiar to the users of the particular catalogue. "See" reference(s) should be made from the other(s); for example, ORNITHOLOGY *see* BIRDS.

6) "See also" cross-references should lead the searcher from a broader term to term(s) designating more specific part(s) of that broader topic; for example, ROCKETS (AERONAUTICS) *see also* GUIDED MISSILES. Cross-references leading from more specific terms to more general ones encompassing them were not recommended by Cutter, but are now common in vocabularies used for machine searching; that is, GUIDED MISSILES *see also* ROCKETS (AERONAUTICS) would not be traditionally acceptable in a list designed for manual searching.

7) "See also" references should be used to link related concepts at about the same level of specificity; for example, MARKETING *see also* COM-

MODITY EXCHANGES, as well as COMMODITY EXCHANGES *see also* MARKETING.

These "rules" are still the basis of current subject indexing practice in manually searched bibliographic lists. Even thesauri for computer-based systems depend heavily on them, though with modifications to favour post-coordinate searching. Unlike rules for name entries, however, these are not rules capable of ensuring uniformity of application since they cannot specify which exact terms are to be used. Rather, they have been the basis on which lists of approved headings and cross-references have been developed.[10]

Characteristics of Subject Headings Lists

Hundreds of subject headings lists have been compiled following the above principles. Some few attempt to cover all of knowledge; most exist primarily to provide verbal control over the concepts of limited fields. Vocabularies have been developed for almost every conceivable specialist subject/form/audience area. There are lists for city planning materials, for libraries of Judaica, for children's books, and for uniquely Canadian usage and topics. A general list, covering all subjects and forms, poses particular difficulties both in compilation and in use; it must reconcile the terminologies of all disciplines within a single compatible vocabulary. Two such lists have predominated in North America throughout the twentieth century: (1) the list of the headings in use in the catalogues of the Library of Congress, and (2) a list originally compiled for use in smaller libraries by Minnie Earl Sears.[11]

Although there are some differences in the terminology authorized by the two, LCSH and Sears are largely compatible, both being based on Cutter's principles.

10. The above principles have been glossed and explained in every subject cataloguing text. They were modernized after Cutter and incorporated into the 1931 code of the Vatican Library: *Vatican Library Rules for the Catalog of Printed Books,* trans. from the second Italian ed. by Thomas J. Shanahan [et al.], ed. Wyllis G. Wright (Chicago: American Library Association, 1948). The official, but now outdated, explanation of the Library of Congress's application of these principles is David Judson Haykin, *Subject Headings, a Practical Guide* (Washington: Government Printing Office, 1951); it was replaced by Lois Mai Chan, *Library of Congress Subject Headings: Principles and Application,* Research Studies in Library Science, no. 15 (Littleton, Colo.: Libraries Unlimited, 1978). The introductory "Suggestions for the Beginner in Subject Heading Work" by Bertha Margaret Frick, which appears as an introduction to recent editions of the *Sears List of Subject Headings* (cited in the next footnote), is a good elementary guide.

11. The current printed edition of the *Library of Congress Subject Headings* (hereafter LCSH) is the 9th (Washington: Library of Congress, 1980). Cumulating supplements are issued regularly. A microform version is also published, of which each quarterly issue incorporates all changes to date. The 9th printed edition, and the microform version as of mid-1982, are incomplete and must be used with *Library of Congress Subject Headings, a Guide to Subdivision Practice* (Washington: Library of Congress, 1981). *Sears List of Subject Headings* (hereafter Sears) is now in its 12th ed., ed. Barbara M. Westby (New York: Wilson, 1982).

The most noticeable difference is that LCSH specifies many times more headings than Sears. In the latter, FOOD CONTAMINATION and FOOD POISONING are adjacent authorized headings, separated only by five cross-references. In LCSH, these two headings are separated by eleven authorized headings and fifteen cross-references, examples of the additional headings being FOOD HABITS, FOOD IN LITERATURE, and FOOD MIXES. Sears, being designed for smaller public and school libraries, presupposes that documents on highly specific subjects in any field, particularly in technology and in the more esoteric academic disciplines, will not be acquired, and therefore headings do not need to be prescribed for them. For the same reason, it sometimes conflates into one heading concepts divided between two or more in LCSH. A single complete heading from LCSH is shown in Figure 69 to illustrate the application of this list, and by analogy Sears, in detail.

Many authorized subject headings are omitted from both lists. Any name, whether proper or common, is an acceptable subject heading. The lists do not include proper names, including geographic ones, except for a sample to show authorized subdivisions, since such name forms are established by applying a cataloguing code as described in Chapter 7. LCSH prints a great many common names, for example SIAMESE CAT; Sears does not, but assumes their applicability as needed.

Pre-Coordinate and Post-Coordinate Headings

The great majority of headings in both LCSH and Sears designate single-term concepts such as YOUTH, CHURCH WORK, and LIBRARY ASSOCIATIONS. Though composed of two words, CHURCH WORK is a single subject term because neither "work" nor "church" has the same meaning in isolation as it does when in association with the other word. Other headings are pre-coordinated (see pages 163–165). They define multi-term concepts such as CHURCH WORK WITH YOUTH, UNIVERSITIES AND COLLEGES—TAXATION, and PHOTOGRAPHY OF ANIMALS. Here each term, whether composed of one or of several words, preserves its independent meaning within the subject heading. CHURCH WORK can be associated with any object of such work: CHURCH WORK WITH THE INDIGENT, CHURCH WORK WITH RURAL PEOPLE, CHURCH WORK IN FOREIGN COUNTRIES, etc. Similarly, YOUTH has an independent meaning and use as a subject term, but writers frequently associate it with other concepts in books, articles, films, etc. YOUTH—EMPLOYMENT, YOUTH IN ART, ETIQUETTE FOR CHILDREN AND YOUTH, and PHOTOGRAPHY OF YOUTH are pre-coordinate terms expressing some of these concept associations.

One should not mistake every longish heading containing a grammatical link such as a conjunction for a pre-coordination. MEDICAL INSTRUMENTS AND APPARATUS INDUSTRY is merely a five-word expression of a single concept for which no shorter term has been authorized. FREE WILL AND DETERMINISM is not

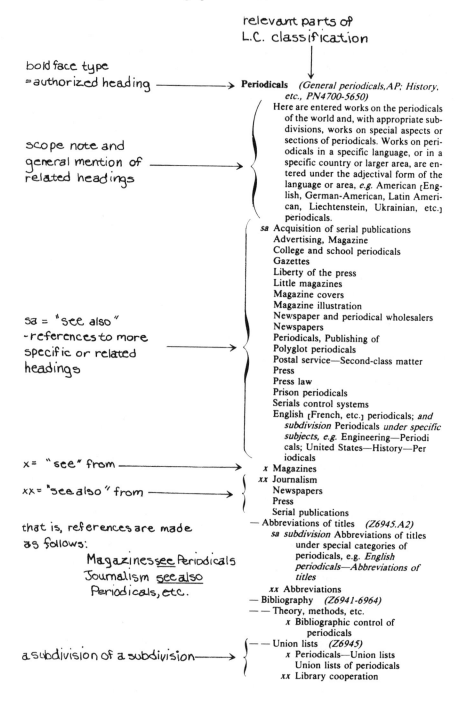

relevant parts of
L.C. classification

bold face type
= authorized heading ⟶ **Periodicals** *(General periodicals,AP; History, etc., PN4700-5650)*

Here are entered works on the periodicals of the world and, with appropriate subdivisions, works on special aspects or sections of periodicals. Works on periodicals in a specific language, or in a specific country or larger area, are entered under the adjectival form of the language or area, *e.g.* American ₍English, German-American, Latin American, Liechtenstein, Ukrainian, etc.₎ periodicals.

scope note and
general mention of ⟶
related headings

sa Acquisition of serial publications
Advertising, Magazine
College and school periodicals
Gazettes
Liberty of the press
Little magazines
Magazine covers
Magazine illustration
Newspaper and periodical wholesalers
Newspapers
Periodicals, Publishing of
Polyglot periodicals
Postal service—Second-class matter
Press
Press law
Prison periodicals
Serials control systems
English ₍French, etc.₎ periodicals; *and subdivision* Periodicals *under specific subjects, e.g.* Engineering—Periodicals; United States—History—Periodicals

sa = "see also"
-references to more
specific or related
headings ⟶

x = "see" from ⟶   *x* Magazines

xx = "see also" from ⟶   *xx* Journalism
Newspapers
Press
Serial publications

that is, references are made
as follows:
    Magazines <u>see</u> Periodicals
    Journalism <u>see also</u>
    Periodicals, etc.

— Abbreviations of titles   *(Z6945.A2)*
sa subdivision Abbreviations of titles under special categories of periodicals, e.g. *English periodicals—Abbreviations of titles*
xx Abbreviations
— Bibliography   *(Z6941-6964)*
— — Theory, methods, etc.
x Bibliographic control of periodicals

a subdivision of a subdivision ⟶
— — Union lists   *(Z6945)*
x Periodicals—Union lists
Union lists of periodicals
xx Library cooperation

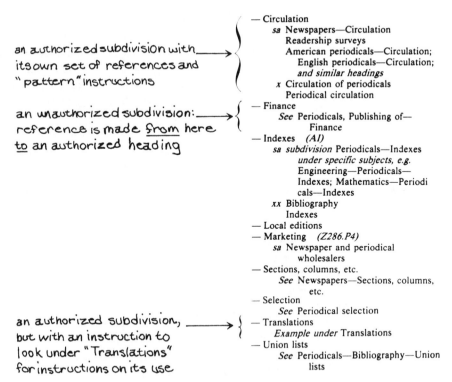

an authorized subdivision with its own set of references and "pattern" instructions →

an unauthorized subdivision: reference is made <u>from</u> here <u>to</u> an authorized heading →

an authorized subdivision, but with an instruction to look under "Translations" for instructions on its use →

— Circulation
   sa Newspapers—Circulation
   Readership surveys
   American periodicals—Circulation;
     English periodicals—Circulation;
     and similar headings
   x Circulation of periodicals
   Periodical circulation
— Finance
   See Periodicals, Publishing of—
     Finance
— Indexes *(AI)*
   sa subdivision Periodicals—Indexes
     under specific subjects, e.g.
     Engineering—Periodicals—
     Indexes; Mathematics—Periodi
     cals—Indexes
   xx Bibliography
   Indexes
— Local editions
— Marketing *(Z286.P4)*
   sa Newspaper and periodical
     wholesalers
— Sections, columns, etc.
   See Newspapers—Sections, columns,
     etc.
— Selection
   See Periodical selection
— Translations
   Example under Translations
— Union lists
   See Periodicals—Bibliography—Union
   lists

FIG. 69. A single complete heading, with its subdivisions, from LCSH. The style of presentation in LCSH and in Sears is essentially the same.

a pre-coordination, but a statement of two opposites which necessarily occur in conjunction with one another when either is written about. CITIES AND TOWNS is a joining of terms so close in meaning to one another that there is no particular point in trying to find a dividing line between them. These would need to be treated as single search terms in any system: a post-coordinate one-term descriptor is not necessarily a single word.

The use of pre-coordination in subject headings is directly related to the analysis of literary warrant. When enough material is written about two concepts in relation to one another, a manual subject analysis system should provide a pre-coordinate heading to designate it as a single class, since such a heading is more specific for the body of existing documents than the separate more general headings would be. If pre-coordinate subject headings were not permitted, a user searching for the topic "youth in literature" would be forced to make a post-coordinated search, looking under YOUTH, then under LITERATURE, and noting which items are listed under *both* terms.

In general, LCSH and Sears lean in favour of pre-coordination, since they were devised for manually searched catalogues, but when to authorize a pre-coordinate heading is the most difficult and subjective issue in verbal subject control. If there exists no substantial literary warrant for a particular pre-coordination it, would be foolish to authorize it because it would not serve the needs of a significant number of searchers. No subject heading is ever established for a particular search, only for a group of documents of similar subject scope. Thus even in LCSH there is no subject heading pre-coordinating the name "Blake, William" with the concept "light." If in fact there exists any book or article specifically on this combination, it is presumably to be given two authorized LCSH headings: BLAKE, WILLIAM, *and* either LIGHT IN ART or LIGHT AND DARKNESS (IN RELIGION, FOLKLORE, ETC.) These must be post-coordinated, whether manually or on a computer terminal, by the student doing the term paper on "light in the imagery of Blake." Yet LCSH, because it is a list intended to deal with highly specific topics, contains some perhaps surprising examples of pre-coordination, headings few users would likely seek on a first search for the topic, such as EPISCOPACY AND CHRISTIAN UNION and DEFICIENCY DISEASES IN POULTRY. There can be no doubt that these have been authorized on the grounds of literary warrant.

Lists of controlled-vocabulary access points devised primarily for computer-based post-coordinate searching and manipulation tend to be composed almost exclusively of single-term headings, each of which may of course contain more than one word. Since the term "subject heading" preserves overtones of pre-coordination and the manual technology, the terms "descriptor" (for the individual access point) and "thesaurus" (for the list of them) are more in favour in the literature of computerized information retrieval. The *Thesaurus of Engineering and Scientific Terms* is an early work of this kind whose careful planning and execution has been a model to many similar efforts in other fields.[12] Figure 70 is an example from a modern thesaurus illustrating the conventions typical of such a list.

New Headings and Topical Subdivision

Subdividing existing more general subject headings gives rise to new headings when literary warrant for this is evident. Subdivision of a concept is usually accomplished by creating new headings in other places in the alphabet. When there came to be a substantial body of material about postsecondary education in the 1960s, the available heading UNIVERSITIES AND COLLEGES was increasingly general for some of it. Headings such as DIPLOMA MILLS, JUNIOR COLLEGES, SMALL COLLEGES, and UNIVERSITY EXTENSION were therefore newly authorized in LCSH.

12. (New York: Engineers Joint Council, 1967).

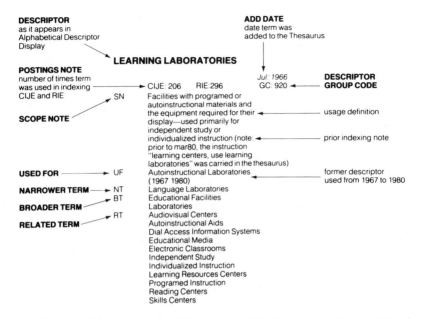

DESCRIPTOR
as it appears in
Alphabetical Descriptor
Display

ADD DATE
date term was
added to the Thesaurus

LEARNING LABORATORIES

POSTINGS NOTE
number of times term
was used in indexing
CIJE and RIE

SN

SCOPE NOTE

CIJE: 206   RIE:296

Jul: 1966
GC: 920

DESCRIPTOR
GROUP CODE

Facilities with programed or
autoinstructional materials and
the equipment required for their
display—used primarily for
independent study or
individualized instruction (note:
prior to mar80, the instruction
"learning centers, use learning
laboratories" was carried in the thesaurus)

usage definition

prior indexing note

USED FOR   UF

NARROWER TERM   NT

BROADER TERM   BT

RELATED TERM   RT

Autoinstructional Laboratories
(1967 1980)
Language Laboratories
Educational Facilities
Laboratories
Audiovisual Centers
Autoinstructional Aids
Dial Access Information Systems
Educational Media
Electronic Classrooms
Independent Study
Individualized Instruction
Learning Resources Centers
Programed Instruction
Reading Centers
Skills Centers

former descriptor
used from 1967 to 1980

FIG. 70. A sample entry from the *Thesaurus of ERIC Descriptors,* 9th ed. (Phoenix: Oryx Press, 1982), showing the significance of its parts. A comparison with Figure 69 on pages 248–249 shows some differences between a thesaurus and a subject headings list.

The first publication to appear on such a new topic does not warrant its own specific access point immediately; hence it is not uncommon for the earliest material on a topic to appear in a subject index under an access point different from the one established for later material. New terms must be added quickly to a vocabulary used for indexing periodical and newspaper articles, even at the risk of choosing for a new topic a term which may later have to be revised. It is interesting, for example, to locate the terms used to index the topic of artificial objects in space in the years following their first appearance in 1957. By the time a topic is the principal subject of a number of monographs and a term for it is needed in Sears or LCSH, the shifting terminology has usually settled.

Subdividing an existing term is another way of adding new terms. One or more subject subheadings (not form subheadings, for which see page 252) are added to an existing term to create new terms, for example ELECTRIC CIRCUITS—ALTERNATING CURRENT and ELECTRIC CIRCUITS—DIRECT CURRENT.

Common subdivisions applicable to headings of the same kind are easily established. Thus if a subdivision such as —POLICE, or —RESTAURANTS, or —SOCIAL POLICY is admitted for one city, logically it must be applicable to all city names. Separate lists of common subdivisions accompany the basic alphabet in LCSH and Sears so that they do not need to be repeated under each heading to which they apply. In LCSH they are called the *free-floating subdivisions*. Selected "key" names (of persons, places, etc.) are also listed with all possible subdivisions in order to show the pattern of their application.

Form Headings and Form Subdivision

Form subdivision is desirable when material on a subject in one form is likely to have a quite different use than material in a different form, for example OHIO—BIBLIOGRAPHY, OHIO—HISTORY, OHIO—STATISTICS, and OHIO—YEAR-BOOKS. The subject in all four cases is Ohio in general. The writing of Ohio's history is, of course, a subject in its own right, whose subject heading is OHIO—HISTORIOGRAPHY.

Some authorized headings in any list are in their entirety form headings. For example, the formerly authorized heading CANADIAN LITERATURE—COLLECTIONS designates a class containing no material about the collecting of Canadian literature, nor in fact any writing *about* Canadian literature at all. Rather, it is the class consisting of anthologies of creative writing done in Canada. In some cases the same words could be used to connote either subject or form, and one must pause to think of which must be the case. The scope note at BIBLIOGRAPHY in LCSH, reproduced in Figure 71, shows how that list deals with the need to reflect both form and subject in relation to this term.

Geographically Oriented Topics

A geographic area may be a subject in its own right. It may also be a useful subdivision of a topical subject since writings on so many subjects are geographically oriented. Is it evident that the authorized heading should be BIRDS—CANADA, or CANADA—BIRDS? If it seems better to group all material about birds together, does consistency then demand LITERATURE—CANADA, FOREIGN RELATIONS—CANADA, and HISTORY—CANADA? Cutter's inconclusiveness on this matter was mentioned on page 164. Present-day lists show the effects of generations of ad hoc judgements as to which would be the better entry element in each instance. In general, scientific material tends to be filed under topic; cultural material under place.

When a geographic name is to be used as a subdivision of a topic, Sears suggests only that it identify the specific territory dealt with in the item being indexed. Thus the authorized forms are ARCHIVES—CHICAGO and ARCHIVES—GENEVA. This is called "direct" geographic subdivision. In contrast, LCSH often specifies that geographic division be "indirect." It authorizes ARCHIVES—ILLINOIS—CHICAGO and ARCHIVES—SWITZERLAND—GENEVA, thus introducing a classified aspect to geographic division. This classified aspect is controlled by rules governing which political division should come at the top of the hierarchy for grouping.

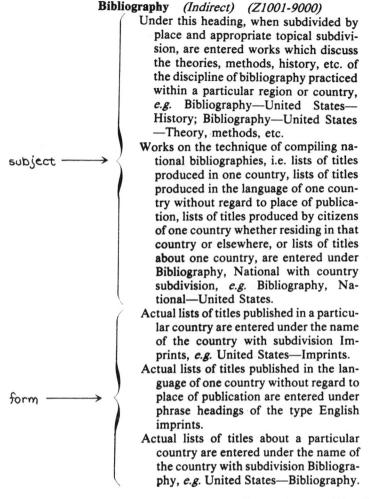

Bibliography *(Indirect)* *(Z1001-9000)*

subject →

Under this heading, when subdivided by place and appropriate topical subdivision, are entered works which discuss the theories, methods, history, etc. of the discipline of bibliography practiced within a particular region or country, *e.g.* Bibliography—United States—History; Bibliography—United States—Theory, methods, etc.

Works on the technique of compiling national bibliographies, i.e. lists of titles produced in one country, lists of titles produced in the language of one country without regard to place of publication, lists of titles produced by citizens of one country whether residing in that country or elsewhere, or lists of titles about one country, are entered under Bibliography, National with country subdivision, *e.g.* Bibliography, National—United States.

form →

Actual lists of titles published in a particular country are entered under the name of the country with subdivision Imprints, *e.g.* United States—Imprints.

Actual lists of titles published in the language of one country without regard to place of publication are entered under phrase headings of the type English imprints.

Actual lists of titles about a particular country are entered under the name of the country with subdivision Bibliography, *e.g.* United States—Bibliography.

FIG. 71. An LCSH scope note illustrating the difference between "form" and "subject."

Changes in Subject Headings Practice

Both Sears and LCSH, but principally the latter, have undergone shifts in their application of one of Cutter's principles (the third, on page 245) over the years.

In the matter of geographic subdivision, a recent policy change affecting LCSH eliminated the direct geographic subdivision once permitted for many headings, replacing it with the now universal indirect subdivision. As an example, the formerly authorized CHRISTIAN SCIENCE—PARIS has been replaced with CHRISTIAN SCIENCE—FRANCE—PARIS.[13] Although Sears tends to imitate the trends set in LCSH, it does not automatically copy them. It has not changed to the practice of indirect geographic subdivision.

Another change is perhaps even more significant. Early in the century there was more of an attempt to group headings logically through the use of inverted forms such as LIBRARIES, CHILDREN'S and LIBRARIES, SPECIAL. J.C.M. Hanson, responsible for the early application of alphabetic subject headings at the Library of Congress, wrote in 1909:

> There is undeniably a strong tendency in the Library of Congress cata-
> log to bring related subjects together by means of inversion of headings,
> by combinations of two or more subject-words, and even by subordina-
> tion of one subject to another. Yes, the tendency at times is so notice-
> able that it may seem as if an effort were being made to establish a
> compromise between the dictionary and the alphabetic-classed cata-
> log. . . . the student and the investigator . . . are best served by having
> related topics brought together so far as that can be accomplished with-
> out a too serious violation of the dictionary principle.[14]

More recently, as new headings were required, practice changed to the use of the natural language form of the term without concern for the grouping of concepts. Thus in the same LCSH appear the authorized headings SCHOOL LIBRARIES and SCIENTIFIC LIBRARIES. Of course, all the inverted headings should have been changed to direct ones as soon as the first heading of the latter type was established, but they were not. Much has been written about the official policy of superimposition described on pages 224–225, a policy followed by the Library of Congress between 1967 and 1980 in its name catalogues. This example shows that an analogous policy, largely unrecognized as such and never formally named, has long been applied to subject access points. The rule is the pragmatic one: "If it costs too much to change it, leave it alone."

Clearly, the issue will never be definitively settled. Even Cutter's principles leave much room for interpretation. A report of Library of Congress policy in 1981 on this issue states:

> . . . the Subject Cataloging Division prefers inverted word order for
> headings, enhanced by topical or form subdivisions, emphasizing that
> this approach renders a service to the user by grouping topics in one
> place.[15]

13. *Cataloging Service,* bulletin 121 (spring 1977):14.

14. "The Subject Catalogs of the Library of Congress," in *Papers and Proceedings of the Thirty-first Annual Meeting of the American Library Association Held at Bretton Woods, New Hampshire, Bulletin of the American Library Association* 3 (September 1909):389–90.

15. Rose Marie Clemandot, reporting comments made by Paul Weiss at the meeting of the Technical Services Special Interest Section of the American Association of Law Libraries, June 28–July 1, 1981, reported in *Library of Congress Information Bulletin* 40 (27 November 1981):421.

How Many Headings? Monographs versus Journal Articles

The subject indexing of monographs in library catalogues and that of journal articles in specialized bibliographies do not require controlled vocabularies based on different principles. Indexers who wish to use a pre-coordinate vocabulary have been able to start with a general one such as LCSH for indexing all levels of material in almost any subject field, supplementing it with specialized additions as needed. Even those who compile the indices within individual books commonly start from a common general vocabulary, although such indexing is often more ideosyncratic and may be based entirely on the terminology of the work itself.

It may be assumed that at least one subject or form heading is desirable for every item listed in a bibliography or catalogue. It is a tradition in library cataloguing, however, that no subject heading is applied to an individual work of the creative imagination, nor to a group of such works by a single author published together. Thus a novel, play, etc., or a collection of such by one author, is listed only under its author/title elements, unless by special exception the cataloguer thinks it desirable to indicate its subject using a form subheading, for example NAPOLEON—FICTION, or MATHEMATICS—POETRY. Music is a frequent exception: one can normally expect to find a recording of Beethoven's fifth symphony under the form heading SYMPHONIES in the subject catalogue of either a music or a general library, although one should not expect to find Dickens' *David Copperfield* under NOVELS. Many factors enter into an explanation of this apparent inconsistency, not all of them relevant to any given library. Anthologies of creative works by many authors are consistently given form headings, for example AMERICAN DRAMA.

At the other end of the spectrum, an upper limit has traditionally been applied to the number of subject headings used for a monograph in a general catalogue or bibliography. This is the "rule of three," an arbitrary practical, not a theoretical, limit. Operating in conjunction with the principle that subject access points should apply to the work as a whole, it tends to limit the average number of headings applied per document. Thus a book on light and heat would properly be listed under both headings, rather than under the (too) general one PHYSICS. But if four branches of physics (but not all its branches) were the subjects of the work, the more general heading PHYSICS would be applied.

The practical result of this "rule" is that the number of subject headings applied to the monographs in a general library's catalogue is an average of about one and a half if one of the standard pre-coordinate lists is used as the controlled vocabulary. Recent Library of Congress policy decisions have tended to increase this number slightly. For example, a biography once characteristically received only one subject heading; now it is common for both the name of the biographee and a topical designation to be applied. About two-fifths of all items in a general collection are listed under only one subject heading. About one-fifth, the creative writing, do not appear in the subject catalogue at all. About a quarter are listed under two headings, usually because no one heading pre-coordinating the aspects or topics of the work as a whole is authorized by the controlled vocabulary used. The remainder warrant three or more subject access points.[16]

In a post-coordinate system, the average number of subject access points per document must automatically be higher. These systems are still primarily used for the control of specialized journal and report literature, and post-coordination is not the only reason for using a higher number of access points for such items. Thirty years ago the designer of the much praised automated retrieval system for medical information, MEDLARS/MEDLINE, wrote:

> The more limited scope of periodical articles, as compared to books, is apt to require a more intensive degree of subject analysis. While this intensification may occasionally need to be met by a greater degree of specificity in the main subject heading used, it may more frequently be solved by increasing the multiplicity of headings assigned, or by resort to topical subdivision, required in only some areas of the book catalog.[17]

This may seem paradoxical, but it makes sense that since there is no internal index to consult within a journal article, that article should normally appear in an external index under as many access points as represent significant discrete concepts within the article, usually a quite manageable number. To do the same for a single longer monograph would usually require dozens, if not hundreds, of access points; and to no particular advantage since one can consult the internal index once one has been led to the monograph by means of a more general indication of its relevance.

The PREserved Context Indexing System

With the advent of bibliographic automation, the *British National Bibliography* sought to automate the production of its verbal subject index. Since the bibliography would continue to be issued in print for manual searching, the use of a completely post-coordinate system was not feasible. Pre-coordinate subject headings of the LCSH type were not the way to a greater degree of automation

16. These figures are taken from the largest quantitative study of subject heading application to date: Edward T. O'Neill and Rao Aluri, "Library of Congress Subject Heading Patterns in OCLC Monographic Records," *Library Resources & Technical Services* 25 (January/March 1981):63–67, 70–80. A fuller report of the same study exists as ERIC document ED 184 592.

17. Frank B. Rogers, "Application and Limitations of Subject Headings: The Pure and Applied Sciences," *The Subject Analysis of Library Materials,* ed. Maurice F. Tauber (New York: School of Library Service, Columbia University, 1953), pp. 81–82.

either, and in any case the verbal index from its inception in 1950 had been constructed according to S.R. Ranganathan's *chain indexing* technique. This is based on classification principles and results in a larger average number of search terms per document than LCSH would generate. Chain indexing theory, based on the coordination of terms in a specified order, seemed adaptable to computer technology. The result was the Preserved Context Indexing System, or PRECIS, which takes its place symbolically in this chapter between verbal indexing and classification because it is a hybrid, sharing features of both. It is verbally expressed and its terms are alphabetized, but its purpose is to display concept relationships within a document, not merely to indicate the existence of isolated specific subjects.

PRECIS also straddles the distinction between pre-coordination and post-coordination. A PRECIS ''string'' looks very much like a pre-coordinate subject heading, for example

    CANADA
        PAPER INDUSTRIES. PERSONNEL

> The two-line display of many PRECIS entries is significant. This avoids possible ambiguity, since a term following another on the same line is always to be taken as the more general context of that term.

Yet the *rotation* (or *shunting* as it is called in the system) of a string produces an index looking like the output from an online post-coordination. The above string will also appear in two other places in the alphabet:

    PAPER INDUSTRIES. CANADA
        PERSONNEL

and

    PERSONNEL. PAPER INDUSTRIES. CANADA

PRECIS is a hybrid in yet a third way. It does not adhere rigidly to a controlled vocabulary for its indexing terms, yet it does not restrict itself to the use of the natural language of titles. In practice there is a tendency toward trying to keep the vocabulary consistent over large numbers of items indexed, but this is left to the experience and judgement of the individual indexer working from precedent, not to a pre-determined list.

In the above example there are three terms in the ''string,'' each representing a concept. There are therefore six possible post-coordinations, but only the three shown above result in index entries. The sequence CANADA. PERSONNEL. PAPER INDUSTRIES, for example, does not appear and would not be wanted. It is the function of the indexer to determine which combinations are to appear. This is done not by inputting the selected combinations directly, but by inputting each desired term along with a code expressing its semantic relationship to the other selected terms. This coding ensures that the computer constructs and prints all, but only, the desired coordinations. What differentiates PRECIS from a KWIC index (see pages 173–174) is therefore that (1) the terms displayed are professionally selected, not mechanically taken from the item, and (2) the context in which each term is displayed is also determined by professional judgement, not by the sequence of words in a title or abstract.

The codes used to designate the appropriate semantic relationships are called *role operators*. They accomplish much the same purpose as prescribed punctuation in ISBD or tags in MARC; they let the computer know how to manipulate the following term in displaying it with the other terms in the string. The more than two dozen role operators include codes to indicate the existence of such factors as processes, points of view, superior or dependent relationships, agents, environments, etc. The system is therefore a fairly thorough and sophisticated one, as may be seen in the subject indices to the *British National Bibliography* and the *Australian National Bibliography*.[18] PRECIS is not an inexpensive system to operate, partly because it results in a higher number of index terms per document than using, say, LCSH. Rigorous training is required to master it. Its use is not widespread, although programs capable of shunting coded PRECIS strings exist for MARC-based computer systems. A few libraries in various parts of the world have incorporated PRECIS into their catalogues with apparent success.

The Systematic Approach: Classification

A subject classification is used for the same purpose as verbal subject headings, namely to identify and to isolate classes based on subject, form, and/or intended audience. Dogs as a biological species are designed 599.74 in the Dewey Decimal Classification, or TUS in Rider's International Classification, or K[5791] in the Colon Classification not merely to locate this subject close to the related subject "wolves" but also, as with a subject heading, to provide an unequivocal term for a specified concept in a particular context. Any classification notation is a controlled vocabulary, there being no possibility of a natural language in systematic arrangement.

Defining Classes: Characteristics of Division

Within any larger agglomeration, the relationship of one subgroup to another is defined by the application to the whole of some *characteristic of division*. The characteristic "colour of binding" is used to distinguish red books from green or blue ones; the characteristic "country of origin" applied to novelists

18. The official manual for the application of the system is by its originator: Derek Austin, *PRECIS, a Manual of Concept Analysis and Subject Indexing* (London: Council of the British National Bibliography, 1974).

distinguishes Japanese novelists from Colombian or Balinese ones. Red books are said to be a *focus* in the colour *facet* of the universe "books," and Japanese are a focus in the nationality facet of "authors." The application of any characteristic of division gathers, but it also separates. Anything without a red binding is not in the class of red books, no matter what other qualities of similarity it may have with members of the class (a red book and a green one may be by the same author, or on the same subject, or even contain the same text). To classify means, in practical terms, to choose and to define characteristics of division relevant to the purposes of the scheme.

Problems of definition tend to be less troublesome if the application of a given characteristic of division results in two, and only two, mutually exclusive classes. This is *dichotomy* in classification, a process which usually results in a neat "tree of knowledge." The classification illustrated in Figure 72 shows it.

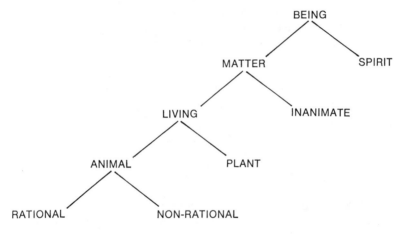

FIG. 72. A classification illustrating dichotomy.

Few topics are amenable to such cut-and-dried definition. In zoological classification, the family "sciuridae" is distinguished within the order "rodentia" as rodents with bushy tails, but how thick does the tail hair have to be to warrant being called "bushy?" It may be easy to distinguish a rat from a squirrel on these grounds, but is a chipmunk's tail bushy enough to deal with this species according to the definition? It may be easy to divide human beings in a societal context into dichotomous classes on objective biological grounds (sex, the division resulting in males and females). The problem is made more difficult if slightly vague, but still conventionally recognizable, grounds are used (age, the foci being children, adults, seniors, etc.) If quite subjective grounds are used, the division will be fraught with problems of definition (for example political opinion, resulting in a division between conservatives and radicals).

Bibliographic Classification

Intellectual classification is the serious study, and often the plaything, of philosophers and logicians. Theoretically, one can divide anything into anything following the formal rules of logic, and in the process often come upon insights and relationships well worth pursuing. Looking directly to the purposes of a given job, scientists and librarians must choose and define characteristics of division with a practical end in mind. What purpose is served by grouping porcupines with hamsters as "rodents," but wolves with terriers as "canines?" Are there purposes for which terriers and hamsters might better be thought of as together in one class (domesticity being the characteristic of division) and wolves and porcupines in another (the class of wild animals)? Is there a point in separating out all the books in a library collection which contain poems, dividing them from those containing plays? Or are there purposes for which it would be preferable to establish a class of English poems and plays, separating them from German poems and plays? Only one characteristic of division can logically be applied at a time. Classification separates as it gathers.

Cross-Classification; Discipline Orientation

The intellectual content of a book, periodical article, or any other library material rarely isolates a logical and simply defined concept, but is a welter of cross-classification. This may be illustrated by the need to establish a group, or class, for "female radicals." The topic results from the application of two (or more) characteristics of division simultaneously, and the classifier must decide whether sex or political opinion should predominate in the placing of the topic. A bibliographic classification scheme cannot be a neat structure, as an intellectual classification of ideas can. It is inevitably a messy arrangement of pragmatic compromises, largely because of the need to accommodate cross-classification.

Furthermore, a subject is necessarily treated in documents within a particular context or discipline. This factor is usually irrelevant to the selection of a subject heading for the document, but is vital to its systematic arrangement within a context. Every significant classification scheme for bibliographic purposes permits the same *subject* to be grouped within each different *discipline* to which it may be relevant.

As an example of both cross-classification and discipline orientation, a book or article is likely to deal with a topic like "working girls of lower-class background," a subject which incorporates three different characteristics of division. The topic may be treated from the point of view of economics (how much the girls are paid and what this means to the industrial economy); from the point of view of history (a description of the situation of such girls in nineteenth-century England); from the point of view of social forces (the impact of the condition of such workers on family life, etc.); and probably from other points of view as well. A discipline-oriented classification recognizes these points of view as predominant reasons for grouping, and forces the classifier to decide whether the item belongs in the history section, the economics section, or the sociology section. The searcher using such a classification must recognize that all material about working girls will not be in any one section. Thus bibliographic classifications are even less able than subject headings lists to define classes in a way that places neat and logical boundaries around each subject.

Arranging Classes

Once the classes which might be useful for the purpose have been defined in the context of a discipline, they must be assigned a sequence in relation to each other. Here, once again, bibliographic classification differs from many classifications devised for other purposes. The classification in Figure 72 on page 259 is shown as a "tree." How to flatten it out, or arrange its results in a linear sequence, is not self-evident. If it is difficult to say that any one citation order is correct for this simple "tree" class, it is much more difficult to determine the correct order for a group of classes showing cross-classification, a variable number of subclasses for each main class, etc.

The linear arrangement of classes is normally accomplished by adopting general principles of logic to the degree possible, modifying these in the light of literary warrant. It is almost universal to attempt to locate the more general before its specific parts, the cause before its effects, the thing before its properties, the process before its agents, etc. Geographic and chronological sub-arrangements are very appealing because they are simple. Fortunately, they are often useful because they are so readily recognized, so easily applied, and so often a part of the point of view of the content of actual documents. Not all subjects lend themselves to these relatively clear principles of citation order, but whenever a user is able to sense the "direction" in which the sequence is leading, the user can employ that knowledge to predict the availability of other aspects of the topic in the classification. The excerpt from the abridged version of the Dewey Decimal Classification reproduced in Figure 73 may illustrate these points.

Classification and the User

The principal difficulty in searching a classified arrangement, whether on the shelves or in a catalogue, is that the average user feels unfamiliar and unconfident. How can one know what is comprised within a given class? Its definition was created by someone else, probably by a specialist with a Ph.D. in the subject in question. How can the nonspecialist predict the location of a particular subtopic within a larger group spanning many shelves of books? These

| 331 | *Economics* | 331 |

▶ **331.3–331.6 Labor force by personal characteristics**

Class here labor force and market; wages, hours, other conditions of employment; specific industries and occupations, labor unions, labor-management bargaining with respect to special classes of workers

Unless other instructions are given, class complex subjects with aspects in two or more subdivisions of this schedule in the number coming first in the schedule, e.g., aged Chinese women 331.3 (*not* 331.4 or 331.6)

Class comprehensive works in 331.1

.3   Workers of specific age groups

Children, young adults, middle-aged, aged 65 and over

Class apprentices in 331.5

.4   Women workers

.5   Special categories of workers

Prisoners, ex-offenders, veterans; contract, migrant, casual workers; apprentices; workers suffering mental and physical handicaps

Class training of apprentices in 331.25

For categories of workers by racial, ethnic, national origin, see 331.6

.6   Categories of workers by racial, ethnic, national origin

Including immigrants

Class migrant workers in 331.5

.7   Labor by industry and occupation

Professional, managerial, white-collar, service, industrial, agricultural, unskilled occupations

Including government employment, choice of vocation

Do not use standard subdivisions

Class a specific element of labor in a specific industry or occupation with the subject, e.g., wages 331.2; studies of vocational interest in 158.6, vocational counseling in schools in 371.4, job hunting in 650.1; description of a specific occupation with the subject, using "Standard Subdivisions" notation 023 from Table 1, e.g., accounting 657.023

FIG. 73. From *Abridged Dewey Decimal Classification and Relative Index.* edition 11, ed. under the direction of Benjamin A. Custer (Albany: Forest Press, 1979).

difficulties stem from an external source: the fact that no two scholars see the logical relationships among parts of their own field of specialization in precisely the same way. If everyone agreed what "felines" are (probably most people do), and that they should precede "canines" in any arrangement of carnivores (here is where the cat-and-dog fights begin), then the use of classified arrangements would be as natural to users as is the use of the alphabet. Until one becomes quite familiar with a topic, one needs an alphabetic word index to any classified arrangement. Many library users search the catalogue under a subject heading merely to find one or two class numbers which lead them to shelf locations for browsing. This is also why LCSH and Sears show class numbers beside many of the subject headings.

There are other limitations of any bibliographic classification, among them the following:

1) The requirement of placing classes in a linear sequence prevents the user from seeing the rich variety of cross-relationships among those items which cannot be located next to each other (for example, the item on working-class girls is probably of interest to the economist, the social worker, and the historian, but can only be located in one of these disciplines).

2) Knowledge is not static; documents ostensibly on the same topic but dating from much different periods may in fact be on quite different topics. No arrangement of a subject and its parts is permanently valid.

3) There is a psychological tendency for any deviser of a classification scheme, and for any classifier using one, to skew the system (or its application) in a direction based on the person's own subject knowledge, interests, and prejudices.

4) Each collection of materials has been brought together for a specific purpose; hence the location of any given item in that collection cannot be an absolute, based on its content alone—the reason for its inclusion must also be considered. The same item may rightly be classified differently in two different collections, even if the same classification scheme is used in both.

The Classification Schemes of Melvil Dewey and the Library of Congress

There exist as many classification schemes as subject headings lists, and for the same reasons. As with subject headings lists, the economics of cooperation and standardization have tended to limit the number of schemes in widespread use. In North America, it is almost certain that a general library, whatever its size, uses either of two schemes: (1) the Dewey Decimal Classification (DDC), or (2) The Library of Congress Classification (LCC). Many classified bibliographies are arranged by DDC or by its offshoot the Universal Decimal Classification (UDC).[19] Nevertheless, many individual classified bibliographies, and older libraries outside North America, are arranged according to schemes devised for a single purpose or location.

Both DDC and LCC are very widely used because unlike most of the other general schemes they are constantly kept up to date. Ultimately, however, their popularity, as well as that of LCSH, depends even more on the fact that the Library of Congress and other national agencies issue bibliographic records bearing subject designations according to these schemes for most contemporary English-language publications. Today it would be economic folly for any general (all-subject) library in the English-speaking world to adopt any other classification scheme, and both schemes are widely used outside the English-speaking world as well.

LCC was, of course, devised by and for the Library of Congress. DDC was also originally devised for a particular library, Amherst College Library, where Melvil Dewey was librarian in 1876 when the scheme was first published. It has long been the property of a private company (Forest Press, Inc., established by Dewey to perpetuate the scheme), but its editing and updating were entrusted in 1923 by that company to the Decimal Classification Office at the Library of Congress. Thus the Library of Congress in effect maintains both classification schemes here under consideration.

LCC is revised almost daily in the process of its application in the Subject Cataloging Division of the Library of Congress, although individual volumes of the classification are fully revised only very infrequently. A completely re-edited DDC is published every five to ten years, but the profession is given a few years' advance warning in the cataloguing literature of any major proposed changes. Both schemes show their age, LCC far more than DDC. The inertia which prevents any list of subject headings from being always timely and relevant operates with classification schemes too! Nevertheless, DDC in its last three editions has come a long way to expressing the twentieth-century classification theories developed by librarians, logicians, semanticists, and mathematicians. The most significant of these was S.R. Ranganathan, whose Colon Classification, chain indexing theory, and general publications on classification have been far more influential than their small readership in North America would indicate.

LCC is more a ''grassroots'' scheme based in literary warrant than is DDC. From the beginning its classes and their arrangement have been based on the existing collections at the Library of Congress. DDC acknowledges the existing

19. The current (19th) edition of DDC was cited on page 11. The current abridged version is *Abridged Dewey Decimal Classification and Relative Index,* 11th ed. (Albany: Forest Press, 1979). LCC consists of almost forty separate publications in various editions and dates as well as a quarterly amendment service. A list is available from the Cataloging Distribution Service, The Library of Congress. UDC also consists of many separately published parts; the full English edition is published by the British Standards Institution.

literature, but has always been more a classification developed theoretically from ideas to documents, than vice versa.

The differences in their notation express this difference in approach. DDC assigns a digit from 1 to 9 to each major discipline (1, Philosophy; 2, Religion; 3, Sociology; etc.). The tenth digit, 0, represents generalia and precedes the others. Each digit of the notation is divided decimally as the hierarchy of knowledge is constructed. Thus 7, Fine Arts, is divided into 71, Civic and Landscape Art; 72, Architecture; 73, Plastic Arts and Sculpture; etc.

This system of decimal notation is undoubtedly the factor which first gave DDC superiority over the many other late-nineteenth century library classification schemes. The notation is easy to remember. It makes the order of classes very visible, encouraging the searcher to be conscious of the classification. It makes additions relatively easy to accommodate. It makes possible, within the same notational base, the *broad classification* of a topic at a general level (using few decimal places) or the *close classification* of the same topic in detail (using many decimal places).

Thus a large library might wish to apply the DDC number 551.710971241 to an item on the geology of lake sediments in Northern Saskatchewan, but if that specific a breakdown of its content were deemed unnecessary, the shorter number 551.71 still expresses the focus of this item's subject, precambrian stratigraphy. In other words, DDC's notation makes it easy to classify at various levels of specificity depending on the needs of the individual collection and/or users. DDC notation is printed on Library of Congress entries in segments to indicate where the number may reasonably be shortened if broader classification is acceptable.

The notation adopted by LCC has almost none of the virtues of the DDC notation except that it does not get as long as a DDC number can sometimes become for a specific topic. An LCC class number does, however, have a larger average number of characters than a DDC one. It is simply a serial numbering, within a one-to-three-letter base which expresses the discipline and immediate subdiscipline. LCC notation does have the virtue of not "tying down" the development of a concept onto the procrustean bed of a nine-unit base.

Class Numbers and Call Numbers

The primary purpose of classification is to group concepts. Its use to "mark and park" the physical items containing those concepts, while a natural by-product, has often been confused with this primary purpose, although the two functions are totally different (see pages 237–238). Nevertheless, any arrangement of either physical items or their entries according to a subject classification requires a class number to be supplemented, so that a unique call number can isolate each item or entry. Since by definition a class comprises more than one individual item (even if the particular library only owns one in that class), a class number cannot in itself identify just one document.

The most natural division of a class is into the works which comprise it. Thus if 540 (DDC) or QD31 (LCC) identifies the class of works about chemistry in general, the most useful characteristic by which to subdivide them is the author's name, since that is a prime identification of the work for all cataloguing purposes. Traditionally, a designation is added to the class number corresponding to the main entry heading applied to the item. This designation is in a kind of shorthand, of which there are several systems in common use. Thus the call number for Saither's book on chemistry might be 540.S2, or 540.S158, or even 540 SAI. Charles Ammi Cutter devised an alphanumeric shorthand of the kind represented by the first two of these examples which has come to be called the *Cutter numbering* system. Further designations may be added in order to distinguish editions (a date is the usual notation), resulting in a call number such as QD31.S3 1982. A library will add to this any relevant volume number, copy number, and branch location information, in order to construct a complete and unique identification for each physical object in the collection for circulation and inventory purposes.

IV Creating and Sharing Bibliographic Records

9

COOPERATIVE DATABASE CONSTRUCTION; NETWORKING

Who Creates Bibliographic Records?

Throughout this book two types of agencies creating bibliographic records have been differentiated: the abstracting and indexing services and the library community. The latter includes the so-called national bibliographic agencies, those responsible for generating national bibliographies. In some ways they treat bibliographic information similarly; in other ways their purposes and methodology differ. An abstracting/indexing service may be either a commercial or a nonprofit organization, and its work may or may not be subsidized in some way, but they all create and disseminate bibliographic information as a business. Each focuses on an area, only occasionally in competition with others, where there is a perceived need for in-depth author-title or subject indexing. It is usually a broad subject area and the type of material covered normally includes, and is often restricted to, journal articles, technical reports, conference proceedings, and the like.

Before the abstracting and indexing services existed, libraries committed their resources heavily to this same type of indexing. They gradually, but consciously, departed the field of analysis as commercial services entered it since the latter quickly showed they could serve the field more successfully than could libraries (see pages 102 and 233). For one thing, they are able to employ full-time indexers expert in specialized fields of knowledge. From the economic point of view, even a generation ago there was neither a technology nor an accepted method of financing available for the kind of cooperative venture which would have been required if libraries had continued indexing a broad range of journal and report literature. How much things have recently changed in these respects is the focus of the remainder of this chapter.

It is not unusual for an indexing service to create more bibliographic records in a year than does the Library of Congress. That it does not require as large a staff per thousand records created as would any library is a reflection of the specialized types of material involved, a generally less "fussy" attitude toward authority control, and the relatively standard bibliographic nature of most of the documents handled by any one indexing service. Since each of these agencies is recovering some or all its costs by selling a product, it must consider what the potential customers are willing to pay for the product's scope, coverage, and adherence to quality standards. These standards have hitherto tended to be individually developed. Each producer has a proprietary interest in its own records, and records created by these services have only recently begun to be amalgamated into common databases. Computerization is enforcing new and compatible standards on these services as it has among libraries. The UNISIST Reference Manual and the Common Communication Format described on pages 147–149 have arisen from the need of the abstracting and indexing community for communication formats.

A hundred years ago each library also created all its own bibliographic records, according to its individual choice of rules. A method of reproduction (pen, typewriter, printing) was selected, and the product was formatted in whatever way seemed best suited to the physical medium chosen (cards, books, sheaves). Each of a thousand copies of the same book was separately catalogued in each of a thousand libraries, using various rules and formats. Since no consideration was given to the potential for sharing costs and products, there was no need for rules or practices which could be called standards even in the loosest meaning of that term. Then in 1898 the Library of Congress began its project of total bibliographic reorganization, incorporating its own new rules and a then modern technology, the printed unit-entry card. Three years later it began to sell copies of its bibliographic records on card stock to any purchaser, putting into practice a suggestion made fifty years earlier by Charles Jewett of the Smithsonian Institution. As a production/distribution facility, it was soon supplying a standard physical product purchased for filing into local catalogues everywhere.[1] Just as quickly it was accepted as the originator/arbiter of standard practices to be imitated throughout the United States and elsewhere; the Anglo-American cataloguing code of 1908 already incorporated rules specifically reflecting Library of Congress application and interpretations.

In filling a vacuum and becoming the de facto leader of the English-speaking

1. The one major bibliographic convention represented on Library of Congress entries which was widely resisted was its classification scheme. Libraries which had adopted one of the other then new classifications (those of Dewey or Cutter) saw little reason to change again to an unfinished scheme, and even new libraries of smaller size tended to adopt Dewey, seeing the Library of Congress Classification as too "large" for their purposes. (It was only in the educational expansion of the 1950s and 1960s that libraries in post-secondary institutions tended to open with the Library of Congress classification in imitation of the larger neighbouring universities which had for the most part adopted the scheme by then.)

world in the techniques of bibliographic control, the Library of Congress gave practical meaning to what has become the first law of cataloguing administration: "Never create a bibliographic record for a document if you can more cheaply acquire and use a satisfactory record originating elsewhere." For a given item to be catalogued only once anywhere was recognized as the ideal situation. The abstracting and indexing services generally saw that this was so for the materials they handled, and in the past twenty years it has become much more the case among libraries as well.

The term *derived cataloguing* refers to the use by one institution of a catalogue entry created somewhere else. It also refers to the entries themselves, which are located and adapted for the local catalogue (by adding local book number and copy information, branch locations, filing headings, etc.) usually by clerical or subprofessional help under supervision. Derived cataloguing is relatively inexpensive. The term *original cataloguing* refers to the local creation of a catalogue record in its entirety. It normally requires professional staff and is therefore relatively expensive.

Every library tries to achieve as high a "hit rate" for derived cataloguing as possible, that is, to locate as high a proportion as possible of its acquired materials in an acceptable bibliographic database by the time it feels it must catalogue each item. Thus, for example, the administrator speaks of "a hit rate of sixty percent in the *Weekly Record* within one month of acquisition." The Library of Congress is the preferred source of derived cataloguing in North America, and to a considerable extent elsewhere, for several reasons:

1) *scope*—The comprehensiveness and vigour of its collecting policies mean that it is one of the world's largest libraries. It can be expected to produce an entry for most United States and many foreign titles soon after their publication.

2) *quality*—It offers a reliable and consistent product based not only on sound rules, but also on a more thorough reference search during authority control work than most smaller libraries can attempt or afford. High clerical standards and physical quality of the product are also evident.

3) *cost*—The real cost of its entries has never been fully assessed to their purchasers. For a long time the cost of creating the entry was entirely absorbed by the Library of Congress. It now adds a percentage of this cost to the price of its bibliographic services, but considering the large quantities involved, the amount per unit is small. Charges for the recoverable costs (physical manufacture, distribution, etc.) also reflect the economies possible in high-volume turnover.

4) *standardization*—The beginning of a national union catalog in 1902 as a card file at the Library of Congress showing the holdings of many important North American libraries was a strong impetus toward stan-

dardization. Since the entries added by the Library of Congress itself to this catalogue are its single largest component, and where possible are the ones on which the holdings of other libraries are recorded, they have always been accepted as the model for all cataloguing, at least in the contributing libraries.

5) *adaptability* —The Library of Congress has been responsive to the fact that other libraries use its catalogue entries in various contexts. It has never lost sight of the fact that the prime purpose of its bibliographic activities is to support its own reference services, not the technical services of other libraries. Nevertheless, it has accommodated itself increasingly to the latter function since it first began to apply Dewey Decimal Classification class numbers to many of its entries in 1930.[2]

Acquiring Derived Cataloguing without Automation

Entries originating with a national bibliographic agency (for example the Library of Congress, the National Library of Canada, the British Library) are now commonly called *source records*. These are assumed to be records of the highest quality and bibliographic veracity. In the printed unit-card format intended for manual catalogues, Library of Congress entries poured out from Washington by mail to all points in increasingly large numbers for seventy years. More than a hundred and twenty million cards a year were being sold or deposited before the flood was stemmed by the availability of more economical means of reproducing Library of Congress copy locally. The Canadian and British national agencies also sold separate card-format entries by the 1960s but with less success; most of the items they catalogued, and far more, could be identified on Library of Congress entries.

But the national agencies were never the only sources of derived cataloguing. Before the introduction of automation, the sharing of entries on a large scale among individual libraries was not practicable, but commercial agencies and a few library consortia and state/provincial libraries were solidly established as suppliers of derived cataloguing in card form. These often provided entries complete with call numbers, branch locations, headings, etc., "ready to file" into individual library catalogues. Some merely enhanced and distributed records originating elsewhere (usually source records). Others did original cata-

2. Where relevant, Library of Congress entries now also include the following features, none of them germane to its own internal handling of the item in question: (1) class numbers and subject headings generated by the National Library of Medicine using its own schemes, (2) alternate class numbers reflecting the subjects of bibliographies classed in Z, (3) class numbers displaying the monographic aspect of items classed as series, and (4) a summary and alternate juvenile subject headings for children's materials (see example on page 124).

loguing of items for which source records were unavailable, or catalogued everything according to different (usually simpler) standards. A commercial agency limiting the scope of its activities to entries for relatively simple and popular materials could keep unit costs low enough to charge a competitive price and even make a profit, despite the fact that source records are subsidized. From 1938 through 1975 the H.W. Wilson Co. created entries for such materials and was the principal supplier of catalogue cards to the public and school libraries of North America (Figure 2 on page 17 is an illustration of a Wilson entry). Some commercial agencies linked the sale of catalogue entries with the sale of books or other services, often using cataloguing services as a loss-leader to attract the more profitable business, the orders for materials. Unlike Wilson cards, this method of acquiring derived cataloguing with the items themselves from a commercial vendor is surviving the change to automation.

Cataloguing in Publication

The usefulness of derived cataloguing was always tempered by the fact that acquiring actual physical catalogue cards from a distant source involves significant direct and hidden costs, and often intolerable delay. Academic libraries have long had to apply routines for making items available to users while awaiting derived cataloguing. Idealists wondered whether there could be found a practical way of incorporating within a document at the time of its publication some or all of the elements of a standard catalogue entry, particularly name and subject access points established according to standard rules. In that way the bibliographic data most costly to create locally would always be available at the same time as the item and at no extra cost. An experiment involving a few thousand printed monographic trade publications was launched in the United States in 1958. The Library of Congress produced prepublication cataloguing information to be printed in the books. This *Cataloging-in-Source* experiment did not become operational after its trial period because the technology for transforming the data economically into usable catalogue entries in individual libraries was not yet available.

The experiment showed, however, that United States publishers and the Library of Congress could cooperate in preparing cataloguing copy for an item before its publication. Page or galley proofs of the item, or at least of its bibliographic preliminaries, and data sheets completed by the publisher are the basis for the work. As a result, since 1960 the publication of a United States trade item is normally recorded in the trade bibliography *Weekly Record* (a part of *Publishers Weekly* until August 1974) using a Library of Congress catalogue entry. Administrators soon stopped thinking of Library of Congress *copy* and the Library of Congress *card* as synonymous terms. Thus even before automation, many libraries devised in-house routines and systems for using the former without acquiring the latter, locally photographing or retyping an entry from copy found in the *National Union Catalog* or elsewhere.[3]

Cataloging-in-Source in its 1958 form had attempted too much, giving rise to the unfulfilled expectation that a physical card could be mechanically reproduced directly from it. In its 1970s form as Cataloging in Publication (CIP), it became internationally successful. All access points (both name and subject) are established, but elements of the ISBD description included in CIP are restricted to the title proper and, if applicable, series title(s) and notes. Having this much information in the item as published makes it possible to produce a full catalogue entry locally using subprofessional help to complete the ISBD description. In some libraries CIP data are used only to provide a shelf location and perhaps temporary catalogue access until full derived cataloguing is available. Examples of CIP data are found on the verso of the title leaf and on page 125.

In a score of countries, CIP is now an operational bibliographic service through the cooperation of the country's publishing industry and the national bibliographic agency. As well as appearing in the items themselves, the CIP entries are usually incorporated immediately into the national bibliography, where it is of course expanded to include publication information. There, CIP is an aid in selection and current awareness services. When the item is published, its CIP entry is upgraded to a complete bibliographic record; occasionally some corrections are necessary, for example when the item as published has a title page different from the copy submitted before publication.

The National Program for Acquisitions and Cataloging

It is self-evident that the Library of Congress could never be solely responsible for the production of all cataloguing copy used in the United States. Yet such expectations appear to have been a subliminal part of the psychology of American librarianship until quite recently, and the Library of Congress has attempted over the years to go some distance toward fulfilling them. As early as the 1930s, entries prepared by other agencies were printed and distributed by the Library of Congress. In 1966 under the Shared Cataloging Program, now known as the National Program for Acquisitions and Cataloging (NPAC), The Library of Congress began to accept for inclusion in its own database bibliographic descriptions copied directly from selected national bibliographies around the world. The inauguration of NPAC led directly to the creation of ISBD as a means of ensuring greater consistency since various national

---

3. Under United States copyright law, the Library of Congress cannot claim any rights of ownership in its bibliographic entries. Anyone is free to transcribe or otherwise reproduce them from any source. This is not true of bibliographic records originating with private commercial sources, institutions, or agencies of many other governments. See The Commerce in Bibliographic Data, pages 289–290.

agencies were in effect contributing to the same database. (Access points, both name and subject, were not automatically accepted; they continued to be established in Washington in conformity with the standards and local practices of the Library of Congress.) The conviction typical of the North American cataloguer at the time, that only his/her own local department or the Library of Congress was capable of creating a satisfactory catalogue entry, was finally shaken, and the door to cooperative database construction was unlocked, if not immediately opened.

Automation, Derived Cataloguing, and Cooperative Database Construction

The creation and dissemination of cataloguing copy by national agencies does not constitute cooperation, but only centralization. The cooperative production and exchange of bibliographic records among libraries has had a long history in the form of the union catalogue to which various libraries would send entries, usually a copy of each unit entry on card stock. But a manually maintained union catalogue housed in one physical location was awkward even for reference librarians to use by mail or telephone. It was essentially useless as a source of cooperatively produced derived cataloguing. It is in any case now almost obsolete. The *National Union Catalog* illustrates the change in the use of a bibliographic database occasioned by its changing physical forms. While it existed only as a card file in Washington, D.C., it served the reference librarian's purposes awkwardly and inconveniently; it served the cataloguer's purpose not at all. When it became a continuing book-form (and later in part microform) publication available for local purchase, it could be used for both purposes, but information on current titles only reached the potential user after a considerable delay required for its production and distribution, and in the inconvenient form of slowly cumulating monthly issues. Though relatively efficient for retrospective cataloguing, it was inefficient for current cataloguing, hence the need for CIP to supplement it.

Automation soon provided new incentives and methods for cooperative database construction, but putting its methods into practice requires a total reassessment of manual practices and a change of many of them. When the Library of Congress began to sell its bibliographic records to other institutions in 1901, the technology involved was the 7.5 × 12.5 cm. catalogue card. To make this technology functional, the only local requirements were enough catalogue cabinets and staff to file the entries acquired. In 1969 the Library of Congress added to its services the weekly shipment of newly created records through a different technology: data in LC MARC format on magnetic tape. This technology required its users to have expensive hardware, sophisticated software, and a new class of professional systems and programming personnel. Few if any libraries had or could quickly acquire such resources. Much professional talk revolved around the possibility that a package of MARC-handling computer programs could be produced for use by any library, but ultimately it became apparent that differences between computers and the absence of a suitable efficient higher-level language would make such a goal unattainable (which it still is).

Two streams of development could soon be discerned. There was a small number of libraries, including some of the very largest research libraries and the smallest most specialized ones, each of which began to develop its own independent automated system for bibliographic control (acquisitions, cataloguing, serials and circulation control, etc.). These libraries used locally owned or leased hardware and developed the software in-house. The largest libraries had the resources to undertake such development.[4] The special libraries, usually restricted to the computing resources of their parent agency and in any case outside the mainstream of library cooperation, had no choice but to develop individualized systems.

Participating in the second type of development was a much larger number of libraries, originally almost always academic libraries within a region. They began to form *consortia* or *networks* whose goals were the development of online bibliographic control systems and the cooperative creation of bibliographic databases. In doing so they acknowledged that to develop systems independently would be too expensive, that sharing with similar institutions would not necessarily mean accepting an inferior system or database, and that there are positive benefits to cooperation.

Processing Facilities

Thus MARC acted as a catalyst, bringing into prominence two new kinds of bibliographic organization, both of them essentially agencies established by and for cooperation in the new context of automation. A processing facility, now often called a *bibliographic utility,* owns computers and acts as an online gatherer and transmitter of bibliographic records. (The second new type of organization, the regional service centre, is described on pages 281–282.) In

4. Among these were of course the national libraries. The Library of Congress developed the Multiple Use MARC System (MUMS) for its in-house processing operations and the Subject-Content-Oriented Retriever for Processing Information On-line (SCORPIO) for its in-house reference searching operations. The British Library, on its founding in 1973, began to develop the British Library Automated Information Service (BLAISE), both for in-house operations and to support online information searching by it and other libraries. The National Library of Canada and the Canada Institute for Scientific and Technical Information have jointly developed a modification of the Dortmunder Bibliothekssystem (DOBIS) for a wide range of processing and information retrieval purposes. A national agency has little need, of course, for features such as a circulation control module.

1967 the Ohio College Library Center (OCLC) was established as the process-ing facility for a consortium of the academic libraries of Ohio. It purchased hardware, hired a staff to develop programs, and subscribed to Library of Congress MARC tapes. It offered to disseminate source records as well as attaching local holdings information to them in the central database in order to construct a machine-readable union catalogue. By 1970 OCLC was able to produce printed catalogue cards on demand. Its online service began in 1971; a user at any display terminal could search for any record in the database using a compression code as described on pages 178–180.

OCLC's purpose at the time is described in the term *cataloguing support system* originally applied to it, that is, an agency to make computer services available for the generation of individual-library catalogues. A derived cata-loguing record located by a library in the OCLC database, but not satisfactory in every respect to the local cataloguer, could be modified: both the data in, and the print form of, a record produced for a particular catalogue are under local control. If no record is located in the database, the system's storage and printing facilities are still employed. The local cataloguer creates an original record online, prompted by an automated worksheet displayed on the terminal by the OCLC programs. This new record, coded to identify the originating library, becomes a part of the master database available to reference librarians wishing to locate items for interlibrary loan, and to other cataloguers wishing to use it as derived cataloguing.

Thus within a very short time the machine-readable bibliographic database, centrally stored and maintained but cooperatively created, has become a basic tool of librarianship. It can be consulted from a distance and entries can be copied to or from a distant input/output device. The reference librarian's use of it as a union catalogue for locating a wanted item not in the local collection has merged with the cataloguer's use of it as a source of derived cataloguing. Source records created by the national agencies are the most important compo-nent of the central database. They now account for perhaps two-thirds of the entries created or copied by the typical larger academic library in the United States, and more than ninety percent of those used by the typical smaller public or school library. But sales of Library of Congress entries on card stock dropped from a high of almost eighty million in 1968 to less than a quarter that number within just over a decade. The Library of Congress decided not to enter the business of distributing machine-readable records as it had distrib-uted its entries on cards, namely on a one-by-one, or ''selected'' basis. It has left that function to the bibliographic utilities. (In contrast, both the National Library of Canada and the British Library do offer the service of selling individual machine-readable records from their databases.)

The North American Utilities Today

The immediate success of OCLC attracted worldwide attention. It represented a marked advance in the art of bibliographic control, both in the sophistication of its technology and in the development of a businesslike and equitable approach to the sharing of local resources in cooperative ventures. Other individual agencies and groups dropped plans to develop processing facilities in favour of purchasing services from OCLC. The geographic scope of the facility quickly spread beyond the borders of the state of Ohio to serve single libraries and consortia across the United States, thus justifying a change of name to "Online Computer Library Center." Its single file of more than eight million bibliographic records is now searched online from more than six thousand terminals. OCLC output products include catalogue cards, spine labels and book cards, and MARC-formatted magnetic tapes known as *archival tapes* of a single library's contributions to the common database. The latter may be used to generate other products, for example COM catalogues, regional union catalogues, and files for use in circulation systems and stand-alone online catalogues. An interlibrary loan system passes requests from the terminal of a would-be borrower to the terminal of the proposed lender, using bibliographic data from the central file.

The gathering and dissemination of machine-readable bibliographic data soon became a competitive business, although among nonprofit organizations. That OCLC was the first bibliographic utility gave it an advantage over those developed later, but events have proved that others could compete on the grounds of different services, different systems characteristics, etc. OCLC has remained largely a United States facility despite recent marketing efforts in the United Kingdom.

Whether for nationalistic or other reasons, Canadian libraries seeking a comparable facility turned to the University of Toronto, whose University of Toronto Library Automation Systems (UTLAS) began to offer online bibliographic services to customers in 1973. Like OCLC, UTLAS makes available source records from various national agencies and accepts for dissemination original records input by its customers. Unlike OCLC, in whose files limited local data are attached by individual libraries to a single master record, the UTLAS system is designed to provide a separate file for each user (or consortium of users, as they desire), into which records from any other user's file may be copied. Where appropriate a charge is levied for the use of the records: source file records are automatically available at nominal cost, but any arrangement to copy the records of another local agency is negotiated and fixed by legal agreement between the libraries concerned.

Thus UTLAS's fourteen million records include many duplicates because they exist in some two hundred separate files. All access points are, however, loaded into unified files and are therefore searchable with a single command.

Online authority control (see pages 183–185) is available, permitting a user to browse in the access point files and to change headings in these files without needing to alter the files of bibliographic records. One of the files used on UTLAS hardware for authority control is a Shared Authority File (SHARAF) to which records in the Canadian MARC Authorities format are being contributed by a number of UTLAS users. UTLAS provides a range of cataloguing products broader than OCLC's, including custom-produced COM and printed book catalogues for individual users, and union catalogues for groups of users.

Another online bibliographic control system is the Washington Library Network (WLN), an agency of the Washington State Library. WLN has emphasized quality of data by imposing manual authority control on its users; each new record submitted to the system must be approved by the editorial staff in Olympia, Washington. WLN's database is considerably smaller than that of OCLC or UTLAS, but it pioneered in offering such services as an integrated acquisitions system with fund accounting, and it has experimented with a vendor-supplied online circulation system using data derived from the cataloguing database. Its searching techniques are also more sophisticated than those of OCLC, and its software permits searching on many more search keys (including subject search keys) than is true of either OCLC or UTLAS.

WLN permits membership only in the Pacific Northwest of the United States, including Alaska. It does not intend to expand beyond that region, although it hopes that similar regional networks will be established, using the WLN software, in other locations. The WLN software is designed for *replication,* that is, transportation to and implementation in other locations using local computer hardware there. A copy of the software may be purchased directly from WLN and is also available with suitable computer hardware as a package through a commercial company. Users of the WLN software include several universities, a regional network, and the National Library of Australia.

The fourth major North American processing facility used to support a cataloguing network is operated by the Research Libraries Group (RLG). The network function is now called the Research Libraries' Information Network (RLIN). Rather than develop its own software, RLG acquired Stanford University's system, Bibliographic Automation of Large Library Operations using a Time-sharing System (BALLOTS), which it has since revised extensively. It provides cataloguing functions, acquisitions with fund accounting, and serials control. Its search commands are particularly well developed and permit the use of boolean operators. Rather than trying to appeal to all types of libraries, as do OCLC and UTLAS, or a specific region as does WLN, RLIN is available only to a select group of research libraries, although it allows access by other libraries to its database on a "search only" basis. RLIN is an active partner in current research into means of dealing with the Sino-Japanese script in automated bibliographic work.

Each of these four computer facilites started as a cataloguing support system.

However, each has developed other services which differ significantly from one another. The characteristics described above were true as of mid-1982. At that time OCLC's interlibrary loan system had no counterpart in the other facilities; RLIN's search capability was more flexible and powerful than the others; WLN's software was available for sale; and UTLAS's varied catalogue-production services were attracting customers from other systems including a number of RLIN users. Each system is constantly developing improved features and new functions, suggesting that as time passes each will look more and more like the others.

Periodic growing pains are characteristic of all the systems. In part these are caused by the growing complexity of hardware and software. Communication problems are particularly troublesome in countries as vast as Canada and the United States, where a number of different communication companies may be involved in the transfer of data from a terminal to a central computer, and where lines capable of reliable high-speed transmission of electronic data are still only available among major centres.

Managerial and systems-design problems are also common within any dynamic enterprise dependent on ever-changing technology. A common symptom of such problems is the existence of unfulfilled claims for new or improved services. Librarians without experience in automation tend to take at face value promises of features to be introduced in just a few weeks or months, and often unwisely assume that all the functions and features described in the sales brochures and manuals are already operating normally and satisfactorily. Nevertheless, any informal survey of the users of the processing facilities reveals that they work well most of the time. Librarians appear to have unbounded optimism that the future will see steady improvements, just as the systems of the present are significantly better than those of even the recent past.

Expanding the Size and Scope of the Utilities' Databases

Records enter the North American utilities' databases from outside sources; none of them does any original cataloguing, though some undertake the technical function of input from manual sources. Source records are acquired by every utility from one or more national agencies, and are loaded into the database at relatively low unit cost. The unique value of any database therefore comes from the number and quality of records other than source records in it. In order to encourage member libraries to input timely original cataloguing into the database, the utilities all incorporate a credit in the form of a lower use-fee for each insertion of an original record. This practice is intended to counter a natural tendency to put the item aside if it is not found in the database, and wait for some other institution to create and input original cataloguing for it.

Today's systems still fall far short of providing complete cataloguing support. They have raised expectations beyond those applied to manual systems for communicating bibliographic information. Most of the databases originating with and for libraries still comprise principally records for newer monographic printed trade publications. A cataloguer hoping to achieve as high a hit rate for derived cataloguing for sound recordings or other nonprint materials, government publications, analytics for microform sets, older publications, etc., will not be satisfied for a number of years to come. Nevertheless, systematic expansion of the databases is now underway. Many individual libraries are committed to conversion, or *recon,* projects to bring existing manual catalogues under full or partial computer control, and much of this converted data is housed in the databases of the processing facilities.

The utilities also have the computer capacity and the searching/output systems which make it possible for them to act much like the abstracting and indexing services, and it is inevitable that they should seek out areas not yet covered by the latter for their own activity. "More is better" both for interlibrary loan locating purposes and for derived cataloguing; therefore each utility or consortium has an interest in amassing ever larger quantities of bibliographic records of any kind into its database.

Major projects in indexing, like reconversion projects, cannot normally be undertaken within existing institutional budgets, but efforts to find outside funding on an ad hoc basis have been successful in many instances. A master database of standard machine-readable bibliographic descriptions for serial publications is growing through a project known as CONSER; major steps are being taken to analyze the contents of microform sets; a project to index Festschriften has received funding; and there is now a machine-readable index to current art sales catalogues. Such developments are rapidly expanding the content of the databases controlled by one or another of the bibliographic utilities.

Regional Service Centres

Regional consortia of libraries have long existed in some areas. Examples of these in the United States are the New England Library Network (NELINET) serving six New England states, the Five Area University Libraries (FAUL) in New York, and the Cooperative College Library Center (CCLC) with headquarters in Atlanta. OCLC expanded so quickly in its early years that it was not prepared to deal with each new member library outside Ohio on an individual basis; rather, it was content to let existing regional organizations act as brokers for its services within their areas. Other network organizations were soon established specifically to assist member libraries in their dealings with a processing facility. They include the Southeastern Library Network (SOLINET) serving more than three hundred libraries in ten states, the Federal Library and Information Network (FEDLINK) serving more than three hundred federal libraries in over forty states, and the State University of New York (SUNY) network with almost two hundred New York members; all of these being OCLC-linked centres. The Cooperative Library Network, part of the California Library Authority for Systems and Services (CLASS), acts as a broker for RLIN services. In Canada, the British Columbia Union Catalogue Project (BCUC) and the Réseau informatique de bibliothèques/Library Information Network (RIBLIN) in Quebec act as intermediaries between their member libraries and UTLAS.

Network functions undertaken by many of these regional centres in conjunction with the processing facility now include assisting in the purchase, installation, and testing of computer hardware and other equipment, providing staff training sessions and supplementary documentation such as instructional materials, distributing materials from the processing facility, and helping to introduce new system features. Many of them undertake other related functions such as assisting members in the production of printed or COM catalogues, gaining access to the online systems servicing the abstracting and indexing databases, developing tools to facilitate interlibrary cooperation (for example union catalogues, union serials lists, interlibrary loan networks, and coordinated acquisitions programs), selecting and implementing stand-alone computer systems including vendor systems, and so on. Some regional centres have begun to acquire computer hardware themselves in order to maintain their own databases, to offer automated services direct to their members, and to provide a high-speed communication link to the central computer facility.[5] In return for these services the regional organization usually charges an annual membership fee, and many add a surcharge to the charges of the central processing facility.

Maintaining Standards

As described in earlier chapters, libraries have adopted somewhat more complex standards for both description and authority work than have the abstracting and indexing services in general. These standards are not onerous when compared with those adopted by the rare-book bibliographer who spends days or weeks on a single item; still, the cost of adhering to them is a source of constant dismay to the administrator. Accepting derived cataloguing is the major way of reducing the cost, but all libraries find some original cataloguing necessary. The first symptom of a library's inability to support a given standard of bibliographic control is an ever-increasing backlog of unprocessed materials. When this symptom becomes troublesome, there is a strong temptation either to shortcut the application of the bibliographic standards applied, or in extreme cases even to seek revision of the standards themselves.

5. See Joseph Ford, "Network Service Centers and Their Expanding Role," *Information Technology and Libraries* 1 (March 1982):28–36.

The rules for description developed over the first third of this century and codified in the 1941 preliminary second edition of the *A.L.A. Catalog Rules* were too demanding of the personnel and financial resources available during World War II. They were never developed further, but were replaced by the considerably simpler 1949 *Rules for Descriptive Cataloging in the Library of Congress* (see page 111). The Library of Congress could not even apply the latter rules to all materials during the period of severe professional staff shortages of the 1950s, and from 1948 to 1963 it applied a policy it called "Limited Cataloging" to items in specified categories. [6]

It is more difficult to justify the shortcutting of name authority work. As was true of the earlier challenge to the 1941 code (see page 115) and of the later acceptance of descriptions from other sources under NPAC (see page 274), the limited cataloging policy did not apply to the choice or form of access points. These were still subject to the full application of the rules then current. But modification of the rules themselves was already underway. An important aspect of AACR in both its editions is its simplification of name authority work by reducing the reference search involved (see page 195) and by removing inconsistencies embodied in earlier codes. This was not intended as a stage in the continuing deterioration of bibliographic standards, but rather as a search for realistic ones valid in the context of the services expected from them.

Finally, subject access is an area where shortcuts are often taken: items left without verbal subject access, items placed in file folders under general subject headings, items assigned to general classifications instead of specific ones. In any period of institutional retrenchment it is difficult to decide whether standards or backlogs set the priorities. In 1981 the Library of Congress announced a new policy called Minimal Level Cataloging under which no subject cataloguing or name authority work would be initiated. [7] Should one praise them for attempting some control over material which would otherwise stay uncatalogued, or should one decry another abrogation of standards?

Of course there are a great many other libraries facing the same problem and the same dilemma, but whose solutions are not published. One increasingly popular solution at present, a solution facilitated by automation and the use of COM, is to establish two catalogues: one of complete listings observing all standards and containing the entries which are part of a cooperative database in the bibliographic utility, and another in-house brieflisting of low-priority material in which one or many shortcuts are taken. Some brieflisting efforts have been raised well beyond the level of in-house stopgap measures, for example the Canadian cooperative scheme of compiling a machine-readable index of government publications and similar reports, called CODOC.

6. The inauguration and termination of the policy are described in *Cataloging Service*, bulletins 13 (December 1947), 14 (January 1948), and 61 (September 1963).

7. *Library of Congress Information Bulletin*, 40 (30 October 1981):382–383.

Quality control, or rather its lack, has always been a significant stumbling block to true cooperation in the creation of a bibliographic database. The single greatest incentive to maintaining high standards in North American libraries during most of the twentieth century has been the fact that Library of Congress entries formed so large a part of so many library catalogues. If a library does not wish to conform to the same standards in its original cataloguing, its decision is of no concern to anyone else until the library in question inputs its records into a union catalogue or other common database. Then it becomes a matter of concern to all who have access to that database. The advent of the bibliographic utilities was therefore attended by moves toward some kind of policing to ensure that the same standards are adhered to by member libraries.

This policing is sometimes left to the computer. Some systems are programmed to displace a locally created record in favour of a source record automatically, without any judgement being made concerning the quality of either. (Searching algorithms designed to identify that two records refer to the same bibliographic item are, of course, never perfect.) In other cases, consortia attempt to ensure the application of common standards by discussion and persuasion.

Deviation from a standard is more likely to consist of the failure to include a data element than to use a different rule for its input. Coding in the control fields, for example (see Appendix I, pages 303–307), is of full value only in online post-coordinate searching. It adds virtually nothing to what appears on a visible entry output from the format. Many libraries do not envision online post-coordinate searching as a use of their catalogue databases in the near future, and question the need to spend time on filling in the suggested codes.

Yet if cooperative input and use of the fullest possible measure of derived cataloguing are to be part of contemporary bibliographic control, all must agree on what constitutes an acceptable record. The effort of formulating such agreement is not technical, but political; hence if the resultant animosity toward cooperation becomes too great, it might not be worth the cost. This effort has been undertaken in the United States with some success. It has resulted in the adoption of the concept of a *National Level Bibliographic Record,* thus far specified for books, films, music, maps, and serials. The stated purpose is worth quoting:

> This document contains specifications for the data elements that should be included by an organization creating cataloging records for books in machine-readable form with the intent of sharing those records with other organizations or for contributing them to a nationwide data base. . . . It should be noted that these specifications are designed only for records to be contributed to a national data base, not necessarily for records for local use.[8]

8. *National Level Bibliographic Record—Books* (Washington: Library of Congress, 1980), p. iii.

Integrated Bibliographic Searching

The processing facilities and the regional service centres came into existence to provide libraries with a level of computer service which almost no individual library could afford to develop or maintain alone. For the same reason, organizations like Dialog and Orbit in the United States and QL Systems in Canada originated at around the same time (the mid-1970s) as service organizations through which an abstracting and indexing service with a machine-readable database could offer it online without having to develop an individual system for the purpose. Differences between these *online searching services* and the library processing facilities are superficially great, but in fact are essentially few and rapidly diminishing. This reflects the fact that the original purposes of the two types of operation were originally very different, but are now converging.

The library processing facilities began as cataloguing support systems, designed only to facilitate the acquisition of derived cataloguing. For this purpose they required relatively limited searching potential, just enough to enable a clerk with a citation, or with the item in hand, to locate a complete entry. A compression code, ISBN, LC Card Number, or exact title proper sufficed as a search key.

The online searching services, on the other hand, originated as aids to subject investigation; they had to begin with the whole range of natural-language and controlled-vocabulary searching potential, including post-coordination and the use of boolean operators, in order to serve their purpose. As librarians recognized the potential of a machine-readable database for purposes other than derived cataloguing, they pressed the bibliographic utilities to expand the searching potential of their systems. As noted on page 279, the newer ones (WLN and RLIN) began with searching potential almost identical to that of the online searching services.

Thus computerization has brought the data control methods of the abstracting and indexing services, of the national bibliographic agencies, and of libraries very close together. It is already possible to use the same searching techniques on their bibliographic databases. For example the Library of Congress MARC database is now among the ones offered by the Dialog online searching service, alongside Excerpta Medica, Pollution Abstracts, Management Contents, and more than a hundred and fifty others. Conversely, the expansion of the databases of the library processing facilities described on page 281 is making these more similar to the databases of the online searching services.

Database Management Systems

Many of the cooperative developments described on the last eleven pages were occasioned by the fact that only an organization with access to a large mainframe computer could store and maintain large indexed bibliographic files and provide the sophisticated searching techniques necessary to retrieve records from them. But in recent years an increasing number of database management systems (often abbreviated to DBMS) have become available for virtually any computer, from mainframe to microcomputer.

Each DBMS consists of a group of programs designed to permit the user to create, maintain, and search indexed files. Some DBMS have powerful command languages to permit the user to specify the options desired; in fact, a few of these languages are sufficiently complex that a trained intermediary is required to specify the desired options to the system. Other DBMS, especially those specifically designed for untrained users and the less sophisticated systems available for microcomputers, are far less complex and offer fewer options.

The typical DBMS allows the user to determine the input format to be used, the number and size of fields to be stored and indexed, and the number and layout of various output products to be produced, although all of these are subject to limitations imposed by the hardware as well as by the software. The user can often load pre-existing bibliographic (or other) records by causing an automatic translation of their format to that required by the DBMS.

The commercial availability of DBMS, including several recently developed specifically for library use, is encouraging both libraries and the abstracting and indexing services to support their own databases, and to offer online access to remote users through computer terminals, modem-equipped microcomputers, and keypad-equipped television sets. The computer system used to channel the information to a television set would be one of the large-scale videotex systems now being developed at the national level, such as Telidon, Prestel, and Antiope. The synthesis of cable television and computer technologies promises a future that will see vast files of bibliographic records made available to users in their schools, offices, and homes, as well as in their libraries.

Compatibility of Systems and Standards

The creation of the complete bibliographic record is governed by the half dozen or more major standards or quasi-standards introduced in this book. Each of them is authorized, sponsored, or issued by a different library-oriented group or committee. The descriptive cataloguing code, AACR2, is maintained by a four-country committee, and was written by an international committee more broadly representative than perhaps any other technical committee in the history of librarianship. Most of the national MARC formats are maintained by, or in consultation with, broadly based user committees. Committees of IFLA and

---

9. An annotated bibliography of almost two hundred published standards for bibliographic description and/or name access points is *Standard Practices in the Preparation of Bibliographic Records,* compiled by the IFLA International Office for UBC. Occasional Papers, no. 9 (London: The Office, 1982).

UNISIST are concerned with compatibility among the MARC formats, and between them and the UNISIST Reference Manual. ISBD falls under the nominal control of the IFLA International Office for UBC. Although its provisions are now incorporated into many cataloguing codes such as AACR2 and are therefore to a degree released from parental control, the IFLA office is conducting regular reviews of ISBD.

Filing rules are only now emerging from a chaotic state in which it could not be predicted that two libraries of the same size or type would use the same rules. Because few libraries wished to pursue vested interests in filing rule standardization during a period of widespread abandonment of existing rules and of manual catalogues, national or national-agency committees have been able to propose new filing standards already widely accepted for computer output.

Standards for subject analysis systems are the most complex and nebulous of all, and seem to resist large-scale committee efforts. LCC and LCSH are maintained on an ad hoc basis by the personnel of the Subject Cataloging Division of the Library of Congress; the editor of DDC is advised by a small but representative international Editorial Policy Committee. PRECIS is in the control of the British Library and the people who originated it, and Sears is still the product of a single editor. The Universal Decimal Classification appears to be seriously encumbered by its loose international committee framework within the International Federation for Documentation.

Finally, each of the above standards and guidelines requires some local interpretation and the application of ad hoc judgement in use. Libraries tend to look to the decisions of the national agencies for guidance in matters where more than one interpretation is possible. Whether these decisions take the form of existing bibliographic records seen as precedents, of authority files, or of published policy statements, they affect everyday practice in the local library. These standards must be in harmony with one another, for although each touches on a different part of the bibliographic record, there are overlapping functions. This harmony has generally come about, but it takes constant effort to maintain it, and it has never been complete.

Each committee working with one given standard or interpretation is to a degree isolated from the others, and does its work within a time period and a context of persons and situations different from the others. Some of the resultant discrepancies have been mentioned in earlier pages, and others will appear in the two appendices to this book, but most are not stumbling blocks large enough to be noted in this brief overview of bibliographic control. Nevertheless, large and numerous committees, each attacking particular detailed problems at different times and often looking for compromise solutions, are inherently incapable of weaving an entirely consistent fabric of standards.

The situation in the more technical world of computer hardware and software is not much different, though there a standard can usually be more quantitatively expressed and more rigidly defined. Computer systems comprise hardware, communication links, and software, the latter including programs and data. The many standards governing these elements are largely outside the control of librarians or other users of bibliographic information, except of course for the data formats such as MARC. In many of the technical areas there are as yet no standards, and there are some areas where more than one standard exists. For example there are three incompatible methods of storing data on videodisks. There are characters that appear in different places on different terminal keyboards.

Any computer places its own limitations not only on the number of records that may be stored online, but also on the format of those records. Similarly, programming languages and database management systems place limitations upon data manipulation: some limit the number of fields that may occur in a single record or the number of characters in a field, while others make it impossible to handle indicators stored with the data or to find subfield codes embedded in a field. Early experiments in bibliographic automation necessarily preceded the establishment of standards, and practices arising from those experiments still exist. As a result there are still systems that cannot accept records or cannot output records in a standard format, systems that can accept input only online or only in batch, systems that output bibliographic data contaminated with system messages, systems designed to work only with a specific type of intelligent terminal or with a specific piece of software not commonly found in computing centres, and systems incorporating incompatible types of terminals.

All of these states contribute to the lack of compatibility which has become a major hindrance to the development of integrated bibliographic systems. The list of incomiatibilities seems endless. As a result of them, scarce financial and personnel resources are constantly being expended on converting data from one format to another, on rewriting existing programs in a different language or for a new operating system, on connecting various kinds of computer hardware and communication equipment together, etc. Although virtually any kind of hardware incompatibility can eventually be overcome provided a sufficient number of programs are written to accomplish the required code conversions, some kinds of software incompatibility are so deeply embedded in the program design that they cannot be overcome without redesigning and rewriting substantial parts of the system.

Meanwhile, many of the existing standards are widely ignored, and the bodies that create them are attacked for not representing the interests of their constituents and for stifling creativity and ingenuity. Yet except for the existence of a small number of programs available to convert data from the format of one bibliographic system to that of another, the few standards that do exist are all that prevent computerized bibliographic systems from collapsing into a state where cooperation is, however desirable, technically impossible.

The Commerce in Bibliographic Data

If incompatibility of standards and systems is a still-unsolved problem, the method of financing shared bibliographic services is another. How the cost of using bibliographic data in machine-readable form should be apportioned, and to whom, is a principal issue of debate in librarianship as this book is being written. The arrival of videotex systems to deliver such data to the home is merely adding another facet to the issue even before its original outline has been clarified. This brief section cannot pretend to isolate trends, but can only cite the factors visible in early 1982.

The technological developments of the past decade have had a profound effect on the economics of creating and distributing bibliographic records. Public, school, and academic libraries traditionally viewed the ones they created with public funds as information to be freely shared with each other and with any user, provided the material costs of reproduction are not too great. Private-sector special libraries tended toward the same view, and the national bibliographic agencies normally subsidize both their bibliographic product and its dissemination. On the other hand, the abstracting and indexing services and the private cataloguing agencies have always had to treat the bibliographic records they create as property protected by copyright and made to be sold (originally of course in the form of printed volumes).

Huge capital investment has been required for the development of the computer-based services described in this chapter. As a result, public-sector libraries are now also being forced to lean toward a view of bibliographic records as commodities. It is the method of financing their storage, distribution, and output, not their original creation, which has caused the change. The agencies focusing attention on the problem are the processing facilities since they must justify the cost of their services to members who once absorbed these costs internally and by very different accounting methods. That the start-up, systems designing, and original programming costs of most of the processing facilities were largely underwritten by grants or subsidies hid, for a time, the effect of the new economics of library processing. Because records created by the Library of Congress are not subject to copyright protection, a number of small-scale attempts to establish commercial computer-based bibliographic services using only Library of Congress MARC-formatted records were inaugurated in the early 1970s. The database thus available in the public domain was not small, but these early commercial ventures were quickly superseded by the processing facilities and the online searching services, both of which could offer a much more valuable product with their larger and cooperatively constructed databases and their sophisticated searching software.

The library community has had only a few years' experience of any but the national public agencies as creators of original cataloguing to be shared. How to pay the new contributors to shared databases for the use of their information (whether for reference search, interlibrary loan, or derived cataloguing) is far from settled. The partial remission of the use-fee by the processing facility mentioned on page 280 was merely a stop-gap first step. The larger question of the ownership of a bibliographic database or of the individual records in it has now become a contentious issue, and the use of such data as a permanently revenue-generating activity is a development not even thought of in the days when printed bibliographies and indices were consulted in a reference department.

National Planning

Since incompatibilities of so many kinds exist in the spheres of standards, technology, and economics, it is worth concluding with some reflection on what might constitute compatible national and international bibliographic networks. In the near future, virtually every national library will have its own in-house online bibliographic system. Below the national level, online processing facilities, commercial jobbers, abstracting and indexing services, networks of libraries, and individual libraries in increasing numbers are using online computer systems. Technical systems and standards compatibility would make it possible, indeed simple, to transfer messages (such as inquiries and responses) and data freely back and forth among them, as well as between institutions and their users, many of whom will have their own interactive terminals. An automated accounting system would keep track of charges, apportioned according to equitable and standardized agreements and incorporating at least the levels of public subsidy available at present.

Unfortunately, these situations do not exist today, at least not in Canada and in the United States. Bibliographic networks have grown up in these two countries without the benefit of any national plan or framework. In the early days of network development their national libraries appear to have made conscious decisions not to form national online networks, but rather to limit their activities to developing formats, setting standards, and distributing the bibliographic records they create in MARC format for other libraries and networks to use. A different model appears to be developing in the United Kingdom, where the British Library is taking a more active role in providing a computer system for centralized services. The national libraries are now in regular communication through an organization named the Association of Bibliographic Agencies of Britain, Australia, Canada, and the United States (ABACUS), which provides a forum for their exchange of information on the rational application of standards for network development within their countries.

Now that databases and online systems exist on a large scale in a large number of diverse organizations in North America, attempts are being made to plan national bibliographic networks. A new forest of acronyms is growing. The National Library of Canada has its Network Development Office (NDO), the Librarian of Congress is being advised by a Network Advisory Committee

(NAC) which also makes recommendations to the Council on Library Resources. The Council is providing a major incentive by funding a Bibliographic Service Development Program (BSDP) to coordinate projects involving all the major library-oriented automated bibliographic services, and to help sidestep the sensitive issue of economic reciprocity for the time being.

The concept of a National Level Bibliographic Record introduced on page 284 is one of the necessary foundations for national planning. So is technical systems compatibility. So are close attention to standards compatibility and agreement on a standard formula for sharing the cost of handling bibliographic information. The extent to which it will be possible to bring about a greater measure of national planning in an already established yet constantly developing automated bibliographic world remains to be seen.

Appendices

THE CANADIAN MARC FORMAT: A DETAILED EXAMINATION

The characteristics of a variable-field format in general, and of the national MARC formats in particular, are described in Chapter 5. This appendix is a detailed analysis of their application in the Canadian MARC communication format for bibliographic records (hereafter CANMARC). It illustrates all the technical features of any variable-field format conforming with the requirements of ISO 2709 (see pages 142–144). CANMARC is very close to LC MARC in almost every major respect and is identical in most. At the level of detail presented in this appendix, CANMARC and LC MARC are the same unless features needed to accommodate French-language equivalents are involved, or unless a difference is specifically noted.

The numbering sequence of the tags, uses of indicators, etc., adopted for the original MARC format reflected closely the arrangement and uses of data on the pre-1968 Library of Congress printed unit-entry catalogue card, and this has remained true. It is desirable, however, and sometimes even necessary, to code data into a machine-readable record which is not explicit on a manual entry. The machine-readable record serves two purposes: (1) it contains the data from which visible records can be output on COM, cards, a video terminal of any kind, or any other medium, and (2) it is a database capable of being used for information retrieval employing any searching technique described in Chapter 6. These two purposes are not identical. For example, the language of an item need not be explicitly stated on a visible catalogue entry if it can be assumed from other elements. The reader who recognizes a title proper in the French language correctly assumes that the text of the item is in French, especially if the place of publication is, say, France or Quebec. The computer cannot recognize a French-language title as such, and it would be uneconomic (as well as an imperfect means to the end) to provide it with a list of places where publication in French is common.

Thus, if a post-coordinate search is to be made in which only items in French are wanted, each MARC record must be explicitly coded for the language(s) of the item. The coding of data elements for post-coordinate machine retrieval is an important feature of every MARC format. Even if the institution does not at the moment use its catalogue records in this way, the loading of MARC-formatted databases into online searching systems or into local database management systems as described on pages 285–286 make it certain that such uses will soon become common. All the national agencies, most larger libraries, and even many smaller ones are now willing to undertake the cost and trouble of doing "extra" coding, and even of incorporating more data than they would have included on catalogue cards, in the expectation that the cost will eventually be returned as integrated systems offer services ranging from accounting to online reference inquiry.

The Leader and the Directory

As is true of all ISO 2709-based communication formats, a CANMARC record is laid out in three parts in sequence, namely (1) the leader, (2) the directory, and (3) the data fields.

The Leader

Each record begins with the 24-character leader, or label, specified in ISO 2709. It contains the following information which describes the record itself, not the bibliographic item being described:

0–4[1]   The total number of characters in the record, including the leader, directory, all terminators, etc., right-justified with leading zeroes.

5   Record status code; one of the following:
     n – new record
     a – previously partial record
     c – corrected or revised record
     p – previously CIP (Cataloguing in Publication) record
     d – deleted record

6   Type of record code; one of the following:

---

1. It is a convention of designating addresses in computer formats that the first *character position* is numbered 0, not 1. The second character is therefore in position 1, etc. This facilitates the mathematical calculation of addresses, since the beginning address of every field is then the starting character position of the previous field plus the number of characters in that field. See The Directory, pages 298–299, for an example of how this calculation works.

a – printed language material
b – manuscript language material
c – music scores
d – music manuscripts
e – printed cartographic material
f – manuscript cartographic material
g – projected media (slides, videorecords, etc.)
i – sound recordings (nonmusic)
j – sound recordings (music)
n – instructional media (models, charts, games, etc.)
o – kits

7   Bibliographic level code; one of the following:

a – analytic record
m – monograph
c – collection
p – pamphlet (this code is not in LC MARC)
s – serial

8–9   **[2] (Two blanks: These two positions are not yet defined by ISO 2709).

10   Indicator count: the numeral 2

There are two indicators at the beginning of each variable field. This 2 tells the computer that each address of a variable field must be incremented by two to reach the subfield code of the first data element in that field.

11   Subfield code count: the numeral 2

Every subfield code consists of two characters. The first is the one shown in this appendix as a dollar sign ($) (see page 134); the second is a lower-case alphabetic character. The number 2 here in the leader tells the computer that when a subfield is recognized by the $, two characters must be skipped in order to reach the first character of data in the element.

12–16   Base address of data, right-justified

This number is the starting-character position of the first control field, the field immediately following the leader and directory, in

---

2. Throughout this appendix an asterisk denotes a blank; that is, a space. This is also a "character," different from a zero and of course significant to any computer program. An equally common convention for designating a blank in print is to use the letter b with a slash through it: (ƀ). A zero is also commonly shown with a slash (0) in order to distinguish it from the letter O.

relation to the beginning of the whole record. In the directory, the address of each field is indicated in relation to this base address of data, *not* to the beginning of the record. That is, the directory described next always indicates the address of the first control field, tag 001, as 00000.

17   Encoding level code; one of the following:
          0 – full level, catalogued from the work in hand
          1 – full level, catalogued without the work in hand
          3 – abbreviated record; for example a subordinate record for a contents note, or a record for a pamphlet not fully catalogued
          5 – partial record; for example a record containing full descriptive information but no subject analysis
          8 – a CIP record, and therefore incomplete

18   Descriptive cataloguing form code, for example:
          a – full ISBD format, AACR2
          i – ISBD format, before AACR2
          * – non-ISBD format

19   Record link code, to note relationship to another MARC record, for example:
          * – this is the only record for the item; there are no related records

20–23   Entry map: 4500
          The digits 00 are at present without significance; the 4 and 5 refer to the lengths established for the second and third parts of each unit of the directory described next.

The Directory

The directory, or record directory, begins immediately following the leader, with the 25th character of the record (in character position 24). It consists of a series of units, one for each field of data in the record. Its final character is the first field separator in the record. Each unit in the directory is 12 characters long, but the directory *as a whole* is of variable length since each data field in the record has its separate 12-character unit and there may be any number of such data fields. Each 12-character directory unit consists of the following elements:

TAG	LENGTH	STARTING POSITION
3 characters	4 characters	5 characters

The first three characters are the tag identifying a particular data field (whether a control or a variable field). Next come four characters giving the length of that field including (for a variable field) its two indicators, all subfield code(s), all bibliographic data in the field, and the field separator or record terminator. Finally, five characters specify the starting character position of the field, not relative to the beginning of the record but relative to the base address of data (see character positions 12–16 in the leader). Thus the first unit of the record directory contains the starting character position 00000. Subsequent units have starting character positions incremented by the field length of the previous entry.

The last entry in the directory is followed by a field separator so that the computer knows where the directory ends and the data fields begin. If, for example, the last field in a record bears the tag 650, is 47 characters long, and begins at character position 732 (relative to the start of the first data field), then the unit in the directory describing that field is:

| PREVIOUS UNIT | 650004700732 | F |

Input and Coding

Only the programmer and the systems librarian need concern themselves with the structure of the leader and directory. The cataloguer assigns six of the codes in the leader, but at the time the record is input to the computer using a standard input program all the other calculations and code assignments forming the leader and directory are accomplished automatically.

The cataloguer's responsibility is to establish the identification and the desired processing of the bibliographic elements by assigning the tags, indicators, and subfield codes in the data fields as described in the remainder of this appendix. The cataloguer must therefore learn that, for example, the Title and Statement of Responsibility Area (ISBD Area 1) is identified by tag 245; within that tag the title proper is input into the first subfield, designated $a, each parallel title, subtitle, or unit of other title information is in a separate subfield designated $b (this subfield being repeatable), and the statement(s) of responsibility together comprise a single subfield designated $c. The cataloguer also learns that in this tag the first indicator is to be set at 1 if an added entry is wanted in a multiple-entry catalogue under the title proper, otherwise at 0. Finally, the number used as the second indicator in this tag is the number of characters to be ignored when filing the title (including, of course, any spaces and/or diacritics).

Following is a title and statement of responsibility area composed according to AACR2 rule 1.1:

```
A dictionary of library terms / by John H. Smith. -
```

Since these data comprise Area 1 in ISBD/AACR2, the applicable tag is 245. A title added entry heading is wanted, so the first indicator is shown as 1. Ignoring the article when filing the title means skipping two characters, so the second indicator is shown as 2. There exist subfields $a and $c in this particular example of the area. As the computer stores the formatted information on a tape or disk, the indicators, subfield codes, and data are all jammed together. The number of the tag itself (245) does not appear with the data; the input program places that number into the record directory, where it also places the result of counting the number of characters in the field (55 in this example, including a field separator) and the address of the first character of the field (which for a variable field is always the first indicator). The data field containing this information therefore appears as follows in computer storage:

```
12$aA*dictionary*of*library*terms*/$cby*John*H.*Smith.F
```

There is a very close correspondence between a tag/subfield code combination and a bit of prescribed punctuation in the ISBD/AACR2 system of description. It should therefore be possible to program the computer to generate the ISBD punctuation automatically from the tags and subfield codes, or vice versa. However, the final version of ISBD came several years after many of the MARC formats had been implemented, and the conventions of input/output programs were fairly well fixed by then. The correspondence between ISBD elements and the tags/subfield codes is also unfortunately not absolute. As a result, the following have become conventional input/output practices, more for convenience and standardization than out of technical necessity. They are the ones applied in the above example:

1) The ISBD prescribed punctuation is included as part of the data, with two exceptions:
   a) The *final* space of each mark of ISBD punctuation, as well as the space-dash-space of the area separator, is not input; the output program supplies these or, optionally, starts a new paragraph where it strips out the relevant content designator
   b) The parentheses of the series area (ISBD Area 6) are not input; they are left for the output program to supply as print constants around any field designated by a tag beginning with a 4 (these are the only tags for Area 6 data)
2) ISBD prescribed punctuation is input at the end of an element, not at the beginning; and the two-character subfield code is automatically replaced by a space when it is stripped out by the output program. The coding is therefore

```
          Signs*:$ba*colouring*book*/$cby ...
not
          Signs$b:*a*colouring*book$c/*by ...
```

3) Brackets surrounding a uniform, romanized, or supplied collective title are not input; the output program supplies them as print constants in association with the appropriate tags (240, 241, or 243)
4) Dashes within subject headings are not input; the output program changes the appropriate subfield codes into dashes
5) Arabic and roman numeration for subject and added entry tracings is not input; the output program automatically supplies the required numbers in sequence.

Figure 74 shows a hypothetical entry as it would appear in print in the traditional paragraphed unit-entry style, and as the data and coding would appear on a typical cataloguer's completed work sheet. The blank work sheet supplied to the cataloguer very likely has printed on it a typical sequence of tags and subfield codes, partly as an aide-memoire, and partly to save the time of writing the frequently used ones repeatedly. If the cataloguer works directly online at a terminal, an interactive cataloguing support system will likely prompt the cataloguer for the next unit of information by suggesting in sequence the next tag or subfield which may need data coded into it (an override is always available to bypass this prompt).

The Data Fields

Like most other MARC formats including LC MARC, CANMARC divides the data fields of ISO 2709 into control fields and variable fields. It is the variable fields which contain the information normally selected and assembled from the machine-readable record for display in a visible catalogue entry. The control fields serve exactly the same purpose as in the simplified format illustrated on pages 138–140; they compress certain housekeeping and identification data into fixed-length, fixed-location units. They have neither indicators nor subfield codes. In Figure 74, "onc" stands for "Ontario, Canada," and is the place-of-publication code, always to be found as the fifth element of control field 008, occupying its character positions 15, 16, amd 17. Each control field as a whole is treated as if it were of variable length, and each one therefore has its unit in the directory. The number of characters of coding defined for a control field does in fact vary; for example, CANMARC uses one character more than LC MARC in the 008 field.

The content of the control and variable fields is defined and described below. Some infrequently used tags are omitted, but everything necessary to enable

745.1'0971   NK1125

Smith, Jean, 1923-
    Collecting Canada's past / Jean & Elizabeth
Smith ; photography by Ken Bell. - Scarborough,
Ont. : Prentice-Hall of Canada, c1974.
    220 p. : ill. (some col.) ; 27 cm. - (The
Hobbyist's handbooks ; no.5)
    Includes bibliographical references.
    ISBN 0-13-140467-9 : $29.95.
    1. Collectors and collecting.
    1. Collectionneurs et collections.
    I. Smith, Elizabeth, 1947-   jt. auth.
    II. Bell, George Kenneth, 1914-   ill.   III.
    Title.   IV. Series.

                                    C75-1023-1

LEADER			namOa*
001			750010231
008			750611
			s
			1974
			****
			onc
			a***
			[etc.: this field has 20 fixed-length elements]
020	**	$a	0131404679
		$c	$29.95.
055	0*	$a	NK1125
082	**	$a	745.1'0971
100	10	$a	Smith, Jean,
		$d	1923-
245	10	$a	Collecting Canada's past /
		$c	Jean & Elizabeth Smith ; photography by Ken Bell.
260	0*	$a	Scarborough, Ont. :
		$b	Prentice-Hall of Canada,
		$c	c1974.
300	**	$a	220 p. :
		$b	ill. (some col.) ;
		$c	27 cm.
440	*4	$a	The Hobbyist's handbooks ;
		$v	no. 5
504	**	$a	Includes bibliographical references
650	*0	$a	Collectors and collecting
650	*6	$a	Collectionneurs et collections
700	10	$a	Smith, Elizabeth,
		$d	1947-
		$e	jt. auth.
700	11	$a	Bell, George Kenneth,
		$d	1914-
		$e	ill.

FIG. 74. Above, a unit entry in a traditional catalogue-card format. Below, a typical cataloguer's worksheet containing the same bibliographic data but also the coding required for input in the CANMARC format.

one to understand the coding of entries for most printed monographs is included. Many of the complete tables of codes employed are shown here only with selected examples. Hence the following cannot replace a complete coding manual in practice.[3] Coding for serials and nonprint material requires some additional or different tags and subfields, although the patterns established for printed monographs are followed to the extent possible. The format for authority control records is quite different and is not introduced here at all.

The following summary is keyed to the application of AACR2. Whenever reference to an AACR2 rule or its examples would help in the interpretation of the definition or application of a code, indicator, etc., the appropriate rule number is given in parentheses. Since CANMARC was originally devised for use with AACR1 (and even earlier rules because of superimposition, see pages 224–225), it contains some elements and codes irrelevant to entries prepared according to AACR2. These are identified as "(pre-AACR2)" or are given with a fuller explanation.

Control Fields

001 Control number

This field contains a character string by which the computer identifies the particular record itself. It does not matter what the number is, but it must be unique for each record in a given database. This means it can also be used in linking entry fields (see pages 123 and 184–185) to associate two or more records to each other automatically. In-house, the National Library of Canada uses the *Canadiana* serial number, while the Library of Congress uses the LC Card Number. An individual library (or a consortium contributing to a union catalogue) may have its computer assign, in sequence or at random, any unique character string. Some control numbers are formatted; in Figure 74, the cataloguer has coded 750010231, but the output program adds as print constants the C for *Canadiana* and the hyphens separating the first two digits (the year of cataloguing) and the last one (a check digit). (See tags 010 and 015 below for the relationship between these tags and 001.)

---

3. The official publication of the CANMARC format is cited on page 146. In any practical cataloguing situation, coding is done in the context of a particular set of local and/or network requirements which may be prescribed in part by the processing facility used. Some additional coding and interpretation manuals are therefore inevitably required. For example, the CANMARC bibliographic and authority formats are related to the use of the UTLAS input-output systems in *UTLAS MARC coding manual for monographs,* 1st ed. (Toronto: UTLAS, 1982– [looseleaf]); and *SHARAF Authorities Coding Manual for Use with the UTLAS Authority System* (Richmond, B.C.: British Columbia Union Catalogue, 1979– [looseleaf]).

008   Fixed-length data element codes, sometimes called the fixed fields

These are principally the codes to facilitate post-coordinate searching referred to on page 296. Tags 007 and 009 carry additional fixed-length elements for audiovisual materials, sound recordings, etc., and the detailed content of tag 008 varies according to which type of material is in question and whether the item is monographic or serial. The codes in character positions 6 and 7 of the leader inform the output program which of the possible sets of meanings of 008 data is intended in a particular record. CANMARC uses 41 characters in 008, the first 40 being the same as in LC MARC. There are 20 groups, each consisting of one to six characters. Many cataloguers refer to a group by its place in the sequence, for example "fixed field five in 008." Both this sequential numeration of the 20 groups and the character positions occupied by each are shown below. A character position is coded with a blank (*) if no other code applies.

1   (0–5)   Date of entering the record on the file, in the year-month-day style; for example, Sept.15, 1982, is coded 820915.

2   (6)   A code designating the nature of the year or years contained in the eight following characters, for example:[4]

s – there is a single date of publication (1.4F1);[5] the year in question is input as the next four characters, the following four being coded with blanks

c – there are both publication and copyright dates (1.4F5); the former appears in the next four characters, the latter in the following four

r – the work was previously issued (for example, a reprint); the date of reissue is entered in the next four characters, the original publication date in the following four

m – there is a multiple or open-ended date to be coded (1.4F8); in the latter case, Date 2 is coded 9999.

3   (7–10)   Date 1: a year only (see explanation above).

4   (11–14)   Date 2: a year only (see explanation above).

5   (15–17)   Country of publication code. A two-character code exists, the

4. "For example" means that a complete coding manual offers codes or alternatives in addition to those selected for this summary. "One of the following" means that all the possible alternatives are stated here.

5. The numbers in parentheses are AACR2 rule numbers.

characters being left-justified; for example, Chile is cl*. In the case of Canada, the United Kingdom, the United States, and the Soviet Union, the first two characters are the code for a province, state, etc., and the third is the code for the country; for example, Ontario is "onc" and California is "cau."

6 (18–21) Illustration codes (2.5C1–2). Up to four such characteristics may be coded. If fewer, they are left-justified with blanks. For example:

a – illustrations	h – facsimiles
b – maps	j – genealogical tables
c – portraits	k – forms

7 (22) Intellectual level code; one of the following:

j – juvenile	u – primary grades
v – secondary	

(If none is applicable, the code is a blank (*).)

8 (23) Reproduction format; one of the following:

a – microfilm	g – punched paper tape
b – microfiche	h – magnetic tape
c – micro-opaque	i – multimedia
d – large-print	z – other
f – braille	

(If not a reproduction, the code is a blank (*).)

9 (24–27) Form of contents; up to four (left-justified), for example:

b – bibliography	l – legislation
c – catalogue	m – thesis
d – dictionary	p – programmed text
j – patents	r – directory
k – official standards	y – yearbook

10 (28) If the item is a government publication, the level is coded, for example:

i – international body	s – state, provincial body
f – federal, national	l – local body

(If not a government publication, the code is a blank (*).)

11 (29) If the item is the proceedings, report, or summary of a conference or meeting, the code is 1; if not, 0.

12 (30) If the item is a festschrift, the code is 1; if not, 0.

13 (31)   If the work contains an index, the code is 1; if not, 0. (But if the work *is* an index, code "i" in character position 24/27 above.)

14 (32)   [Any code here other than 1 is unlikely if the description is in the ISBD format.]

15 (33)   If the item is a literary publication, the type is coded, for example:

d – drama   i – letters
f – fiction   p – poetry
h – humour, satire   s – speeches

(If not literary, the code is a blank (*).)

16 (34)   If the item is biographical, the code is one of the following:

a – autobiography   c – collective biography
b – individual biography   d – contains biographical
                                 material

(If no biographical content, the code is a blank (*).)

17 (35–37) Language (or major language) of the text. A three-character mnemonic code exists, for example, English is "eng" and French is "fre." If the text is in more than one language, or if it is a translation, variable field 041 is used to convey complete information (the principal or first language is still coded here).

18 (38)   A code to indicate whether the entry as input to the computer in MARC format is in any way different from that produced on a catalogue card; for example, an "r" code means that the MARC record is romanized, although the manual record is in a nonroman script.

19 (39)   A code to indicate the source of the cataloguing data; for example, the Library of Congress is "l", any library reporting to the Canadian Union Catalogue is "r," etc. Additional information may be given in variable field 040, for example the fact that one particular cataloguing agency has modified another's entry. This information is particularly useful in shared database construction.

20 (40)   A code to indicate the use of *fill characters* in the MARC record. These are characters used in place of data which would be present if fuller input coding had been done. LC MARC has

no provision for these, hence this character is also lacking in its use of the 008 field.

Variable Fields

Tags 010 through 999 identify the fields in which the data may be of any length. Just over a hundred of these tags are defined in the CANMARC monographs format (which accommodates also the nonprint media); there are an additional three dozen in the serials format. Hence there is plenty of room for additions, although few can be foreseen. The variable fields are divided into the following groups, roughly corresponding in numerical order to the arrangement of the printed Library of Congress unit-entry card.

010–099   Various numeric and alphanumeric codes associated with the item or the cataloguing agency. Included here are Area 8 of the ISBD (the ISBN, ISSN, and related qualifiers), national bibliography numbers, plate numbers (for music scores), label numbers (for sound recordings), codes for the instrumentation of the music in a score or sound recording, classification numbers in any classification scheme, local call numbers, codes designating the geographic and/or chronological scope of the content of the item, etc. Of the almost 30 tags defined in this group, only the few most commonly used are described below in detail.

1XX[6]   Main entry heading (AACR2 Chapter 21, and see pages 217–220 in this work). There is one such field for each item, except that no 1XX field exists for an item whose title proper (tag 245, subfield $a) is its main entry heading (see AACR2 rule 21.1C).

2XX   Tags 210 through 243 cover uniform titles and other constructed title forms useful as access points (sometimes in conjunction with other name access points). The remainder (tags 245 through 265) contain ISBD Areas 1 through 4.

3XX   ISBD Area 5.

4XX   ISBD Area 6.

5XX   ISBD Area 7.

---

6. The designation 1XX means any tag beginning with a 1, although only four tags numbered between 100 and 199 in fact exist. The 1XX, 6XX, 7XX, 8XX, and the 2XX tags preceding 245, are tags for access points. The content of these fields is treated in this book in Chapters 7 and 8. The 3XX, 4XX, 5XX, and the 2XX tags beginning at 245 contain data whose form is governed by ISBD and/or other rules discussed in Chapter 5.

6XX Verbal subject analysis: subject headings in any system or from any list, PRECIS strings, etc. If an indicator elsewhere in the record generates the desired subject tracing and heading automatically, the corresponding 6XX tag is not used; see for example the second indicator in tag 100, for an autobiography.

7XX Tags 700 through 740 contain name added entry headings for persons, corporate bodies, and titles other than series titles. If an indicator elsewhere in the record generates the desired added-entry tracing and heading automatically, the corresponding 7XX tag is not used; see for example the first indicator in tag 245, already noted on page 300. Tags 760 through 787 are "linking" tags (see page 123) used to associate one record with another record describing a related item.

8XX Tags 800 through 840 contain series-title added entry headings. If a tag from 400 through 440 exists, the corresponding 8XX tag is not used, since those 4XX tags "trace" their content automatically. Tag 850 contains serials holdings information. Tags following 850 differ in CANMARC and LC MARC, and are used for miscellaneous purposes.

9XX These tags appear in the CANMARC format but not in LC MARC. They can be used for authority control, to generate name cross-references and/or history notes, etc., although fully developed authority systems with separate MARC-type formats are increasingly being used for that purpose.

Each variable-field tag has two one-digit indicators associated with it, also one or more two-character subfield codes. There are many patterns and mnemonic features in the assigning of tags, indicators, and subfield codes. For example, the indicators and subfield codes relevant to a personal name are the same whether that personal name is used as a main entry heading (tag 100), a subject heading (tag 600), an added entry heading (tag 700), the first element of a series heading (tag 400 or 800), or a language-equivalent in a 9XX tag. In the case of subfield codes, $l is always the name of a language, $p is always the name of a part, $d is always a date of some kind, etc. The alphabetic order of the subfield codes is not necessarily related to the desired output display order, since the output program can instruct the computer to present them in whatever sequence is called for by the application of the cataloguing rules or local policy. The first (or only) subfield in *every* tag is automatically $a.

Many tags and subfield codes are repeatable; they may be used more than once in the same record or field. These have ® following them in the list below (the ® is not a part of the tag or subfield designation). Repeating the tag 650 for multiple subject headings, for example, means that there are two or more separate 650 tags in the record, each with its own indicators, subfields, etc., and each containing one subject heading. A repeated subfield means that within a single use of a tag, the same subfield may occur more than once; for example, each of several subheadings forming part of a single corporate heading is subfield $b within the one 110 field.

The principal variable-field tags used in common situations follow, along with their possible indicators and subfields.

010   Library of Congress Catalog Card Number. Both indicators are blanks; the number is in $a. If the number has been used in tag 001, it is not repeated here.

015®   A national bibliography number from any national bibliography. Preceding the number is an alphabetic code identifying the bibliography, for example B stands for the *British National Bibliography*. Both indicators are blanks; the number is in $a. If the number has been used in tag 001, it is not repeated here.

020®   International Standard Book Number. Both indicators are blanks. There are three subfields:
> $a – the ISBN (without hyphens, since the output program can supply them as print constants) followed in parentheses by its qualifier(s) (1.8B, 1.8E)
> $b – binding (1.8E)
> $c – price, etc., with its qualifier(s) (1.8D, 1.8E)

050®   Call (class) number(s) according to the Library of Congress Classification, as assigned by the Library of Congress. The first indicator shows whether the Library of Congress owns or does not own the item; the second is a blank. The class number is in $a, the book number in $b. A class number according to the Library of Congress Classification but assigned by the National Library of Canada is input in tag 055.

082   Dewey Decimal Classification class number. Both indicators are blanks; the number is in $a.

090   This tag is not defined in CANMARC. It is used by many libraries and consortia to contain local call number, copy, and location information. It is internally subfielded at the discretion of the library or processing facility.

The tags between 100 and 880 normally required for coding printed monographs are displayed below in concise tabular form. The first column is the tag, the next two show the values permissible for its two indicators, and the fourth shows the subfield codes which may be assigned within the tag (omitting the "$" common to all). The brief verbal explanations in the final column following a colon (:) briefly define the indicators. Those following an equals sign (=) or without punctuation define the subfields.

There is a group of subfields applicable to any uniform title, whether it occurs alone as an access point or in conjunction with a personal or corporate name in a name-title heading. These are described in the section Common Subfields on page 317, and are referred to under the tags where they may be applicable.

TAG	1st IND	2nd IND	SUBF CODE	
			: – meaning of indicator	
			= – content of subfield	

100 – Personal name as main entry heading (hereafter m.e.h.) (21.1A2; Chapter 22 as to its form)

0				: name has no surname (cf. 22.8,10–11,17)
1				: name has a single surname
2				: name has a multiple surname (cf. 22.5C)
	0			: m.e.h. is not the subject of the work
	1			: m.e.h. is also the subject of the work
		a		= the whole name: surname with forename(s), initial(s), etc.
		q		= parenthetical expansion of initials (22.16)
		b		= numeration, as for popes, rulers, etc. (22.17A2)
		c		= titles, qualifiers, etc. (22.12–15,17,19)
		d		= dates (22.18)
		e		= relator, for example "joint author" (mostly pre-AACR2, though a few are still optional)

110 – Corporate name as m.e.h. (21.1B2; Chapter 24 as to its form)

0		: heading begins with a personal surname followed by forename(s) and/or initial(s) (pre-AACR2)
1		: heading is a place name, with or without subheading(s) (AACR2 allows this form only for governments and their agencies; cf. 24.18)
2		: corporate name in direct order, including any geographic or other qualifier(s) (24.1–4,6,9–11)
	0,1	: second indicator the same as for tag 100
	a	= the name, or only the main heading if there are subheadings
	b®	= subordinate unit(s) represented as subheading(s) (24.13–14,18–19)

TAG	1st IND	2nd IND	SUBF CODE	: – meaning of indicator = – content of subfield

111 – Conference or meeting name as m.e.h. (21.1B2d; 24.7–8 as to its form)

      2   : name is in direct order (any other first indicator impossible under AACR2, and rare under former rules)

            0,1   : second indicator the same as for tag 100

                    a   = the conference name (24.7)

                    n   = number (24.7B2)

                    d   = date (24.7B3)

                    c   = place (24.7B4)

130 – Uniform title as m.e.h. without a personal or corporate name preceding it (cf. 21.1C; Chapter 25 as to its form)

    *   0,1   : second indicator the same as for tag 100

                    a   = the uniform title

    [See also Common Subfields, page 317]

240 – Uniform title for a work, following a name heading

      1   : no added entry under the uniform title

      3   : added entry to be made under the uniform title

            0–9   : number of characters ignored in filing

                    a   = the uniform title

    [See also Common Subfields, page 317]

241 – Title in romanized form

      0   : no title added entry under romanized form

      1   : added entry to be made under romanized form

            0–9   : number of characters ignored in filing

                    a   = the romanized title

243 – Collective uniform title, following a name heading

      0   : the collective title is "Works" (25.8,11)

      1   : several complete works published together (cf. 25.9–11, 25.35–36)

      2   : extracts from a work or works (cf. 25.9–11, 25.35–36)

      3   : other collective titles

            0–9   : number of characters ignored in filing

                    a   = the collective title

    [See also Common Subfields, page 317]

TAG | 1st IND | 2nd IND | SUBF CODE | : – meaning of indicator
= – content of subfield

245 – Title and statement of responsibility area (1.1) If there is no 1XX tag for the record, this tag is the main entry heading and the first indicator is set at 0.

    0   : no title added entry made under the wording in this tag (cf. tag 740)

    1   : title added entry made as worded here

        0–9   : number of characters ignored in filing

          a = title proper (1.1B)

          b = parallel title(s), other title information (1.1D–E)

          c = remainder of the area—statement(s) of responsibility, etc. (1.1F; cf. 1.1G)

          h = general material designation (GMD) (1.1C)

250 – Edition area (1.2)

    *   *   a = edition statement (1.2B)

          b = statement(s) of responsibility (1.2C)

260 – Publication, distribution, etc., area (1.4)

    0   *   : publisher is not the m.e.h.

    1   *   : publisher is the m.e.h.

          $a^{®}$ = place (1.4C)

          $b^{®}$ = name of publisher, etc. (1.4D–E)

          c = date(s) (1.4F; cf. tag 008, character positions 6–14)

          e = place of manufacture (1.4G)

          f = manufacturer (1.4G)

300 – Physical description area (1.5, 2.5, etc.)

    *   *   a = extent of item (pagination, etc.)

          b = other physical details (ill., etc.)

          c = dimensions

          d = accompanying material and its physical characteristics (1.5E1d)

$400^{®}$ – Series statement traced as given here; consists of personal name plus title (pre-AACR2)

    0–2   : first indicator (type of personal name) the same as for tag 100

        0   : author of series is not the m.e.h.

        1   : author of series is the m.e.h.

        personal name subfields, the same as for tag 100

          t = title

        [See also Common Subfields, page 317]

TAG	1st IND	2nd IND	SUBF CODE	: – meaning of indicator = – content of subfield

410® – Series statement traced as given here; consists of corporate name plus title (pre-AACR2)

   0–2   : first indicator (type of corporate name) the same as for tag 110

     0,1   : second indicator the same as for tag 400

      corporate name subfields, the same as for tag 110

      t = title

      [See also Common Subfields, page 317]

411® – Series statement traced as given here; consists of name of conference, etc., plus title (pre-AACR2)

   2   : first indicator the same as for tag 111

     0,1   : second indicator the same as for tag 400

      conference name subfields, the same as for tag 111

      t = title

      [See also Common Subfields, page 317]

440® – Series statement beginning with a title, and traced as given here (1.6)

   * 0–9   : number of characters ignored in filing

      a = the series title

      v = numbering within the series

      x = ISSN

490® – Series statement, untraced or traced differently

   0 *   : series not traced

   1 *   : series traced differently from the wording here (if this indicator is used with tag 490, an 8XX tag is also required; it contains the traced form of the series heading)

      subfields a,v,x the same as for tag 440

500® * * a = general note (any note not designated by one of the other 5XX tags, of which only those most frequently used in cataloguing printed monographs are represented here)

502   * * a = dissertation note (2.7B13)

503   * * a = notes on sequels, adaptations, other editions of the work, etc. (cf. 2.7B7)

504   * * a = bibliography note (2.7B18, first 2 examples)

TAG | 1st | 2nd | SUBF | : – meaning of indicator
IND | IND | CODE | = – content of subfield

505 – Contents note (2.7B18)

    0   *   : complete contents note
    1   *   : incomplete contents note
    2   *   : partial contents note
                a   = the note (omitting the words "Contents," etc., which are supplied as print constants via the first indicator)

520 – Abstract, annotation, or summary (2.7B17)

    *   *   a   = the annotation or summary

600® – Subject heading which consists of, or begins with, a personal name

   0–2   : first indicator (type of personal name) the same as for tag 100
        0   : the heading is from LCSH
        1   : children's heading from LCSH supplement
        2   : National Library of Medicine "MESH" heading
        3   : National Agricultural Library heading
        4   : other heading from foreign source
        5   : heading from *Canadian Subject Headings*
        6   : French language heading, from *Repertoire des vedettes-matière*

       personal name subfields, the same as for tag 100
       t   = title
       [See also Common Subfields, page 317]
       $x^®$ = general subdivision
       $y^®$ = period subdivision
       $z^®$ = place subdivision

610® – Subject heading which consists of, or begins with, a corporate name

   0–2   : first indicator (type of corporate name) the same as for tag 110
       0–6   : second indicator (source of subject heading) the same as for tag 600
       corporate name subfields, the same as for tag 110; plus subfields x,y,z the same as for tag 600
       t   = title
       [See also Common Subfields, page 317]

TAG 1st   2nd SUBF   : – meaning of indicator
     IND   IND CODE   = – content of subfield

611®– Subject heading which consists of, or begins with, the name of a con-
       ference, meeting, etc.
              2   : first indicator the same as for tag 111
                  0–6   : second indicator (source of subject heading) the
                                     same as for tag 600
                     conference name subfields, the same as for tag 111; plus
                     subfields x,y,z the same as for tag 600
                     t   = title
                     [See also Common Subfields, page 317]

630®– Subject heading which begins with a uniform title
          *   0–6   : second indicator (source of subject heading) the
                                 same as for tag 600
                     a   = the uniform title
                     [See also Common Subfields, page 317]

650®– Topical subject heading
          *   0–6   : second indicator (source of subject heading) the
                                 same as for tag 600
                     a   = the topical subject heading
                     subfields x,y,z the same as for tag 600

651®– Subject heading which consists of, or begins with, a geographic name
       (political jurisdictions as such, with or without corporate subdivisions,
       are considered corporate bodies and tagged 610)
          *   0–6   : second indicator (source of subject heading) the
                                 same as for tag 600
                     a   = the geographic name or place element
                     subfields x,y,z the same as for tag 600

700®– Added entry heading which consists of, or begins with, a personal name
          0–2   : first indicator (type of personal name) the same as
                                 for tag 100
                  0–2   : second indicator designates subtle differences re-
                                 quired in some filing arrangements
                     personal name subfields, the same as for tag 100
                     t   = title
                     [See also Common Subfields, page 317]

TAG   1st   2nd   SUBF   : – meaning of indicator
     IND   IND   CODE   = – content of subfield

710® – Added entry heading which consists of, or begins with, a corporate name

     0–2   : first indicator (type of corporate name) the same as for tag 110

         0–2   : second indicator the same as for tag 700

         corporate name subfields, the same as for tag 110

         t   = title

         [See also Common Subfields, page 317]

711® – Added entry heading which consists of, or begins with, a conference name

     2   : first indicator the same as for tag 111

         0–2   : second indicator the same as for tag 700

         conference name subfields, the same as for tag 111

         t   = title

         [See also Common Subfields, page 317]

730® – Added entry heading which begins with a uniform title

     *   0–2   : second indicator the same as for tag 700

         a   = the uniform title

         [See also Common Subfields, page 317]

740® – Added entry heading which consists of a title different in wording from the content of 245 $a

     *   0–2   : second indicator the same as for tag 700

         a   = the title as required in the heading

800–830 – The four tags in this group contain series tracings, except those provided for by the existence of tags 400 through 440. The existence of one of these 8XX tags depends upon the existence of a 490 tag with its first indicator set at 1. The first indicator and all subfield codes for 800, 810, 811, and 830 are exactly as for 400, 410, 411, and 440 respectively. The second indicator in each of these 8XX tags is a blank.

800® – Series added entry heading which consists of a personal name plus a title

810® – Series added entry heading which consists of a corporate name plus a title

811®– Series added entry heading which consists of a conference name plus a title

830®– Series added entry heading which begins with a title or uniform title

880 – This tag is used when the information given in another tag cannot be used for filing purposes exactly as it appears there. Thus, if one wants the roman numeral "IV" to file as either the arabic numeral "4" or the word "four," rather than as the word "iv," the appropriate *sort key* (the character string to be used in filing) is put into tag 880, and linked to the location of the data it replaces via a code in control field 005. LC MARC does not contain tags 005 or 880.

Common Subfields

n   number or designation of the work—the serial, thematic, or opus number of a piece of music; the numeration of the section or part of a series. (The latter is not a common situation; see 1.6H2. It is not the numbering *within* a series, which appears in subfield $v.) The number of a conference or meeting is now also put into this subfield in conference-name tags (cf. tag 111).

p®   the part of the work (1.1B9, 25.6A2, 25.18A1–9, 25.32)

l   language (25.5D, 25.18A10, 25.31B6–7)

s   version (25.18A11–12)

k   a form subheading such as "Selections" (25.10, 25.18A9, 25.36C)

f   date of the work (25.5B–C, 25.18A13, 25.31A6)

g   miscellaneous information, for example the name of a second party to a treaty (25.16)

d   date of a treaty signing (25.16B1, 25.16B3)

m   medium of performance, for music (25.29)

o   arranged (arr.), in a music heading (25.31B2)

r   key signature, for music (25.31A5)

h   general material designation (GMD) (1.1C, 25.5E)

v   volume or part numbering within a series (1.6G)

x   ISSN of a series (in the cataloguing of monographs this applies only in the 4XX, 7XX, and 8XX tags; in the record for a serial itself, the ISSN is in tag 022)

These subfields are relevant to titles. Most of them are peculiar to uniform titles because these are arbitrarily structured by the addition of various elements for file organization. One or more of these subfields is therefore likely to be needed in tags 130, 240, 243, 630, 730, and 830, where the title, being the first element of the field, is in $a. They also apply to the title portion of a name-title heading (cf. AACR2 21.30G and 21.30M, and subject headings similarly constructed). Name-title headings can occur, though they are not common, in tags 600, 610, 611, 700, 710, and 711. They are inevitable in tags 400, 410, 411, 800, 810, and 811. Since subfield $a in these twelve tags is reserved for the first element of a personal, corporate, or conference name, the title subfield is designated $t. Thus the subject heading SHAKESPEARE, WILLIAM. HAMLET—SOURCES is coded:

      600 10 $a SHAKESPEARE, WILLIAM. $t HAMLET $x SOURCES

This listing is not necessarily in the order in which the elements would appear in a heading.

Complete Example

Figure 75 shows the record used as an example in Figure 74 on page 302 as it would look in the CANMARC format, if it were stored sequentially on a length of magnetic tape. (The data would of course be in binary code.) It is blocked out here in units of data, and a numbering system for its addresses is added in subscript in order to help interpret its parts in conjunction with the preceding description of the format. The address "205=0" indicates that the 206th character from the beginning (character position 205) is the base address of data referred to in character positions 12 through 16 of the leader. It contains the first character of the data fields. All subsequent addresses are calculated relative to it, and each is stored in its respective unit of the directory.

0 0 7 4 3 n a m * * 2 2 0 0 2 0 5 0 i * 4 5 0 0 0	0 0 1 0 0 1 4 0 0 0 0 0 24	
0 0 8 0 0 4 2 0 0 0 1 4 36	0 2 0 0 0 2 6 0 0 0 5 6 48	0 5 5 0 0 1 1 0 0 0 8 2 60
0 8 2 0 0 1 5 0 0 0 9 3 72	1 0 0 0 0 2 4 0 0 1 0 8 84	2 4 5 0 0 8 2 0 0 1 3 2 96
2 6 0 0 0 5 8 0 0 2 1 4 108	3 0 0 0 0 4 1 0 0 2 7 2 120	4 4 0 0 0 3 8 0 0 3 1 3 132
5 0 4 0 0 4 1 0 0 3 5 1 144	6 5 0 0 0 3 1 0 0 3 9 2 156	6 5 0 0 0 3 6 0 0 4 2 3 168
7 0 0 0 0 4 0 0 0 4 5 9 180	7 0 0 0 0 3 9 0 0 4 9 9 192	F * 7 5 0 0 1 0 2 3 1 * 205 = 0

* * F 7 5 0 2 0 6 s 1 9 7 4 * * * * o n c a b * * * * * * * * * 0 0 0 1
14

* * e n g * * * F * * * $ a 0 1 3 1 4 0 4 6 7 9 * : $ c $ 2 9 . 9 5 . F 0
56   82

* $ a N K 1 1 2 5 F * * * $ a 7 4 5 . 1 ' 0 9 7 1 F 1 0 $ a S m i t h , *
93   108

J e a n . $ d 1 9 2 3 - F 1 0 $ a C o l l e c t i n g * C a n a d a ' s
132

* p a s t * / $ c J e a n * & * E l i z a b e t h * S m i t h * ; * p h

o t o g r a p h y * b y * K e n * B e l l . F 0 * $ a S c a r b o r o u
214

g h , * O n t . * : $ b P r e n t i c e - H a l l * o f * C a n a d a ,

$ c c 1 9 7 4 . F * * $ a 2 2 0 * p . * : $ b i l l . * (s o m e * c o
272

l .) * ; $ c 2 7 * c m . F * 4 $ a T h e * H o b b y i s t ' s * h a n
313

d b o o k s * ; $ v n o . * 5 F * * $ a I n c l u d e s * b i b l i o g
351

r a p h i c a l * r e f e r e n c e s . F * 0 $ a C o l l e c t o r s *
392

a n d * c o l l e c t i n g . F * 6 $ a C o l l e c t i o n n e u r s *
423

e t * c o l l e c t i o n s . F 1 0 $ a S m i t h . * E l i z a b e t h
459

, $ d 1 9 4 7 - $ e j t . * a u t h . F 1 1 $ a B e l l , * G e o r g e
499

* K e n n e t h , $ d 1 9 1 4 - $ e i l l . R

FIG. 75. A complete entry for the item illustrated and coded in Figure 74 on page 302, as it would appear on a length of machine-readable tape.

Index to MARC Coding

The following is an index to the leader elements, tags, indicators, and subfield codes tabulated in the preceding appendix. The ''common subfield'' codes are on page 317.

ALPHANUMERIC ARRANGEMENT: FILING

Chapters 6, 7, and 8 discuss the establishment and use of access points in bibliographic files. Whether these access points are names, titles, concepts, or the symbols of a classification scheme, every manual retrieval system stores them in alphabetic or alphanumeric order. Computer retrieval systems tend to do the same, not because the computer requires alphanumeric order for its internal searching functions, but because such an arrangement facilitates computer programming for most bibliographic purposes, and because the results of a search are most conveniently displayed for human consultation in this order. It is the most universally recognized means of arranging any name or concept which can be represented in words or digits. That M follows L and 5 follows 4 is arbitrary and conventional. It is neither a rational nor a logical arrangement, but is useful because unlike any other possible arrangement, it is almost independent of language and subject knowledge.

Alphanumeric arrangement is not, unfortunately, totally independent of language. Semantic elements have crept into almost every filing rule ever devised, though they are not essential to one. The only linguistic problem inevitable in alphabetic arrangement is the fact that there are hundreds of forms of the alphabet, among them the Arabic, Cyrillic, Devanagari, Hebrew, Roman, and Thai forms. Few people know the characters and their conventional arrangement in each existing form.[1] Fortunately, the twenty-six-character roman alpha-

---

1. Non-phonetic writing systems may employ objective criteria for establishing the order of characters, for example the use of the number of strokes in a Sino-Japanese kanji as one factor in determining its dictionary location. There may even be more than one accepted arrangement for the elements of a script, as is the case with the Japanese phonetic hiragana. Even roman-alphabet letters can be a problem when they are modified (for example, ł, đ, and letters with accents, umlauts, etc.), since there are single-language conventions concerning their order. The Danes, for

bet is very widely known and is commonly used even where it is not the means of expressing the native language, and standard conventions of transforming characters from other forms into roman characters are widely applied (see Romanization, pages 220–223). A conventional order for the ten decimal digits (0–9) and their numeric combinations is universally accepted, although some rules governing the interfiling of numbers and words prefer to translate numbers into words so that a single sequence suffices instead of separate numeric and alphabetic ones within the same file.

Filing Rules

The most basic of all filing issues which needs to be settled by a rule (rather than by universal convention) is whether a space shall constitute a significant character or not. In *letter-by-letter filing,* it does not: "Newfoundland" precedes "New York." In *word-by-word filing,* it does: "New York" precedes "Newfoundland" since the space after the "w" in New York is considered and is located before the "f" in Newfoundland. Word-by-word arrangement is sometimes called nothing-before-something filing: the space (nothing) is considered a twenty-seventh character of the alphabet, filing before A (something). Letter-by-letter filing is not at all uncommon. Most telephone directories and many encyclopaedias adopt it, for example; but it is unusual in bibliographic practice. Library filing rules, like so many other technical services applications, owe much to the ideas of Charles Ammi Cutter, whose influence lingers through the many changes recently wrought by the computer.[2] He established word-by-word arrangement as the basic principle.

The treatment of punctuation is logically the next matter on which a rule is needed. Should a mark of punctuation act as a second space? The question of punctuation arises because of the need to interfile names, titles, and (in dictionary catalogues) subject terms. A telephone directory needs concern itself only with problems of filing names, most of which have a conventional structure. Even in an encyclopaedia whose headings include both names and subject terms, problems of subarrangement are not numerous. Corporate subheadings, titles, and multiword and subdivided subject terms are the ones causing difficulties with punctuation. Cutter prescribed that punctuation should play a significant role in any name or subject heading whose form is established by the cataloguer. In fact, he prescribed in his cataloguing rule what punctuation to include in a name heading precisely so that his filing rule could take account of

---

example, traditionally file ø after z; the Germans traditionally file ü as if it were "ue"; etc. The distinction between upper- and lower-case forms of letters, when it exists, is almost universally ignored in arranging the characters.

2. Cutter's filing rule appears in his *Rules for a Dictionary Catalog,* pp. 111–129 (rules 298–344).

it. (Since a title is not formulated by the cataloguer, punctuation within it is not predictable and is therefore ignored in filing.) Thus the heading "Vancouver. Police Department" is filed by Cutter's rule as if it were "Vancouver [two spaces] Police Department." This location precedes "Vancouver Art Gallery" and is far from "Vancouver Police Department" without a period.

The third and final basic issue is how to arrange words which are the same up to the first significant mark of punctuation. Cutter prescribed the following order: (1) person, (2) place, (3) subject, (4) title. Thus his arrangement of:

```
Vancouver. [a one-word title]
Vancouver. City Engineer's Dept.
Vancouver, George
```

is:

```
Vancouver, George
Vancouver. City Engineer's Dept.
Vancouver. [title]
```

The presence of punctuation means that only the word "Vancouver" is taken into consideration in first instance: its use as a personal name precedes its use as a place name and, finally, its use as a title.

A fuller example shows considerable differences in arrangement when the three basic issues described here are solved in various possible ways:

Letter-by-Letter

```
WOOD [a subject heading]³
Wood [a one-word title]
WOOD--BIBLIOGRAPHY
Wood, Daniel
Wooden shoes and windmills [a title]
Wood frame house construction [a title]
Wood, Henry
Wood Lake (Neb.) [a two-word place name in Nebraska]
Woodlawn Cemetery
Wood (Pa.) [a one-word place name in Pennsylvania]
Woodward Stores and British Columbia retailing
Woodward Stores, Ltd.
Wood, William
```

3. Subject headings are given in full capitals. Strict letter-by-letter or word-by-word filing does not prescribe whether a subject heading should precede or follow a title which consists solely of the same word(s). In practice, they would traditionally be arranged by whatever element follows the heading in the complete entry. The order of "WOOD" and "Wood" is therefore arbitrary in this example and the second.

Word-by-Word, Disregarding Punctuation

```
WOOD
Wood
WOOD--BIBLIOGRAPHY
Wood, Daniel
Wood frame house construction
Wood, Henry
Wood Lake (Neb.)
Wood (Pa.)
Wood, William
Wooden shoes and windmills
Woodlawn Cemetery
Woodward Stores and British Columbia retailing
Woodward Stores, Ltd.
```

Word-by-Word, Regarding Punctuation

```
Wood, Daniel
Wood, Henry
Wood, William
Wood (Pa.)
WOOD
WOOD--BIBLIOGRAPHY
Wood
Wood frame house construction
Wood Lake (Neb.)
Wooden shoes and windmills
Woodlawn Cemetery
Woodward Stores, Ltd.
Woodward Stores and British Columbia retailing
```

Every departure from letter-by-letter filing represents an attempt to ensure that the user will find logical groupings of material together in an alphabetically arranged file. Cutter was not the first person to think this would be desirable, but he systematically developed such groupings in his widely imitated rule. This led in the early twentieth century to the incorporation of more and more interpretive requirements in rules designed for very large catalogues. Some examples from various rules, including Cutter's own, show how filing rules became in many details rules to file "as if," not "as is:"

1) numbers transcribed as arabic numerals, and symbols such as the ampersand (&), are filed as if written in letters in the language of the element in which they occur
2) an entry is filed in one grouping if it is a main entry, but in a different one if it is an added entry, even though the same access point is used for both
3) entries for editions, translations, etc., of the same work are filed in a single group, regardless of the sequence of the words of the entry

4) an acronym is filed as a word if it is commonly spoken as a word, but as a series of initial letters if not.

In some instances, the "improved" grouping intended is not particularly logical, but merely technical, perhaps meaningful to a bibliographically trained person but not to the average searcher (for example, the separation of main from added entries). The complex manual filing rule developed by and for the card catalogues of the Library of Congress represents the greatest extension of the use of interpretive considerations for the benefit of trained searchers using a huge catalogue.[4] That it should have been imposed on freshmen students in dozens of small colleges throughout North America was certainly never intended by its creators.

Once entries have been arranged considering only their access points, rules for subarrangement are needed when more than one entry is to be filed under the same access point. Thus, if there are five different items in the file under the access point "Smith, John," or "University of British Columbia. School of Librarianship," or the title "Principles of Chemistry," the filing rule must determine whether they are to be subarranged by (1) the title proper in the descriptive part of the entry, or (2) the date of publication, or (3) the main entry heading, or (4) some other characteristic. Possible criteria and recent trends in subarranging the entries within a single access point grouping are discussed in the section Filing Rules as Determinants of Coordination on pages 162–163.

The main entry heading constitutes an important factor in subarrangement in the unit entry system illustrated in Figure 2 on page 17. Rules of the past tended to be written considering only this system of displaying entries. Except when the title proper is itself the main entry heading, it is always preceded by the name of the principal author of the work and/or perhaps by a uniform title. These elements are thus linked as a single unit for filing purposes unless the filing rule explicitly specifies otherwise. Few manual filing rules made any exceptions to this linking: after all, a principal reason for codifying the choice of main entry heading in a cataloguing code was precisely to pre-coordinate these elements for filing purposes throughout the listing.

Even before the unit entry format began to disappear along with card catalogues, it had become more and more commmon to file by rules which bypass the main entry heading/title link. In many library catalogues, entries under the same subject heading are now subarranged first by date, not by main entry heading. Name headings are now more often arranged without regard to their function as main or added access points, and are subarranged by a title, ignoring an intervening main entry heading if there is one. Figure 76 shows the differences between the arrangements described.

---

4. This rule appeared in its final published form as: Library of Congress, Processing Department, *Filing Rules for the Dictionary Catalogs of the Library of Congress* (Washington: Library of Congress, 1956).

③
Davis, E. Allan.
Andrew, Frank.
  Trigonometric analysis / by Frank Andrew
and E. Allan Davis. - ...

    ②
    Davis, E. Allan.
      A university course in trigonometry / by
    E. Allan Davis. - ...

        ①
        Davis, E. Allan.
          Essentials of trigonometry / by E. Allan
        Davis and Jean J. Pedersen. - ...

FIG. 76. On entries 1 and 2, "Davis, E. Allan" is the main entry heading. On 3, it is an added entry heading, "Andrew, Frank" being the main entry heading. In the arrangement shown here, the added entry files after all the main entries bearing the same access point. An arrangement more favoured by modern rules files entry 3 *between* 1 and 2.

Filing by Computer

In the past, librarians and many publishers of commercial bibliographies treated filing rules as a matter of individual choice, provided there was internal consistency within any one catalogue or bibliography. Even though many adhered to common cataloguing codes so that access points might be the same in different catalogues, there existed an astonishingly large number of manual filing rules for library card catalogues, many differing from one another only in minor details. The reasons for the variants may originally have been real or supposed user needs in a particular situation, reflecting for example the differences between a dictionary and a divided catalogue. The cost of refiling an existing card catalogue perpetuates local variations or practices now considered obsolete. Many libraries, notably the Library of Congress, have been pleased to be able to abandon old filing rules at the time of closing or freezing card catalogues in favour of either new card catalogues or some computer-output product.

In his rules, Cutter integrated the techniques and purposes of both authority control and filing in order to produce a consistent result since he saw them as two faces of the same coin. For example, his intention that administrative departments of a jurisdiction should file together is reflected both in his cataloguing rule for the formulation of the required headings (establishing government agencies normally as subheadings under the name of the jurisdiction in question) and in his filing rule (considering as significant the period which separates the name of the jurisdiction from the subheading). As cataloguing rules and subject headings patterns have changed over the years, filing rules have also had to change; and as in those cases, the advent of the computer has been a major cause of the change.

Filing is basically a routine and clerical operation. Because of this, it is highly desirable to transfer it to the computer; people who do it for long periods begin to make an unacceptable number of clerical errors as the mind wanders from the boredom of the task. The increasing cost and uncertainty of manual filing have been reason enough for many libraries to abandon the card form of the catalogue, which cannot be computer-arranged, to a form which can be.

However, interpretive requirements such as Cutter had introduced were a barrier to the mechanization of filing since it takes complex programming and longer execution times to accomplish the judgements called for. Commercial publishers, including the abstracting and indexing services, used computers for filing earlier than most libraries, because they were willing to sacrifice subtleties of arrangement if it meant cheaper computer runs and simpler programming. A fairly easy-to-program filing rule produces the following results when applied to a number of typical catalogue access points:

```
The 2 x 2 game
19th century prints and drawings
35-cent thrills
1940: the world in flames
A.L.A. booklist
Abbott, Susan
The ALA accreditation process
France & Belgium fight together
France. Ambassade (United States)
France, Anatole
La France au Canada
FRANCE--BIBLIOGRAPHY
France. Direction des forets
The nineteenth century in Europe
The thirty-nine steps
Two by two into the ark
U.S. see also United States
U.S. Grain Marketing Research Laboratory
The U.S. health system
The uninvited
United States. Army
UNITED STATES IN LITERATURE
United States Lutheran-Roman Catholic Dialogue (group)
United States national security policy in the decade ahead
UNITED STATES--NEUTRALITY
United States. Office of Education
United States Soccer Federation
UNITED STATES--TERRITORIAL EXPANSION
```

Librarians at first scorned such a lax approach. To program a computer to file according to the principles then in vogue in library practice is possible, and was for a time pursued.[5] Ultimately, however, such attempts led to the conclusion that existing rules were unnecessarily complex, not only for computers but also for human searchers. The simplicity of the filing arrangements such as the one above, adopted by many commercial tools of the 1960s and 1970s, came to be seen as a virtue rather than a weakness even for library catalogues. It has become clear that the untrained user adapts easily to such former heresies as, for example, filing a number before the letter A, interfiling personal and place names along with titles without distinctions based on punctuation, and providing more cross-references instead of attempting the logical grouping of visually unlike headings. The trained professional who understands and has become accustomed to the more classified groupings is the person more likely to be disconcerted by the computer-based style. Whether the catalogue should be constructed primarily for that trained professional or for the average searcher remains a dilemma in this, as in many areas of the presentation of bibliographic files.

Whatever the benefits of the former practices, filing rules for library purposes slowly followed the lead of commercial directories, etc. The 1968 American Library Association filing rule was simpler than its predecessor, but chiefly because of the simplified heading structures prescribed in the then new cataloguing code, the first edition of AACR. Computer considerations were not much of a factor in it. It found little application in practice because increasing numbers of libraries were soon using catalogue records generated and filed by computers, even if still often refiled into card catalogues. In 1973 a Computer Filing Committee was formed in the American Library Association (the word "Computer" was later dropped from the name, perhaps in recognition that soon all filing would be done this way). Its rules, published in 1980, are designed for computer application in more than one way: they make extensive use of MARC tags and subfield codes to identify elements for arrangement. The results of their application are very similar to those in the example on page 329.[6]

Filing by computer could not be entirely standardized within a mere decade. There remain differing practices depending on the degree to which it is considered feasible and desirable to program more complex subroutines and "translation" tables. Punctuation and nonalphabetic symbols are the usual areas of difference. The *ALA Filing Rules* of 1980 depart most significantly

5. See, for example, William R. Nugent, "The Mechanization of the Filing Rules for the Dictionary Catalogs of the Library of Congress," *Library Resources & Technical Services* 11 (spring 1967):145–166.

6. The three filing rules published by the American Library Association are *A.L.A. Rules for Filing Catalog Cards*, 1942; *ALA Rules for Filing Catalog Cards*, 2nd ed., 1968; and *ALA Filing Rules*, 1980. Each is a committee effort. The third bears no edition number, in recognition of the fact that it is an essentially different work.

from the Cutter tradition in that punctuation (and therefore any difference between types of heading) is ignored. The results show a marked similarity in the treatment of the basic issues to the example on page 326 of filing word-by-word, disregarding punctuation. By contrast, the new computer filing rule published by the Library of Congress (also in 1980) retains the traditional grouping of types of headings (surnames, jurisdictions with subdivisions, etc.)[7] Both sets of rules recognize that there are advantages and disadvantages to either approach. The retention in the new Library of Congress rules of some complexities sacrificed in the new American Library Association rules reflects two assumptions: (1) that more attention needs to be paid to logical groupings in a very large catalogue where it is harder to see the "forest" for the "trees," and (2) that the catalogue of a national institution is more likely to be searched by persons well versed in bibliographic practices than by casual untrained users.

It seems unlikely that a third major set of computer filing rules will be devised for library use in North America. In the United Kingdom, the British Library has published its own rules, the results of which closely approximate those of using the Library of Congress rule.[8] In the late nineteenth century, Cutter provided a single integrated system for establishing and for arranging name and subject headings. Since his time, the work of the individual has become the work of the committee, and the groups concerned with filing rules have tended to be different from those concerned with formulating cataloguing rules, format requirements, etc. Nevertheless, the arrangement of access points has consistently come up for consideration each time major changes have occurred in the other facets of bibliographic organization, and filing committees have always based their decisions on the completed work of the others.

7. *Library of Congress Filing Rules,* prepared by John C. Rather and Susan C. Biebel (Washington: Library of Congress, 1980). In reviewing both the 1980 ALA and LC rules, John F. Knapp shows how human interpretation and judgement are still required to a degree in their application: *Journal of Library Automation* 14 (June 1981):126–129.

8. *BLAISE Filing Rules,* by the British Library Filing Rules Committee (London: British Library, 1980).

INDEX

Please refer to the detailed table of contents on pages ix–xv for a systematic survey of this book.

This index does not cover the tabulation of the MARC format which occupies most of Appendix I. It is separately indexed on pages 320–322.

In general, examples and secondary sources are not indexed, but significant concepts and primary sources are indexed even if mentioned only in figures or footnotes.